Data Science in Healthcare

Data science is transforming every aspect of modern life, from healthcare and urban planning to finance and governance. This comprehensive book provides an accessible yet rigorous exploration of the principles, methodologies, and applications of data science. It introduces readers to the evolution of data science, the role of artificial intelligence, and the philosophical foundations underpinning data-driven discovery. By bridging theory and practice, this book provides a unique perspective on how data can be harnessed to solve complex, real-world problems.

Unlike other texts, this book integrates technical foundations with ethical, regulatory, and societal considerations. It covers the entire data science lifecycle, from acquisition and processing to advanced analytics, application development, and decision support. Real-world case studies—including a detailed example of using electronic health records in Rwanda—illustrate how data science can drive impact in low- and high-resource settings alike.

Key Features:

- Comprehensive coverage of data science fundamentals, machine learning, and advanced analytics.
- In-depth exploration of ethical, governance, and regulatory challenges.
- Practical insights into developing applications and decision support systems.
- Global case studies demonstrating applied data science in healthcare and public policy.
- Clear explanations suitable for multidisciplinary audiences.

This book is ideal for students, researchers, and professionals in data science, healthcare, public policy, and technology development. It equips readers with both the technical and ethical tools needed to navigate today's data-rich world and to leverage data for innovation, problem-solving, and societal good.

CHAPMAN & HALL/CRC DATA SCIENCE SERIES

Reflecting the interdisciplinary nature of the field, this book series brings together researchers, practitioners, and instructors from statistics, computer science, machine learning, and analytics. The series will publish cutting-edge research, industry applications, and textbooks in data science.

The inclusion of concrete examples, applications, and methods is highly encouraged. The scope of the series includes titles in the areas of machine learning, pattern recognition, predictive analytics, business analytics, Big Data, visualization, programming, software, learning analytics, data wrangling, interactive graphics, and reproducible research.

Recently Published Titles

Explanatory Model Analysis, Explore, Explain, and Examine Predictive Models
Przemyslaw Biecek and Tomasz Burzykowski

An Introduction to IoT Analytics
Harry G. Perros

Data Analytics, A Small Data Approach
Shuai Huang and Houtao Deng

Public Policy Analytics, Code and Context for Data Science in Government
Ken Steif

Data Science, An Introduction
Tiffany-Anne Timbers, Trevor Campbell, and Melissa Lee

Tree-Based Methods, A Practical Introduction with Applications in R
Brandon M. Greenwell

Data Science for Infectious Disease Data Analytics, An Introduction with R
Lily Wang

Urban Informatics, Using Big Data to Understand and Serve Communities
Daniel T. O'Brien

Data Science in Healthcare, A Complete Guide
Gayathri Delanerolle, Yassine Bouchareb, Konstantinos V. Katsikopoulos, and Peter Phiri

For more information about this series, please visit: https://www.routledge.com/Chapman--HallCRC-Data-Science-Series/book-series/CHDSS.

Data Science in Healthcare

A Complete Guide

Gayathri Delanerolle, Yassine Bouchareb,
Konstantinos V. Katsikopoulos, and Peter Phiri

CRC Press
Taylor & Francis Group
Boca Raton London New York

CRC Press is an imprint of the
Taylor & Francis Group, an **informa** business
A CHAPMAN & HALL BOOK

Designed cover image: Shutterstock

First edition published 2026 by CRC Press
2385 NW Executive Center Drive, Suite 320, Boca Raton FL 33431

and by CRC Press
4 Park Square, Milton Park, Abingdon, Oxon, OX14 4RN

CRC Press is an imprint of Taylor & Francis Group, LLC

ISBN: 9781032799599 (hbk)
ISBN: 9781032786063 (pbk)
ISBN: 9781003494737 (ebk)

DOI: 10.1201/9781003494737

Typeset in Times
by codeMantra

Contents

About the Authors

Gayathri Delanerolle is a Chartered Scientist with interdisciplinary expertise. Her research connects women's health with data science to address critical gaps that impact the life-course of women. Her work spans across low-, middle-, and high-income countries, with a strong focus on equity, digital health, health system strengthening, and developing evidence-based culturally sensitive interventions promoting health equity. She has developed several evidence-based tools using advanced analytics.

Yassine Bouchareb is a Senior Scientist and a Medical Physics Expert (RPA2000 #1032, UK) with over 25 years of experience in Medical Imaging and Medical Physics. He has worked at world-leading institutions in the UK, Germany, France, and Qatar, and currently serves as Associate Professor at Sultan Qaboos University, Oman.

Dr. Bouchareb holds a PhD in Medical Imaging from René-Descartes University, Paris, and an MBA in Healthcare Services Management from Greenwich Management School, London. Author of numerous high-impact scientific publications, his research focuses on the development and assessment of advanced image processing techniques, estimation and optimisation of patients and occupational radiation doses, evaluation of the efficacy of new drugs for cardiovascular diseases, neurological disorders, and cancer, as well as the development of artificial intelligence and radiomics-based imaging solutions for COVID-19 and cancer.

He has served as a keynote speaker at several international conferences. He has been involved in teaching and training Radiology and Ophthalmology residents, and supervising undergraduate, master, and PhD students and postdoc researchers. He is a member of several professional bodies, scientific societies, a founding member of scientific associations, and serves as a scientific reviewer for famous international journals (*PMB*, *EJNMMI*, *BPEX*, *EURA*, *IEEE TNS*, *JCM*/MDPI).

Konstantinos V. Katsikopoulos is Professor of Behavioural Science at the Department of Decision Analytics and Risk of the University of Southampton Business School, where he has also been the Associate Dean for Research. He is a world-leading researcher in the interdisciplinary study of decision-making. His research connects behavioural science with analytics by employing psychological experiments to understand lay and expert decision-making under conditions of radical uncertainty, harvesting this understanding to build simple mathematical models of how such decisions should be made, and testing multiple models using machine learning methodologies. This approach is enjoying a rare success—the models are accurate and at the same time transparent. He is a fellow of the Psychonomics Society (US), the Chair of the Behavioural OR Group at The Operational Research Society (UK), and has received a German Science Foundation Fellowship for Young Researchers. Before joining the University of Southampton, he worked as Visiting Assistant Professor at the University of Massachusetts Amherst, the Naval

Postgraduate School, and the Massachusetts Institute of Technology, as well as a Senior Research Scientist and Deputy Director at the Centre for Adaptive Behavior and Cognition of the Max Planck Institute for Human Development. Currently, he serves as Editor-in-Chief of *Mind and Society* (the official journal of the Herbert Simon Society) and Associate Editor for the *Journal of Mathematical Psychology* and *Judgment and Decision Making*. His previous books include *Classification in the Wild* and *Cognitive Operations*.

Peter Phiri, BSc (Hons), CBT DipHE, RMN, PhD, is a Clinical Academic and Psychotherapist affiliated with the University of Southampton's Faculty of Medicine, School of Primary Care, Population Sciences & Medical Education. He supervises doctoral researchers in the UK and globally. He has co-authored two key academic books: *Cultural Adaptation of CBT for Serious Mental Illness: A Guide for Training and Practice* (2015) and *Clinical Trials and Tribulations* (2023).

With more than two decades of experience in the NHS, he has worked extensively in settings serving adults with severe mental illness, including inpatient, community, and forensic services. Upon completion of a postgraduate diploma in cognitive therapy for severe mental health problems at the University of Southampton, he became accredited by the British Association for Behavioural and Cognitive Psychotherapies (BABCP). He has led National Institute for Health Research (NIHR)-funded clinical trials such as POMET, STEPWISE, and SCIMITAR. His research interests centre on the cultural adaptation of evidence-based psychological interventions, global mental health and data science, student well-being, and the application of psychological methodologies across diverse populations.

Acknowledgements

We would like to express our sincere gratitude to Ms Vindya Pathiraja and Dr David Ikwuka for their valued contributions to *Data Science in Healthcare*. Their support, insight, and commitment to advancing interdisciplinary approaches at the intersection of healthcare, technology, and data-driven innovation have been greatly appreciated throughout the development of this work. We are grateful for their willingness to contribute intellectual and supporting materials to this book and acknowledge their role in strengthening its multidisciplinary perspective and broader translational relevance. Their engagement reflects the collaborative spirit required to advance modern healthcare research, innovation, and evidence-based practice.

1 An Introduction to Data Science

KEY POINTS

- Understanding the evolution, and philosophy of data science
- Differentiating data science from related fields like data analysis, machine learning, and deep learning
- Exploring the impact of data science on various domains, including healthcare, business, and technology
- Introduction of core data science methodologies and models

1.1 INTRODUCTION TO DATA SCIENCE

Data science or "information science" is a multidisciplinary field that draws upon advanced analytical techniques, machine learning (ML), and scientific principles to uncover insights that guide synthesis, visualisation, and interpretation to gain insights to support decision-making. At its core, it merges statistics, computing, and domain-specific expertise to convert raw data into actionable knowledge. Whether applied in healthcare to improve patient outcomes or in urban policy to optimise resource distribution, data science services are a compass for navigating complex, data rich environments.

Far from being a purely technical domain, data science has philosophical roots that reach deep into antiquity. Thinkers like Plato and Aristotle, in their quest to systematise knowledge, laid the intellectual groundwork for today's logic-driven, evidence-based methods. These early epistemologies, concerned with classification, inference, and the nature of truth, echo in the algorithms and models we now use to make sense of data-saturated realities.

1.2 HISTORICAL EVOLUTION OF DATA SCIENCE

1.2.1 Ancient Origins to the Industrial Era

The historical origins of modern data science emerged from the study of statistical probabilities in the 1920s, and later via sociological use during the industrial revolution [1]. Victorian times in Britain also enhanced the use of data science with the advances in accurate actuarial tables, better gambling strategies, and reporting better ways to secure agricultural yield [2]. This was furthered by way of the methods such as bootstrapping and Markov chain Monte Carlo simulations and parametric assumptions that aided in developing computational methods and power [3].

DOI: 10.1201/9781003494737-1

From this perspective, the development of algorithms and automation to determine patterns within large datasets rejuvenised the logic and progression of data science.

1.2.2 The Evolution of Data as a Concept

Once confined to counting objects or measuring speeds, data has since evolved into a universal language, one that transcends geographic, cultural, and linguistic boundaries. More than just numbers, data now underpins how we understand, model, and respond to the world. Philosophers such as Pythagoras, who declared,

> 'Everything is number,' anticipated this transformation, where symbolic representation, be it in digits, graphs, or code, mediates our relationship to objective reality. In today's digital ecosystem, data functions as both the substrate and syntax of meaning-making.

1.2.3 The First Data Revolution (Scientific Data)

The first data revolution emerged alongside the rise of modern science, marking a turning point in the relationship between knowledge and empirical evidence [4]. During this era, data collection and analysis became indispensable for understanding natural phenomena grounded in mathematical modelling and increasingly precise instrumentation. Scientific inquiry transformed into a rigorously data-driven endeavour, where the validity of hypotheses hinged not only on logic but also on measurable proof. This shift wasn't merely methodological; it redefined science as a language of numbers and models, bridging abstract theory with observable reality.

1.2.4 The Second Data Revolution (Big Data)

The second data revolution, unfolding in the 21st century, is driven by the exponential growth of "big data", an era where information is generated, stored, and analysed at scales that overwhelm traditional methods [4]. Characterised by its sheer volume, velocity, variety, and value, big data redefines how patterns are detected, decisions made, and futures predicted. No longer reliant on hypothesis-first models, this revolution favours data-led discovery, uncovering correlations before causation is fully understood. Its influence extends beyond industry and science, thus shaping governance, ethics, and even our philosophical notions of objectivity and truth.

Crucially, big data allows for the prediction of changing trends in significant events that were traditionally analysed only after their occurrence. Its defining features include volume (huge data amounts), variety (diverse and complex characteristics), velocity (rapid generation speed), and value (economic and scientific values). Compared to the first data revolution, the second one is comprehensive, transforming scientific research paradigms and providing quantitative research methods for social sciences. It has the potential to bring about significant changes in various social science domains like economy, society, and military affairs. In natural sciences, big data has reshaped traditional research paradigms, offering a scientific method known as Gray's fourth scientific paradigm. Big data has the potential to revolutionise social science research, making it more empirical and quantitative, thus shedding the label of "pseudoscience." Big data's impact extends beyond the technical realm, influencing management philosophy, operating methods, and more. "Data-driven social management" is a novel management mode, requiring data collection and analysis as fundamental components for grassroots-level management departments. Big data plays a pivotal role in healthcare, public security, smart city construction, prevention of terrorism, national defence, and governance against social corruption. From data to knowledge, business intelligence has evolved, and the "decision-support system" now relies heavily on data and information. Compared to traditional data, the resource character of big data is remarkably outstanding and is considered as critical as energy and material resources. Data is not just the basis for producing information, knowledge, and wisdom, but is inherently connected to them. In the information age, the challenge is not the lack of information but dealing with information desolateness, a challenge that big data sharing and standard management can potentially overcome. Despite its rapid development and innovation in data analysis technologies, big data, like any new technology, poses social risks such as individual privacy concerns, data objectivity and accuracy, and potential misuse. Big data exhibits uncertainty, diversity, complexity, and regularity, and its virtual nature makes it uniquely influential, raising ethical and philosophical considerations. General features of big data include objective existence, internal structure and mechanisms, causality, correlation, mining capabilities, resource character, virtuality, and potential risks. The exploration, development, and use of big data are primarily motivated by its objective existence and value, providing a new way to understand the laws and rules of things' development.

Data science encompasses the application of advanced analytics and scientific principles to extract valuable business insights from data [5]. The primary focus of advanced analytics is to anticipate future events by identifying patterns within data. While basic analytics provide a general description of data, advanced analytics delve deeper, offering a more profound understanding and analysis of granular data. Various types of analytics, including descriptive, diagnostic, predictive, and prescriptive analytics, are prevalent in the field of data science. The integration of ML techniques, a significant component of artificial intelligence (AI), plays a crucial role in the Fourth Industrial Revolution (Industry 4.0) by enabling smart computing and automation. In the current era of "data science and advanced analytics," our daily lives are extensively recorded in various digital forms, encompassing business, financial, healthcare, multimedia, IoT, cybersecurity, and social media data. This data, ranging from structured to unstructured, continues to grow exponentially. Data science serves as a comprehensive concept unifying statistics and data analysis to comprehend and analyse real-world phenomena. Described as the "science of data," data science involves creating data products that offer insights, predictions, services, or guidance in decision-making. The popularity of data science, as illustrated by Google Trends data over the past five years, is steadily rising. The figure also depicts increasing trends for related areas such as data analytics, data mining, big data, and ML. This surge in popularity, supported by statistical information and the practical applicability of data-driven decision-making in various domains, motivates a closer examination of data science and ML-based advanced analytics. Fast-forward to the 21st century, data science has co-evolved with medicine, healthcare, and other specialist domains in addition to influencing the development of computer science and AI. Data science combines a variety of techniques, methods, and methodologies from statistics and mathematics. The combined knowledge and information extracts have structured and unstructured source data, resulting in pooled datasets that can help better answer complex problems. However, there is scepticism around "problems" and "solutions," as often the demarcation of these areas can be non-specific, given that some deem minimalist and others maximalist accounts to condition and carve the data. In particular, maximalist accounts characterise ontologies and taxonomies—sometimes also called domains—well to construct a data pool before any analyses is conducted, while the minimalist approach embraces a narration of the identified data rather than a said method.

Methods such as ML modelling, natural language processing (NLP), sentiment analysis, neural networks, and deep learning (DL) are employed to develop data-driven intelligent applications. Their study encompasses various advanced analytics methods, including regression analysis, classification, clustering, association rules, time-series analysis, sentiment analysis, behavioural patterns, anomaly detection, factor analysis, log analysis, and DL. The importance of ML modelling for extracting valuable insights and facilitating data-driven decision-making is highlighted. This chapter provides a comprehensive overview of data science, detailing different analytic methods and their applicability in various real-world data-driven domains, such as business, health, IoT, behavioural, and urban data science. The key contribution lies in understanding data science modelling and elucidating analytic methods for practical solutions in diverse application areas. The overarching goal is to serve as a guide for academia and industry professionals interested in studying, researching, and developing automated and intelligent applications or systems within the realm of data science.

1.2.5 The DTOP Model (Data–Theory–Observation–Phenomenon)

1.2.5.1 Quaternion, the Phenomenon of Data–Theory–Observation

Beyond the sweeping history of scientific development lies a quieter, yet equally profound, question: *How do we come to "know" something in the age of data?* The DTOP model—short for Data–Theory–Observation–Phenomenon—offers one philosophical response. Building on traditions from logical positivism to falsificationism, it recognises data not as a passive record but as an active participant in the shaping of theory. Where classical models emphasised a binary of theory and observation, DTOP proposes a fourfold interaction: theories emerge from data, observations refine theories, and phenomena both inspire and challenge their interpretation. Data, in this model, is not neutral; far from it, it is infused with human judgement, theory-leadenness, and technical constraints. This insight prompts us to ask the following question: *Can objectivity exist in data?* Or, must we accept that even our most "empirical" tools carry the imprint of choice, bias, and abstraction?

DTOP invites us to reconsider the presumed objectivity of data. It suggests that data is not a neutral mirror but a mediated construct, filtered through theoretical frameworks, disciplinary norms, and technical systems. The same dataset, for example, might serve as raw input in computer science, derived insight in sociology, or contested evidence in legal studies. This fluidity underscores the model's core claim: that data and theory are co-constructive, each shaping and reshaping the other across context. In a world increasingly reliant on data-driven claims, this recursive relationship matters, not only for science but for society's trust in knowledge itself.

In today's digital landscape, data rarely stands alone. It enters a layered system of transformation; data becomes information when contextualised, knowledge when synthesised, and wisdom when ethically applied. This progression, known as the "data, information, knowledge, and wisdom (DIKW) hierarchy, challenges us to ask: at what point does raw input become actionable insight? And who gets to decide? As algorithms digest terabytes of information in milliseconds, the risk isn't merely data overload; it's meaninglessness masquerading as certainty. The DIKW model reminds us that value emerges not from accumulation but from interpretation, judgement, and human-centred discernment."

Data emanates from the outcomes of human cognitive activity, serving as the subjective reflection of objective phenomena and acting as a logical language to characterise these phenomena. Beyond being a quantitative representation, data is intrinsic to understanding things and forms a highly unified language, surpassing traditional text languages in communication efficiency due to its simplicity and accuracy. Originating from observations and measurements, data inherently possesses the features of things, and while its objectivity is influenced by human subjectivity, it has been a fundamental component since the birth of numbers. Data functions as a connection between the objectivity of things and human subjectivity, serving as a bridge for humans to comprehend the world. With the rapid advancement of computing methods and information technology, big data has emerged as a crucial resource for analysis, management, decision-making, and more in various domains. Big data represents a new paradigm for knowledge discovery, creation, and understanding the world. The significance of data is indisputable, as it is omnipresent in our surroundings, reflecting a return to the ontological idea. Analogous to the value of science, the value of data necessitates that individuals handling and managing data bear responsibility for its use, sharing, operation, and management.

As data becomes an integral part of human existence, philosophical reflections on data are deemed essential. The primary framework of the philosophy of data should aim to elucidate the nature, general laws, rules of data, and the philosophical challenges arising in its utilisation. Exploring the historical evolution, ontology, epistemology, methodology, factuality, ethics, and sociology of data will constitute crucial aspects of the philosophy of data. The study of the philosophy of data will span multiple disciplines, including the history of science and technology, natural philosophy, philosophy of science, philosophy of technology, philosophy of engineering, cognitive science, sociology, methodology, ethics of science and technology, economics of technology, psychology, and relevant natural sciences, exhibiting the typical characteristics of interdisciplinary sciences.

For many visual applications, pose estimation is a crucial procedure. In augmented reality mapping, a rigid body's spatial orientation is often depicted using six degrees of freedom (6 DoF), which encompass translation and a sequential series of rotations known as Euler angles. Initially, these rotations may seem intuitive, as they denote rotations around the principal axes. However, sequential rotations pose inherent issues, such as gimbal lock or the loss of a degree of freedom. Moreover, there exist 12 alternative combinations of rotations that can produce a specific spatial orientation, leading to confusion and complicating computations for inverse or forward dynamics. While calculating the rates of change of Euler angles for a given rotation sequence is feasible, it presents a significant mathematical challenge. In industries as varied as chemistry, robotics, space shuttle control, 3D gaming, and virtual reality, quaternions emerge as the preferred rotation operator. Particularly valuable in real-time or key-frame animations and AR applications, quaternion multiplication proves computationally efficient, enabling swift and seamless interpolation of orientations. Quaternions offer an algebraic representation of arbitrary rotational operations on oriented spatial data, addressing challenges that arise with Euler angles in traditional GIS systems. Through quaternion operations, a solution is provided for the rotational transformation of complex spatial data, offering a more efficient alternative to the sequential steps and rules of thumb involved in traditional GIS graphics techniques. The utility of quaternions extends to pose estimation, where algorithms based on quaternions can yield unique solutions to camera pose estimation problems. Fathian et al. [6] pioneered a quaternion-based approach for representing rotation, facilitating easier recovery of rotation and translation parameters. This method enables faster and more accurate pose estimation compared to traditional techniques, enhancing tracking systems' ability to estimate object rotation accurately and mitigate drift effects during static states. Seo et al. [7] further improved tracking system accuracy by introducing quaternion-based orientation estimation, effectively eliminating drift effects during static states. The limitations of GIS in handling rotation and interpolation of orientation are addressed by De Paor et al. [8] through the incorporation of quaternions. Quaternions-based pose representation emerges as a more effective method for solving general nonlinear least squares optimisation problems involving unit quaternion functions. To reduce computational requirements, a Kalman filter utilising quaternion-based orientation estimation from MARG sensors is proposed, offering a method for incorporating inertial measurement unit data into quaternion-based orientation estimation algorithms. Quaternions possess the capability to express precise spatial relationships and geometry. A novel linear pose estimation based on quaternions enhances the accuracy and efficiency of camera pose estimation algorithms for 3D to 2D line and point correspondences [9]. Additionally, for the visualisation of indoor navigation, a quaternion-based precise 3D modelling method for path networks is proposed, enabling the automatic generation of highly recognisable 3D models. Quaternions possess the capability to describe the rotation of any vector axes, facilitating the rotation of oriented spatial data and expressing differences at the surface level of directional spatial data. However, previous published studies concerning quaternion-based pose estimation for spatial data have primarily focused on a single spatial object (Figure 1.1).

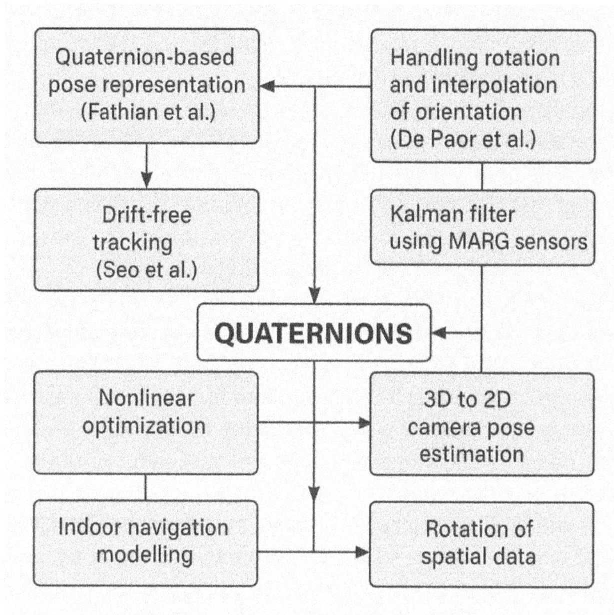

FIGURE 1.1 Uses of quaternions for visualisation.

1.3 DATA SCIENCE DEFINITIONS AND MODELLING METHODS

In the rapidly evolving ecosystem of data science, terminology matters. Words like data analysis, data mining, data analytics, big data, advanced analytics, ML, and DL are often used interchangeably. Yet each represents a specific methodological stance, technical toolset, and epistemological assumption. This section aims to clarify those distinctions and provide a conceptual map for understanding how data science operates at the intersection of theory, method, and application.

"Data analysis" in its traditional sense refers to the interpretation of data using statistical tools to summarise key features. It answers the question, "What does the data show?" without necessarily extrapolating future trends or diagnosing root causes. "Data analytics," by contrast, digs deeper, incorporating advanced statistical models and domain knowledge to generate actionable insights. It is less about raw description and more about uncovering embedded patterns that might inform decision-making.

"Data mining" goes a step further, as a practice emerging from data theory and AI, it seeks to discover previously unknown patterns and knowledge within large datasets. It is often described as the non-trivial extraction of implicit, previously unknown, and potentially useful information. This method relies heavily on automation and is often considered a precursor or sibling to ML.

The term "Big data" refers to datasets with unique characteristics such as massive volume, high dimensionality, heterogeneity, and complexity. Coined to describe datasets too large, fast, or complex for the traditional data-processing software, it encompasses the famed "3 Vs," volume, velocity, and variety with some scholars adding veracity, value, and variability. Big data does not merely describe scale; it also denotes a qualitative shift in how data is generated (e.g., through sensors, social media, and IoT devices), how it is processed (real-time analytics), and how it reconfigures industries from marketing to medicine.

"Advanced analytics" stands as a bridge between traditional data analysis and emergent AI methods. It encompasses techniques like predictive modelling, prescriptive analytics, and optimisation algorithms, and thus extends our ability to forecast outcomes and test hypothetical scenarios. Where descriptive analytics tells us "what happened, and diagnostic analytics seeks to explain why, advanced analytics ventures into what will happen" and "what should be done".

"Machine learning (ML)" and "Deep learning (DL)" form the technical backbone of most modern data science initiatives. ML involves creating algorithms that allow systems to learn from and make decisions based on data. These can range from linear regressions to support vector machines to random forests. DL, a subfield of ML, utilises neural networks with many layers, mimicking the structure of the human brain to handle highly complex tasks such as image and speech recognition.

It is essential to note that while ML and DL are critical to data science, they are not synonymous with it. Data science is broader, as defined by Cao [10], it is an interdisciplinary field that synthesises statistics, informatics, computing, communication, management, and sociology to transform data into actionable insights. It is both a science of data and a methodology for applying that science to real-world problems.

In practical terms, data science projects follow a lifecycle understanding the problems, acquiring data, cleaning and preprocessing it, modelling, evaluating, deploying, and iterating [11]. The process starts with domain immersion, whether in healthcare, finance, or agriculture, to understand the questions that data might help answer. This is followed by data acquisition from sources like APIs, public repositories, or proprietary systems. Obtaining ethical approvals, CAG, or indeed local governance approvals is critical before access is provided. Cleaning data is arguably the most labour-intensive phase, involving tasks like handling missing values, correcting inconsistencies, and standardising or harmonising formats (where multiple systems are used to access data).

Once the data is prepped, exploratory data analysis (EDA) begins. This includes visualisations, summary statistics, and hypothesis testing to identify patterns and anomalies [12]. EDA is not merely technical but interpretive; it requires domain knowledge to ask the right questions and contextualise the answers. Modelling, then, involves selecting appropriate algorithms based on the nature of the data and the problem, for instance, regression for prediction, clustering for segmentation, classification for decision-making, and so forth.

Evaluation metrics differ based on the modelling goal. For classification, metrics like accuracy, precision, recall, and F1-score are common. For regression, we consider RMSE or R-squared. Beyond numerical scores, models are judged on interpretability, scalability, and ethical considerations. For example, a high-performing model that acts as a "black box" may not be acceptable in fields like healthcare or law [13].

Deployment moves models from notebooks to production environments, embedding them in apps, websites, or enterprise systems. This phase includes monitoring for data drift, re-training models, and ensuring system robustness. Iteration is continuous; models must evolve as new data becomes available and business needs change.

The field also contends with philosophical debates, such as the tension that exists between minimalist and maximalist approaches to data. The minimalist sees data as narrative valuable when tied to context and meaning. In contrast, the maximalist sees data as infrastructure, raw material to be structured and analysed en masse. Both perspectives have merit and reflect deeper epistemological divides.

Databases used in data science can range from structured (e.g., spreadsheets, Sequence Query Language (SQL), databases) to unstructured (e.g., free text, images, audio) to semi-structured (e.g., HTML, XML, JSON). Metadata, that is, data about data, is increasingly crucial, guiding how data is interpreted and ensuring traceability. Real-world applications are diverse, for instance, Network Security Language—Knowledge Discovery in Databases (NSL-KDD) for cybersecurity, MIMIC for healthcare, or Kaggle repositories for general-purpose modelling.

Examples include cybersecurity datasets like NSL-KDD, UNSW-NB15, and Bot-IoT, smartphone datasets covering phone call logs and mobile application usage, IoT data, health data encompassing conditions like heart disease, diabetes, and COVID-19, as well as datasets from agriculture and e-commerce.

Data science, as an umbrella term encompassing advanced data analytics, data mining, ML, and related disciplines like statistics, plays a crucial role in real-world business processes. Data science, an encompassing term for advanced data analytics, data mining, and related disciplines, significantly impacts real-world business processes. The modelling process involves key stages, starting with a comprehensive understanding of the business problem, its implications, and the formulation of relevant questions. Business intelligence is applied to enhance decision-making. Understanding the available data follows, including assessing its quality, relevance, and types. EDA, employing visualisation and statistical tools, helps develop hypotheses and ensures data readiness. Data preprocessing techniques clean, transform, and enrich the data for modelling. ML models are then designed and evaluated using metrics like accuracy and precision. Advanced analytics methods, such as feature engineering, algorithm tuning, and ensemble methods, enhance model performance. The ultimate output is a data product, representing a discovery, prediction, service, or tool, aiding in making smarter business decisions and contributing to automation. In summary, data science modelling drives positive changes in business practices, requiring a deep understanding of the business problem. Data scientists play a vital role in interpreting and managing data, uncovering answers to complex questions, and designing advanced analytics tools for intelligent computing processes.

Descriptive analytics provides hindsight, revealing trends and anomalies. Diagnostic analytics probes causality. Predictive analytics forecasts probabilities. Prescriptive analytics recommends actions. Together, they form a hierarchy of understanding that moves from observation to intervention. This analytics stack is used across sectors, from identifying fraud in banking to predicting equipment failure in manufacturing.

Ultimately, the value of data science lies not just in technical competence but in critical thinking, ethical sensitivity, and the capacity to bridge abstract models with human needs. As we become increasingly data-driven, the challenge will be to stay meaning-driven. Data science is not just about answers; it is also about asking better questions (Figure 1.2).

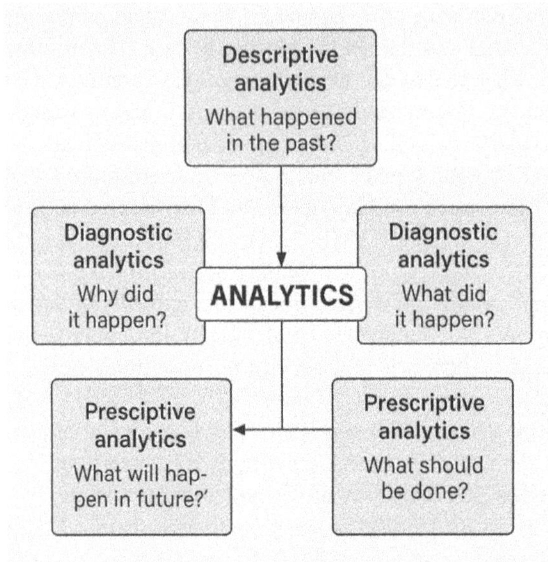

FIGURE 1.2 A taxonomy of analytics.

1.4 DATA SCIENCE IN MEDICINE

The digital evolution has ushered in an era where vast amounts of medical data are generated daily in the form of electronic health records (EHRs), diagnostic images, genomics data, wearable device outputs, prescription histories, and public health records, just to name a few sources. This abundance of health-related data presents both opportunity and risk. On the one hand, ML algorithms and predictive analytics can identify hidden patterns in clinical data, enabling earlier diagnosis, personalised treatment plans, and more effective public health interventions. Conversely, questions of data privacy, algorithmic bias, and equitable access to these technologies remain pressing.

The integration of big data analytics into medicine is reshaping the field in profound ways. Health Information Exchanges now allow for the consolidation of patient data from multiple sources, creating comprehensive profiles that clinicians can access in real time. These systems support not only clinical decision-making but also population health management, enabling healthcare providers to track disease outbreaks, identify at-risk groups, and allocate resources more efficiently.

Moreover, the rise of mobile health (mHealth) technologies, including smartphone apps, wearable sensors, and remote monitoring devices, has expanded the boundaries of healthcare beyond the clinic. Individuals can now track vital signs, monitor chronic conditions, and share real-time data with their care teams, fostering more proactive and participatory models of care.

Yet these advances come with significant technical and ethical challenges. The three Vs of big data, volume, velocity, and variety, are especially pronounced in healthcare where datasets are not only large and fast-moving but also heterogeneous, encompassing structured records, free text notes, images, genetic sequences, and streaming sensor data. Managing this complexity requires sophisticated tools for data integration, storage, and analysis.

Crucially, the veracity of health data, that is, its accuracy and reliability, can vary widely, with implications for patient safety and research integrity. Errors in data entry, mismatches across systems, and incomplete records can compromise the quality of insights derived from analytics. Thus, ensuring data quality is as vital as developing predictive models or decision-support algorithms. Furthermore, big data in medicine raises philosophical and societal questions. Who owns health data? How can patient autonomy and privacy be preserved in an era of ubiquitous data collection? How do we ensure that data-driven healthcare does not exacerbate existing inequalities?

ML models trained on biased datasets may inadvertently reinforce health disparities, particularly if underrepresented populations are insufficiently represented in training data. Addressing these concerns requires a commitment to transparency, inclusivity, and continual auditing of algorithms.

Despite these complexities, the potential benefits of data science in medicine are substantial. Predictive analytics can help identify individuals at high risk for diseases such as diabetes, cardiovascular conditions, or cancer, facilitating early intervention. NLP tools can extract critical insights from unstructured clinical notes. AI-driven diagnostic tools, including computer vision systems for medical imaging, are achieving expert-level performance in detecting conditions like diabetic retinopathy or certain cancers.

Ultimately, the responsible application of data science in healthcare holds the promise of more precise, efficient, and equitable care. However, realising this vision requires more than technical expertise; it demands thoughtful governance, interdisciplinary collaboration, and a patient-centred ethos that prioritises ethics alongside innovation.

1.5 DATA SCIENCE AND APPLICATION USE

The influence of data science extends well beyond its technological origins, permeating nearly every sector of contemporary life. As data generation accelerates, industries from agriculture to astrophysics grapple with both the promise and complexity of this information abundance. In the corporate world, businesses leverage data science to gain a competitive advantage, optimise operations, and drive innovation. Retailers apply predictive analytics to forecast consumer demand, personalise marketing campaigns, and refine supply chain logistics. Financial institutions use ML models to detect fraudulent transactions, assess credit risk, and automate investment strategies through algorithmic trading.

Manufacturing industries, propelled by Industry 4.0, integrate data-driven systems to enhance predictive maintenance, streamline production, and enable smart factories [14]. Sensors embedded in machinery generate continuous streams of data, which, when analysed in real time, minimise downtime and improve efficiency. Urban environments are similarly transformed. Smart cities harness data from transportation networks, energy grids, public safety systems, and citizen services to optimise resource allocation and improve quality of life. Traffic patterns are analysed to reduce congestion, sensor data informs waste management, and environmental monitoring supports sustainability initiatives.

In agriculture, precision farming employs data science to monitor soil conditions, predict crop yields, and manage resources with unprecedented accuracy [15]. Satellite imagery, IoT devices, and ML converge to optimise planting schedules, irrigation, and pest control, enhancing food security while minimising environmental impact.

Environmental science and climate research also rely heavily on data-driven methodologies. Vast datasets from satellite observations, climate models, and sensor networks enable scientists to track environmental changes, predict extreme weather events, and inform mitigation strategies for climate resilience.

Education, too, is undergoing a data-driven transformation. Learning analytics track student engagement, performance, and retention patterns, allowing educators to personalise instruction and improve outcomes. Predictive models identify at-risk students, enabling timely interventions to support academic success [16].

Similarly, public policy increasingly depends on data-informed decision-making. Governments use data science to model economic trends, manage public health crises, and enhance emergency response systems [17]. The COVID-19 pandemic exemplified how real-time data analytics shaped policies on mobility, healthcare resource allocation, and vaccination strategies.

Scientific research itself has entered a new era, which some term the "Fourth Paradigm," where data-intensive discovery complements theory, experimentation, and simulation [4]. Disciplines like bioinformatics, computational social science, and astroinformatics exemplify how data science accelerates knowledge creation, from understanding genetic pathways to mapping the cosmos.

Yet the proliferation of data across domains is not without challenges. Data governance, privacy concerns, algorithmic accountability, and the digital divide persist as pressing issues. Moreover, the sheer volume and heterogeneity of data raise questions about storage, interoperability, and meaningful interpretation.

Ethically navigating these complexities requires interdisciplinary collaboration, robust regulatory frameworks, and a commitment to equity. As data becomes a ubiquitous resource, societies must grapple with who benefits, who is left behind, and how to ensure that data-driven progress aligns with broader social values. Thus, the application of data science across domains illustrates its dual nature: a catalyst for innovation and a crucible for ethical reflection. Harnessing its potential demands not only technical acumen but also cultural, philosophical, and institutional wisdom.

1.6 HUMAN FACTORS AND DATA SCIENCE

While data science is often framed in terms of algorithms, models, and computational infrastructure, its success and ethical impact are inextricably linked to human factors. Behind every dataset lies human decision-making: in what data is collected, how it is labelled, how algorithms are designed, and how outputs are interpreted and acted upon.

Cognitive biases, organisational culture, user behaviour, and societal norms profoundly shape how data-driven systems operate in practice. Even the most sophisticated model is vulnerable to human oversight, poor communication, or misaligned incentives. One critical human factor is *data literacy*. As data science permeates workplaces, policymaking, and daily life, the ability of individuals and organisations to understand, question, and responsibly use data becomes paramount. Data illiteracy can lead to misinterpretation of results, over-reliance on automated systems, or uncritical acceptance of algorithmic outputs.

Moreover, *diversity* within data science teams enhances both technical robustness and ethical sensitivity. Inclusive teams are better equipped to anticipate unintended consequences, detect algorithmic biases, and design systems that serve diverse populations. Conversely, homogenous groups risk blind spots that can embed inequities into technological infrastructures.

Human trust in data-driven systems is another essential consideration. Black-box algorithms, opaque data practices, and inconsistent communication erode public confidence. Transparent model development, explainable AI techniques, and participatory design approaches help build trust and ensure that data science aligns with societal values.

Behavioural factors also influence how individuals engage with data-driven tools. Interface design, feedback mechanisms, and cognitive load affect whether users adopt systems effectively or disregard recommendations. Human-centred design principles must guide not only algorithm development but also user experience engineering.

Additionally, organisational dynamics play a role in how data science initiatives unfold. *Leadership support*, cross-functional collaboration, resource allocation, and ethical governance structures determine whether data projects succeed or exacerbate operational silos and systemic risks.

Finally, the global nature of data science requires sensitivity to cultural differences, legal variations, and geopolitical contexts. Ethical norms, data privacy expectations, and regulatory frameworks differ across regions, influencing how data-driven technologies are designed and deployed. In short, data science is as much a human enterprise as it is a technical one. Recognising and integrating human factors at every stage, from data collection to algorithm deployment, enhances system effectiveness, fosters ethical resilience, and ensures that technological advancement remains accountable to human dignity and social good.

Case Study: Leveraging EHRs for Epidemiological Research in Rwanda

A CASE STUDY DEMONSTRATING THE USE OF ELECTRONIC HEALTHCARE RECORDS TO CONDUCT EPIDEMIOLOGY RESEARCH IN RWANDA

INTRODUCTION

The healthcare landscape is constantly evolving, and EHR represents a big change, transitioning from traditional paper records to digital ones. Rwanda has progressively adopted EHR systems in its healthcare facilities, and this represents a concrete framework for epidemiological research. The introduction of EHRs has provided a rich source of data that is crucial for tracking, understanding, and mitigating disease patterns [18]. As Rwanda moves towards comprehensive digital health coverage, EHRs have facilitated efficient data management and improved patient care, while supporting extensive epidemiological studies [19]. This case study examines how EHR is employed for epidemiological research in Rwanda, using non-communicable diseases as an example, to demonstrate their potential for addressing health disparities, informing policy, and improving outcomes.

Implementation of EHR in Rwanda

The Rwandan Ministry of Health prioritised the integration of EHRs as part of its broader e-Health strategy, which aligns with the World Health Organization's digital health guidelines. The EHR system has been widely adopted across Rwandan healthcare facilities, particularly in rural areas. Rwanda's commitment to digitising health records across health facilities, including primary care centres, enables the collection of consistent data nationwide, supporting large-scale epidemiological studies. According to Nzarama et al., the country's EHR system enables data linking and matching across facilities, ensuring that even mobile patients maintain a continuous health record that aids in tracking health outcomes across provinces [20].

CASE STUDY ON THE USE OF EHRs IN EPIDEMIOLOGY: NON-COMMUNICABLE DISEASES RESEARCH

The utilisation of EHR in Rwanda has enhanced tracking and management of healthcare programmes, especially in child immunisation through the electronic immunisation registry (e-Tracker) [21]. The e-Tracker system is designed to track immunisation schedules across health facilities, allowing healthcare providers to keep track of vaccine administration and identify vulnerable populations for targeted interventions. This case study examined healthcare workers' experiences with the e-Tracker system in Rwanda. It focused on the usability, challenges with duplicate data entry, and the impact of EHR on immunisation data completeness and timeliness [21]. The study also highlighted areas of improvement in EHR functionalities to improve health outcomes and programme monitoring for children in Rwanda.

Data Collection and Analysis

The e-Tracker EHR system that is used across health facilities in Rwanda targets the childhood immunisation programme, and the system enables live tracking and updates on immunisation records, inclusive of doses given, and follow-up prompts. The study included healthcare workers across various health facilities in Rwanda who frequently interacted with the e-Tracker system for childhood immunisation tracking. Data was collected via healthcare worker feedback on system usability, satisfaction, and associated challenges with using the e-Tracker. Emphasis was placed on how duplicate data entry (into both electronic and paper systems) affected healthcare workers' workload and satisfaction with the system.

Key Findings

The use of EHRs in this epidemiological study was instrumental in several ways:

1. **Data Accuracy and Completeness**: The e-Tracker EHR system was reported to improve the completeness of immunisation records by providing a centralised, digital record system. It reduces the reliance on paper records and allows for a more comprehensive tracking of each child's immunisation history.
2. **Improved Data Timeliness**: Real-time entry of data into the e-Tracker system decreases delays in immunisation status reporting, which is vital for time-sensitive public health interventions. For example, if a child missed a vaccination, the e-Tracker allowed healthcare workers to promptly identify this and arrange follow-ups.
3. **Challenges in Dual Data Entry**: Despite the benefits, health workers reported challenges with the double entry requirements of both digital and paper records. This double entry not only increased the workload but also sometimes led to a mismatch between the electronic data and paper, hence affecting data quality.
4. **Health Worker Satisfaction and Usability**: The healthcare workers' user feedback suggested that while e-Tracker helped provide easier access to immunisation records, the double-entry requirement decreased satisfaction and usability, as it lengthened the data entry process and at times resulted in redundant workflows.
5. **Targeting High-Risk Populations**: EHR data facilitated healthcare workers to identify children who were behind schedule on immunisations, and supporting targeted outreach to high-risk populations. This functionality is important for epidemiological monitoring, as it allows public health officials to allocate resources to areas with low immunisation rates or high dropout rates in the vaccination schedule.

Implications and Future Directions for Epidemiological Research

The e-Tracker system's ability to maintain complete, centralised, and timely data presents significant benefits for epidemiological research in Rwanda:

- By providing accurate records of immunisation uptake, EHR data from the e-Tracker helps epidemiologists assess coverage levels across different regions of the country. This insight is critical for determining where additional resources or interventions are needed to enhance vaccination rates.
- Through real-time data, epidemiologists can analyse patterns in immunisation dropout rates, missed appointments, and setbacks in vaccine administration. These insights will inform public health strategies to prevent outbreaks and strengthen immunity in populations at risk.
- The e-Tracker EHR system enables researchers to evaluate the effectiveness of immunisation programmes by monitoring trends over time. Researchers can also identify progress or declines in immunisation rates, helping to assess the impact of recent public health interventions or policy changes.

This case study also demonstrates the potential for expanding EHR use in researching other pressing health issues in Rwanda, such as maternal health, infectious disease outbreaks, and mental health conditions [22]. Moving forward, addressing the current limitations of EHRs can enhance their utility in epidemiology. Investment in digital infrastructure, particularly in rural areas, could improve data completeness and accuracy. Moreover, ongoing training for healthcare providers on EHR management will ensure more consistent data entry. Implementing advanced data analytics, including ML algorithms, could also enhance the analytical capacity of EHRs, enabling predictive modelling for disease prevention and intervention [22].

CONCLUSION

The use of EHRs in epidemiological research represents a crucial advancement for Rwanda's healthcare system. The implementation of the e-Tracker EHR system demonstrates the potential of electronic records to support epidemiological research and also enhance healthcare delivery in Rwanda and beyond. Despite certain challenges with double data entry, the e-Tracker system's ability to give comprehensive and timely data on immunisation schedules enables epidemiologists and public health officials to make timely informed decisions, targeting vulnerable areas, and ultimately improve child health outcomes across the country. This case study illustrates how EHRs can serve as a foundational tool in low- and middle-income countries like Rwanda, supporting both clinical care and epidemiological research to address pressing public health needs.

2 Data Science and Artificial Intelligence

2.1 INTRODUCTION TO ARTIFICIAL INTELLIGENCE

The father of "Artificial Intelligence (AI)" is considered to be John McCarthy, although the evolution began in the 1940s. This is first up in our lane in the timeline of AI. The *Bombe* machine, designed by Alan Turing during World War II, was certainly the turning point in cracking the German communications encoded by the Enigma machine. It helped in speeding up the decoding of messages. Hence, this allowed the allies to react and strategise within a few hours itself rather than waiting for days/weeks. His entire formula of breaking the code was with the observation that each German message contained a known piece of German plain text at a known point in the message. Gunn's pioneering investigation in 1976 marked the initial exploration of AI technology in the realm of surgery, particularly in diagnosing acute abdominal pain through computer analysis. Over the past two decades, there has been a significant uptick in interest and activity surrounding medical AI. In contemporary medicine, a significant challenge lies in managing the vast amount of knowledge required to address intricate clinical issues. The evolution of medical AI has been closely linked to the creation of AI programs aimed at aiding clinicians in diagnosing conditions, making treatment decisions, and forecasting outcomes. These programs are tailored to assist healthcare professionals in their daily responsibilities, particularly in tasks that involve processing data and knowledge. Various systems, such as Artificial Neural Networks (ANNs), fuzzy expert systems, evolutionary computation, and hybrid intelligent systems, have been developed to fulfil this role.

In the past two decades, ANNs have emerged as the most prevalent AI technique in the medical field, as evidenced by the volume of publications. ANNs are computational tools inspired by the biological nervous system, comprising interconnected computer processors known as "neurons." These networks conduct parallel computations for data processing and knowledge representation. Their capacity to learn from historical examples, analyse non-linear data, handle imprecise information, and generalise has rendered them highly attractive in medicine. The inception of artificial neurons dates back to 1943 when McCulloch and Pitts developed the first artificial neuron employing simple binary threshold functions. A significant advancement occurred with the introduction of the perceptron by psychologist Frank Rosenblatt in 1958, which served as a practical model. While numerous variations of the basic perceptron network have been proposed, the multilayer feedforward perceptron model has gained popularity. These networks consist of layers of neurons, typically including an input layer, one or more hidden layers, and an output layer, all fully interconnected. Neurons are linked by connections, each associated with a numerical weight, and the network learns through iterative adjustments of these weights.

DOI: 10.1201/9781003494737-2

One notable characteristic of ANNs is their ability to learn from experience in a training environment. However, the utilisation of multilayer feedforward Perceptrons was hindered by the absence of a suitable learning algorithm until Paul Werbos introduced "backpropagation" learning in 1974. Other popular network designs include Hopfield networks, Radial Basis Function networks, and the Self-Organising Feature Map. ANNs have demonstrated a broad range of applications in real-world scenarios. Their exceptional capability to classify and recognise patterns accurately has drawn researchers to employ them in addressing various clinical challenges. Recognising that diagnosis, treatment, and outcome prediction in many clinical scenarios depend on complex interactions among clinical, biological, and pathological variables, there is a growing demand for analytical tools like ANNs that can leverage these intricate relationships. Baxt was among the first researchers to explore the clinical potential of ANNs. He developed a neural network model that accurately diagnosed acute myocardial infarction and subsequently validated his findings with similar accuracy in prospective studies. Since then, ANNs have been utilised across virtually every field of medicine. ANNs have been applied across various domains in clinical settings, including diagnosis, image analysis in radiology and histopathology, data interpretation in intensive care settings, and waveform analysis. Stamey et al. developed a neural-network-based classification algorithm known as the ProstAsure Index, capable of distinguishing between benign and malignant prostates [23]. This model, validated in prospective studies, demonstrated a diagnostic accuracy of 90%, with a sensitivity of 81% and specificity of 92%. Other clinically relevant diagnostic applications of ANNs include the assessment of abdominal pain and appendicitis, identification of retained common bile duct stones, diagnosis of glaucoma, and the evaluation of back pain. Furthermore, ANNs have been instrumental in diagnosing cytological and histological specimens. PAPNET, an automated screening system based on neural networks, aids cytologists in cervical screening and has been commercially promoted. Various types of cells, including breast, gastric, thyroid, oral epithelial, urothelial, pleural, and peritoneal effusion cytology, have been analysed using neural networks, with varying degrees of success. In radiology, ANNs can utilise both human observations and direct digitised images as inputs. They have been employed to interpret plain radiographs, ultrasound images, CT scans, MRI scans, and radioisotope scans, contributing to enhanced diagnostic capabilities in radiology practice.

AI, also known as machine intelligence, refers to the capacity of computer systems to learn from input or historical data. The term AI is commonly employed when a machine replicates cognitive behaviours associated with human brain functions during learning and problem-solving. In contemporary times, biological and chemical scientists extensively integrate AI algorithms into the drug design and discovery process. Computational modelling based on AI and machine learning (ML) principles offers significant opportunities for identifying and validating chemical compounds, target identification, peptide synthesis, drug toxicity and physiochemical properties evaluation, drug monitoring, drug efficacy and effectiveness assessment, and drug repositioning. The emergence of AI principles, along with ML and deep learning (DL) algorithms, has streamlined the virtual screening (VS) of compounds from chemical libraries containing over 106 million compounds, making it more efficient and less time-consuming. Moreover, AI models address toxicity concerns arising from off-target interactions. This discussion briefly outlines the evolution of AI from ML to DL and the substantial involvement of Big Data in revolutionising the drug discovery process. It further provides an overview of the integration of AI and conventional chemistry to enhance drug discovery and highlights various AI applications throughout the drug design and discovery processes, including primary and secondary screening, drug toxicity assessment, drug release and monitoring, drug dosage effectiveness and efficacy evaluation, drug repositioning and polypharmacology, and drug–target interactions.

In September 2015, Google search revealed that following the modern (re)introduction of ML, AI became the most searched term. Some describe ML as the primary application of AI, while others see it as a subset of AI. AI serves as an umbrella term encompassing computer programs capable of processing information and possibly also behaving like humans, whereas ML goes beyond this by enabling machines to learn from input data with algorithms such as Naïve Bayes, decision trees (DT), hidden Markov models, and others, without explicit programming. With the advent of neural networks, machines gained further ability to classify and organise input data, as the human brain can do. In the 20th century, Igor Aizenberg and colleagues introduced the term "deep learning" (DL) while discussing adaptive neural networks. ML utilises supervised learning, where models are trained using labelled data, and unsupervised learning, where models find recurring patterns in unlabelled data. Other approaches include semi-supervised learning, self-supervised learning, reinforcement learning, and DL, which comprises many layers, requiring substantial computational power and Big Data for training [24–53].

The origins of ML trace back to 1943 when McCulloch and Pitts proposed the first mathematical model of a neural network. Alan M. Turing introduced the concept of ML in his seminal 1950 paper. In 1952, Arthur L. Samuel popularised the term "machine learning" with a checker-playing program for IBM. Frank Rosenblatt developed the perceptron in 1957 for image recognition. Henry J. Kelley introduced the continuous backpropagation model in 1960, further simplified by Stuart Dreyfus in 1962. In 1965, Ivakhnenko and Lapa developed the first working DL networks. Around 1980, Kunihiko Fukushima created neo-cognitron, an ANN with a multi-layered design for recognising visual patterns, and the first convolutional neural network (CNN) based on the organisation of the visual cortex in animals.

In 1986, David Rumelhart, Geoffrey Hinton, and Ronald J. Williams published a groundbreaking paper titled "Learning Representations by Back-propagating Errors," showcasing the potential of backpropagation to enhance shape recognition and word prediction. Despite initial successes, there were setbacks, but Hinton persisted through the challenges of the second AI Winter, earning himself the moniker "Godfather of DL." In 1989, Yann LeCun demonstrated backpropagation practically at Bell Labs. Concurrently, Christopher Watkins introduced Q-learning in his thesis "Learning from Delayed Rewards," refining reinforcement learning [54]. In 1995, Corinna Cortes and Vladimir Vapnik developed support vector machines (SVMs) for recognising similar data, followed by Jürgen Schmidhuber and Sepp Hochreiter's creation of long short-term memory (LSTM) for recurrent neural networks (RNNs) in 1997 [55]. In 1999, the launch of graphic processing units (GPUs) marked a pivotal moment, initially designed for accelerating 3D graphics processing but later repurposed for parallel computing, becoming essential for DL. The emergence of Big Data was foreseen in 2001, urging preparation for the influx of data. Nvidia's introduction of CUDA in 2007 facilitated the utilisation of GPUs for general-purpose computing, enabling DL operations due to high memory bandwidth and parallel processing capabilities. Fei-Fei Li's launch of ImageNet in 2009 provided a vast labelled image database for research. Around 2012, Alex Krizhevsky developed AlexNet, a CNN that significantly improved speed and dropout with rectified linear units. In the same year, Google Brain's "cat experiment" highlighted DL's limitations, with networks recognising less than 16% of presented objects. In 2014, Nvidia introduced cuDNN, a CUDA-based DL library, and "Deep Face" achieved 97.5% accuracy in face identification [56]. Generative adversarial networks (GANs) debuted the same year, revolutionising data authentication. In 2016, Cray Inc. utilised Microsoft's neural network software on its XC50 supercomputer, powered by 1000 Nvidia Tesla P100 GPUs, capable of rapid processing [57]. Nvidia's Tesla V100 GPU, introduced in 2017, featured tensor cores for accelerated AI operations [58]. Despite significant advancements, DL continues to evolve, requiring innovative ideas for further progress.

2.1.1 The Turing Years

Alan Turing, widely regarded as the world's foremost computer scientist and mathematician, proposed yet another experiment to assess machine intelligence. His aim was to determine whether a machine could exhibit human-like thinking capabilities and make decisions with comparable rationality and intelligence. In this test, an interrogator must discern which responses originate from a human and which from a machine. If the interrogator cannot reliably distinguish between the two, the machine would pass the test by being indistinguishable from a human. In Turing's era, there was a lively debate among mathematicians about the feasibility of constructing a single, all-purpose machine capable of solving any computable problem. These problems ranged from finding the most energy-efficient route for a car to predicting how a sequence of amino acids would fold into a three-dimensional protein structure. Another example was the computability of whether larger numbers could be expressed as the product of smaller ones, a crucial aspect of modern encryption, where the distinction between prime and composite numbers plays a pivotal role. Several prominent mathematicians proposed intricate designs for universal computers that would operate according to complex mathematical rules. However, the prospect of constructing such machines seemed dauntingly challenging. It was Turing's brilliance that illuminated a path forward, demonstrating that a remarkably simple machine could effectively compute anything that is computable. This hypothetical device came to be known as a "Turing machine." At the heart of the Turing machine lies a strip of tape divided into individual boxes, each containing a symbol such as letters representing the genetic code (A, C, T, and G) or blank spaces. This tape serves a dual purpose: initially representing the input data for the problem at hand and acting as the computer's memory. As the computation progresses, the Turing machine writes and reads data on the tape, manipulating symbols to perform the necessary calculations. This rudimentary yet ingenious concept laid the groundwork for modern computing, with the tape analogy akin to today's hard drives storing and accessing data. The device operates by reading individual symbols on the tape and executing instructions based on the current state of the machine. These instructions dictate whether to alter the symbol, leave it unchanged, and move to the next symbol. For instance, to determine if the tape contains the text string "TC," the machine scans forward, transitioning between states such as "previous letter was T" and "previous letter was not C." If, while in the state "previous letter was T," it reads a "C," the machine transitions to a state labelled "found it" and stops. Conversely, if it encounters a blank symbol at the end of the input, it transitions to the state "did not find it" and halts. In modern terms, we recognise this set of instructions as the machine's program. After some time, it became evident to everyone that Turing's insight was correct: the Turing machine could indeed compute everything that appeared computable. No matter how many additions or enhancements were made to the machine, its computing capabilities could not be expanded beyond its fundamental design.

Turing's early investigations into computation were influenced by the programme outlined by David Hilbert at the 1928 International Mathematical Congress. Hilbert posed three fundamental questions concerning logic and mathematics: whether mathematics was complete, meaning that any mathematical assertion could be proven or disproven; whether it was consistent, implying that false statements could not be derived from valid steps; and whether it was decidable, indicating the existence of a definite method to determine the truth or falsity of every mathematical assertion. Within three years, Kurt Gödel demonstrated that the axioms of arithmetic were neither complete nor consistent, and by 1937, both Alonzo Church and Alan Turing had proven the undecidability of specific mathematical assertions. While Gödel and Church relied on mathematical calculi to establish their results, Turing pursued an unconventional approach by considering mathematical proof as a product of human reasoning. He conceived of a physical machine that mimicked a human mathematician using pen and paper, along with a set of instructions. Turing then expanded this concept to create a universal machine capable of emulating all other computing machines. He utilised this construct to illustrate that certain functions could not be computed by such a universal machine, thereby demonstrating the undecidability of assertions related to these functions. At the core of Turing's universal machine lies a model of human calculation. This decision laid the groundwork for subsequent discussions regarding the extent to which computers might achieve more sophisticated human-level reasoning. The onset of World War II presented Turing with an unprecedented opportunity and resources to devise and test a machine capable of replicating human reasoning. Serving as the UK's primary decryption hub during the war, Bletchley Park had enlisted a cadre of the nation's top mathematicians in a concerted effort to decrypt German military communications. By 1940, the Bombe machine, a collaboration between Turing and Welchman, was operational and adeptly deciphering messages using methods previously executed manually by human codebreakers. Rooted in Turing's background in Mathematical Logic, the Bombe design operated on a principle of reductio ad absurdum, simplifying the hypothesis space of the Enigma machine's 263 possible settings to a manageable number based on recorded message transcriptions. The hypothesis elimination approach employed by the Bombe machine was further refined in the development of the Colossus I and II machines.

The declassified Tunny report reveals that a significant technical advancement in Colossus was the integration of Bayesian reasoning to guide the search through hypothetical settings for the Lorenz encryption machine. This fusion of logical hypothesis generation with Bayesian evaluation later became central to methodologies employed within ML. Notably, the Bletchley Park decryption efforts laid the groundwork for the post-war emergence of machine intelligence and subjective probabilistic reasoning, with two key figures from the Tunny report, Donald Michie and Jack Good, assuming pioneering roles in these fields. During numerous informal gatherings at Bletchley Park, Turing engaged in discussions about the concept of machine intelligence with Michie and Good. According to Turing's biographer, Andrew Hodges, these meetings provided an opportunity for Turing to refine ideas on chess-playing machines, which had originated in his 1941 conversations with Jack Good. The trio frequently explored the mechanisation of thought processes, integrating theories of probability and weight of evidence familiar to Michie. Turing's focus shifted towards envisioning a machine capable of learning, rather than merely executing complex tasks—a concept that would profoundly influence the trajectory of AI research [59–77].

In Turing's 1950 paper, he begins by posing the question: "Can machines think?" He then proceeds to delineate a philosophical framework in the subsequent six sections as shown below [78]:

1. **The Imitation Game**: Commonly known as the "Turing test," this parlour game involves a human interrogator questioning both a concealed computer and a concealed person to discern their identities alternately. The aim of the Imitation Game is to provide an objective assessment for determining whether machines possess the capacity for thought.
2. **Critique of the New Problem**: Turing examines the game's advantages in adjudicating whether machines and humans could be credited with thinking equally, employing impartial human judgement.
3. **The Machines Involved in the Game**: Turing specifies that he intends for digital computers to be the sole type of machine eligible to participate in the game.
4. **Digital Computers**: The characteristics of the contemporary digital computers, exemplified by the Manchester machine, are elucidated and juxtaposed with Charles Babbage's designs for an Analytical Engine.
5. **Universality of Digital Computers**: Turing elucidates how digital computers can simulate any discrete-state machine.
6. **Contrary Views on the Main Question**: Turing introduces and summarily dismisses nine traditional philosophical objections to the assertion that machines can engage in thought.

Over the past six decades, the endeavour to engineer software addressing the central question posed by Turing's paper has been at the forefront of AI research. In the final section of his 1950 paper, Turing delves into the motivation and potential approaches for such endeavours. His departure from the purely philosophical tone of the preceding sections is marked by the following transition:

> The only truly satisfactory support for the viewpoint expressed at the beginning of section 6 will be provided by awaiting the end of the century and then conducting the experiment described. But what can we say in the meantime?

Turing proceeded to discuss three distinct strategies that may be considered capable of realising a thinking machine. These strategies can be characterised as follows: (1) AI by programming, (2) AI by ab initio ML, and (3) AI using logic, probabilities, learning, and background knowledge. In the subsequent three sections, we explore Turing's strategies in relation to the various phases of AI research conducted over the past half-century. Turing contemplates an argument regarding the memory requirements for programming a digital computer with a capacity similar to that of a human being. He acknowledges that the crux of the issue lies in programming, although advancements in engineering will also be necessary, he expresses confidence that these advancements will likely be sufficient for the task. Estimates of the brain's storage capacity range from 10^{10} to 10^{15} binary digits, with Turing leaning towards the lower end of the spectrum. He suggests that only a small fraction of this capacity is used for higher-level thinking, with the majority likely devoted to retaining visual impressions. Turing speculates that no more than 10^9 digits would be necessary for effective participation in the imitation game, especially against a blind opponent. He asserts that a storage capacity of 10^7 would be feasible even with present-day techniques. Additionally, he argues that there may not be a need to increase the speed of operations of the machines, as parts of modern machines analogous to nerve cells already operate about a thousand times faster than the latter. This discrepancy should provide a sufficient "margin of safety" to cover potential losses of speed in various scenarios. The challenge, then, lies in programming these machines to play the game. Turing estimates his own productivity at around a thousand digits of program code per day, implying that a dedicated team of around 60 programmers working steadily for 50 years could potentially complete the task, assuming no setbacks. However, Turing recognises that this approach may not be the most efficient, hinting at the need for a more expedient method. In hindsight, it's remarkable that Turing anticipated the advent of computers with gigabyte storage capacities by the end of the 20th century, and he suggests that memory capacity, rather than processing speed, would be critical in achieving human-like intelligence. Nevertheless, Turing also foresaw that manual composition of a program capable of passing the Turing test would not be the most expedient method, acknowledging the challenges and uncertainties inherent in the process of debugging computer programs, a lesson learned from his experience with the early pilot ACE computer.

Turing's profound influence on the evolution of AI from the 1960s to the 1980s is exemplified by the *Machine Intelligence* book series, which served as a pioneer in cutting-edge AI research during this era. Donald Michie, the series' Executive Editor, was not only a colleague of Turing's at Bletchley Park but also played a pivotal role in shaping AI research in Europe. In the 1960s, Michie founded Europe's first Department of Artificial Intelligence in Edinburgh, and in the 1980s, he established the Turing Institute, a renowned AI research institution in Glasgow [79]. Michie curated topics for the machine intelligence workshops that closely mirrored discussions he and Jack Good had with Turing during the war. Good, a frequent contributor to the series, explored Turing-inspired topics such as Computer Chess. The opening volume of *Machine Intelligence 5* featured Turing's previously unpublished article "Intelligent machinery," in which Turing envisaged designing intelligent robots capable of learning from their experiences, illustrating his visionary approach to AI. Turing's Version 1 Programming method was the dominant paradigm for AI research until the mid-1980s. Research during this period centred on three main areas: reasoning, physical perception, and physical action. Simon and Newell's General Problem Solver (GPS) was an influential attempt to program a universal problem solver capable of tackling various formal symbolic reasoning problems. However, while GPS could handle simple tasks, its reasoning capabilities were quickly overwhelmed by the complexity of more challenging problems. Consequently, researchers pursued diverse approaches to enhance the efficiency of search and planning, as well as developing specialised techniques for theorem proving and chess playing. Addressing Turing's concerns about writing effective and efficient AI programs led to the emergence of several high-level languages during this period. These languages varied from λ-calculus-based systems like LISP to stack-based languages such as POP1, as well as those founded on first-order predicate calculus like Prolog. The development of heuristic programming, exemplified by systems like Dendral and MYCIN, employed rule-based constraints to create systems capable of reasoning at the level of human experts, marking a significant milestone in AI achievements during the early 1980s. During the 1960s to 1980s, there were several pioneering attempts to develop programs capable of recognising three-dimensional objects within digital images. However, these efforts were primarily limited to analysing simple polygons, and there was uncertainty regarding their applicability to recognising real-world objects like trees, cars, or people. Simultaneously, significant progress was made in the field of natural language generation and understanding. Early systems aimed to directly address one of the fundamental aspects of Turing's imitation game by enabling responses to questions posed in natural language. However, similar to the challenges faced in computer vision, these natural language systems were constrained by the complexity of the grammars provided by their programmers. In terms of physical action, Turing had envisaged intelligent machines capable of autonomous learning while roaming the countryside. One notable project from this period was Stanford's Shakey project (1966–1972), which focused on mobile robotics. In contrast, Edinburgh's Freddy assembly robot employed a different approach, with a fixed robot arm and digital camera, while a platform carrying sequentially assembled parts was directed to move past it under computer control [80].

In his 1950 paper, Turing foresaw the challenges inherent in manually programming a digital computer to achieve AI. He proposed an alternative approach: rather than attempting to replicate the workings of the adult mind, why not strive to simulate the learning process of a child? Turing suggested that if a machine could mimic the learning trajectory of a child and undergo a suitable educational regimen, it could eventually develop into an adult-like brain. Turing likened the child's brain to a blank notebook obtained from a stationery store, containing minimal pre-existing mechanisms and mostly empty pages. He hypothesised that the simplicity of the child's brain might facilitate its emulation through programming. Turing's optimism stemmed from the belief that the child's brain possesses a level of mechanistic simplicity that lends itself to straightforward programming. He proposed that the educational process required to shape the machine's development would be similar in scope and effort to that of a human child. During the 1970s, the expert systems movement experienced considerable success. However, this progress was increasingly hindered by the prohibitive costs associated with involving experts in the development and upkeep of large rule-based systems. This issue came to be known as "Feigenbaum's bottleneck." Interestingly, in the 1990s and beyond, researchers such as Gerd Gigerenzer and Peter Todd, realised and demonstrated empirically that systems with very few simple rules, inspired by human expertise, can achieve performance that competes very well with that of established ML models such as Naïve Bayes, Classification and Regression Trees (CART), and Random Forests [81]. Nevertheless, early experiments with systems like Meta-Dendral and later Michalski's Soy-Bean expert system demonstrated that machines could autonomously learn rules from observations. Moreover, Michalski showcased that this automated learning approach not only offered a more efficient means of constructing and managing expert systems but also yielded rules that surpassed the accuracy of those generated by human experts. This breakthrough sparked the inception of a new series of workshops known as ML, spearheaded by Ryszard Michalski, Jaime Carbonell, and Tom Mitchell. Initially modelled after Donald Michie's Machine Intelligence workshops, these gatherings evolved into the International Conference on Machine Learning. In the standard ML framework, a common practice is to initiate learning from scratch, as Turing puts it, akin to starting with "blank sheets." This typically involves using a set of vectors associated with positive and negative classifications. However, Turing offers a cautionary note, inspired by mathematics, regarding this approach. He suggests that employing punishments and rewards can, at best, serve as a component of the teaching process. Essentially, if the teacher lacks alternative methods of communication with the student, the amount of information conveyed to the student is limited by the total number of rewards and punishments administered. Turing illustrates this concept by likening it to a scenario where a child is learning to recite a poem. If the only way for the child to learn the correct text is through a "Twenty Questions" technique, where every incorrect response is met with a punitive consequence, the child would likely experience significant discomfort and distress by the time they successfully memorise the poem. Turing's understanding of information theory [42] allowed him to foresee certain constraints that were later elucidated in the 1980s by Valiant's theory of learnability. Specifically, Turing anticipated that effective ab initio ML would be inherently limited to the creation of relatively small units of knowledge. However, Valiant's work also revealed that, with an ample supply of examples, the expected accuracy of the acquired knowledge could reach arbitrarily high levels. Nonetheless, this brings us back to Turing's fundamental question: How can we program the approximately 10^{12} bits of memory necessary to attain human-level intelligence? Despite advancements in understanding the theoretical underpinnings of learning, the practical challenge of achieving human-like intelligence remains a daunting task.

Turing proposed a solution to the challenges of ab initio ML, building upon the quote provided in the previous section. He argued that it is essential to establish alternative "unemotional" channels of communication. With these channels in place, it becomes feasible to train a machine through a system of punishments and rewards to adhere to commands given in a symbolic language. By transmitting these commands through the "unemotional" channels, Turing contended that the use of a symbolic language would significantly decrease the number of punishments and rewards needed for effective learning. His assertion was that employing such an "unemotional" symbolic language could potentially reduce the number of examples required for learning. The next pertinent question concerns the appropriate form and function of the symbolic language to be utilised. Turing's insights on this matter follow directly from the previous quote. There may be differing opinions regarding the complexity deemed suitable for the child machine. One approach might aim to keep it as simple as possible while remaining consistent with overarching principles. Alternatively, one could opt for a comprehensive system of logical inference that is "built in." In the latter scenario, the machine's memory would predominantly consist of definitions and propositions. Alan Robinson's introduction of resolution-based automatic theorem proving in 1965 sparked significant interest in using first-order predicate calculus as a framework for reasoning within AI systems. Aligned with Turing's concept of employing "built-in" logical definitions, Gordon Plotkin's thesis explored the use of resolution theorem proving as a context for investigating a form of ML involving the generation of logical axioms from observations and background knowledge. During the era of Logic Programming in the 1980s, Plotkin's early inquiries were revisited by Shapiro, who explored the use of inductive inference for automatically revising Prolog programs. However, it wasn't until the 1990s that the field of Inductive Logic Programming delved deeply into this approach as a highly expressive paradigm for ML. A recent survey of the field underscores the maturity of theory, implementation, and applications in this domain. Turing offers intriguing insights into the uncertainty inherent in learned rules, noting that learned processes do not yield absolute certainty of outcomes; otherwise, they wouldn't be subject to unlearning. This observation underscores the dynamic and evolving nature of learning. In recent years, there has been a growing interest in incorporating probabilities into Inductive Logic Programming. These probability values serve to quantify the uncertainty associated with learned rules, providing a nuanced understanding of their reliability. Moreover, Turing addresses the seeming paradox of a learning machine, acknowledging that some may find the concept perplexing. He clarifies that while the rules governing the machine's operation are typically regarded as static and time-invariant, the rules subject to change during the learning process possess only temporary validity. This distinction elucidates the transient nature of learning and adaptation within machine intelligence. The inherent meta-logical interpreter function of a Universal Turing machine is crucial. This property enables the treatment of rules as data, facilitating their alteration and updating. A recent paper authored by the researcher demonstrates that the meta-interpretive capability of the Prolog Logic Programming language can efficiently support the integration of auxiliary "invented" predicates and recursion within the framework of learning complex grammars. This highlights the adaptability and versatility of programming languages in facilitating advanced computational tasks such as learning complex structures. Many of the challenges Turing discusses in the final section of his paper have been thoroughly explored in the AI literature.

However, one of the ML challenges he raises remains completely unresolved. Turing presents an analogy involving an atomic pile, where an injected idea corresponds to a neutron entering the pile. In a subcritical pile, the disturbance caused by such an idea dissipates over time. However, in a super-critical pile, the disturbance grows and may lead to the destruction of the entire pile. Turing speculates whether there is a similar phenomenon for minds and machines. He notes that most human minds appear to be subcritical, meaning that an idea typically gives rise to less than one new idea in response. However, some minds are super-critical, where an idea can lead to the generation of multiple secondary, tertiary, and more remote ideas. Turing poses the question: Can a machine be made to be super-critical? This query remains an open challenge in the field of ML, reflecting the ongoing pursuit of creating AI systems capable of generating complex and innovative ideas beyond the input they receive. Turing's challenge to develop a machine capable of being "super-critical" appears to be most relevant within the framework of the Version 3 approach to AI. In this scenario, where a new observation sparks the creation of a cascade of interconnected ideas, a machine would require not only an alert and agile mind but also an extensive reservoir of relevant background knowledge. Equipping a machine with such abundant background knowledge presents a significant challenge. However, the emergence of the World Wide Web provides a readily available source of information, assuming that this vast repository of data can be accessed and leveraged effectively for the purposes of inductive reasoning. In this context, the task lies in developing AI systems capable of harnessing the wealth of information available on the web to fuel the generation of complex and innovative ideas, akin to the super-critical state described by Turing.

Turing concludes his paper on the Mind with a poignant statement: "We can only see a short distance ahead, but we can see plenty there that needs to be done." This reflection reveals Turing's forward-thinking perspective, acknowledging the vast territory of uncharted research awaiting exploration. While Turing's vision was certainly expansive and prescient, it's worth noting that a conclusive demonstration of a computer passing the Turing test remains elusive. Present-day computers often lack the sophisticated natural language capabilities required to engage in the type of nuanced conversation described by Turing. However, in our contemporary era, individuals commonly turn to computers or smartphones when confronted with challenging questions, relying on the collective intelligence of the World Wide Web. This reliance underscores the significant role of computers in augmenting human cognition. Modern computers excel at searching vast databases, identifying objects in images, discerning patterns in user behaviour, and offering translations in foreign languages—capabilities that have roots in the research conducted by AI laboratories. In essence, Turing's legacy extends beyond the concept of the Universal Turing machine, which laid the foundation for the computer industry. His visionary ideas about intelligent machines have spurred the development of the digital assistants ubiquitous in the modern world, shaping the landscape of technology as we know it today. We owe Turing a debt of gratitude for his profound impact on both hardware and software, shaping the digital landscape that surrounds us.

2.1.2 The McCarthy Era

John McCarthy [82] occupies a prominent place in the history of AI. An American computer scientist, he introduced the term "Artificial Intelligence" in his proposal for the Dartmouth Conference, the inaugural AI conference convened in 1956. The primary objective of this conference was to conceptualise a machine capable of human-like thinking and reasoning. McCarthy held the belief that this scientific breakthrough would undoubtedly occur within the span of 5–5,000 years. Additionally, he pioneered the creation of the Lisp computer language in 1958, which subsequently became the standard programming language for AI.

The widespread availability of GPUs revolutionised parallel processing, making it faster, more cost-effective, and more potent. Concurrently, the era of "Big Data"—encompassing images, text, bioinformatics, medical records, financial transactions, and more—entered the mainstream, accompanied by nearly limitless data storage capabilities. These developments sparked a significant resurgence of interest in AI across academic and industrial domains beyond traditional computer science. Once again, AI captures the zeitgeist and stands poised to revolutionise various sectors, including medicine, at fundamental, clinical, healthcare management, and financial levels. The terminology surrounding these technologies continues to evolve and can be perplexing for non-computer scientists. AI is broadly categorised into two types: general AI, which involves machines replicating human thought, emotion, and reasoning (still largely relegated to science fiction); and narrow AI, which comprises technologies capable of performing specific tasks as well as/or better than humans. ML refers to the study of computer algorithms that can discern complex relationships or patterns from empirical data and make accurate decisions. Instead of encoding specific sets of instructions to accomplish a task, ML algorithms are "trained" using extensive data and algorithms, enabling them to learn how to perform the task. Unlike traditional algorithms, in ML, the data dictates what the "correct answer" is, and learning occurs without explicit programming. John McCarthy, the creator of Lisp, a standard programming language widely used in robotics, various scientific applications, and Internet-based services like credit-card fraud detection and airline scheduling, holds a significant place in the history of computing. Lisp gained prominence among the original hackers, who employed it in their efforts to teach rudimentary IBM machines of the late 1950s to play chess. This contributed to Lisp's revered status in the programming community. ML problems are typically classified as supervised learning or unsupervised learning. In supervised ML algorithms, such as face recognition, the machine is presented with numerous examples of "face" or "non-face," allowing the algorithm to learn to predict whether an unseen image depicts a face or not. In contrast, unsupervised learning involves presenting the machine with unlabelled data, where the algorithm discerns patterns or relationships without predefined categories. McCarthy's work on Lisp was pivotal for his other major contribution: the concept of computer time-sharing, or utility computing. In an era when personal computers were only a dream in science fiction, McCarthy envisioned a central computer capable of accommodating multiple simultaneous connections, a concept that laid the groundwork for the future Internet. At Stanford University, McCarthy established an AI laboratory where he focused on early iterations of a self-driving car. He also delved into topics such as robot consciousness, free will, and enhancing programs' ability to understand or mimic human common-sense decision-making. McCarthy's contributions extend to the development of an early system of computer time-sharing and networking, allowing numerous users to share data by connecting to a central computer. His foresight in 1960, when he suggested that "computation may someday be organised as a public utility," laid the conceptual foundation for cloud computing. In 1966, John McCarthy, the pioneer of AI, garnered global attention by organising a series of four simultaneous Computer Chess matches against opponents in Russia, conducted via telegraph. Spanning several months, these matches concluded with McCarthy losing two and drawing two. Although McCarthy passed away on October 24, 2011, his enduring legacy in the AI field continues to inspire and shape the work of researchers and innovators worldwide. Despite his efforts, McCarthy's system did not enable him to achieve his ultimate objective: having a computer pass the Turing test. In this test, a person communicates via a computer screen and if they cannot distinguish whether the responses are from a human or a machine, then the machine is considered intelligent. To date, no computer has successfully passed this test. Towards the latter part of his career in 1978, McCarthy had to relinquish his idealistic notion of AI [83–86].

> To succeed, artificial intelligence needs 1.7 Einstein's, 2 Maxwells, Five Faradays and the funding of 0.3 Manhattan projects
>
> *John McCarthy*

2.1.3 Evolutionary Computing

Evolutionary computation encompasses a range of computational techniques inspired by natural evolutionary processes, mimicking mechanisms like natural selection and survival of the fittest to address real-world problems. Among these techniques, Genetic Algorithms, conceptualised by John Holland in 1975, stand out as one of the most prevalent forms in medical applications. These algorithms, rooted in biological evolution principles, are stochastic search and optimisation algorithms. Genetic Algorithms operate by generating numerous random solutions to a given problem, with this population evolving from one generation to the next until a satisfactory solution is achieved. Superior solutions are retained while inferior ones are discarded, and through iterative refinement among the better solutions, the population continually improves and adapts to the problem space. In medical decision-making, where scenarios often involve navigating vast and complex solution spaces, Genetic Algorithms prove invaluable. For instance, in cytology, where a cytologist must assess cell features to determine malignancy, Genetic Algorithms efficiently explore the myriad possibilities to facilitate accurate diagnoses. These algorithms find application in tasks such as diagnosis, prognosis, medical imaging, signal processing, and planning and scheduling. The principles of Genetic Algorithms have been applied to predict outcomes in critically ill patients, lung cancer, melanoma, and response to medications like warfarin. They have also been utilised in computerised analysis of mammographic microcalcifications, MRI segmentation of brain tumours to assess treatment efficacy, and the analysis of computerised 2D images to diagnose malignant melanomas.

Each AI technique possesses its unique strengths and weaknesses. Neural networks excel in learning, fuzzy logic in handling imprecision, and evolutionary computation in search and optimisation. By combining the advantages of these technologies, hybrid intelligent systems can be created to work in a complementary manner. Their synergy enables hybrid systems to incorporate common sense, extract knowledge from raw data, utilise human-like reasoning mechanisms, address uncertainty and imprecision, and adapt to rapidly changing and unknown environments. There are numerous hybrid systems available, with popular ones including using ANNs for designing fuzzy systems, fuzzy systems for designing ANNs, and Genetic Algorithms for automatically training and generating neural network architectures. Once again, the application of hybrid intelligent systems has been explored in various clinical scenarios. Examples include breast cancer diagnosis, analysis of microcalcifications on digital mammograms, diagnosis of coronary artery stenosis, assessment of myocardial viability, and control of anaesthesia depth.

Over the last two decades, the development of efficient and advanced systems for delivering therapeutic agents with maximum efficacy and minimal risk has presented a significant challenge among chemical and biological scientists. Additionally, the cost and time involved in developing novel therapeutic agents have posed further obstacles in the drug design and development process. To mitigate these challenges, researchers worldwide have turned to computational approaches such as VS and molecular docking, also referred to as traditional methods. However, these techniques also present challenges, including inaccuracies and inefficiencies. Consequently, there has been a surge in the adoption of novel techniques capable of addressing the limitations of traditional computational approaches. AI, encompassing DL and ML algorithms, has emerged as a potential solution to overcome the obstacles in the drug design and discovery process. Moreover, drug discovery and design involve complex and lengthy steps, such as target selection and validation, therapeutic screening and lead compound optimisation, preclinical and clinical trials, and manufacturing practices, all of which pose significant challenges in identifying effective medications for diseases. Thus, the primary concern for pharmaceutical companies is managing the cost and expediting the process. AI has provided answers to these challenges in a straightforward and scientific manner, reducing both time and cost. Furthermore, the increasing digitisation of data in pharmaceutical companies and the healthcare sector further incentivises the implementation of AI to address the complexities of data analysis.

2.1.4 Drug Discovery and Artificial Intelligence

Big Data encompasses datasets too vast and complex for conventional analysis software, tools, and techniques. Its three main characteristics are volume, velocity, and variety. Volume refers to the massive amount of generated data, velocity to the speed of reproduction, and variety to the heterogeneity within the datasets. With the emergence of microarray, RNA-seq, and high-throughput sequencing technologies, the biomedical field faces an influx of data daily, propelling drug discovery into the era of Big Data. Target identification, the initial step in drug discovery, involves pinpointing relevant targets like genes or proteins implicated in disease pathophysiology, aided by access to numerous biomedical data repositories. The evolution of AI facilitates Big Data analytics, offering a plethora of ML techniques to extract valuable features, patterns, and structures from these vast biomedical datasets. Gene expression serves as a prominent feature for target identification, elucidating disease mechanisms and identifying disease-related genes. Repositories such as NCBI Gene Expression Omnibus (GEO), The Cancer Genome Atlas (TCGA), and ArrayExpress host extensive gene expression data. Analysis of gene expression signatures unveils target genes associated with various disorders, exemplified by van IJzendoorn et al.'s [87] discovery of novel biomarkers and potential drug targets for rare soft tissue sarcoma using ML approaches and gene expression data. Genome-wide association studies (GWAS) explore the correlation between genomic variants and complex disorders, with repositories like GWAS Central and NHGRI-EBI GWAS Catalog housing GWAS data. GWAS aids in identifying disease-associated genetic loci, with genes linked to these loci emerging as potential therapeutic targets. Li et al. [88] utilised GWAS catalogues, gene expression, epigenomics, and methylation data to identify target genes associated with juvenile idiopathic arthritis loci through ML analysis. Genes with mutations leading to severe diseases present promising therapeutic targets. Risk genes can be identified through analysis of various genome and exome sequencing data, with repositories like the Sequence Read Archive and the National Cancer Institute Genomic Data Commons containing sequencing data, particularly related to cancer. Leveraging Big Data and AI, Han et al. [89] developed DriverML, a supervised ML tool pinpointing driver genes associated with cancer.

Moreover, published literature can serve as a resource for target identification, with PubMed being a significant repository of various biomedical literature. Data mining of PubMed can aid in identifying targets for different disorders. Once an appropriate target is identified and validated, the subsequent step involves finding suitable drugs or drug-like molecules capable of interacting with the target and eliciting the desired response. In the era of Big Data, numerous large chemical databases are available for this purpose. PubChem, for instance, is a freely accessible chemical database containing data on various chemical structures, including their biological, physical, chemical, and toxic properties. Similarly, the ChEMBL database offers an extensive collection of data on bioactive compounds with drug-like properties, encompassing information on absorption, distribution, metabolism, and excretion (ADME), toxicity properties, and target interactions. DrugBank, another open-access pharmaceutical data repository, houses data on various drugs, their targets, and mechanisms. The library of integrated network-based cellular signature (LINCS) L1000 provides information on changes in gene expression signatures of human cell lines when treated with different chemical compounds. Its data-driven search engine, L1000CDS2, contains data on drugs capable of reverting the expression of differentially expressed genes, thus serving in drug discovery efforts. The protein data bank (PDB) is a freely accessible online repository containing data on three-dimensional structures of proteins, DNA, and RNA. PDB data are commonly utilised to assess protein–ligand interactions and identify appropriate inhibitors for target proteins. Xu et al. [90] combined ML and molecular docking techniques to identify inhibitors of the COVID-19 3CL proteinase, obtaining the crystal structure of the proteinase from PDB for their analysis.

In the pharmaceutical industry, AI has emerged as a potential solution to challenges stemming from traditional chemistry or chemical space, which can hinder drug discovery and development. With advancements in technology and the advent of high-performance computing, AI algorithms ranging from ML to DL have found increased application in computer-aided drug design (CADD). AI isn't a novel technique for scientists in drug discovery and development, nor is it a new desire for chemists to accurately predict chemical activity–structure relationships. Historically, scientists like Hammett and Hansch have explored methods to forecast chemical activity–structure relationships. For instance, Hammett correlated equilibrium constants with reaction rates, while Hansch pioneered computer-assisted prediction of physicochemical properties and biological activity of drug compounds. Hansch's success paved the way for research focusing on detailed identification and prediction of chemical structure, along with characterising properties such as pharmacophores and three-dimensional structure. Additionally, scientists aim to hypothesise complex mathematical equations linking chemical representation to the biological activity of predicted compounds. In the contemporary era, the primary goal is to enhance the drug discovery and development process with high accuracy and confidence scores through ML algorithms rooted in classical chemistry principles. This encourages chemists to harness AI techniques to answer critical questions in medicinal chemistry, such as determining the next compound and its synthesis process. Over the past two decades, numerous techniques and tools for computational drug discovery, quantitative–structure activity relationship (QSAR) methods, and free-energy minimisation techniques have been developed. For example, some studies have utilised machine intelligence methods such as DT, random forest (RF), CNNs, SVMs, LSTM networks, and gradient boosting machines to classify compound cell activity. Advancements in automated drug discovery methods involving AI and ML have made it easier to distinguish existing drugs from novel chemical structures. For instance, computational approaches have been applied to screen hepatotoxic ingredients in traditional Chinese medicines and analyse phylogenetic relationships, structure–toxicity relationships, and herb–ingredient networks. Recent efforts include computational analysis against novel coronaviruses, where compounds biologically active against severe acute respiratory syndrome (SARS) were identified and subjected to ADME as well as docking analysis. These studies highlight the potential of combining conventional chemistry-oriented drug discovery concepts with computational drug design, creating a promising platform for future research. Collaboration between system biology, chemical scientists, and computational scientists is crucial in developing modern ML algorithms and principles to advance drug discovery and development further.

The future of clinicians and researchers as ML and DL technologies advance is poised to be transformative. With the continual increase in data, ML will undoubtedly become integral to its interpretation and utilisation in healthcare. However, there are legitimate concerns and considerations regarding the implications of AI technologies [91]. Professor Stephen Hawking's assertion that AI could be "either the best, or the worst thing, ever to happen to humanity" encapsulates the dual nature of AI. While AI holds immense potential for improving healthcare outcomes and efficiency, there are also valid anxieties regarding its impact on governance of data, automation, and the future of work and employment. It is also noteworthy that, contrary to common assumptions, AI might lack not only in transparency, but also in other currencies. For example, a review of prediction of human behaviour in domains such as politics and law—as in predicting election outcomes, criminal profiling, and granting bail—has found that AI algorithms are less predictively accurate than simple rules of thumb. The Royal Society's commissioned report on AI and ML underscores these concerns while recognising the technology's pivotal role in managing Big Data. As AI continues to advance, clinicians and researchers must grapple with its implications for the practice of medicine. While medicine encompasses more than diagnosis and treatment algorithms, ML is poised to both transform and complement the delivery of care. In essence, while AI technologies offer unprecedented opportunities for innovation in healthcare, it is imperative to address the ethical, social, and practical challenges they present. Clinicians and researchers must navigate these complexities to harness the full potential of AI while ensuring that patient care remains at the forefront of technological advancement.

2.2 ML AND MODEL DEVELOPMENT

ML encompasses the development of algorithms and models that facilitate computers in learning from data and enhancing their performance without the need for explicit programming. ML, a discipline within computer science, focuses on extracting patterns from data with the aim of enhancing performance across diverse tasks. Unlike conventional programming, where developers provide specific instructions for computers to execute, ML algorithms enable computers to learn from examples and data, allowing them to identify patterns and make predictions or decisions autonomously. There are several distinct approaches within ML. Supervised learning, for instance, involves algorithms learning from labelled data, where each input is associated with a corresponding output. By understanding these input–output relationships, the algorithm can generalise patterns and make predictions or decisions on new, unseen data, thereby enabling tasks like classification and regression. On the other hand, unsupervised learning algorithms operate on unlabelled data, without predefined correct outputs. Instead, these algorithms aim to discern inherent structures or patterns within the data, such as clustering similar data points together or reducing the dimensionality of the data, without explicit guidance. Semi-supervised learning bridges the gap between supervised and unsupervised learning. In this approach, the algorithm is trained on a combination of a limited amount of labelled data and a larger pool of unlabelled data. By leveraging the labelled data to learn initial patterns, the algorithm then extends its understanding to the unlabelled data, thereby improving performance through a combination of supervised and unsupervised learning techniques. Reinforcement learning represents a unique paradigm within ML, where an agent learns to make decisions by interacting with an environment to maximise cumulative rewards in a sequential task such as playing chess or driving a car. Through a process of informed trial and error, the agent receives feedback in the form of rewards or penalties based on its actions, thereby refining its decision-making strategy over time. Active learning is another related category within ML where the agent chooses the feedback it wants to receive.

2.2.1 Supervised Learning

Supervised ML is a type of ML approach where the algorithm learns from labelled data, meaning each input data point is associated with a corresponding output or target. The goal of supervised learning is to learn a mapping or relationship between the input variables (features) and the output variable (target) so that the algorithm can make predictions or decisions on new, unseen data. N supervised learning, the algorithm is trained on a dataset containing input–output pairs. During the training process, the algorithm adjusts its internal parameters based on the input–output pairs to minimise the error between the predicted output and the actual output. This process continues iteratively until the algorithm achieves a satisfactory level of performance, typically measured using metrics such as accuracy, precision, recall, or others depending on the specific task.

Supervised learning is utilised to delineate predictive tasks, as its primary objective is to anticipate or classify specific outcomes of interest, such as the presence or absence of mental disorders. This methodology has been extensively applied to vast datasets encompassing demographic, clinical, and social indicators, aiming to construct risk scores that forecast the onset and progression of various mental disorders, including anxiety, depression, trauma-related disorders, and suicidal behaviour. Moreover, supervised learning has been instrumental in devising prognostic scores, gauging the likelihood of individuals responding favourably to specific mental health interventions, such as cognitive behavioural therapy for depression or programmes targeting obsessive-compulsive disorder. Such risk and prognostic scores serve as valuable tools for identifying individuals necessitating preventive interventions or tailored and intensive treatments, contingent upon their predicted risk or prognosis levels. While many studies formulate risk and prognostic scores based on predictors assessed at a single time point, various approaches exist to integrate repeated measures, or time-varying predictors, into supervised learning algorithms. This may entail operationalising predictors relative to the timing preceding the outcome or employing a person–time data structure.

2.2.2 Unsupervised Learning

Unsupervised learning algorithms use the structure in a dataset to assign observations into various groups. The goal is to assign observations so that observations in one group are more "similar" to other observations in the same group than they are to observations in other groups. For example, in dermatology, a supervised learning algorithm might assign moles into different groups according to characteristics of their visual appearance. Such assignments might help doctors to better diagnose and treat moles.

2.2.3 Causal Inferences

Causal inference entails the estimation of effects by contrasting outcomes among the exposed group with the counterfactual outcomes that would have occurred had they not been exposed. For instance, one might seek to gauge the suicide rate that would have been observed if all individuals in a study population had undergone a psychosocial suicide prevention intervention, juxtaposed with the suicide rate in the absence of such intervention. This process involves determining the effect of treatment exposure on a particular outcome. To explore such causal inquiries, clinical psychologists commonly employ a randomised controlled trial (RCT) design alongside conventional statistical methodologies.

However, causal inference can extend to observational (i.e., non-randomised) data in a manner that mirrors a hypothetical randomised trial. While causal inference methods have been in existence for decades, the incorporation of supervised learning methods is a more recent development. For instance, techniques such as CART, along with random forests, have been leveraged to construct propensity score models, aiding in the adjustment of treatment effect estimates based on individual variances in the (non-random) likelihood of receiving a specific intervention. An increasingly favoured approach in causal inference is targeted maximum likelihood estimation (TMLE). TMLE holds appeal due to its double robustness property, wherein the average treatment effect remains unbiased as long as either the exposure regression or outcome regression is accurately estimated. Simulation studies have demonstrated that implementing TMLE through supervised learning techniques, such as ensemble methods, helps mitigate bias in treatment effect estimates. It is also worth noting that methodologies exist to employ TMLE and supervised learning in developing optimised treatment rules, derived from either RCT or observational data, to match patients with the intervention most likely to yield benefit.

2.2.4 Recursive Partitioning

One of the most popular approaches to supervised learning is decision tree methods, known for their non-parametric nature and high flexibility. For instance, CART operates by segmenting all possible values for each predictor into distinct, non-overlapping regions within the predictor space. This process, known as recursive partitioning, automates the detection of main effects, including non-linear associations and interactions. A decision tree is then constructed based on these non-overlapping regions, with terminal nodes, or distinguishable subgroups, at the bottom of the tree. In the case of categorical outcomes, observations are predicted to belong to the most frequently occurring class or category within a node. For continuous outcomes, observations within a particular node are predicted to have the mean of the response values associated with that node. Various criteria can be employed to grow a decision tree. Using CART, for example, splits are determined by minimising classification error (for categorical outcomes) or residual sum of squares (for continuous outcomes). In contrast, conditional inference trees grow based on the strength of univariate associations. In general, trees are considered, due to their visual nature, transparent to all sorts of decision makers, including those that might have less of a quantitative background, even though empirical evidence on this issue is relatively scarce. A particular type of DT, called fast-and-frugal DT can also be induced by standard methods and are especially designed to be simpler and thus hopefully more transparent.

Individual DT offer high visual interpretability and are valuable for identifying non-linear associations and interactions between variables. However, random forests present an alternative approach, functioning as a collection of individual DT for prediction purposes. Random forests, classified as an ensemble method, combine multiple models, such as trees, into a single entity. This is achieved by creating bootstrapped copies of the original data, with a single tree estimated in each bootstrap. Random forests mitigate the risk of overfitting, a phenomenon where a model closely mirrors a specific dataset but fails to accurately predict events in new samples. This is accomplished by averaging multiple trees to yield more accurate and stable predictions. While random forests lack the visual interpretability of individual trees, they compute measures of variable importance, offering insights into how each predictor impacts model accuracy or discrimination ability. It's important to note that alternate parameterisations of CART and random forests algorithms, along with variable importance metrics, are advisable for data structures comprising a mix of binary, categorical, and continuous variables, such as conditional inference trees.

Recent applications of recursive partitioning in psychology and psychiatry have demonstrated its utility in predictive modelling. For instance, Gradus and colleagues [92] utilised classification trees and random forests to forecast death by suicide using Danish population-based registry data. The classification trees unveiled specific combinations of risk factors linked to a heightened risk of suicide, such as individuals not prescribed antidepressants, antipsychotics, or anxiolytics, but with a history of suicide attempts and lower income. Meanwhile, random forests identified the most crucial variables for accurately predicting suicide deaths, including antipsychotic prescriptions, alcohol-related disorders, and schizophrenia. In another application, Walsh, Ribeiro, and Franklin [93] leveraged electronic medical records to anticipate suicide attempts among 5,167 adult patients with a claim code for self-injury. They observed that prediction accuracy improved as the suicide attempt became more imminent, ranging from 720 days to 7 days prior to the event, with predictor importance shifting over time. For instance, certain predictors such as psychotic disorders, recurrent depression, and poisoning remained consistently important across time, while others gained significance only several months or years before the suicide attempt, such as prescriptions for selective serotonin reuptake inhibitors, benzodiazepines, acetaminophen, and recent inpatient, outpatient, and emergency department visits.

2.2.5 Support Vector Machines

SVMs are designed for classification tasks involving two classes, such as cases and controls, within a multidimensional space encompassing numerous variables. To discern between classes, SVMs delineate a hyperplane—a boundary that maximally segregates the classes or outcome categories. Employing a data transformation,

SVMs project the data into a higher-dimensional space to ascertain a separating decision surface. This transformation process is facilitated by a kernel function. While SVMs can yield highly accurate predictions, especially when utilising flexible non-linear kernels, they exhibit limitations due to their "black box" nature. In other words, SVMs do not furnish metrics elucidating how predictors are amalgamated to optimise the hyperplane. In one of the pioneering studies in psychopathology forecasting, Galatzer-Levy and colleagues [94] employed SVMs and longitudinal data to predict the chronic trajectory of PTSD symptoms among individuals admitted to an emergency department following a traumatic event. This study compared the prediction accuracy of three models: one using all available predictors ($n = 68$), another utilising a subset of predictors selected through a predictor selection algorithm ($n = 16$), and a third incorporating only acute stress disorder symptoms. Surprisingly, the model with only 16 predictors, including factors such as event/injury characteristics, use of tranquilisers, and psychological symptoms, performed comparably well to the model using all available predictors. This suggests that accurate forecasting of PTSD may be achievable with a limited number of clinical assessment tools. There is, in fact, a growing body of empirical evidence, not only from medicine but also other areas challenging for prediction, such as politics, law, economics, and finance, that simpler models can often achieve higher predictive accuracy than more complex ones. The explanation is that simpler models may strike a better balance between fitting too much noise in the data while also capturing enough of the signal in the data. In another application of SVMs, Månsson and colleagues [95] investigated neural predictors of long-term treatment outcome among patients with social anxiety disorder one year after completing Internet-delivered cognitive behavioural therapy. SVM classification revealed that the initial blood oxygen-level-dependent responses to self-referential criticism in the anterior cingulate cortex accurately predicted long-term response with high precision.

2.2.6 Regularisation

Regularisation, or penalisation, methods represent an extension of traditional regression techniques aimed at shrinking coefficients towards zero to enhance prediction accuracy while curbing model overfitting. Methods such as least absolute shrinkage and selection operator (LASSO) regularisation, ridge regularisation, and elastic net strike a balance between optimising prediction accuracy and preventing excessive model complexity. LASSO, ridge, and elastic net employ regularisation terms that penalise models for increasing complexity, such as having more predictors than observations or a large number of collinear predictors. This is advantageous because overly complex models may capture trivial patterns specific to the dataset (noise) rather than generalisable trends applicable to external datasets. LASSO is often favoured for variable selection, particularly in scenarios with numerous predictors and limited observations, aiming to produce sparse models with only a subset of variables influencing the outcome. However, LASSO's capability to arbitrarily shrink predictor coefficients to zero among highly correlated sets can be a limitation, especially when dealing with well-established or conceptually significant predictors. In contrast, ridge regression may lead to non-parsimonious models retaining all predictors. Elastic net was developed to address the shortcomings of both LASSO and ridge regression by combining their penalties, facilitating the creation of parsimonious models with enhanced stability and accuracy compared to either method alone. Elastic net determines the optimal penalty term using an internal cross-validation procedure. An example of the application of regularisation methods comes from Kessler and colleagues [96], who employed elastic net to identify a subset of predictors for accurately predicting suicides within 12 months following psychiatric hospitalisation among U.S. Army soldiers. The aim was to enhance post-hospital care targeting. Elastic net was specifically utilised to address multicollinearity issues within the original set of hundreds of predictors. The most effective model encompassed various sociodemographic characteristics (such as male gender and late age of enlistment), criminal offenses (e.g., weapons possession, verbal violence), prior suicidality, aspects of prior psychiatric inpatient and outpatient treatment, and specific disorders diagnosed during hospitalisations. Regularisation methods have also been instrumental in predicting the trajectory of depressive symptoms, as demonstrated by Chen and colleagues [97]. They applied elastic net to identify 25 out of 164 variables that optimally predicted changes in three empirically defined depressive symptom clusters over treatment: core emotional symptoms, sleep problems, and atypical symptoms like psychomotor agitation. A less developed, but promising approach is to construct hybrids of heuristics and regularisation. Lichtenberg and Şimşek [98] explored this direction by considering the effects of a penalty term that is minimised when regression coefficients are set to be equal. The results were remarkable in that this hybrid of regression and the heuristic of simply tallying predictors outperformed a number of state-of-the-art regularised regressions (e.g., elastic net) even under conditions that are usually unfavourable to heuristics, such as intermediate-to-large training sets.

2.2.7 Algorithm Comparison and Stacking Methods

While we've explored some of the most prevalent supervised ML algorithms in clinical psychology and psychiatry literature, a myriad of other approaches exist, including neural networks and gradient boosting. It's important to recognise that different algorithms may yield varying performance levels, underscoring the necessity of testing and comparing multiple algorithms. Most supervised learning methods are versatile enough to handle complex data structures comprising a mix of categorical and continuous predictors. However, certain methods have been tailored to accommodate predictors with differing scales of measurement or varying numbers of categories. For instance, conditional inference trees represent an adaptation of CART specifically designed for such scenarios. Moreover, the performance of some methods may be influenced by whether the predictors are binary or continuous. Researchers interested in comparing different algorithms may thus find it necessary to operationalise predictors using diverse approaches. This could entail using continuous predictors directly alongside creating dummy variables based on which quintile a score falls into. By adopting such strategies, researchers can conduct comprehensive evaluations of algorithm performance across different predictor types and data structures.

In a recent application, Rosellini and colleagues [99] utilised super learning to develop algorithms predicting the onset of internalising disorders between Waves 1 and 2 of the National Epidemiological Survey on Alcohol and Related Conditions ($n = 34{,}653$). Risk scores were developed for five disorders (generalised anxiety, panic, social phobia, depression, mania) using over 200 predictors and a library of nine different supervised learning algorithms. As expected, the composite super learner ensemble resulted in better prediction than individual algorithms from which it was developed. However, the difference in performance across algorithms was sometimes small, including when compared to logistic regression. Nevertheless, it's important to note that other studies have found substantially better performance of super learning relative to individual algorithms, including logistic regression.

ML has become a pivotal aspect of AI, enabling computers to learn from data and make decisions or predictions without being explicitly programmed for the task. The development of ML models involves various methods, each suited to different types of problems and data structures. This essay explores the primary methods of ML used for developing models, namely supervised learning, unsupervised learning, semi-supervised learning, reinforcement learning, and DL [100–103].

2.2.8 Supervised Learning

Supervised learning is one of the most widely used methods in ML, where the model is trained on a labelled dataset. This means that for each input in the training dataset, the corresponding output is known. The objective of supervised learning is to learn a mapping from inputs to outputs, which can then be used to predict the output for unseen inputs. Common algorithms used in supervised learning include linear regression, DT, SVMs, and neural networks. Linear regression is often used for continuous output prediction, while DT and SVMs are typically used for classification tasks. Neural networks, particularly in their DL form, are highly versatile and can handle both regression and classification problems with great accuracy, especially when dealing with large datasets.

2.2.9 Unsupervised Learning

In contrast to supervised learning, unsupervised learning deals with unlabelled data. The model is tasked with identifying patterns or structures within the data without any explicit guidance. Unsupervised learning is commonly used for clustering and association tasks. Clustering involves grouping similar data points together, with algorithms such as K-means, hierarchical clustering, and DBSCAN being commonly employed. Association learning, on the other hand, aims to discover interesting relations between variables in large datasets, with the Apriori algorithm being a well-known method in this domain.

Unsupervised learning is particularly useful in exploratory data analysis, where the goal is to discover hidden patterns or intrinsic structures in the data. It also plays a crucial role in applications such as market segmentation, anomaly detection, and image compression.

2.2.10 Semi-Supervised Learning

Semi-supervised learning is a method that falls between supervised and unsupervised learning. It involves using a small amount of labelled data along with a large amount of unlabelled data. This approach is particularly beneficial when labelling data is expensive or time-consuming, but unlabelled data is readily available. The model leverages the labelled data to make predictions on the unlabelled data, gradually improving its accuracy as it learns.

Techniques such as self-training, co-training, and graph-based methods are common in semi-supervised learning. These methods have been effectively applied in various fields, including text classification, speech recognition, and image classification, where obtaining large amounts of labelled data is challenging.

2.2.11 Reinforcement Learning

Reinforcement learning is a distinct method of ML where an agent learns to make decisions by interacting with an environment. The agent receives rewards or penalties based on the actions it takes, and the goal is to learn a policy that maximises the cumulative reward. Unlike supervised learning, where the model learns from a fixed dataset, reinforcement learning involves a continuous interaction with the environment, making it more dynamic.

Reinforcement learning has been successfully applied in areas such as robotics, game-playing, and autonomous driving. Algorithms like Q-learning, deep Q-networks, and policy gradient methods are commonly used in reinforcement learning. One of the most celebrated achievements in this area is the development of AlphaGo, a reinforcement-learning-based system that defeated human world champions in the game of Go.

2.2.12 Deep Learning

DL, a subset of ML, has gained immense popularity due to its success in handling large-scale and complex data. It involves the use of deep neural networks, which are neural networks with multiple hidden layers. These networks are capable of learning hierarchical representations of data, making them highly effective for tasks such as image and speech recognition, natural language processing (NLP), and more.

DL models, particularly CNNs and RNNs, have revolutionised fields like computer vision and NLP. The depth of these models allows them to capture intricate patterns in data, leading to state-of-the-art performance in various applications.

The development of ML models is a multifaceted process that involves choosing the appropriate method based on the nature of the data and the specific problem at hand. Supervised learning, unsupervised learning, semi-supervised learning, reinforcement learning, and DL each offer unique advantages and are suited to different types of tasks. As ML continues to evolve, these methods will likely see further refinement and innovation, leading to even more powerful and versatile models.

2.3 DL AND MODEL DEVELOPMENT

2.3.1 What Is Deep Learning?

DL is a subset of ML that employs ANNs with multiple layers to analyse various forms of data. This approach is particularly effective for handling complex patterns and large datasets. Unlike traditional ML models, which often require manual feature extraction, DL algorithms automatically discover hierarchical patterns in the data through their layered architecture [101].

At its core, DL uses neural networks, inspired by the human brain's structure. These networks consist of layers of interconnected nodes or neurons, where each layer transforms the input data in increasingly abstract ways. For instance, in image recognition tasks, lower layers might detect edges, while higher layers identify shapes or objects.

DL has demonstrated remarkable success across various applications, such as NLP, computer vision, and speech recognition. This is due to its ability to learn from vast amounts of data and its robustness in feature extraction and representation. However, it requires substantial computational resources and large datasets to perform effectively.

2.3.2 What Are the Methods of DL for Developing Models?

DL encompasses several methods and architectures for developing models, each tailored to specific types of data and tasks. These methods leverage neural networks with multiple layers to extract and learn intricate patterns. The primary methods include CNNs, RNNs, and GANs, among others. Each method is distinct in its approach and application [41,44,101,102,104–110].

2.3.2.1 Convolutional Neural Networks

CNNs are particularly effective for image and video analysis. They utilise convolutional layers to detect local patterns and features in the data. A CNN typically consists of multiple layers, including convolutional layers, pooling layers, and fully connected layers. The convolutional layers apply filters to the input data, detecting patterns such as edges or textures, which are then pooled to reduce dimensionality and computational complexity. This method has achieved significant success in tasks like image classification and object detection, as exemplified by the ImageNet competition.

2.3.2.2 Recurrent Neural Networks

RNNs are designed for sequential data, such as time series or natural language. Unlike feedforward networks, RNNs have connections that loop back on themselves, allowing them to maintain a form of memory of previous inputs. This capability makes them suitable for tasks where context or order is important, such as speech recognition or language modelling. However, traditional RNNs suffer from issues like vanishing and exploding gradients, which can hinder learning over long sequences. To address these challenges, variations such as LSTM networks and

Gated Recurrent Units have been developed, which incorporate mechanisms to better manage long-term dependencies.

2.3.2.3 Generative Adversarial Networks

GANs are a class of DL models used for generating new data samples that resemble a given distribution. GANs consist of two networks: the generator and the discriminator. The generator creates synthetic data, while the discriminator evaluates its authenticity against real data. These networks are trained simultaneously in a competitive setting, with the generator improving its ability to produce realistic data and the discriminator becoming better at distinguishing real from fake. GANs have been utilised in various applications, including image generation, style transfer, and data augmentation.

2.3.2.4 Autoencoders

Autoencoders are neural networks used for unsupervised learning, particularly for dimensionality reduction and feature extraction. They consist of two main components: the encoder, which compresses the input data into a lower-dimensional representation, and the decoder, which reconstructs the original data from this compressed form. Autoencoders can be applied in anomaly detection, data denoising, and even generating new samples from learned representations [107]. Variants like variational autoencoders introduce probabilistic elements to the model, enabling more flexible data generation.

2.3.2.5 Transformers

Transformers represent a significant advancement in handling sequential data, particularly in NLP. Unlike RNNs, transformers use self-attention mechanisms to weigh the importance of different parts of the input data, allowing for parallelisation and improved efficiency in training. This method has led to breakthroughs in language understanding and generation, with models such as BERT (Bidirectional Encoder Representations from Transformers) and GPT (Generative Pre-trained Transformer) achieving state-of-the-art results in various NLP tasks.

2.3.2.6 Deep Reinforcement Learning

Deep Reinforcement Learning combines neural networks with reinforcement learning techniques, enabling models to learn optimal actions through interaction with an environment. In this approach, an agent receives rewards or penalties based on its actions and adjusts its strategy accordingly. This method has been applied to complex tasks such as game-playing and robotic control, with notable successes like AlphaGo, which defeated professional human players in the game of Go.

DL methods provide a diverse set of tools for model development, each suited to specific types of problems and data. From CNNs for image analysis to Transformers for NLP, these methods leverage the power of neural networks to learn from and make predictions about complex data. As research continues to advance, new methods and improvements to existing techniques are likely to further enhance the capabilities and applications of DL.

2.4 ALGORITHM DEVELOPMENT AS CLINICAL DECISION-MAKING TOOLS

An algorithm is a set of step-by-step instructions designed to perform a specific task or solve a particular problem. In the context of clinical decision-making, algorithms are increasingly used as tools to aid in diagnosis, treatment planning, and patient management. They help standardise processes, reduce variability in care, and improve patient outcomes by providing evidence-based recommendations [111–118].

2.4.1 Understanding Algorithms

Algorithms in healthcare are typically designed to analyse patient data and provide recommendations based on predefined criteria and logic. They can be as simple as a flowchart for initial triage or as complex as ML models that predict disease progression. Fundamentally, an algorithm involves input data, a series of logical operations or calculations, and output results.

For instance, a clinical decision support algorithm might use patient symptoms, history, and test results to suggest possible diagnoses or treatment options. These algorithms can be integrated into electronic health records (EHRs) to provide real-time assistance to clinicians, helping them make informed decisions quickly.

2.4.2 Developing an Algorithm

The development of a clinical algorithm involves several key steps:

1. **Defining the Problem**: The first step is to clearly define the clinical problem or decision-making challenge the algorithm aims to address. This involves understanding the clinical context, including the specific decision that needs support and the data available for making that decision.
2. **Gathering and Preparing Data**: Effective algorithms require high-quality data. This data may include patient demographics, medical history, laboratory results, and imaging studies. The data must be accurate, comprehensive, and relevant to the problem at hand. Data preparation involves cleaning and organising this data to ensure it is suitable for analysis.
3. **Designing the Algorithm**: This step involves determining the structure of the algorithm. For rule-based algorithms, this means defining a set of rules or DT based on clinical guidelines and expert knowledge. For data-driven approaches, such as those involving ML, this step involves selecting and configuring the appropriate model. This may include defining features, choosing a learning algorithm, and specifying parameters.
4. **Training and Validation**: For algorithms that use ML, the next step is training the model on a dataset. This involves using historical data to teach the algorithm how to make predictions or decisions. Validation is crucial to ensure that the algorithm performs well on new, unseen data. Techniques such as cross-validation are employed to assess the algorithm's accuracy and generalisability.

5. **Testing and Evaluation**: Once trained, the algorithm undergoes rigorous testing to evaluate its performance in real-world scenarios. This involves comparing its recommendations to actual clinical outcomes and assessing its usability and effectiveness in the clinical setting. Feedback from healthcare professionals is crucial in refining the algorithm and ensuring it meets practical needs.
6. **Implementation**: After successful testing, the algorithm is integrated into clinical practice. This might involve embedding it into EHR systems, providing training for healthcare providers, and establishing protocols for its use. Implementation also requires ongoing monitoring and evaluation to ensure the algorithm continues to perform well and adapts to new clinical evidence or changing practices.
7. **Continuous Improvement**: Clinical algorithms require continuous updates and improvements. This is because medical knowledge evolves, and new data may become available. Ongoing monitoring and feedback mechanisms help ensure that the algorithm remains accurate and relevant.

2.4.3 Challenges and Considerations

Developing algorithms for clinical decision-making is not without challenges. Ensuring data quality and managing biases are significant concerns. The algorithm's recommendations must be interpretable and aligned with clinical guidelines. Moreover, ethical considerations regarding patient privacy and the potential impact on clinician–patient relationships must be addressed [116].

Algorithms are powerful tools in clinical decision-making, capable of enhancing the efficiency and accuracy of healthcare delivery. The development of these tools involves a systematic approach, from defining the clinical problem to continuous improvement post-implementation. As healthcare increasingly relies on data-driven solutions, understanding and effectively developing these algorithms will be critical in advancing patient care and optimising clinical outcomes.

Developing algorithms, particularly for clinical decision-making tools, involves a range of techniques that cater to different types of data and problem-solving needs. The techniques used can vary from rule-based systems to advanced ML methods. This summary outlines key techniques and provides a structured approach to developing a clinical decision-making tool [112,113,115,119–125].

2.4.3.1 Techniques for Developing Algorithms

1. **Rule-Based Systems**

   Rule-based algorithms use predefined rules to make decisions based on input data. These rules are often derived from clinical guidelines and expert knowledge. A rule-based system processes input data through a series of "if-then" statements to generate outputs. For instance, in a clinical decision support system (CDSS) for diagnosing a condition, a rule might state: "If the patient has a fever and a cough, then consider influenza as a possible diagnosis" [126]. Rule-based systems are straightforward and interpretable but can be limited by the complexity of rules and their inability to adapt to new data without manual updates.

2. **Statistical Models**

   Statistical models use mathematical techniques to analyse data and make predictions based on observed patterns. Techniques such as logistic regression, linear regression, and survival analysis are commonly used in clinical settings. For example, logistic regression might be employed to predict the likelihood of a patient developing a certain condition based on various risk factors [122]. These models are useful for understanding relationships between variables but may require assumptions about data distribution and linearity.

3. **Machine Learning**

   ML techniques are increasingly used in developing clinical algorithms due to their ability to handle large and complex datasets. Key methods include the following:

   - **Supervised Learning**: In supervised learning, algorithms are trained on labelled data, where the outcomes are known. Techniques such as DT, random forests, and SVMs are applied to predict outcomes based on input features. For instance, a random forest algorithm could be used to predict patient outcomes based on historical data.
   - **Unsupervised Learning**: This method involves finding patterns or groupings in data without predefined labels. Clustering techniques like K-means or hierarchical clustering can identify patient subgroups with similar characteristics. Unsupervised learning is useful for exploratory analysis and pattern discovery.
   - **DL**: A subset of ML, it employs neural networks with multiple layers to model complex relationships in data. CNNs are used for image analysis, while RNNs are applied to sequential data like EHRs. DL models can automatically learn features from raw data but require substantial computational resources and large datasets.

4. **Natural Language Processing**

   NLP techniques are used to process and analyse unstructured data from clinical notes, research papers, and patient records. NLP algorithms can extract meaningful information from text, such as identifying mentions of symptoms or diagnoses. This is valuable for integrating textual data into clinical decision-making tools.

2.4.3.2 Developing a Clinical Decision-Making Tool

1. **Define the Objective**

   The first step in developing a clinical decision-making tool is to clearly define the objective. This involves understanding the specific clinical problem to be addressed, such as diagnosing a condition, predicting patient outcomes, or recommending treatments. Engaging with clinicians and stakeholders is crucial to ensure that the tool meets practical needs and aligns with clinical workflows.

2. **Collect and Prepare Data**
   Data collection and preparation are critical for developing effective algorithms. This involves gathering relevant data from sources such as EHRs, clinical trials, and patient surveys. Data must be cleaned and preprocessed to ensure quality and consistency. This step may include handling missing values, normalising data, and encoding categorical variables.
3. **Choose the Appropriate Technique**
   Based on the objective and data, select the appropriate algorithmic technique. For structured data with well-defined features, statistical models or ML methods may be suitable. For unstructured text, NLP techniques are more appropriate. The choice of technique will depend on factors such as data complexity, interpretability, and the need for real-time processing.
4. **Develop and Train the Model**
   Develop the algorithm or model by implementing the chosen technique. For ML methods, this involves splitting the data into training and validation sets, training the model on the training set, and tuning hyperparameters to optimise performance. It is crucial to evaluate the model using metrics such as accuracy, sensitivity, and specificity to ensure it performs well on unseen data.
5. **Test and Validate**
   Thorough testing and validation are essential to ensure the tool's reliability and effectiveness. This involves evaluating the tool in real-world clinical settings, comparing its recommendations to expert opinions, and assessing its impact on patient outcomes. Feedback from clinicians can provide valuable insights for refining the tool.
6. **Implement and Monitor**
   Once validated, the tool is integrated into clinical practice. This may involve incorporating it into EHR systems, providing training for healthcare providers, and establishing protocols for its use. Ongoing monitoring and evaluation are necessary to ensure the tool remains effective and to address any issues that arise.
7. **Continuous Improvement**
   Continuous improvement is crucial for maintaining the relevance and accuracy of the tool. This involves updating the tool based on new clinical evidence, changes in medical practice, and feedback from users. Regular updates and maintenance ensure that the tool continues to provide valuable support in clinical decision-making.

Developing clinical decision-making tools involves applying a range of techniques from rule-based systems to advanced ML methods. Each technique has its strengths and applications, and the choice depends on the problem at hand and the available data. A systematic approach to defining objectives, preparing data, selecting techniques, and validating models ensures the development of effective and reliable decision-making tools that can enhance clinical practice and improve patient outcomes.

2.5 EVIDENCE-BASED MEDICINE METHODS TO MODEL DATA SCIENCE

Evidence-Based Medicine (EBM) is a systematic approach to clinical practice that integrates the best available research evidence with clinical expertise and patient values to make informed healthcare decisions. The goal of EBM is to improve patient outcomes and optimise healthcare delivery by ensuring that clinical practices are grounded in the most current and rigorous scientific evidence [125,127–133].

2.5.1 Principles of EBM

EBM is based on several core principles. First, it emphasises the use of **best available evidence**. This means that clinical decisions should be guided by research findings from well-conducted studies, rather than anecdotal experiences or outdated practices. Evidence is typically ranked according to its quality, with systematic reviews and meta-analyses of RCTs being considered the highest level of evidence.

Second, EBM incorporates **clinical expertise**. This refers to the skills and past experiences of healthcare professionals in diagnosing and treating patients. Expertise is crucial because even the best evidence must be interpreted and applied in the context of individual patient needs and circumstances.

Third, EBM takes into account **patient values and preferences**. Effective healthcare requires aligning treatment options with the patient's personal values, preferences, and circumstances. This ensures that the care provided is not only clinically effective but also acceptable and meaningful to the patient.

2.5.2 Steps in the EBM Process

The practice of EBM involves a systematic process:

1. **Ask**: Formulate a clear, answerable clinical question. This often follows the PICO format, which stands for Patient/Problem, Intervention, Comparison, and Outcome. For example, a question might be, "In elderly patients with hypertension (Patient/Problem), does medication A (Intervention) compared to medication B (Comparison) improve blood pressure control (Outcome)?"
2. **Acquire**: Search for the best available evidence. This involves conducting a thorough literature review to identify relevant research studies. Resources include medical databases such as PubMed, Cochrane Library, and clinical guidelines published by reputable organisations.
3. **Appraise**: Critically evaluate the evidence for its validity, impact, and applicability. This includes assessing the study design, methodology, sample size, and relevance to the clinical question. Tools such as the Critical Appraisal Skills Programme (CASP) checklists can be useful for this evaluation.
4. **Apply**: Integrate the evidence with clinical expertise and patient preferences to make a decision. This step involves tailoring the evidence to the specific patient context and considering how the findings fit with clinical experience and patient values.

5. **Assess**: Evaluate the outcomes of the decision. This involves monitoring and reviewing the effectiveness of the decision in practice and making adjustments as needed. Continuous assessment ensures that the interventions remain effective and relevant to the patient's evolving needs.

2.5.3 Benefits of EBM

EBM offers several benefits to healthcare practice. By relying on high-quality evidence, EBM helps to reduce variability in clinical practice and improve the consistency of care. It also enhances the likelihood of positive patient outcomes by using interventions that have been proven effective through rigorous research.

Furthermore, EBM promotes a culture of critical thinking and continuous learning among healthcare professionals. It encourages practitioners to question existing practices and seek out the best available evidence to inform their decisions.

2.5.4 Challenges and Limitations

Despite its advantages, EBM faces several challenges. One challenge is the potential for information overload. The sheer volume of medical research can be overwhelming, and it can be difficult to keep up with the latest evidence. Additionally, not all evidence is of high quality, and there may be limitations in the applicability of certain studies to individual patients.

Another challenge is the integration of evidence with clinical expertise. While evidence provides a foundation for decision-making, it must be balanced with the clinician's judgement and the patient's unique circumstances. This balance can be difficult to achieve, particularly when evidence is not clear-cut or when it conflicts with clinical experience.

Lastly, patient values and preferences are not always easy to incorporate. Effective communication with patients is essential for understanding their preferences and values, which requires time and skill.

EBM is a cornerstone of modern healthcare, aiming to improve patient outcomes by integrating the best available research evidence with clinical expertise and patient values. While EBM offers numerous benefits, including improved consistency and patient outcomes, it also presents challenges such as information overload and the need to balance evidence with individual patient needs. By following a systematic process of asking, acquiring, appraising, applying, and assessing evidence, healthcare professionals can make informed decisions that enhance the quality of care.

EBM methods refer to the systematic approaches and tools used to integrate the best available research evidence with clinical expertise and patient values in making healthcare decisions. These methods guide healthcare professionals in applying EBM principles in practice. Here's a breakdown of key EBM methods aligned with the five steps of EBM:

1. **Defining a Clinically Relevant Question (Formulating the Question)**
   - **PICO Framework**: The PICO framework (Population, Intervention, Comparison, Outcome) is a method for structuring clinical questions.

It helps clarify the patient group, the intervention being considered, the comparison intervention (if any), and the desired outcomes. This structured approach ensures the question is precise and researchable.

2. **Searching for the Best Evidence.**
   - **Systematic Literature Search**: This involves using databases like PubMed, Cochrane Library, and others to find high-quality studies. Methods include developing search strategies using relevant keywords and applying filters to narrow down results to the most relevant studies.
   - **Hierarchy of Evidence**: This method helps in prioritising evidence based on study design. RCTs and systematic reviews/meta-analyses are usually at the top, followed by cohort studies, case-control studies, and case reports or expert opinion.
3. **Critically Appraising the Evidence.**
   - **Critical Appraisal Tools**: Tools like the CASP checklists or GRADE (Grading of Recommendations, Assessment, Development, and Evaluation) assess the validity, relevance, and applicability of studies. These tools help evaluate study methodology, bias, and the strength of evidence.
   - **Bias Assessment**: Methods for identifying and mitigating different types of bias (e.g., selection bias, performance bias) in studies are crucial for determining the reliability of evidence.
4. **Applying the Evidence.**
   - **Clinical Guidelines**: Evidence-based clinical practice guidelines synthesise research evidence to provide recommendations for clinical care. Professionals use these guidelines to apply the best available evidence to patient care.
   - **Shared Decision-Making**: This method involves integrating the best evidence with the healthcare provider's expertise and the patient's preferences and values. Tools like decision aids may be used to help patients understand their options and the potential outcomes.
5. **Evaluating the Performance of EBM.**
   - **Audit and Feedback**: This involves reviewing clinical outcomes to determine the effectiveness of EBM in practice. Methods include tracking patient outcomes, adherence to guidelines, and assessing whether the applied evidence led to improved patient care.
   - **Continuous Quality Improvement (CQI)**: A method for ongoing monitoring and improvement in clinical practice. It involves regularly updating practices based on new evidence and evaluating performance metrics to enhance patient outcomes.

EBM provides a systematic framework for integrating the best available scientific evidence with clinical expertise and patient values to optimise healthcare outcomes. It represents a paradigm shift in clinical practice, moving away from traditional approaches that often relied heavily on anecdotal experience or pathophysiological rationale alone, towards a more rigorous, data-driven methodology. The ultimate aim of EBM is to improve patient care by ensuring that clinical decisions are informed by the most reliable evidence available, tailored to the individual patient's circumstances and preferences. This process involves not only applying the evidence to clinical practice but also critically evaluating the outcomes to continually refine and improve treatment strategies [133–137].

At the heart of EBM is the concept that clinical decisions should be based on a careful synthesis of three key elements: the best research evidence, clinical expertise, and patient values. The best research evidence typically comes from well-conducted studies, such as RCTs or systematic reviews, which are considered the gold standard in clinical research. However, clinical expertise remains crucial, as it enables healthcare professionals to interpret and apply the evidence in the context of the specific clinical situation. Moreover, patient values are integral to the decision-making process, ensuring that the chosen interventions align with the patient's preferences, concerns, and expectations.

A fundamental aspect of EBM is the continuous re-evaluation of outcomes following the implementation of an intervention. This step is essential to determine whether the intervention has achieved the desired effect and to assess any unintended consequences. Re-evaluation is typically conducted in the context of the original clinical question, allowing clinicians to measure the efficacy of the treatment in real-world conditions. This feedback loop is vital for refining clinical practices and improving patient outcomes over time. Moreover, when applied to larger populations, re-evaluation can inform public health recommendations and guidelines, which are then disseminated to improve care at a broader level.

Population-level recommendations in EBM are often graded based on the strength of the underlying evidence. Various grading schemes exist, each with its own methodology for ranking the quality of evidence and the strength of recommendations. One widely used system is the GRADE framework, which categorises recommendations into four levels: high, moderate, low, and very low. Recommendations graded as "high" are supported by robust evidence from multiple RCTs or meta-analyses, indicating that further research is unlikely to change the confidence in the estimate of effect. Conversely, recommendations graded as "low" or "very low" are based on weaker evidence, such as observational studies or expert opinion, and are more susceptible to change as new evidence emerges.

The use of grading schemes in EBM is crucial for translating research findings into clinical practice. These schemes provide clinicians with clear guidance on the reliability of the evidence supporting different treatment options, helping them to make informed decisions that are consistent with current best practices. However, it is important to critically assess these grading systems and the evidence they are based on. Not all RCTs or systematic reviews are of equal quality, and the context in which the research was conducted may not always be applicable to every patient population. For instance, a well-conducted RCT may provide strong evidence for the efficacy of a treatment in a controlled environment, but its applicability to a diverse patient population in a real-world setting may be limited.

Moreover, the emphasis on high-quality evidence can sometimes marginalise other valuable forms of knowledge. For example, qualitative research, which explores patients' experiences, beliefs, and preferences, is often rated lower in traditional evidence hierarchies but is essential for understanding the human dimensions of healthcare. This type of evidence is crucial when considering patient values, which are a core component of EBM. Therefore, while grading systems are valuable tools, they should be used in conjunction with a broader assessment of all relevant evidence, including patient-reported outcomes and contextual factors.

The implementation of EBM also faces challenges related to the dynamic nature of medical evidence. As new research is published, previously accepted guidelines may need to be revised or even discarded. This requires a commitment to continuous learning and adaptation on the part of healthcare providers, who must stay informed about the latest developments in their field. The rapid pace of medical research can make this difficult, highlighting the need for accessible, up-to-date resources that synthesise the latest evidence in a user-friendly format. EBM represents a powerful approach to improving healthcare outcomes by integrating the best available evidence with clinical expertise and patient values. The continuous re-evaluation of interventions and the grading of recommendations based on the quality of evidence are fundamental to this process. However, the application of EBM requires a critical approach, recognising the limitations of the evidence and the need for a holistic view that incorporates both quantitative and qualitative research. As medical knowledge evolves, so too must the practices and guidelines that underpin patient care, ensuring that EBM remains a dynamic and responsive framework for clinical decision-making.

EBM and data science are both pivotal in advancing modern healthcare, each contributing unique methodologies to improve patient outcomes. Integrating EBM methods with data science enables the development of optimal models that can transform clinical decision-making, making it more precise, personalised, and effective. This integration, however, requires careful consideration of the principles underlying both fields, ensuring that data-driven models are not only technically robust but also clinically relevant and aligned with the core tenets of EBM. At the core of EBM is the systematic use of the best available evidence to inform clinical decisions. This evidence typically comes from well-designed clinical studies, such as RCTs, systematic reviews, and meta-analyses. Data science, on the other hand, leverages vast amounts of data, advanced algorithms, and computational power to identify patterns, predict outcomes, and optimise decision-making processes. By combining these approaches, we can develop models that are both evidence-based and data-driven, thereby enhancing their reliability and applicability in clinical settings [134,138–141].

2.5.4.1 Evidence Synthesis and Model Development

One of the primary ways EBM methods contribute to data science is through evidence synthesis, which involves systematically reviewing and aggregating data from multiple studies to produce a comprehensive understanding of a given clinical question. This synthesis is crucial for model development, as it ensures that the data used to train and validate models is based on the highest quality evidence. For instance, systematic reviews and meta-analyses can provide the necessary input data for developing predictive models, ensuring that the underlying data reflects the best available evidence rather than isolated or biased studies.

Moreover, the PICO framework, a fundamental EBM tool, can guide the formulation of research questions that inform model development. By clearly defining the population, intervention, comparison, and outcomes of interest, researchers can ensure that the models they develop are tailored to specific clinical contexts. This alignment with clinical questions enhances the relevance and utility of the models in real-world practice.

2.5.4.2 Data Quality and Model Validation

Another critical aspect where EBM methods intersect with data science is in the emphasis on data quality and model validation. In EBM, the quality of evidence is paramount, with tools like the GRADE system used to assess the strength of evidence. Similarly, in data science, the quality of the data used to train models directly impacts their performance and generalisability. EBM methods encourage a rigorous evaluation of data sources, ensuring that the data used in model development is accurate, relevant, and free from significant biases.

Model validation is another area where EBM provides valuable insights. In EBM, the validity of clinical evidence is often tested through replication in different populations and settings. This principle can be applied to data science models by validating them across diverse patient datasets to ensure their robustness and generalisability. Cross-validation techniques, which are standard in data science, align with this EBM principle by testing models on multiple subsets of data to prevent overfitting and ensure that the models perform well on unseen data.

2.5.4.3 Personalisation and Clinical Relevance

The integration of EBM with data science also enables the development of personalised models that consider individual patient characteristics, preferences, and values—an essential aspect of EBM. Data science techniques such as ML can analyse large datasets to identify patient subgroups with different risk profiles or treatment responses. This capability allows for the creation of personalised predictive models that align with the EBM goal of tailoring treatment to individual patient needs.

However, the challenge lies in ensuring that these data-driven models are clinically relevant and actionable. EBM emphasises the importance of clinical judgement and patient preferences in decision-making, which must be reflected in the models. It is not enough for a model to be technically accurate; it must also provide insights that are meaningful to clinicians and patients. This requires close collaboration between data scientists and clinicians throughout the model development process to ensure that the models address clinically relevant questions and support shared decision-making.

2.5.4.4 Ethical Considerations and Transparency

Finally, the ethical considerations inherent in EBM are equally important in data science. EBM advocates for transparency in reporting research methods and results, which is critical for building trust in clinical practice. Similarly, data science models must be transparent, with clear documentation of how they were developed, validated, and tested. This transparency is essential for clinicians to understand the limitations and strengths of the models they use, ensuring that they can make informed decisions when applying these models in patient care.

Moreover, the use of data science in healthcare raises ethical issues related to data privacy, consent, and bias. EBM's focus on patient-centred care and ethical standards can guide the responsible use of data in model development. For instance, ensuring that models do not perpetuate existing healthcare disparities requires careful consideration of the data used and the potential biases it may introduce. EBM principles can help ensure that data science models are developed and applied in ways that are equitable and just.

In conclusion, the integration of EBM methods with data science holds significant potential for developing optimal models that can improve clinical decision-making. By synthesising high-quality evidence, ensuring rigorous data quality and model validation, personalising models to individual patients, and upholding ethical standards, we can create data-driven tools that are both scientifically robust and clinically relevant. However, this integration must be approached with caution, ensuring that the principles of EBM—such as the primacy of patient values and the importance of clinical judgement—are not lost in the pursuit of technological advancement. By maintaining a critical perspective, we can harness the power of data science to enhance, rather than replace, the human elements that are central to effective healthcare.

2.6 CLINICAL TRIALS FOR ARTIFICIAL INTELLIGENCE TOOLS

Clinical trials are a fundamental component of medical research, serving as the primary method for testing the safety, efficacy, and overall impact of new treatments, interventions, and medical devices on human health. These trials are meticulously designed studies that follow a structured protocol to ensure that the results are reliable and applicable to broader patient populations. The primary goal of clinical trials is to generate robust evidence that can inform clinical practice, guide healthcare policy, and ultimately improve patient outcomes. Given their critical role in advancing medical knowledge, clinical trials are subject to rigorous ethical standards and regulatory oversight [142–145].

2.6.1 The Clinical and Scientific Need for Clinical Trials

The need for clinical trials arises from the necessity to translate basic scientific research into tangible medical benefits. While preclinical studies—such as those conducted in laboratories using cell cultures or animal models—provide valuable insights into the mechanisms of diseases and the potential effects of new treatments, they cannot fully predict how these interventions will perform in humans. Clinical trials bridge this gap by providing the essential data needed to evaluate whether a new treatment is safe and effective in the human population.

From a clinical perspective, clinical trials are indispensable for advancing patient care. They enable healthcare professionals to move beyond anecdotal evidence and intuition, grounding their practice in scientifically validated knowledge. For instance, clinical trials are crucial in determining the appropriate dosages of medications, understanding side effects, and identifying which patient populations are most likely to benefit from a particular treatment. Without clinical trials, the adoption of new therapies would be based on conjecture, potentially leading to ineffective or harmful practices.

Scientifically, clinical trials contribute to the body of evidence that forms the basis for EBM. They provide a controlled environment where variables can be carefully managed, ensuring that the outcomes observed are genuinely due to the intervention being tested rather than external factors. This level of control is critical for establishing causality, which is essential for developing new treatments and improving existing ones. Moreover, clinical trials often reveal unexpected findings, such as additional benefits or risks of a treatment, which can lead to new avenues of research and innovation.

2.6.2 Classifications of Clinical Trials

Clinical trials can be classified in various ways, depending on their design, purpose, and the phase of development of the intervention being tested. The most common classification is based on the trial's phase, which ranges from Phase I to Phase IV, each serving a distinct purpose in the development of new treatments.

- **Phase I Trials**: These are the first trials conducted in humans, typically involving a small number of healthy volunteers or patients. The primary objective of Phase I trials is to assess the safety of the intervention, including its pharmacokinetics (how the drug is absorbed, distributed, metabolised, and excreted) and pharmacodynamics (the effects of the drug on the body). Dose-escalation studies are often a key component of Phase I trials, helping to determine the appropriate dose for further testing.
- **Phase II Trials**: Once a treatment has been deemed safe in Phase I, it moves on to Phase II trials, which involve a larger group of patients and focus on assessing the treatment's efficacy. Phase II trials are often randomised and controlled, comparing the new treatment to a placebo or standard therapy. These trials also continue to monitor safety and side effects, providing a more detailed understanding of the treatment's risk-benefit profile.
- **Phase III Trials**: These are large-scale studies involving hundreds or even thousands of patients across multiple sites. Phase III trials aim to confirm the efficacy of the treatment, monitor side effects, and collect data that will allow the treatment to be used safely in the general population. These trials are typically required for regulatory approval and are designed to provide the definitive evidence needed to change clinical practice. The results from Phase III trials are often published in peer-reviewed journals and form the basis for guidelines and recommendations.
- **Phase IV Trials**: Also known as post-marketing surveillance trials, Phase IV trials are conducted after a treatment has been approved for use in the general population. These trials continue to monitor the safety and effectiveness of the treatment over the long term and in a broader patient population. Phase IV trials can also identify rare or long-term side effects that may not have been apparent in earlier phases.

2.6.3 Other Classifications and Types

In addition to the phase-based classification, clinical trials can be categorised by their design and objectives. For example, RCTs are considered the gold standard for testing the efficacy of new treatments because they minimise bias by randomly assigning participants to different treatment groups. Blinded trials, where participants and/or investigators are unaware of which treatment is being administered, further reduce bias and ensure objective assessment of outcomes. Other types of trials include observational studies, where researchers observe outcomes without intervening, and adaptive trials, which allow for modifications to the trial protocol based on interim results.

2.6.4 Ethical and Regulatory Considerations

Given the potential risks to participants, clinical trials are subject to strict ethical standards and regulatory oversight. Informed consent is a cornerstone of ethical clinical trials, ensuring that participants are fully aware of the risks and benefits before agreeing to take part. Regulatory bodies such as the Medicines and Healthcare products Regulatory Agency (MHRA) in the UK and the Food and Drug Administration (FDA) in the US require rigorous evaluation of clinical trial protocols before they can proceed.

In conclusion, clinical trials are essential for advancing medical knowledge and improving patient care. They provide the critical evidence needed to ensure that new treatments are safe and effective, guiding clinical practice and informing public health policy. The classification of clinical trials into phases reflects the progressive nature of medical research, from initial safety testing to widespread clinical application. Through rigorous design, ethical oversight, and scientific integrity, clinical trials continue to be a cornerstone of modern healthcare, offering hope for new treatments and improved outcomes for patients worldwide.

Clinical trial design is a fundamental aspect of drug development, ensuring that new pharmaceutical interventions are both safe and effective before being introduced to the wider population. The rigour and structure of these designs are paramount, as they directly influence the reliability and applicability of the trial outcomes. While numerous designs exist, each with its own strengths and limitations, a critical appraisal of these methodologies reveals the complexity of translating scientific inquiry into practical healthcare solutions [143,146,147].

2.6.5 Randomised Controlled Trials

RCTs are widely regarded as the gold standard in clinical trial design, particularly in the context of drug development. The core strength of RCTs lies in their ability to minimise bias and confounding variables through randomisation. By randomly assigning participants to either the treatment group or the control group, RCTs ensure that any differences in outcomes can be attributed to the intervention rather than external factors. This is further strengthened by blinding, where neither the participants nor the researchers know which treatment the participants are receiving, reducing the risk of bias in reporting and assessing outcomes. While RCTs are highly valued for their internal validity, they are not without limitations. One significant critique is their often limited external validity. The stringent inclusion and exclusion criteria necessary to ensure a homogenous study population can lead to results that are not easily generalisable to the broader, more diverse patient populations seen in everyday clinical practice. Additional artificial environment of RCTs, where patient care is closely monitored and controlled, may not accurately reflect real-world conditions, potentially limiting the applicability of the findings.

2.6.6 Observational Studies

In contrast to RCTs, observational studies, such as cohort or case-control studies, offer insights into the effects of drugs in real-world settings. These studies are particularly useful for identifying long-term outcomes and adverse effects that may not be apparent in the controlled environment of an RCT. Observational studies can include larger and more diverse populations, enhancing the external validity of their findings. They are also often more ethical and feasible when randomisation is not possible, such as in studies of harmful exposures, or when withholding treatment would be unethical.

Despite these, observational studies are more susceptible to bias, particularly selection bias and confounding. Since participants are not randomly assigned, differences in baseline characteristics between groups can influence outcomes, making it difficult to establish causality. Techniques such as propensity score matching and multivariate adjustment are used to mitigate these issues, but these methods cannot entirely eliminate the inherent biases in observational data.

2.6.7 Adaptive Trials

Adaptive trial designs have emerged as a more flexible approach to drug development, allowing for modifications to the trial procedures based on interim data without compromising the study's integrity. This approach can make clinical trials more efficient by identifying ineffective treatments early, reducing the time and cost associated with drug development. Adaptive designs can also be more ethical, as they may reduce the number of patients exposed to inferior treatments.

However, adaptive designs pose no challenges. The flexibility that is their hallmark can also lead to complexities in trial design and analysis, requiring advanced statistical techniques and careful planning to ensure that the trial remains valid and unbiased. Furthermore, the frequent interim analyses required in adaptive trials can introduce operational biases, and there is a risk that the trial may be stopped prematurely based on incomplete data.

2.6.8 Pragmatic Trials

Pragmatic trials address the gap between the controlled conditions of RCTs and the complexity of real-world clinical practice. These trials are designed to evaluate the effectiveness of interventions in the context of routine healthcare, making them highly relevant for informing clinical practice. Pragmatic trials typically include a broader range of participants and are conducted in settings that reflect typical clinical environments, enhancing the generalisability of their findings.

Despite their practical advantages, pragmatic trial challenges. The broader inclusion criteria and less stringent control over variables can introduce heterogeneity that complicates the interpretation of results. Moreover, while pragmatic trials are designed to reflect real-world practice, the lack of blinding and randomisation in some designs can increase the risk of bias, potentially undermining the validity of the findings.

2.6.9 Master Protocol Trial

Master protocol trial designs represent an innovative approach to clinical research, aimed at improving the efficiency and flexibility of trials, particularly in the context of drug development. Unlike traditional trials, which typically focus on a single treatment for a specific disease, master protocols allow for the simultaneous evaluation of multiple therapies, biomarkers, or patient subgroups under a unified trial structure. This design is especially advantageous in areas like oncology, where multiple treatments and targeted therapies are being developed concurrently [148,149].

There are three main types of master protocol designs: umbrella trials, basket trials, and platform trials. Umbrella trials evaluate multiple targeted therapies for a single disease, stratifying patients based on specific biomarkers or genetic mutations. This design enables the comparison of different treatments within the same disease context, enhancing the precision of therapeutic interventions.

Basket trials, on the other hand, test the effectiveness of a single therapy across multiple diseases that share a common molecular or genetic feature. This approach is particularly useful for rare cancers, where traditional trial designs may be impractical due to limited patient populations.

Platform trials are perhaps the most flexible, allowing the addition or removal of treatment arms as new therapies become available or as interim results suggest modifications. This adaptive design helps to streamline the drug development process by continuously testing new treatments within the same overarching trial framework.

Master protocols offer several benefits, including faster patient recruitment, reduced costs, and more comprehensive data on treatment effects across various patient subgroups. However, they also present challenges, such as increased logistical complexity and the need for sophisticated statistical methods to manage multiple comparisons and adaptively modify the trial.

2.6.10 Regulatory and Ethical Considerations

Ethical and regulatory considerations are integral to all clinical trial designs. The protection of participants through informed consent, safety monitoring, and the ethical review process is paramount. However, the ethical landscape is increasingly complex, particularly with the advent of innovative trial designs such as adaptive and pragmatic trials. Regulatory agencies such as the MHRA in the UK and the FDA in the US have developed guidelines to ensure that these designs are implemented in a manner that protects participants while allowing for scientific innovation.

A critical appraisal of clinical trial designs must also consider the implications of these methodologies. For example, while adaptive designs may reduce patient exposure to ineffective treatments, the complexity of these trials can make it difficult for participants to fully understand the risks and benefits, complicating the informed consent process. Similarly, while observational studies offer insights into real-world drug effects, the lack of randomisation raises ethical concerns about the potential for bias and the misinterpretation of results.

The design of clinical trials for drugs is a complex and multifaceted process that balances scientific rigour with ethical responsibility. RCTs remain the cornerstone of drug development, offering robust evidence of efficacy and safety, but their limitations highlight the need for complementary approaches such as observational, adaptive, and pragmatic trials. Each design has its strengths and challenges, and the choice of design must be tailored to the specific research question, the characteristics of the intervention, and the practical and ethical considerations of the study population. By critically appraising and refining these designs, the scientific and medical communities can continue to advance the development of new therapies that are both effective and safe for the patients who need them.

Designing a clinical method to test AI tools involves a careful balance between traditional clinical trial methodologies and the unique characteristics of AI systems. AI tools in healthcare are often designed for tasks such as diagnostics, treatment recommendations, or predictive analytics, and their evaluation requires rigorous methods to ensure they are safe, effective, and reliable. This process necessitates a clear understanding of both the clinical problem the AI tool aims to address and the specific characteristics of the AI technology itself.

2.6.11 Understanding the Clinical Context and Defining the Objective

The first step in designing a clinical method to test AI tools is to define the clinical context and the specific problem the AI tool intends to solve. This involves identifying the target patient population, the clinical decision or process the AI is intended to assist or automate, and the existing standard of care. The objective of the trial should be clearly articulated, whether it is to assess diagnostic accuracy, improve patient outcomes, or enhance efficiency in clinical workflows. Defining these parameters is crucial for designing a trial that is relevant and meaningful in the clinical setting.

2.6.12 Trial Design: Comparative Studies and RCTs

The design of the clinical trial should consider the nature of AI tools, particularly their ability to learn and adapt. RCTs, the gold standard in clinical research, can be adapted to test AI tools by comparing the outcomes of patients managed with the help of the AI tool versus those managed through standard care without AI assistance. In this design, the AI tool is used in one arm of the trial, while the control group follows standard clinical practice.

However, unlike traditional drugs or devices, AI tools may undergo continuous learning and updates, which can complicate the RCT design. To address this, adaptive trial designs may be appropriate. These designs allow for modifications to the trial procedures based on interim data, which is particularly useful for AI tools that may evolve over the course of the trial.

2.6.13 Performance Metrics and Outcomes

Selecting appropriate performance metrics is a critical aspect of trial design. For diagnostic AI tools, accuracy metrics such as sensitivity, specificity, and the area under the receiver operating characteristic curve are essential. For AI tools designed to predict outcomes or recommend treatments, metrics might include clinical outcomes like mortality, morbidity, or length of hospital stay, as well as process measures such as time to diagnosis or treatment. It is also important to assess the AI tool's impact on healthcare professionals, including usability, interpretability, and the degree of trust clinicians place in the tool's recommendations.

2.6.14 Addressing Bias and Generalisability

AI tools are highly dependent on the data they are trained on, which raises concerns about bias and generalisability. Ensuring that the AI tool has been trained on diverse datasets that reflect the population in which it will be used is essential to avoid bias. The clinical trial should also include a representative sample of the target population to evaluate how well the AI tool generalises to different patient groups. Furthermore, stratified analysis might be necessary to assess the AI tool's performance across different subgroups, such as by age, sex, ethnicity, or comorbidity status.

2.6.15 Ethical Considerations and Regulatory Compliance

The integration of AI into clinical practice introduces unique ethical considerations. Informed consent is particularly challenging, as patients and clinicians must understand not only the clinical intervention but also the role and limitations of the AI tool. The potential for AI to make errors, particularly in critical clinical decisions, must be clearly communicated. Moreover, the AI tool's decision-making process should be transparent, and there should be mechanisms in place to allow clinicians to override AI recommendations when necessary.

Regulatory compliance is another critical aspect, as AI tools may fall under medical device regulations. Regulatory bodies such as the MHRA in the UK and the FDA in the US are developing guidelines to address the unique challenges posed by AI tools, including how they are validated, monitored, and updated. The clinical trial design must align with these regulatory requirements to ensure that the AI tool can be safely and effectively integrated into clinical practice.

2.6.16 Continuous Monitoring and Post-Market Surveillance

Given the dynamic nature of AI tools, continuous monitoring and post-market surveillance are crucial components of the clinical evaluation. Unlike traditional clinical interventions, AI tools may change over time as they are updated with new data or algorithms. Therefore, even after initial validation through clinical trials, ongoing assessment is necessary to ensure that the tool continues to perform as expected and does not introduce new risks or biases. This can be achieved through real-world evidence studies, registries, and long-term follow-up of patients who have been managed with the help of the AI tool.

Designing a clinical method to test AI tools in healthcare requires adapting traditional clinical trial methodologies to account for the unique characteristics of AI. A robust trial design should include a clear definition of the clinical context, appropriate performance metrics, strategies to address bias and generalisability, and considerations for ethical and regulatory compliance. Moreover, given the evolving nature of AI, continuous monitoring and post-market surveillance are essential to ensure that these tools provide safe and effective support in clinical practice. By addressing these challenges, clinical trials can provide the rigorous evidence needed to integrate AI tools into healthcare in a way that enhances patient outcomes and supports clinical decision-making.

2.7 DEVELOPING ARTIFICIAL INTELLIGENCE AS EFFECTIVENESS TOOLS

AI has made significant strides in healthcare, offering tools that enhance diagnostic accuracy, optimise treatment plans, and streamline administrative tasks. AI's effectiveness in various specialisms reflects its potential to revolutionise patient care by harnessing vast amounts of data to deliver insights and predictions. This discussion critically examines some of the most effective AI tools in healthcare, illustrating their applications across different specialisms and evaluating their benefits and limitations [140,150–152].

2.7.1 Diagnostic Imaging AI Tools

1. DL Algorithms (e.g., Google's DeepMind, IBM Watson Health)
2. Radiology AI Systems (e.g., Aidoc, Zebra Medical Vision)

Applications:

- **Radiology**: AI tools in radiology primarily focus on enhancing the interpretation of medical images. DL algorithms are used to detect anomalies in X-rays, MRIs, and CT scans with high accuracy. For instance, Aidoc provides real-time analysis of CT scans to identify acute abnormalities such as pulmonary embolism or fractures, significantly reducing the time to diagnosis and enabling quicker intervention.
- **Oncology**: AI-driven imaging tools are used to detect and classify cancers, particularly in mammography and pathology. Google's DeepMind has developed AI systems that outperform human radiologists in breast cancer detection by analysing mammograms and identifying cancerous lesions with greater precision and fewer false positives.

Critical Evaluation: While these AI tools demonstrate impressive diagnostic accuracy, their effectiveness is contingent upon the quality and diversity of training data. Bias in training datasets can lead to less accurate results for underrepresented populations. Furthermore, reliance on AI requires rigorous validation to ensure clinical reliability and integration into existing workflows without compromising patient care.

2.7.2 Predictive Analytics-AI Tools

1. Predictive Modelling Platforms (e.g., IBM Watson Health, Health Fidelity)
2. Risk Stratification Tools (e.g., Optum, Medial EarlySign)

Applications:

- **Cardiology**: AI predictive models are used to assess cardiovascular risk by analysing patient data, including EHRs, lab results, and lifestyle factors. Tools like IBM Watson Health help predict the likelihood of heart disease and suggest preventative measures based on individual risk profiles.
- **Emergency Medicine**: Risk stratification tools help in predicting patient deterioration, guiding early interventions. For instance, Medial EarlySign uses AI to predict the risk of diseases like sepsis or cancer based on historical patient data, enabling timely and potentially life-saving treatments.

Critical Evaluation: Predictive analytics in healthcare offers significant potential for preventative care and personalised treatment. However, these tools must be validated in diverse clinical settings to ensure their accuracy and generalisability. The integration of AI into clinical practice also raises concerns about data privacy and the potential for over-reliance on algorithms, which could overshadow the clinical judgement of healthcare professionals.

2.7.3 Drug Discovery and Development AI Tools

1. Drug Discovery Platforms (e.g., Atomwise, BenevolentAI)
2. Genomic Data Analysis Tools (e.g., Deep Genomics, Tempus)

Applications:

- **Pharmacology**: AI tools like Atomwise use ML algorithms to predict how different compounds interact with biological targets, accelerating the drug discovery process. BenevolentAI applies AI to analyse biomedical data and identify potential drug candidates for diseases with unmet needs, such as rare or complex conditions.
- **Genomics**: AI is used to analyse genomic data, identifying genetic mutations associated with diseases and predicting responses to treatments. Tools like Deep Genomics and Tempus leverage AI to personalise treatment plans based on genetic profiles, improving the precision of therapies.

Critical Evaluation: AI-driven drug discovery has the potential to significantly reduce the time and cost associated with developing new therapies. However, challenges include the need for high-quality data and the risk of overfitting models to specific datasets, which may limit the broader applicability of findings. Collaboration between AI researchers and clinical experts is essential to ensure that discoveries translate into effective and safe treatments.

2.7.4 Clinical Decision Support AI Tools

1. CDSS (e.g., IBM Watson for Oncology, PathAI)
2. Virtual Health Assistants (e.g., Babylon Health, Ada Health)

Applications:

- **Oncology**: AI systems like IBM Watson for Oncology assist oncologists by analysing vast amounts of medical literature and patient data to recommend personalised treatment options for cancer patients. This tool aims to support clinical decision-making by providing evidence-based recommendations and highlighting relevant research.
- **Primary Care**: Virtual health assistants such as Babylon Health and Ada Health provide patients with initial consultations, symptom checking, and health information based on AI algorithms. These tools help triage patients and provide guidance on whether they need to seek further medical attention.

Critical Evaluation: CDSS enhance the decision-making process by providing comprehensive and up-to-date information. However, reliance on these tools necessitates rigorous validation and integration into clinical workflows to prevent potential biases or errors. Ensuring transparency in AI recommendations and maintaining a human oversight component are crucial for effective patient care (Table 2.1).

AI tools have shown transformative potential across various specialisms in healthcare, from improving diagnostic accuracy to personalising treatment and accelerating

TABLE 2.1
Some AI Tools Used in Healthcare and Their Applications

Specialism	AI Tool	Application	Example
Diagnostic Imaging	Deep Learning Algorithms	Image analysis for disease detection	Google DeepMind, Aidoc
Predictive Analytics	Predictive Modelling Platforms	Risk assessment and early intervention	IBM Watson Health, Medial EarlySign
Drug Discovery	Drug Discovery Platforms	Accelerating drug discovery and development	Atomwise, BenevolentAI
Clinical Decision Support	Clinical Decision Support Systems	Personalised treatment recommendations and health guidance	IBM Watson for Oncology, Babylon Health

drug discovery. Their application ranges from enhancing imaging interpretation and predictive analytics to supporting clinical decision-making and developing new therapies. However, the integration of AI into healthcare systems must be approached with caution, addressing challenges such as data quality, algorithmic bias, and the need for transparent, validated results. Continuous collaboration between AI developers, clinicians, and regulatory bodies is essential to harness the full potential of AI while safeguarding patient safety and enhancing overall healthcare delivery.

2.8 THE USE OF BIG DATA AND DATA PLATFORMS

A Big Data platform is a comprehensive technological framework designed to handle, process, and analyse vast amounts of structured and unstructured data that exceed the capabilities of traditional data management systems. These platforms are crucial in leveraging the potential of Big Data to generate insights, drive decision-making, and enable predictive analytics across various domains. This discussion critically examines the concept of a Big Data platform, its key components, and the challenges and benefits associated with its implementation [153–156].

2.8.1 Definition and Key Components

A Big Data platform integrates a range of technologies and tools to manage the complexities associated with large-scale data processing. The fundamental components of a Big Data platform include the following:

1. **Data Storage**: Big Data platforms utilise distributed storage systems to manage enormous volumes of data. Technologies like Hadoop Distributed File System (HDFS) and cloud-based storage solutions such as Amazon S3 enable the scalable storage of data across multiple nodes or servers. These systems are designed to handle various data types, including structured data (e.g., relational databases), semi-structured data (e.g., JSON, XML), and unstructured data (e.g., text, images).
2. **Data Processing**: To process Big Data, platforms employ frameworks that facilitate parallel processing of data across distributed systems. Apache Hadoop and Apache Spark are prominent examples. Hadoop provides a MapReduce framework for processing large datasets in parallel, while Spark offers in-memory processing capabilities, which can be significantly faster for iterative algorithms and real-time analytics.
3. **Data Integration**: Big Data platforms often include tools for integrating data from disparate sources. Technologies like Apache NiFi and Talend are used to automate the extraction, transformation, and loading processes, enabling seamless integration of data from various sources into a unified platform.
4. **Data Analytics and Visualisation**: Advanced analytics and visualisation tools are critical for extracting actionable insights from Big Data. Platforms typically incorporate ML algorithms and statistical analysis tools.

Technologies such as Apache Hive for SQL-based querying and Tableau or Power BI for visual analytics play a significant role in making data comprehensible and actionable for end-users.

2.8.2 Benefits and Applications

The implementation of Big Data platforms offers numerous advantages. For instance, these platforms can handle data at scale and provide insights that drive business strategies. In healthcare, for example, Big Data platforms facilitate the integration of EHRs, genomic data, and patient history to enhance personalised medicine and predictive analytics for patient care. In finance, they enable real-time fraud detection and risk management by analysing transaction data for suspicious patterns.

Moreover, Big Data platforms support advanced analytics such as predictive modelling and ML. These capabilities allow organisations to identify trends, forecast future outcomes, and optimise operations. For example, retail businesses use Big Data analytics to personalise marketing strategies and manage inventory more effectively.

In the UK, several prominent data platforms have been established to facilitate research and healthcare improvements by providing comprehensive, high-quality data. These platforms, including the Clinical Practice Research Datalink (CPRD), UK Biobank, Akrivia Health, OPEN SAFELY, and ORCHID, serve diverse purposes ranging from epidemiological studies to clinical trials. This discussion critically examines each platform, highlighting their contributions, strengths, and limitations in the context of UK healthcare research.

2.8.2.1 Clinical Practice Research Datalink

The CPRD is one of the largest and most widely used EHR databases in the UK. Managed by the MHRA, CPRD collects anonymised patient data from primary care practices across the UK, covering a wide range of health conditions, demographics, and treatments [157–159].

Strengths:

1. **Comprehensive Coverage**: CPRD provides extensive longitudinal data on patient health records, including diagnoses, prescriptions, and clinical measurements, which are invaluable for epidemiological studies and drug safety research [159].
2. **Integration with Other Datasets**: CPRD data can be linked with other datasets such as hospital records and mortality data, enhancing the depth of research and enabling more comprehensive analyses.

Limitations:

1. **Data Quality and Completeness**: Although CPRD offers detailed records, the quality and completeness of the data can vary depending on the practice. Missing or incomplete data may affect the reliability of research outcomes [158].

2. **Generalisation Issues**: The data primarily comes from general practices that have agreed to participate in CPRD, which may not fully represent the diverse demographic of the UK population, potentially leading to biases in findings [158].

2.8.2.2 UK Biobank

UK Biobank is a large-scale biomedical database containing genetic, lifestyle, and health information from over 500,000 participants aged 40–69 at recruitment. UK Biobank is a large-scale prospective study that recruited 502,000 adults aged 40–69 from the UK general population between 2006 and 2010. Participants provided extensive information on lifestyle, medical history, and other factors, underwent physical measurements, and provided biological samples. The study aims to enable research into the determinants of a wide range of diseases. Participants have been followed for over a decade, with over 52,000 incident cancer cases now recorded. The resource is open-access, allowing researchers worldwide to use the data for health research. UK Biobank continues to be enhanced with repeat assessments, imaging, and conversion of samples to genomic and other "-omic" data. It has already demonstrated value for cancer research and is uniquely placed to transform understanding of cancer development and drive improvements in treatment and prevention. The data includes a range of health metrics, biochemistry, and imaging data, with the goal of understanding the relationships between genetics, lifestyle, and disease.

UK Biobank continually enhances its resource to increase its value for health research. The enhancements are implemented through various means, each contributing to the depth and breadth of available data. A key enhancement involves repeat assessments, wherein approximately 20,000 participants underwent a repeat of the baseline assessment to allow for measurement error adjustments. Additionally, an ambitious imaging sub-study aims to recruit up to 100,000 participants to undergo detailed imaging of the brain, heart, and body, with repeat imaging planned for 60,000 individuals.

To objectively measure physical activity, 100,000 participants wore wrist accelerometers, providing valuable data on activity patterns. The biological samples collected are being analysed for all participants, including genotyping, whole-exome and whole-genome sequencing, and various biomarkers. Furthermore, measurements of 3,000 proteins are being conducted for 57,000 participants initially. Plans are underway to expand linkage to datasets with information on tumour characteristics and treatments, enhancing the cancer data available. Periodic web-based questionnaires capture additional health information, whilst linkage to environmental data provides information on air pollution, noise, and other environmental exposures. To democratise access to the expanding dataset, UK Biobank has introduced a cloud-based Research Analysis Platform. These enhancements significantly expand the depth and breadth of data available, enabling more comprehensive research into disease determinants and potential treatments.

Strengths:

1. **Extensive Dataset**: The breadth and depth of data available, including genetic information and detailed health records, make UK Biobank an invaluable resource for understanding disease aetiology and progression.
2. **Longitudinal Follow-Up**: Participants are followed up for long-term health outcomes, providing insights into how lifestyle and genetic factors influence health over time.

Limitations:

1. **Population Bias**: The majority of participants are of European descent and are generally healthier compared to the general population, which may limit the generalisability of findings to more diverse or less healthy groups.
2. **Data Utilisation**: Although the database is rich, accessing and utilising the data can be complex and may require navigating extensive ethical and logistical procedures.

2.8.2.3 Akrivia Health

Akrivia Health is a newer platform focused on integrating EHRs with other data sources to support research and clinical decision-making. UK-CRIS is a system that provides access to de-identified clinical case records from 12 NHS Mental Health Trusts in the UK. It allows researchers to search and analyse large amounts of EHR data, including both structured information like diagnoses and unstructured text like clinical notes. The system aims to facilitate mental health research using real-world clinical data. UK-CRIS functions by allowing researchers to query and extract relevant information from the de-identified records. It contains data on thousands of patients, with millions of clinical documents available.

Technically, UK-CRIS utilises NLP methods to extract structured information from the unstructured text in clinical notes. This involves steps like defining variables of interest, developing annotation schemas, training NLP models on annotated data, and using active learning to improve model performance. The system allows for complex queries across the structured and unstructured data. It leverages real-world evidence to improve patient outcomes and facilitate drug development.

The NLP pipeline used in UK-CRIS consists of several key steps. First, clinical experts define the variables of interest and develop an annotation schema. Next, a sample of clinical documents is selected and annotated by medical professionals to create a gold standard dataset. This annotated data is then used to train an initial named entity recognition model, which utilises techniques like word embeddings and bidirectional LSTM neural networks. To improve model performance, active learning procedures are employed. This involves using the initial model to identify ambiguous text spans, which are then annotated to provide the most informative additional training data. The model is iteratively fine-tuned through this process. The pipeline also incorporates methods to maximise the information extracted from limited annotations. This includes using string matching algorithms to identify relevant documents and weighting annotation categories based on their frequency.

Finally, the model's performance is validated on a held-out test set, with metrics like precision, recall, and F1 score calculated for each variable category. The pipeline aims to accurately extract structured information on diagnoses, symptoms, medications, and other relevant clinical data from free-text notes.

Strengths:

1. **Integration of Diverse Data Sources**: Akrivia Health combines EHR data with genomic, imaging, and other health-related data, enabling comprehensive analyses and more informed clinical decision-making.
2. **Real-World Evidence**: The platform focuses on real-world evidence, which helps bridge the gap between clinical trials and everyday practice, providing insights that are directly applicable to patient care.

Limitations:

1. **Data Integration Challenges**: The integration of diverse data sources can be complex and may face challenges related to data compatibility and standardisation.
2. **Early Stage**: As a newer platform, Akrivia Health is still in the process of establishing its reputation and proving its utility compared to more established data platforms.

2.8.2.4 OPEN SAFELY

OpenSAFELY is a COVID-19 research platform that uses anonymised patient data from EHRs to study the impact of the pandemic [160]. It was developed rapidly to provide timely insights into the spread, treatment, and outcomes of COVID-19. OpenSAFELY is a secure, transparent, open-source software platform designed for analysing EHRs with a focus on reproducible research. It allows secure analysis of pseudonymised primary care EHRs from England within the EHR vendor's highly secure data centre. OpenSAFELY addresses key challenges in reproducible EHR research through its innovative design. By standardising data preparation workflows and enforcing code sharing, it mitigates issues of inconsistent data processing and lack of transparency. The platform's use of dummy data for development allows full code sharing without privacy risks, overcoming a major barrier in EHR research reproducibility. The integration of tools like ehrQL and Open Code lists enhances reproducibility by standardising data extraction and code list management. However, the lack of direct data access may pose challenges for researchers in problem-solving and code development. While OpenSAFELY mandates some reproducible practices, it maintains flexibility in others, which may lead to inconsistent adoption. The platform's approach to reproducibility goes beyond current norms in the field, potentially driving cultural change in EHR research practices. Overall, OpenSAFELY demonstrates how research platforms can significantly improve reproducibility in

EHR research, though some trade-offs in researcher flexibility exist. Key features of OpenSAFELY that enhance reproducibility include the following:

1. Standardising data preparation workflows
2. Removing barriers to code sharing in secure environments
3. Enforcing public sharing of code and code lists
4. Ensuring consistent computational environments
5. Integrating tools that enable reproducible practices
6. Providing an audit trail of all code run on real data.

OpenSAFELY uses dummy data for code development, allowing all code to be non-disclosive and publicly shared. It integrates with GitHub for version control and code review. The platform also includes custom tools like ehrQL for standardised data extraction and Open Code lists for managing clinical code lists. By design, OpenSAFELY makes reproducible research practices easier to adopt while maintaining patient privacy and data security. This approach aims to improve the transparency, efficiency, and credibility of EHR-based research.

Strengths:

1. **Timeliness**: OPEN SAFELY was designed to rapidly generate insights during the COVID-19 pandemic, providing crucial data on risk factors, treatment efficacy, and vaccine effectiveness.
2. **Data Access and Collaboration**: The platform promotes open access to data and encourages collaboration across research institutions, which has accelerated research findings and public health responses.

Limitations:

1. **Pandemic-Specific Focus**: While highly effective for COVID-19 research, the platform's utility may be limited outside the context of the pandemic, and it may not provide the same level of detail for other diseases.
2. **Data Privacy Concerns**: Managing large-scale data during a pandemic raised concerns about data privacy and security, which needed careful handling to protect patient information.

2.8.2.5 ORCHID

ORCHID (Observational Research in COVID-19) is another platform that provides real-time data on COVID-19 patients, focusing on hospital admissions and outcomes [161]. It supports observational research to improve understanding and management of COVID-19.

Strengths:

1. **Real-Time Data**: ORCHID offers up-to-date data on hospitalised COVID-19 patients, which is crucial for understanding patient management and outcomes in a rapidly evolving situation.

2. **Clinical Insight**: By focusing on hospital data, ORCHID provides valuable insights into the clinical management of COVID-19, including treatment responses and patient trajectories.

Limitations:

1. **Scope Limitation**: ORCHID's focus on hospitalised patients may not capture data from primary care settings or patients not requiring hospitalisation, potentially missing broader epidemiological trends.
2. **Data Integration**: Integrating hospital data with other sources of information, such as primary care records or national datasets, remains a challenge for comprehensive research.

Each of these platforms offers unique strengths and serves different research needs within the UK healthcare system. CPRD and UK Biobank provide extensive datasets for broad epidemiological and genomic research, respectively. Akrivia Health and OPEN SAFELY focus on integrating diverse data sources and addressing specific research needs related to drug development and COVID-19. ORCHID complements these efforts by offering real-time data on hospitalised patients. However, challenges such as data quality, integration, privacy concerns, and generalisability must be addressed to maximise the utility of these platforms. The ongoing development and refinement of these platforms will be crucial for advancing healthcare research and improving patient outcomes in the UK (Table 2.2).

TABLE 2.2
Healthcare Data Platforms and Their Characteristics

Platform	Focus	Strengths	Limitations
CPRD	Primary care data	Extensive coverage, integration with other data	Data quality issues and generalisation bias
UK Biobank	Genomics and health data	Extensive dataset and longitudinal follow-up	Population bias and complex data utilisation
Akrivia Health	Integrated health data	Real-world evidence and diverse data from mental healthcare NHS organisations in the UK	Data integration issues and only mental health data
OPEN SAFELY	COVID-19 research primarily	Timely insights and open data access	Pandemic-specific data and privacy concerns
ORCHID	Surveillance data	Real-time data and clinical insights	Flu and COVID-19 data primarily with limited scope and data integration issues

2.8.3 Challenges and Criticisms

Despite their benefits, Big Data platforms face several challenges. One significant issue is data security and privacy. Handling large volumes of sensitive data, especially in industries like healthcare and finance, raises concerns about data breaches and compliance with regulations such as the General Data Protection Regulation. Ensuring robust security measures and maintaining privacy is critical, but it can be complex and costly. Another challenge is data quality and integration. While Big Data platforms are designed to handle diverse data types, integrating data from various sources can result in inconsistencies and inaccuracies. Ensuring data quality requires rigorous validation and cleansing processes, which can be resource-intensive. Scalability is also a concern. Although Big Data platforms are built to scale, managing and scaling infrastructure to keep pace with growing data volumes can be challenging. Organisations must invest in scalable architectures and continually optimise performance to avoid bottlenecks.

Finally, there is the issue of skill gaps. Leveraging Big Data platforms effectively requires specialised skills in data science, analytics, and engineering. The shortage of skilled professionals in these areas can hinder the successful implementation and utilisation of Big Data technologies. In summary, Big Data platforms are essential for managing and analysing large volumes of data, offering significant benefits across various sectors by enabling advanced analytics and insights. However, their implementation is not without challenges, including issues related to data security, quality, scalability, and the need for specialised skills. Addressing these challenges requires a balanced approach that combines robust technological solutions with effective management practices and a focus on data governance.

3 Ethical Implications and Social Policy

KEY POINTS

- There are many ethical considerations to be made when using data, in particular patient data
- Reusing data requires careful consideration at the point of synthesising, analysing, and interpretation
- Legislations around data gathering, use, and processing vary globally

3.1 INTRODUCTION

The advancement of measurement and data collection processes, alongside the expansion of data storage capabilities and the development of sophisticated tools for data analysis and processing, often in real time, is significantly reshaping our world. This transformation has sparked extensive philosophical and legal debates regarding the appropriate and ethical utilisation of such data. In the absence of a definitive authority to provide guidance, it becomes imperative for us, as creators, suppliers, and users of data, to actively engage with these ethical considerations. The convergence of data science and ethics presents intricate challenges that demand meticulous consideration and deliberate action. Data science offers vast potential to enhance various facets of private and public life, spanning healthcare to environmental sustainability. Yet, this potential must be weighed against ethical concerns to ensure that benefits are realised without encroaching on individual rights or perpetuating harm. Fairness, responsibility, and upholding human rights emerge as focal points, as data science becomes increasingly pervasive and automated. Worries arise regarding fairness in algorithmic decision-making, accountability for automated processes, and safeguarding human rights, including privacy and non-discrimination. It's imperative that ethical data science practices align with the values of open, pluralistic, and tolerant societies. This entails promoting transparency, accountability, and respect for diversity and individual rights in the development and application of data-driven technologies. Prioritising social acceptability and preferability is paramount in data science projects to ensure they resonate with societal values and norms. Learning from past shortcomings, such as the National Health Service (NHS) care.data programme, underscores the importance of contemplating ethical implications and engaging stakeholders to foster trust and support. Striking a balance between safeguarding individual rights and enabling innovation is crucial. While it's essential to protect rights, overly rigid regulations may stifle innovation and limit the potential

DOI: 10.1201/9781003494737-3

social value of data science. Nuanced policymaking and ongoing dialogue between stakeholders are essential to achieve this balance. Examining real-world examples, such as proposed amendments to data protection regulations, can offer valuable insights into the challenges and trade-offs involved in addressing ethical concerns in data science. While the focus commonly leans towards risk mitigation and protection, it is essential to maintain a delicate equilibrium between risk and benefit. Complete elimination of risk can only be achieved at the expense of forsaking any potential benefits, yet the potential advantages offered by new data technologies are immense. As articulated by prominent data ethicists Floridi and Taddeo, "Neglecting ethical issues may lead to adverse impacts and societal rejection … However, excessive emphasis on safeguarding individual rights in inappropriate contexts may result in overly rigid regulations, thereby hindering the ability to harness the societal value of data science" [162].

It is crucial to acknowledge the complexity of moral dilemmas associated with data, understanding that providing simplistic answers to such intricate problems is often unfeasible, particularly given the rapidly evolving nature of the data landscape. Instead, our objective should be to shed light on the issues and strive to eliminate confusion and ambiguity, offering principles that can guide individuals in determining the appropriate course of action in their particular circumstances. Moreover, in grappling with ethical considerations, it is imperative to contemplate both present and future uses of data. The advancement of data science and technology is frequently portrayed as an attainment of a new equilibrium; however, this fails to grasp the perpetual nature of the changes unfolding. Rather than approaching a static state, we are navigating a landscape marked by continual evolution, driven by the application of existing tools and the emergence of novel data technologies, such as blockchain, homomorphic computation, and quantum computing. The pervasive influence of data technologies across various facets of contemporary life underscores the necessity for stakeholders to address ethical concerns. This marks a notable shift, as disciplines like statistics and computer science, pivotal in the data revolution, have traditionally prioritised technical considerations. Yet, the acceptability of the tools being developed and their utilisation is profoundly influenced by nuanced ethical factors. This is evident in the current climate, with a growing scrutiny towards the unfettered operations of social media companies, which have thus far operated with relatively few constraints on their actions and practices [162–167].

A critical consideration in this regard is the inherent uncertainty surrounding the future utilisation of data, as well as the unforeseeable connections they may forge with other datasets. This renders attempts to categorise datasets as either public or non-public, or to predict their potential uses, largely futile, given the limitless and unpredictable nature of such applications. Moreover, the intrinsic characteristics of the data itself cannot serve as a definitive argument against their potential risks. Ethical concerns are not inherently raised by the data alone; rather, it is the manner in which they are employed and the analyses to which they are subjected that give rise to ethical considerations. Several distinctive features of modern data and its utilisation differentiate data technology from other advanced technologies, necessitating meticulous consideration of ethical implications. The widespread prevalence of modern data technology justifies its classification as a component of societal infrastructure, akin to mathematics, language, and transportation. The interconnected nature of data underscores their capacity to transcend their original purposes; for instance, travel data may yield insights beyond mere travel patterns, while purchase data possess broader implications beyond transactions alone. Additionally, the dynamic evolution and accumulation of modern datasets imply their potential to yield discoveries in the future that are not feasible presently. The immediacy of real-time and online data analysis and decision-making processes reflects the agility of data technology, further compounded by the synergistic effects achieved through the merging and amalgamation of diverse datasets. Furthermore, the absence of spatial, temporal, and social context constraints enables the broad applicability of data, regardless of their origin or intended use. However, this flexibility also engenders risks, including the potential for unexpected uses and the revelation of unforeseen information, exemplified by the practice of data mining. Moreover, the proliferation of data across multiple databases heightens concerns regarding privacy infringement and the risk of exploitation for illicit purposes, such as blackmail. Ownership issues surrounding data ownership add another layer of complexity, as data ownership can be ambiguous and fluid, raising questions about individual rights and commercial exploitation. These multifaceted ethical considerations underscore the need for vigilant oversight and robust safeguards in the realm of data technology. It is important to note that the purposes outlined are framed within the context of "professions." Traditionally, professions have established formal codes of practice founded on ethical principles. However, a distinguishing characteristic of modern data science and technology is the absence of a single profession tasked with its governance. While statistics and computer science serve as core disciplines, numerous other fields, including various application domains, contribute to the landscape. Given this diversity, different application domains, such as medicine, social media, retail, and finance, will interpret ethical principles and translate them into practical guidelines in distinct ways. Ethical codes pertaining to data collection, manipulation, and use serve several functions. They offer guidance on navigating challenging circumstances, safeguard privacy in manners acceptable to users and the public, ensure data are utilised to benefit society, instil confidence in an organisation's integrity among customers and the public, and foster a sense of trustworthiness among employees regarding their affiliation with the organisation [168–170].

As evident from this list, there are occasions where these objectives are in tension with each other. A notable example is the utilisation of extensive medical records to infer insights about disease progression and effective treatments. While this undoubtedly benefits the public, it also entails the disclosure of individuals' data, thus posing a potential risk to their privacy. The complexity deepens as public perceptions on such matters vary widely, not only among different groups but also evolving over time, often in response to media coverage and news reports. Attitudes towards data use also evolve positively with an increased understanding of its value and potential applications. In an ideal scenario, precise guidelines could dictate behaviour in diverse circumstances. However, the expansive and rapidly changing landscape of data science precludes the establishment of rigid regulations. A singular, universally applicable set of rules is unattainable, and unforeseen circumstances are inevitable. Therefore, the pursuit lies in delineating ethical principles that require interpretation and instantiation in specific applications. These principles must be translated into actionable guidance, often tailored to particular contexts. A principle-based approach is a common strategy in navigating such dynamic environments. Examples within the realm of data ethics include the original Code of Practice of the UK Statistics Authority, grounded in eight principles, the report by the joint British Academy/Royal Society on Data Management and Use: Governance in the 21st Century, which centres on five principles, the Accenture Universal Principles of Data Ethics comprising twelve principles, and the ACM Code of Ethics and Professional Conduct, which delineates seven general moral principles guiding computing professionals [171–173].

At the highest echelon, ethical principles encompass vital attributes such as integrity, honesty, objectivity, responsibility, trustworthiness, impartiality, non-discrimination, transparency, accountability, fairness, robustness, resilience, usability, efficiency, and independence—all inherently valuable traits. These overarching principles are then distilled into more specific yet still elevated directives. While it is tempting to anticipate and prepare for future challenges related to data, the reality is that such foresight is exceedingly challenging. Legal frameworks typically evolve reactively in response to past issues rather than proactively addressing potential or impending ones; legislation tends to be retrospective. Law prescribes regulations that members of a society must comply with, enforced through penalties. In contrast, ethics serve to guide individuals in their conduct, aiding them in discerning morally upright actions. However, the distinction between ethics guiding what one should do and the law mandating what one must do underscores their intrinsic connection.

The subsequent sections of this chapter are structured as follows: the following section delineates modern data, their inception, and the perception of them as a novel resource or even commodity. Subsequently, personal data, the foundational concept underpinning the General Data Protection Regulation (GDPR), is examined. The notion of data ownership poses a considerable challenge, given the nebulous nature of data ownership and the uncertainty surrounding whether data can indeed be owned.The Consent and Purpose section delves into two pivotal aspects often viewed as guiding ethical data use. However, trustworthiness underpins all these considerations, as elaborated in the Trustworthiness section. Privacy and confidentiality constitute one facet of the risk–reward equilibrium, yet, as elucidated in the Privacy and Confidentiality section, the concept of privacy in a data context is nuanced, with the internet simultaneously enhancing and eroding personal privacy. Finally, the Conclusion section consolidates the discussion, offering a set of recommendations to navigate the intricate terrain of practical data ethics [174–177].

The utilisation of big data in social science research (SSR) presents significant ethical challenges that impact the integrity of research practices. Over recent years, advancements in technology have facilitated the collection and processing of large datasets, offering new opportunities for social scientists. This includes the generation of big datasets as well as the reuse of existing ones obtained from various sources. Social scientists have increasingly benefited from these developments, leveraging big datasets collected by public institutions, federal agencies, social media platforms such as Facebook analytics, and digital device and service developers like Google Trends. However, alongside the opportunities, the integration of big data into SSR raises ethical concerns that must be addressed. One primary ethical challenge involves ensuring the responsible and transparent use of big data in research. The vast amount of data collected from diverse sources raises issues related to informed consent, privacy, and data protection. Researchers must navigate complex ethical considerations regarding data ownership, confidentiality, and the potential for unintended consequences, such as data breaches or misuse. Moreover, the use of big data in SSR may introduce biases and distortions, leading to inaccurate or misleading research findings. The reliance on algorithmic decision-making and automated data processing algorithms can exacerbate existing inequalities and perpetuate social biases. Researchers must critically evaluate the validity and reliability of big data sources and methodologies to uphold the integrity of their research. Additionally, ethical considerations extend to the broader societal implications of SSR using big data. The ethical responsibility of researchers extends beyond individual research projects to encompass the societal impact of their work. Researchers must consider the potential consequences of their findings on vulnerable populations, marginalised communities, and society as a whole. In summary, while the integration of big data into SSR offers unprecedented opportunities for research and innovation, it also poses significant ethical challenges. Addressing these challenges requires a comprehensive approach that prioritises transparency, accountability, and ethical awareness throughout the research process. By upholding ethical principles, social scientists can ensure the integrity and credibility of their research while contributing positively to society. The increasing use and reuse of big datasets in SSR give rise to new ethical concerns that warrant attention and inclusion in research ethics guidelines and protocols. These concerns become particularly relevant when considering studies that source data from countries with differing ethical standards or utilise publicly available data, such as that harvested from social media platforms, without adequately addressing ethical issues. Recent research highlights a lack of attention to ethical considerations in studies utilising big data, with a significant portion failing to discuss ethical issues, often citing the data's public availability. For example, a study found that 64% of studies using big data did not address ethical issues, primarily because they considered the data to be publicly available. Despite the importance of addressing ethical challenges in big data SSR from a research ethics and integrity standpoint, there is a notable gap in the published literature. An exploratory search revealed limited discussion on the ethical dimensions of big data SSR within the existing literature, with the majority of existing discourse focusing on big data ethics in the contexts of health and technology. This discrepancy may be attributed to the historical roots of ethics, which have traditionally been more closely associated with biomedical sciences, as well as the close relationship between big data and discussions surrounding technology. In light of these findings, there is a pressing need for increased attention and discourse on the ethical implications of big data SSR within the research community. Efforts to address these concerns should involve integrating ethical considerations into research guidelines, protocols, and academic discourse to ensure the responsible and ethical use of big data in SSR [178–188] (Figure 3.1).

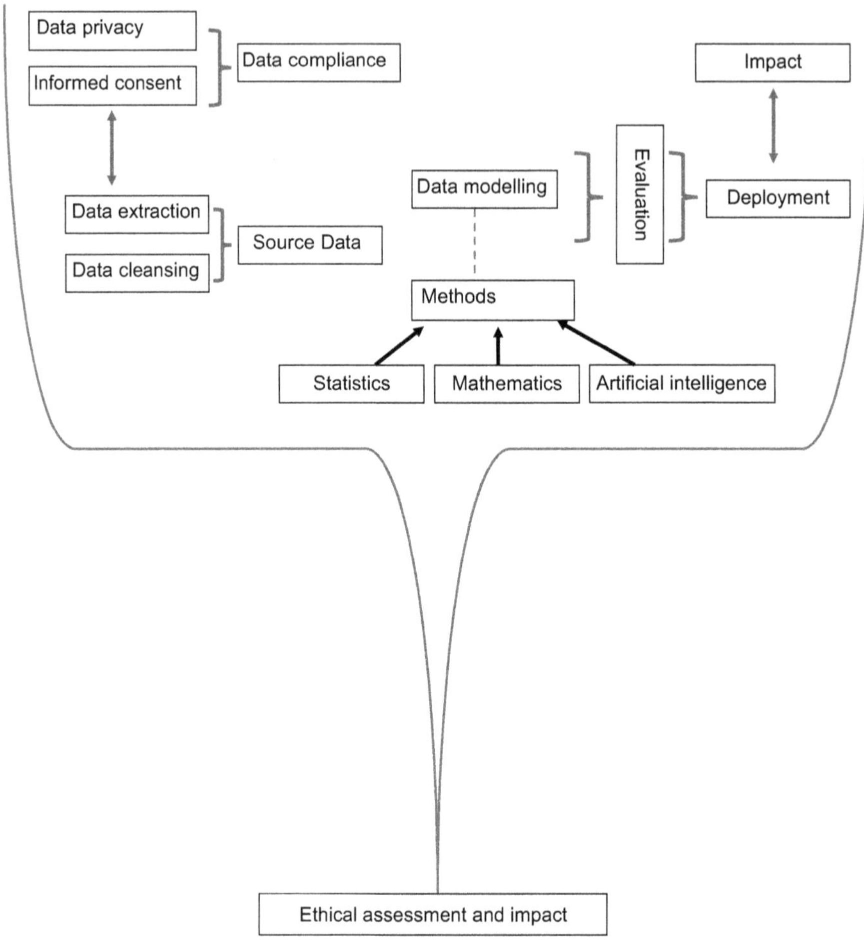

FIGURE 3.1 Healthcare research pathways requiring ethical assessment.

3.2 ETHICAL ISSUES

Analysing the vast amount of data we encounter daily is deeply ingrained in human nature. Recognising and interpreting patterns in our surroundings enables us to make informed decisions, from basic survival instincts to shaping our opinions, preferences, habits, and relationships. With the advent of the digital age, these behaviours have been amplified, and with the proliferation of technologies and software, they have been digitised and stored in a global repository of active information, influencing our actions in ways we may not always be aware of. As the volume of data continues to grow exponentially, with research from 2013 suggesting that approximately 90% of it was generated in the preceding two years, it became evident to pioneers in technological advancement that navigating and deriving insights from this vast trove of data would require a dedicated field. Thus, data science emerged, accompanied by the concept of "big data," which refers to the systematic handling of massive datasets characterised by their volume and variety. Companies collect and curate these datasets to be analysed for valuable insights. By scrutinising patterns within big data, including how data is utilised and transferred, data scientists delve into the fundamental behaviours of our digital interactions, driving continuous innovation and underpinning much of the artificial intelligence that has become integral to our daily lives. When our data is recognised for its scientific and economic value, ethical conduct becomes crucial in safeguarding it within the realm of data science. Anonymised data, which may contain personal information but has been stripped of unique identifiers, operates in a largely unregulated space and can be sold to third parties, including marketing firms or data brokers. These data brokers specialise in purchasing and reselling data to clients, such as businesses seeking to target advertisements to potential customers or financial institutions looking to detect fraud and assess the creditworthiness of loan applicants. While this transactional use of data may seem ethically straightforward as it aligns with capitalist structures, concerns arise when data usage results in excessively targeted profiling of individuals. Despite protective legislation against the misuse of personal data, the industry's interconnectedness means that individually depersonalised identifiers can easily be cross-referenced and re-identified. This reality appears to diminish the ethical challenge of misusing the capabilities of data science amidst the broader pursuit of market success. Ethical principles serve to distinguish between a company employee and a malicious insider, who is often a common cause of data breaches. However, ethics alone may not always prevent data mishandling, whether it occurs internally or through theft. While ethics are fundamental in data science, other factors, often influenced by companies profiting from big data, play significant roles. Enhancing data defences through knowledgeable security personnel and well-maintained hardware can protect the information of individuals unwittingly at the core of research. Yet, the decision to invest in strengthened cybersecurity and a better understanding of data science often hinges, to some extent, on ethical considerations. However, the consequences of security breaches are substantial; statistics from 2020 indicate that the average cost of a data breach is $3.86 million. Consequently, companies most likely to reject or avoid investing in data protection are those with the highest profit margins on their services or products. These companies are also more inclined to collect extensive data while disregarding ethical considerations. Recent significant data breaches, such as Twitter's targeting of 130 high-profile accounts, a security breach at the Marriott–Starwood hotel chain affecting over 5.2 million guests, and Uber's 2016 hack resulting in the theft of information from 57 million users and drivers, underscore the importance of ethical considerations in data handling and security practices [189–197].

Undoubtedly, most ethical dilemmas surrounding data revolve around information concerning individuals. The implementation of the GDPR on May 25, 2018, superseding the UK's Data Protection Act (DPA), constitutes a significant milestone. This European Union (EU)-wide regulation focuses on safeguarding the rights of natural persons in the processing of personal data, defining personal data expansively as any information relating to an identified or identifiable individual. This includes identifiers like names, identification numbers, location data, online identifiers, and even pseudonymised data. The GDPR imposes heightened responsibility and accountability on entities handling personal data, mandating prompt notification of serious data breaches to national authorities, ideally within 24 hours. Moreover, it empowers individuals by granting them easier access to their own data, facilitating data portability between service providers to enhance competition, and establishing the "right to be forgotten," enabling individuals to request the deletion of their data when no legitimate grounds for retention exist. Organisations found in breach of the regulation risk substantial penalties, up to four percent of global turnover [197–202].

The GDPR delves into intricate obligations pertaining to personal data processing and delineates legitimate operations that may be conducted on such data, albeit leaving room for interpretation and debate. GDPR covers three areas to consider:

- Affirms the fundamental right to the protection and legal use of personal data.
- The right is not absolute, emphasising the need to balance it against other fundamental rights in society, guided by the principle of proportionality.
- Underscores that the processing of personal data should ultimately serve humanity.

The UK's Information Commissioner's Office has issued guidelines to ascertain what constitutes personal data, outlining a series of steps or questions to determine the identifiability of individuals from data. These guidelines focus on whether individuals can be identified from the data, potentially by linking to other data sources. Complications arise due to the contextual nature of data; individual data points do not exist in isolation but within a broader context. For instance, while my genetic data may reveal information about other family members, my address and holiday patterns may also indirectly describe other individuals. Similarly, your personal data may indicate group affiliation, but the mere fact of group meetings may not inherently constitute personal data. However, combining various data points can lead to the inference of additional personal information about individuals.

GDPR Recital (7) asserts that "Natural persons should have control of their own personal data," implying a notion of ownership. Prior to the digital age, discussions surrounding data ownership often drew upon concepts from copyright law. Occasionally, datasets were safeguarded against duplication by incorporating unique features. For instance, mathematical tables might contain occasional inaccuracies in the fourth digit, while maps could include fictional towns or non-existent bends in roads. More recently, techniques like "digital watermarking" have been employed, embedding identifying signals within data, akin to steganography where information is concealed within data. While these methods are effective when ownership of a dataset is clear, unfortunately, in the realm of data, ownership is often ambiguous. In other contexts, ownership is typically attributed to the creator or the entity commissioning the work. For instance, a mining company owns the coal it extracts, a software company possesses the code its employees develop, and a furniture manufacturer retains ownership of the chairs it produces. However, when it comes to personal data—information "about" individuals—the ownership dynamic becomes murky. If a shop records a customer's purchase history for billing purposes, who owns that data? Similarly, should Google claim ownership over search histories and individual user data, or should Amazon be considered the proprietor of customer behaviour data? The crux of the matter lies in the personal and identifiable nature of the data. Many scholars, such as Greenwood et al. [171] advocate for the perspective that ownership of personal data rests with the individuals whom the data describe. If the data are anonymised, with no possibility of identifying individuals, ownership typically resides with the researcher or entity that collected the data. However, disputes over the value of data, particularly in the context of open data initiatives, have arisen. Some researchers are reluctant to share their datasets with others, fearing exploitation of their efforts. Conversely, in fields like astronomy, where data collection is a collaborative effort, data are willingly shared via public databases.

In 2007, Alex Pentland proposed to the World Economic Forum that individuals should have control over their personal data, equating it to "money." He envisioned a scenario where a person's data would be analogous to their finances, managed, exchanged, and accounted for in a manner akin to personal banking services. While this idea carries a certain idealistic appeal, its practical feasibility remains questionable, particularly in maximising the potential of data for societal progress. Unlike money, which holds consistent value regardless of its use, the value of data is context-dependent and varies based on its application. Furthermore, with the proliferation of automatic data capture and the impending Internet of Things, assigning individual ownership to each data item presents significant challenges. As previously mentioned, data about one person often imply information about others, complicating the notion of individual ownership. Moreover, the analysis and amalgamation of datasets yield derived data, potentially disclosing further insights about individuals, which would need to be managed within their data accounts. From a technical and statistical standpoint, granting individuals the right to refuse access to their data risks distorting datasets and yielding misleading conclusions. An alternative approach could involve establishing "data commons"—trusted entities tasked with storing data from diverse sources. Analogous to credit bureaus, which aggregate and analyse financial data to produce credit scores, data commons mitigate selection bias risks by integrating data from multiple sources.

Several national initiatives have explored similar models on a smaller scale. For instance, the Administrative Data Research Network (ADRN) in the UK connects data from various government departments and organisations within a secure environment, facilitating approved research projects for scientific and public policy endeavours. The legal dimensions of data ownership are equally intricate. Notably, the GDPR does not explicitly address "data ownership." The EU's Inception Impact Assessment on the European Free Flow of Data Initiative within the Digital Single Market highlights the legal ambiguity surrounding data ownership. While personal data cannot be "owned" in the EU, stringent regulations govern access and usage by entities other than the data subject. Nonetheless, a gap persists concerning the "ownership" of non-personal data, particularly machine-generated data.

Van Asbroeck et al. [177] provide insights into the legal landscape within the EU, highlighting the inadequacy of the current framework concerning data ownership. They note that no specific ownership rights exist for data, and existing data-related rights fail to adequately address the needs of stakeholders involved in the data value cycle. The lack of legal harmonisation across jurisdictions further complicates matters. The complexity of data ownership is compounded by the intricate nature of the data value cycle, which involves multiple stakeholders. Determining who holds ownership rights becomes challenging, as various parties may assert ownership based on different contributions to the data lifecycle. Stakeholders may lay claim to ownership due to their role in data creation, generation, manipulation, compilation, selection, structuring, reformatting, enrichment, analysis, purchase, licensing, or value addition. Ownership, therefore, extends beyond the mere act of data collection to encompass the effort involved in data manipulation and value enhancement. Van Asbroeck et al. [177] offer several conclusions regarding data ownership:

- EU case law does not explicitly acknowledge an ownership right in data.
- Personal data may not necessarily be owned by the individual, opening the possibility for data controllers or processors (as defined in the GDPR) to hold ownership rights, subject to the individual's control over their personal data.
- Traditional principles governing ownership of physical entities may not always be applicable to data.
- Numerous regulations may impact a company's control over, access to, or rights in data.
- Intellectual property rights and trade secrets do not adequately protect ownership in data.

Van Asbroeck and colleagues suggest that addressing these issues through contractual agreements would be onerous and likely unfeasible with legal certainty. Instead, they propose the establishment of a nonexclusive, flexible, and extensible ownership right in datasets, coupled with a data traceability obligation as a protective measure. This concept of traceability appears pivotal in addressing many ethical and non-technical data challenges.

Ethics not only regulate data science but also influence its application. While the collection of sensitive data poses risks of misuse, ethically guided data scientists can leverage it to identify and address systematic prejudices and injustices. By questioning the underlying causes of these issues, tangible progress can be made in resolving larger societal problems reflected in algorithms used across defective societies. Digital algorithms, while not sentient, are susceptible to human bias embedded in their programming by data scientists and previous research. This can perpetuate systemic biases or discrimination within service providers if not ethically considered. Human involvement in data science introduces ethical considerations, enabling the identification and acknowledgement of model flaws. Scientists and organisations can then address these flaws progressively to dismantle institutionalised barriers. Data scientists have demonstrated the importance of ethics in innovative practice by responding to concerns of algorithmic bias and developing methods to detect supposedly neutral functions perpetuating systemic flaws. Ethics within data science foster a culture of progression, contributing to solving unresolved technological and social challenges at an accelerated pace [203–206].

3.2.1 Big Data and Ethical Implications

Concerns regarding the ethics of big data in SSR stem from several key factors. Firstly, there is a noticeable absence of ethical discussion within studies that utilise big data for social science purposes. Many of these studies overlook important ethical considerations, such as sourcing data from countries with differing ethical standards or using publicly available data without thorough ethical scrutiny. Secondly, the literature addressing the ethical challenges of big data in SSR is surprisingly limited. While big data's significance in this field continues to grow, ethical discourse primarily revolves around health and technology, neglecting the unique ethical considerations specific to SSR [207–209]. Lastly, the lack of attention to ethical dimensions in big data SSR highlights the need for increased awareness and integration of ethical principles into research practices. It is essential to foster discourse within the research community and incorporate ethical considerations into research guidelines and protocols to ensure responsible and ethically sound practices in the use of big data for SSR [168,199,210–215].

- Some perspectives in social science define it as the study of societal facts to formulate theories and predictions, yet we align with the perspective that views social sciences as interpreting societal norms and practices through the lens of researchers' values and beliefs. This interpretative approach becomes particularly significant in studies focusing on subjective concepts like culture, behaviour, and social relations. Results from such studies are inherently interpretative and shaped by the cultural context, historical circumstances, and worldviews of the researchers involved. However, interpretative practices also open the door to external influences such as researchers' moral beliefs, prejudices, and values, which can impact the research outcomes. The use of big data in SSR adds another layer of complexity to this issue, as third-party technologies and services used in data collection or analysis may introduce problematic interpretations. Additionally, applying big data processing techniques developed for STEM disciplines to study social phenomena may not always be suitable, further complicating the interpretative nature of SSR. Moreover, the positivist view of data as an objective entity may clash with the interpretative aspects inherent in SSR.
- The concept of raw data or big datasets representing objective facts is contested within the academic discourse. Instead, it is argued that big data is inherently interpreted by those who generate the datasets or by the algorithms and designers involved in their creation. When researchers engage with preprocessed data or reuse existing datasets, they further imbue them with meaning through subsequent analyses, potentially diverging from the original intentions of the data generators. This divergence poses challenges for researchers committed to upholding research ethics and integrity norms, as the dissemination of results from big data SSR may carry unidentified or poorly managed risks. Additionally, algorithmic tools used to analyse big data SSR can influence results based on assumptions that may not align with researchers' or subjects' perspectives. The inherent unpredictability of

big datasets, which may reveal unforeseen connections and patterns, complicates the anticipation of outcomes and consequences for future analyses. These challenges not only threaten the methodological rigour of research but also carry ethical implications when unpredictable results could potentially justify discriminatory or harmful practices. Moreover, the specialised skill of data literacy, which is unevenly distributed among researchers, policymakers, and the public, may lead to confusion among various stakeholders regarding the intended purpose or true meaning of results produced by big data SSR [216–219].

- While methods and devices used to collect health-related information are subject to stringent regulatory oversight and extensive trials to demonstrate their reliability, such rigorous requirements are not typically applied to SSR. Even if applied, they may be deemed inappropriate. Applying a biomedical ethical framework, which focuses on principles such as avoiding harm, obtaining informed consent, and ensuring confidentiality, to SSR could lead to a misunderstanding of the impact of SSR on research subjects and society. This mismatch in ethical approach may result in SSR being used to justify discriminatory policy decisions against research subjects or perpetuate harmful stereotypes about social groups. Particularly concerning is the fact that many researchers engaged in big data SSR lack formal training in social sciences, leaving them ill-prepared to anticipate potential harms arising from their research. Moreover, existing ethical frameworks are often ill-equipped to address the complex ethical issues inherent in big data SSR. Regulatory bodies, Institutional Review Boards, and Research Ethics Committees are also ill-prepared to evaluate the ethical dimensions of big data SSR. The evolving nature of big data technologies presents a challenge in capturing and addressing ethical issues, necessitating continuous revision of guidelines. This dynamic landscape underscores the need for ongoing improvement in current ethical guidelines, even those specifically developed for certain data collection methods like Internet Research: Ethical Guidelines.

To systematically explore the ethical issues of big data SSR, we utilise the normative framework developed by David Resnik in his *Ethics of Science* (2005), comprising twelve principles: honesty, carefulness, openness, freedom, credit, education, social responsibility, legality, opportunity, mutual respect, efficiency, and respect for subjects. While all twelve principles are pertinent to big data SSR, our analysis focuses on six: honesty, carefulness, openness, efficiency, responsibility, and respect for subjects. By examining these six principles in pairs, we aim to systematically address the three most pressing ethical concerns in the context of big data SSR. Specifically, we explore ethical issues related to bias (honesty and carefulness), risks associated with the publication and reuse of big data (openness and efficiency), and ethical considerations regarding individuals and societies (social responsibility and respect for subjects) [220].

Resnik's framework facilitates a distinction between two types of bias relevant to big data SSR. The first type, discouraged by the principle of carefulness, involves biases inherent in research methodologies and techniques, known as methodological biases. The second type, discouraged by the principle of honesty, pertains to researchers' personal values, worldviews, and language, which may influence their observations and conclusions, referred to as prejudice. Given the challenges of big data analysis methods for SSR and the interpretive nature of SSR, distinguishing between these biases helps articulate ethical issues more precisely. These two forms of bias are discouraged by the principles of honesty and carefulness, as detailed below:

Honesty: "Scientists should not fabricate, falsify, or misrepresent data or results. They should be objective, unbiased, and truthful in all aspects of the research process" [emphasis added] (Resnik [220], p. 48).

Carefulness: "Scientists should avoid errors in research, especially in presenting results. They should minimize experimental, methodological, and human errors and avoid self-deception, bias, and conflicts of interest" [emphasis added] (Resnik [220], p. 51).

Resnik's principles of openness and efficiency play a significant role in examining the ethical considerations surrounding the publication and reuse of big data and the associated risks. Openness, as outlined by Resnik, emphasises the importance of scientists sharing data, results, methods, ideas, techniques, and tools, and being open to criticism and new ideas from other researchers. This principle underscores the necessity for transparency and collaboration within the scientific community, allowing for the verification and validation of research findings. Efficiency, on the other hand, underscores the importance of using resources effectively. In the context of big data, efficiency becomes crucial, as large volumes of data require substantial resources for storage, processing, and analysis. Efficient resource utilisation ensures that research efforts are optimised, minimising waste and maximising the potential benefits of data-driven research. When applied to the publication and reuse of big data, these principles highlight the need for responsible data sharing practices that balance openness with efficiency. Researchers must strive to make data accessible to others in a manner that is efficient and effective while also ensuring that appropriate safeguards are in place to protect individual privacy and confidentiality. Additionally, the transparent documentation of data sources, methodologies, and analytical approaches enables the reproducibility of research findings, enhancing the credibility and reliability of the scientific process. However, the pursuit of openness and efficiency in big data research also raises ethical concerns, such as ensuring data security, protecting sensitive information, and mitigating the risks of data misuse or misinterpretation. Thus, while openness and efficiency are essential principles for advancing scientific knowledge through big data research, they must be accompanied by ethical considerations and responsible practices to safeguard the integrity and trustworthiness of research outcomes.

Openness: "Scientists should share data, results, methods, ideas, techniques, and tools. They should allow other scientists to review their work and be open to criticism and new ideas" (Resnik [220], p. 52).

Efficiency: "Scientists should use resources efficiently" (Resnik [220], p. 60).

Furthermore, Resnik's framework encompasses the broader social impacts of SSR, recognising the potential influence of research outcomes on societal and political agendas, in addition to individual harms. This recognition allows for the identification and exploration of two distinct forms of ethical concerns: those pertaining to research subjects, such as issues of dignity and autonomy, and those concerning societies, including potential harms and consequences for broader social welfare. By considering these normative principles within Resnik's framework, researchers can better navigate the ethical complexities inherent in big data SSR, addressing concerns related to data sharing, resource efficiency, and societal impacts while upholding ethical standards and promoting responsible research practices.

Respect for subjects: "Scientists should not violate rights or dignity when using human subjects in experiments" (Resnik [220], p. 61).

Social responsibility: "Scientists should avoid causing harms to society and they should attempt to produce social benefits. Scientists should be responsible for the consequences of their research and they should inform the public about those consequences" (Resnik [220], p. 57).

3.2.2 Prejudice and Biases

Recent advancements in big data technologies have introduced new opportunities for social scientists, but they also bring the risk of introducing subtle forms of prejudice and bias into research outcomes. These biases not only challenge researchers' commitment to honesty and carefulness but may also elude detection even by conscientious researchers. While researchers have some degree of control over the methods used to generate original datasets, they may struggle to identify biases introduced by the technologies they employ. This challenge is particularly pronounced in the realm of big data due to the sheer volume, velocity, and variety of information, which amplifies researchers' reliance on technology while diminishing their control over its impact. Consequently, when utilising datasets generated with the aid of third-party technologies or services, social scientists may encounter specific ethical dilemmas related to bias. Depending on the stage at which third-party technology is integrated into the research process, its inherent biases can distort data collection, study designs, and analysis. For instance, these biases may overlook pertinent characteristics of respondents, such as membership in vulnerable groups or specific political affiliations. Such challenges can impede social scientists' ability to recognise and mitigate methodological biases, as required by the principle of carefulness. To illustrate these biases more concretely, we will examine the use of self-tracking and crowdsourcing platforms in SSR, which further complicate researchers' adherence to principles of honesty and carefulness [221–223].

SSR domains like psychology, anthropology, and sociology of sports and health, researchers utilise automated data collection devices, such as self-tracking devices worn or used by research subjects, to investigate movement, health, and productivity patterns. However, the data collected through these devices may not always be accurate, leading to conclusions that are less objective and unbiased than they appear. Studies indicate that self-tracking devices may fail to reliably detect certain types of movement, resulting in inflated or underestimated activity metrics despite presenting them as accurate and objective. Furthermore, even if self-tracking devices could accurately capture all movements, their designers may categorise and interpret the data differently from researchers. For instance, the definition of intense physical activity and recommended activity levels vary, leading to different parameters used by different technologies to define variables. Consequently, devices from different manufacturers may yield disparate results for the same subject, even in seemingly straightforward measurements like step counting. This discrepancy is exacerbated when considering complex parameters, such as distinguishing between light and deep sleep, which could be crucial information for social scientists investigating the relationship between physical and mental health and the quality of the neighbourhoods where research subjects reside. Despite the potential lack of objectivity and accuracy in these results, they may be interpreted (and subsequently disseminated in popular media) with unwavering confidence upon publication, partly due to varying levels of data literacy among different stakeholders, as numerical expression may give the impression of objective measurement.

Moreover, collected data may lack contextual information because researchers might be unable or unmotivated to examine and disclose contextually relevant factors that influenced the datasets. For instance, while self-tracking data on geolocation and physical activity could be valuable for studying people's mobility and public health risks, it may not encompass all the contextual details necessary to draw accurate conclusions about the studied cohort. A standardised approach to data collection devices may overlook variables such as childcare responsibilities or the injury history of research subjects, which can significantly impact their daily movements and activity levels. Consequently, although some researchers may strive to draw seemingly objective and scientifically based conclusions when utilising big data in SSR, a thorough assessment of the information missing from the datasets and the implications of this absence for the overall conclusions could unveil undisclosed limitations and biases.

Algorithmic bias and limitations of third-party technologies often remain undisclosed, leaving researchers unable to implement measures to counteract biases effectively. Data-generating devices process collected information using algorithms that operate based on the instructions and assumptions of their developers. However, designers of algorithmic tools may be unaware of their own presuppositions and prejudices, or they may not actively take steps to mitigate biases in algorithm design. Consequently, many contemporary technologies have been shown to exhibit various forms of algorithmic bias. For example, self-tracking devices are reported to be accurate only in gathering data related to particular types of activity or specific users, while producing unreliable or even erroneous results for others. Women using wearable fitness trackers or step-counting features in smartphones commonly report that some of their daily movements, such as pushing prams, remain unregistered, or that their smartphones record different statistics when placed in handbags rather than pockets.

Technologies that collect and process data often fail to account for the racial, gender, and age diversity of the general population. For instance, they may be more likely to produce reliable results for white, young, male users if these groups were over-represented in the development process. Moreover, developers rarely disclose the functioning of algorithms and the rationale for the design of hardware used in data-collecting devices. This lack of transparency has implications for researchers attempting to untangle the genealogy of data. However, untangling this genealogy may not always be possible, especially when companies with commercial interests hide the exact technical specifications of their devices and algorithms, or even attempt to mislead users and researchers about the actual operations of their technologies through unclear terms of service and privacy policy documents. As a result, biases inherent in devices and algorithms used for collecting and processing data are likely to manifest in the generated big datasets. However, since data is often framed as accurate and objective, and potential biases or limitations are not diligently disclosed, researchers face challenges in identifying potential biases in generated datasets [224].

3.2.3 Risk of Reusing Data

Reusing datasets in SSR, as advocated by Resnik's principles of openness and efficiency, is a common practice. However, while this approach promotes transparency and resource efficiency, it also introduces risks that may compromise other ethical principles. In this section, we aim to elucidate these risks associated with the reuse of openly available data by third parties, such as researchers or non-academic entities. While some of these risks overlap with those related to individual and social harms, as well as biases discussed in preceding sections, it is crucial to emphasise the specific challenges inherent in the reuse of datasets generated for other studies. However, if an evidence synthesis is completed methodologically, secondary data can still produce high-quality outcomes that can inform prospective research, clinical and health outcomes for a specific period of time that could improve the understanding of disease or treatment trends as well as long-term effectiveness. This is a cost-effective method to use in comparison to conducting a prospective epidemiology study or a clinical trial with a long-term follow-up.

The availability of administrative data from public institutions provides a valuable resource for SSR, offering access to demographic and financial information. For example, platforms like the EU Open Data portal and the American Data.gov catalogue host a vast array of datasets covering diverse topics such as opinion trends, healthcare, mobility, and demographics. Leveraging these datasets, researchers can utilise advanced big data analytics techniques to extract valuable insights without the need for extensive and expensive data collection efforts. However, this abundance of available data raises three ethical dilemmas that warrant consideration. While the efficiency of reusing datasets is undeniable, it comes with a significant epistemic downside: researchers are often not involved in the data collection process, leading to limited insight into how the data was collected. This lack of involvement means that researchers may not anticipate or account for undisclosed biases embedded in the datasets. Especially when datasets lack supplementary information or are not linked to published manuscripts detailing the methodology, researchers are left unaware of potential biases and limitations. Consequently, researchers are unable to assess whether the data was collected diligently and responsibly, posing a threat to the integrity of the research.

The public availability of data offers numerous benefits, including enabling critical scrutiny of results and promoting research efficiency. However, it also exposes data to potential misuse by unethical actors or abusive practices. While making research data FAIR has expanded access to data for both academic and non-academic users, the latter may not be bound by the same norms and values as academic researchers. Unlike academic researchers, non-academic users may not undergo rigorous ethics training or have their research proposals vetted by ethics committees. This disparity in regulation between academic and non-academic research could lead to unforeseen ethical challenges when non-academic users access and reuse data. Additionally, concerns arise regarding the security of publicly available data, as datasets are vulnerable to cyber-attacks and data leaks. Even if researchers take measures to protect data, corrupt individuals or non-academic entities may still attempt to steal or hack data repositories for valuable information. Therefore, while data sharing initiatives promote transparency and collaboration, they also necessitate careful consideration of potential risks and ethical implications.

The availability of data not only enhances research capabilities but also enables data aggregation, leading to the potential for reaching unforeseen conclusions. By combining results from various datasets, researchers can uncover correlations and insights that may not have been apparent otherwise. However, this increased accessibility to data also raises ethical concerns, particularly regarding the potential for inadvertently violating research integrity principles. For instance, when administrative datasets on citizens' earnings are linked with demographic information, researchers may uncover correlations that could lead to biased or prejudiced conclusions. This risk is compounded when researchers use data without obtaining proper consent or ethical approval, potentially violating principles of research integrity. Social scientists utilising big datasets from public institutions, other researchers, or commercial entities must be vigilant about ensuring ethical practices throughout their research processes. This includes obtaining appropriate consent, adhering to data protection regulations, and critically evaluating the potential implications of their research findings. Failure to do so could result in ethical breaches and undermine the credibility and trustworthiness of the research outcomes. Therefore, while data availability offers significant research opportunities, researchers must approach data aggregation and analysis with careful consideration of ethical implications [225].

3.2.4 Individual and Social Harms

SSR raises concerns about the ethical principles of respect for subjects and social responsibility, particularly when it involves exposing participants' personal characteristics and vulnerabilities. Predictive research efforts fuelled by big datasets enable researchers to forecast participants' future behaviour and behavioural patterns, which can have profound implications. When predictive research is driven by commercial interests, it can lead to the unfair exclusion of vulnerable groups from opportunities or predatory marketing campaigns. Moreover, research results may rationalise policies and practices that target or discriminate against specific groups based on data categorisation, even when the data is anonymised. This raises ethical concerns about the potential misuse of data to manipulate or exploit individuals for social, political, or financial gain. The uncertainties surrounding the future processing of datasets pose challenges to upholding principles of social responsibility and respect for subjects. Researchers and other users may employ data processing methods to achieve objectives that participants did not consent to or may use the data in ways that harm participants' interests without regulatory oversight. Examples include prioritising services based on zip code categorisation, gerrymandering to manipulate political dynamics, or increasing insurance premiums based on demographic segmentation, all of which can have far-reaching consequences for individuals and communities.

The use of big datasets in research has facilitated the emergence of questionable research practices such as HARKing (Hypothesizing After Results are Known) and question trolling. Such issues might be compounded by the use of "black-box" or even a-theoretical models, as is often the case in big data analytics. In a rush to "let the data speak for themselves" [203], sometimes spurious correlations are taken more seriously than they should, occasionally even mistaken for causations [226]. These practices involve searching data with multiple constructs or relationships to find notable results, often leading to a shift from hypothesis-driven to hypothesis-free research paradigms. While this may challenge traditional methodological approaches, it also raises ethical concerns regarding respect for subjects and social responsibility. Both HARKing and question trolling undermine individuals' consent by formulating questions or hypotheses after the data has been collected, which may not have been communicated to participants beforehand. In the context of SSR, these practices can exacerbate the harmful effects of research on society by granting more control to those who can access and analyse users' data without their explicit consent. By shifting the focus from hypothesis-driven research to exploratory data analysis, researchers may inadvertently prioritise finding significant results over the ethical considerations of how their research impacts individuals and society. This challenges the principles of respect for subjects and social responsibility, as it can lead to the exploitation of individuals' data without their knowledge or consent, ultimately undermining the integrity and trustworthiness of research outcomes.

The principle of respect for subjects is challenged by projects that gather personal information from users' online activities or fitness trackers and combine it with various evaluation metrics, such as credit history or criminal background records. This amalgamation of data is used to categorise users based on specific characteristics, influencing their access to privileges and services, particularly affecting low-income individuals. These practices result in the creation of digital representations of individuals, known as data doubles, which are formed through pattern recognition methods and used to develop predictive behavioural models at a large scale. Researchers can engage in HARKing by searching for patterns in these datasets, a process commonly referred to as data mining, to maximise predictive power when testing social or psychological hypotheses. The unrestricted processing of data about the behaviour of large groups exposes vulnerabilities and decision-making processes, placing these groups at a disadvantage compared to researchers or institutions with access to and interpretation of this information. This knowledge about cohorts' decision-making allows parties with financial or political agendas to target specific groups with tailored strategies based on predicted behavioural profiles, potentially leading to manipulation facilitated by information derived through HARKing.

From the perspective of the principle of social responsibility, the environmental costs associated with big data storage and processing are often overlooked in discussions about the ethical implications of big data analytics. Dignum and Crawford [227] contends that terms like "cloud computing" may create the misconception that data processing algorithms operate seamlessly and without consequences. However, the devices used to store and process big data require significant quantities of rare minerals, leading to detrimental effects on the environment and local communities where mining occurs. Additionally, these devices consume vast amounts of electricity, contributing to the exacerbation of the climate crisis. The material and energy requirements of big data methods also raise concerns regarding efficiency. While these methods may offer advantages in terms of data analysis and insights, they may not be the most efficient allocation of resources when considering the overall environmental impact of a study. Therefore, from a social responsibility standpoint, it is essential to consider the environmental consequences of big data storage and processing and explore more sustainable alternatives to minimise harm to the environment and local communities.

3.2.5 Consent and Purpose

The concept of consent, particularly informed consent, has been central in research, particularly in healthcare, where interventions require prior consent based on a comprehensive understanding of their implications and potential outcomes. However, the applicability and practicality of this notion in the modern data landscape are debatable for several reasons. Firstly, the essence of modern big data lies in its potential for unforeseen and unspecified future applications, making it challenging to obtain consent for uses that are unknown and perhaps unknowable. Secondly, data often already exists in databases, rendering many studies noninterventional in nature. The GDPR addresses consent in Recital (40), stipulating that lawful data processing should be based on the consent of the concerned data subject or another legitimate basis prescribed by law. However, Recital (54) acknowledges exceptions, allowing for the processing of special categories of personal data in areas of public health without the explicit consent of the data subject, subject to conditions outlined in Article 6. Nonetheless, debates surrounding consent in big data research have produced diverse perspectives, ranging from abandoning informed consent entirely for noninterventional research utilising existing or passively collected datasets, to advocating for the development of statistical methods and research infrastructures to accommodate dynamic consent models. In essence, meaningful consent to data usage necessitates two key conditions: an understanding of potential future uses of the data and an understanding of how the data will be utilised.

The challenge of obtaining informed consent is compounded by the inherent uncertainty surrounding future data usage. As previously discussed, future applications of data are often unknown, and datasets may be merged with others to unveil valuable insights not discernible in isolation. This merging is crucial not only for exploring aggregate population properties but also for individual decision-making processes, such as in clinical trials where aggregated data inform treatment decisions for individuals. Recital (33) of the GDPR attempts to address this uncertainty by acknowledging that the full purpose of data processing for scientific research may not be identifiable at the time of collection. Consequently, data subjects should be permitted to consent to certain areas of research in line with recognised ethical standards, without the need for exhaustive detail. Extending this approach to other domains could involve specifying broad purposes for data usage, such as credit scoring or product recommendations, without delving into intricate specifics. However, this approach risks limiting the potential benefits of the data revolution, as emerging practices like using social media data for credit scoring exemplify the evolving landscape of data usage.

Additionally, the requirement for individuals to understand how their data will be used assumes a level of expertise and knowledge that may not be realistic. Modern data analytics tools, such as neural networks and ensemble systems, are inherently complex and defy simple explanation. Nonetheless, the GDPR mandates that data subjects have access to meaningful information about data processing logic and the right to explanation for decision-making processes. Addressing this challenge could involve strategies like those proposed by Hand and Yu [228], which focus on identifying the variables influencing decisions rather than explaining the intricacies of complex models. Such an approach could facilitate providing explanations of decisions while navigating the complexity of modern data analytics. Data sharing is essential for harnessing the benefits of modern data technology, yet obtaining consent for such sharing presents challenges. While much attention focuses on individuals' privacy concerns regarding data combination, organisations also exhibit reluctance to share their data. This reluctance may stem from a variety of factors, including business model reliance on data value and general caution. For instance, the ADRN faced difficulties in accessing government data for research purposes due to cultural reluctance within some departments. This caution is justified, as data sharing entails risks, and instances of data leakage or theft frequently make headlines. Legislative measures like the Digital Economy Act aim to address these concerns and promote secure data sharing practices. In the context of research, informed consent serves as a crucial step towards fostering accountability, transparency, and responsibility. These pillars necessitate justifying actions, ensuring transparency without secrecy, and upholding obligations to perform actions properly.

While much of the discourse surrounding data ethics focuses on responsible data usage and constraints on its application, there exists a complementary aspect of responsibility: the duty to act upon detecting abuse. Analysis of extensive datasets can potentially uncover early signs of serious crimes like child sexual abuse rings or serial killings, surpassing the scope of analysis for which prior consent was given. In certain circumstances, there may be arguments for granting certain bodies access to wide-ranging datasets, akin to search and wiretapping protocols. However, strict adherence to codes of conduct and due process would be essential to mitigate risks associated with such access. Moreover, if informed consent is feasible in the realm of big data, it cannot be presumed by default; it must be actively obtained. Yet, the prevailing practice of passive consent, wherein individuals tacitly agree to terms and conditions without thorough review, remains common. This passive acquiescence to legalese is often driven by practical considerations, as deciphering complex legal language requires time and technical expertise that many lack.

3.2.6 Data Trustworthiness

Ensuring the trustworthiness of data involves understanding their provenance, or where they originate from, and assessing the reliability of their sources. Properly identified provenance is crucial not only for data but also for other types of information, such as news articles and blog posts, as it can help combat false news and fake facts. Blockchain technology holds promise in providing immutable records that lead back to the origin of data, although integrating multiple data sources can pose challenges. Quality monitoring is more straightforward when data come from a single source, as matching data from different sources is complex and risky. Additionally, data quality is relative and depends on the specific objective; what constitutes high quality for one purpose may not be sufficient for another. Open data initiatives can strengthen provenance assurance by allowing more eyes to scrutinise the data and detect errors or inconsistencies.

Beyond numbers, comprehensive metadata are essential for understanding and trusting data. Adequate description of methods is also crucial for trust, as analyses should be reproducible, meaning others can replicate the results using the same methods and data. Lack of transparency in analysis methods raises concerns about potential biases or omissions. In some cases, data exhaust from operations may not align well with the research question, leading to mismatches between data and objectives. This can result in algorithms that are inherently discriminatory because they are trained on data that do not represent the entire population accurately. An illustrative example is the concept of a "horse" in machine learning, which refers to a system that achieves impressive results by focusing on irrelevant characteristics, rather than the desired features. Such issues highlight the importance of careful consideration and transparency in data analysis methods to ensure trustworthiness.

The distinction between theory-driven and data-driven models is fundamental to understanding the potential pitfalls and benefits of data analysis. Theory-driven models are based on underlying theories of mechanisms, such as Newton's theory of gravitation, while data-driven models rely solely on observed relationships within the data. While data-driven analysis can lead to significant discoveries, it also carries the risk of detecting spurious correlations or chance associations. A poignant example of this distinction is illustrated in David Haig's play "Pressure," which portrays the uncertainty surrounding weather forecasts for the D-Day landings. Meteorologist Irving Krick advocates for a purely data-driven approach based on similarities between current and past weather conditions, while James Stagg argues for a theory-based approach that considers high-altitude wind patterns. This is an ongoing debate even though sometimes more confidence is directly being put in purely data-driven, a-theoretical models. Still, there are cases where this confidence might be misplaced. For example, Lichtman's (1980) history-based tallying appears to be the only model that has predicted the results of all US presidential election outcomes since 1984, notably including the 2016 election results, where all big data models, including Nate Silver's five-thirty-eight site, made the wrong prediction. And naïve forecasting, which uses laypeople's reliance on the most recent observation to predict the next observation in a time series, predicted influenza prevalence in the US more accurately than the computationally intensive Google Flu Trends

[229]. This dichotomy underscores the importance of understanding the limitations of both types of models and recognising that models are simplifications of reality. Ultimately, trustworthiness in data analysis depends not only on the accuracy of the data and the rigour of the methods but also on the integrity and competence of the analysts. Ethical considerations, such as discrimination and dynamic pricing, further complicate the issue, highlighting the need for clear definitions and guidelines. Addressing these ethical challenges requires a multifaceted approach that includes training, accreditation, and ongoing scrutiny of analysts' practices. Trust in both the data and the analysts is essential for maintaining the integrity and reliability of data-driven insights.

3.2.7 Privacy and Confidentiality

Privacy is a multifaceted concept that has been subject to ongoing debate and interpretation. Defined in various ways, it encompasses the right to be left alone, protection from government intrusion, and the power to selectively reveal oneself to the world. This last definition highlights the importance of privacy control in shaping one's identity and how they are perceived by others. In the context of data, privacy becomes even more complex. The capacity of individuals to determine the disclosure and use of their personal data, known as informational self-determination, is considered insufficient for protecting privacy in the face of emerging technologies and associated threats. Privacy, like data, is not absolute and depends on the context, the relationship between the data giver and receiver, and the intended use of the data. Public attitudes towards privacy can change rapidly, especially in response to reports of data leaks or breaches. These fluctuations can impact the value of datasets, as individuals may choose to opt in or opt out of data sharing based on privacy concerns. Additionally, perceptions of privacy vary across different cultures and nations, as evidenced by differences in attitudes towards identity cards between the UK and Scandinavia. The evolving nature of privacy underscores the importance of ongoing dialogue and ethical considerations in the handling and use of personal data. Balancing privacy concerns with the potential benefits of data sharing requires careful consideration of ethical principles and legal frameworks.

The tension between personal privacy and the broader societal good is a fundamental ethical dilemma, particularly in the context of data use. While respecting privacy rights is crucial, there are instances where not utilising available data can be considered unethical. For example, disclosing information about someone's contagious and fatal disease, while potentially infringing on their privacy, may be necessary to protect public health. However, navigating this balance is complex, as the risks and benefits of data use are often unclear and subject to change. Decision-makers must weigh potential gains against potential harms, considering both immediate and long-term consequences. Moreover, excessive caution or enthusiasm in response to these risks and gains can further complicate ethical decision-making.

Modern data technology has amplified this dilemma, as evidenced by the creation of databases like Voter Vault, which revolutionised political campaigning by enabling targeted messaging based on voters' beliefs and opinions. This shift emphasises the importance of what candidates know about voters rather than what voters know about candidates. Recent controversies, such as the Cambridge Analytica scandal involving the alleged manipulation of Facebook data for election purposes, highlight the ethical implications of data use in influencing public opinion and decision-making processes. Ultimately, addressing these ethical challenges requires careful consideration of privacy rights, transparency, accountability, and the broader societal implications of data use. Balancing individual privacy with the societal benefits of data-driven insights is essential for fostering trust and integrity in data practices.

The use of databases for electoral purposes is just one example of their broader application across various contexts. Loyalty cards, for instance, serve as a mechanism for organisations to gather data about consumers' preferences, habits, and behaviour in exchange for discounts and offers. This reflects a balance where consumers willingly provide personal data in return for perceived benefits, rather than exploitation. The privacy paradox, as described by Wittes and Liu, emphasises that technological advancements often offer both privacy-enhancing and privacy-threatening features simultaneously. Consumers possibly navigate this balance by weighing the privacy benefits against the privacy risks associated with using certain technologies. For example, while the internet provides access to sensitive content in a private manner, it also introduces new risks such as online predators and fraudsters. The concept of personally identifiable information (PII) is central to discussions of privacy, typically encompassing data such as names, addresses, and account details. However, the notion that anonymising data by removing PII guarantees privacy is often flawed. With sufficient effort and data matching capabilities, anonymised records can often be re-identified, highlighting the limitations of relying solely on PII for privacy protection. In essence, the notion of "identifying information" may not be sufficient for safeguarding privacy, as any piece of information can potentially be used to identify individuals when combined with other data. This underscores the need for comprehensive privacy measures that consider the broader context and potential risks associated with data sharing and usage.

Striking an appropriate balance between benefit and risk requires careful consideration of who stands to benefit and who bears the associated risks. When these factors are distributed unevenly among different actors, ethical imbalances can arise, potentially leading to disastrous outcomes. It's essential to distinguish between individual and collective benefits and risks, as they may not always align. In the context of public benefit, complexities emerge, such as corporations claiming that promoting their products benefits the public or privacy concerns impeding efforts to prevent wrongdoing. Additionally, social credit systems may offer perceived benefits at a larger scale, but their implementation raises ethical questions and the potential for unintended consequences. Various organisations approach data ethics with different core principles, albeit with related themes. For example, the European Data Protection Supervisor emphasises human dignity as a central guiding principle, viewing it as essential for countering pervasive surveillance and power imbalances in the digital age. Similarly, the Data Governance Working Group prioritises human flourishing as the overarching principle for developing systems of data governance. These principles underscore the importance of prioritising human values and well-being in ethical considerations related to data usage and governance.

Indeed, ethical principles can vary significantly across different countries and regions, leading to diverse approaches to data collection and usage. In some jurisdictions, like the UK, there may be stricter ethical considerations surrounding data governance, which could potentially impede agility in adopting and leveraging emerging data technologies. This phenomenon, often referred to as "ethical drag," suggests that adherence to stringent ethical standards may slow down the adoption or implementation of innovative data technologies. Countries like the UK already have established legal frameworks governing data usage, which include laws and regulations aimed at safeguarding privacy, protecting individual rights, and ensuring data security. For instance, initiatives such as the joint Royal Society/British Academy Data Governance Landscape Review contribute to shaping the ethical and legal landscape surrounding data governance in the UK. While adherence to ethical principles is crucial for maintaining trust and safeguarding individual rights, it's essential to balance ethical considerations with the need for innovation and technological advancement. Striking the right balance between ethical constraints and technological progress is a complex challenge that requires ongoing dialogue and careful consideration of societal values and priorities.

The ethics of data encompass a wide array of ethical challenges arising from the collection and analysis of large datasets. These challenges span various domains, including biomedical research, social sciences, profiling, advertising, data philanthropy, and open data initiatives. One key concern revolves around the potential re-identification of individuals through techniques such as data mining, linking, merging, and reusing of datasets. Additionally, there are risks associated with "group privacy," where identifying characteristics of groups, rather than individual identities, may lead to discrimination and targeted forms of violence. The ethics of algorithms addresses challenges posed by the growing complexity and autonomy of algorithms, particularly in machine learning applications and artificial intelligence. Key issues include the moral responsibility and accountability of designers and data scientists for unforeseen consequences and missed opportunities. Ethical design and auditing of algorithms are increasingly researched areas to mitigate potential negative outcomes like discrimination or the propagation of antisocial content. Lastly, the ethics of practices, which encompass professional ethics and deontology, scrutinise the responsibilities and liabilities of individuals and organisations involved in data processes, strategies, and policies. This branch aims to establish an ethical framework guiding responsible innovation, development, and usage in data science, ensuring ethical practices that advance both the field and safeguard individual and group rights. Consent, user privacy, and secondary use are central issues within this domain of analysis.

The ethics of data, algorithms, and practices are intricately connected, forming a conceptual space where ethical issues intersect and overlap. It is more appropriate to view them as three axes defining this space, rather than distinct lines of research. Many ethical problems do not neatly align with just one axis; instead, they involve considerations from multiple dimensions. For instance, discussions on data privacy invariably touch upon issues of consent and professional responsibilities. Similarly, ethical evaluations of algorithms often entail examining the obligations of their creators, developers, users, and adopters. Therefore, addressing data ethics comprehensively requires considering all three axes simultaneously, albeit with varying degrees of emphasis and focus. Developing data ethics as a macro-ethics from the outset is essential. This macro-ethical approach provides an overarching framework that encompasses the diverse ethical implications of data science in a unified and inclusive manner. It avoids narrow, piecemeal approaches in favour of a holistic perspective that acknowledges the interconnectedness of ethical considerations across the entire spectrum of data-related activities.

3.3 LEGISLATION DEVELOPMENT

The regulatory framework in the UK includes several key pieces of legislation aimed at governing data usage and ensuring transparency, accountability, and privacy;

1. **GDPR**: This regulation sets out rules for data protection and privacy for all individuals within the EU and the European Economic Area (EEA). It addresses the transfer of personal data outside the EU and EEA areas, aiming to give individuals greater control over their personal data and harmonise data protection laws across Europe.

Freedom of Information Act: Case Study: Navigating Ethical Challenges in the MARIE Project on Menopause

BACKGROUND

The MARIE project is a multifaceted, multi-work-package initiative addressing the physical and mental health impacts of menopause across cisgender and transgender individuals [230]. Despite the growing recognition of menopause as a significant health issue, comprehensive research on its diverse impacts and the development of evidence-based interventions remains limited. This case study outlines the ethical challenges encountered during the MARIE project's approval process and the strategies employed to overcome these hurdles.

The MARIE project aimed to fill critical gaps in menopause research by leveraging innovative methodologies and an inclusive framework. It sought to capture menopause experiences across diverse populations and develop interventions to optimise health outcomes [231]. The project's design included multiple work packages to ensure operational efficiency and comprehensive data collection. However, the project faced significant delays due to challenges with ethics committee approvals.

CHALLENGES ENCOUNTERED

1. **Ethics Committee's Limited Understanding of Novel Methodologies**
   - The MARIE project utilised cutting-edge methodologies tailored to address gaps in menopause research. These included advanced mixed-methods designs, digital tools, and inclusive frameworks for capturing diverse experiences.

- The ethics committee condemned the use of novel methodologies, citing their unfamiliarity with these approaches rather than evaluating their scientific merit.
- This lack of understanding created significant bottlenecks for the research team, which had to repeatedly defend its methodologies. These delays caused frustration, diverted resources from research activities, and increased the overall cost and timeline of the project. For researchers, this situation led to diminished morale and heightened stress, as they faced unwarranted scrutiny over scientifically sound approaches.
- The impact extended beyond the research team to the populations the study aimed to benefit. Individuals experiencing menopause—especially those from underrepresented groups—faced further delays in accessing interventions that could improve their quality of life. The lack of timely research perpetuated health disparities and left critical gaps in understanding menopause's multifaceted impacts.

2. **Operational Efficiency Misinterpreted as Complexity**
   - The project's multi-work-package design aimed to consolidate resources and minimise redundant processes. This approach, while efficient, was misinterpreted by the ethics committee as unnecessarily complex and beyond their capacity to assess effectively.
   - Ethics committee members raised concerns about deliverability, citing their own misunderstandings about how integrated work packages function. These delays had cascading effects on project timelines, delaying the delivery of meaningful results to stakeholders and the populations the research intended to serve.
   - As delays mounted, the efficiency of the multi-work-package approach was undermined, increasing operational costs and creating logistical challenges for the research team. Delayed deliverables risked eroding trust with funding bodies and collaborators, further compounding the challenges.
   - Ethics committees, while essential for ensuring ethical standards, are not tasked with determining operational feasibility or resource allocation. By overstepping their remit into areas of project management, the committee created unnecessary obstacles that detracted from their primary role of safeguarding ethical integrity. Such interference underscores the need for clear boundaries and improved training to help ethics committees focus on their core responsibilities.
3. **Lack of Awareness about Cisgender and Transgender Health Needs**
   - Despite the project's inclusivity, the ethics committee lacked understanding of the unique health challenges faced by cisgender and transgender individuals during menopause. This resulted in unwarranted scepticism about the project's objectives and methodologies.
   - The implications of this knowledge gap were profound. Transgender and non-binary individuals, who already experience significant barriers to accessing healthcare, were further marginalised by the delayed approval of research addressing their specific needs. This underscored the systemic lack of

recognition for diverse experiences of menopause, perpetuating inequities in healthcare and research.

STRATEGIES TO ADDRESS ETHICAL CHALLENGES

1. **Challenging the Committee's Scientific Understanding**
   - The MARIE team submitted a detailed rebuttal to the committee's concerns, providing educational materials and evidence supporting the validity and necessity of the proposed methodologies.
   - External experts were consulted to endorse the scientific soundness of the project design.
2. **Advocating for Operational Efficiency**
   - The team highlighted the cost and time implications of pursuing multiple ethics approvals for individual work packages.
   - They emphasised the benefits of integrated research approaches for generating robust and generalisable findings.
3. **Promoting Awareness of Inclusive Health Research**
   - Educational sessions were organised to inform the ethics committee about the health disparities faced by cisgender and transgender populations.
   - Testimonials and evidence from pilot studies were shared to illustrate the importance of inclusive menopause research.

Outcomes: Following rigorous advocacy and engagement, the MARIE project secured ethics approval on the third submission. The revised approval process underscored the importance of improving ethics committees' capacity to evaluate innovative and inclusive research proposals. The project proceeded to generate significant insights into menopause experiences and developed evidence-based tools to support individuals and healthcare providers.

IMPROVING OVERSIGHT AND ACCOUNTABILITY OF ETHICS COMMITTEES

Ethics committees play a critical role in safeguarding ethical research practices, but systemic issues within their structure and operations can hinder research progress and inadvertently reinforce inequities. To address these challenges, the following measures are essential:

1. **Regular Oversight and Auditing**
   - Ethics committees in the UK should be regularly overseen and audited by independent bodies to ensure they adhere to established guidelines and best practices. These audits should assess whether committees are making decisions based on evidence and ethical standards rather than personal beliefs or perceptions.
   - Transparent reporting mechanisms should be implemented to track decision-making processes and identify areas for improvement. This ensures that

committees remain accountable to the research community and the populations served by the studies they review.

2. **Representation of Underserved Populations**
   - Committees should be more representative of diverse populations, particularly those underserved in research. This representation ensures that ethical reviews account for the unique needs and perspectives of all groups, preventing biases that can marginalise certain populations.
   - Diverse representation can also mitigate the risk of committees overestimating their understanding of population needs and imposing their views on research teams who may have direct experience and expertise working with these communities.
3. **Clear Boundaries for Committee Roles**
   - Ethics committees should focus exclusively on evaluating the ethical aspects of research proposals, such as participant safety, consent processes, and risk mitigation. Operational decisions, such as feasibility and deliverability, fall outside their purview and should be left to the research teams and funding bodies.
   - Training programmes should be instituted to help committee members better understand their roles and the potential consequences of overstepping their responsibilities. This ensures that committees support, rather than hinder, innovative and impactful research.
4. **Addressing Personal Biases**
   - Comprehensive training on unconscious bias and cultural competency should be mandatory for all ethics committee members. This helps minimise the influence of personal perceptions and beliefs on decision-making processes, fostering more objective and equitable reviews.

Outcomes: Following rigorous advocacy and engagement, the MARIE project secured ethics approval on the third submission. The revised approval process underscored the importance of improving ethics committees' capacity to evaluate innovative and inclusive research proposals. The project proceeded to generate significant insights into menopause experiences and developed evidence-based tools to support individuals and healthcare providers.

LESSONS LEARNED

1. **Education and Advocacy Are Key**
   - Bridging knowledge gaps within ethics committees is crucial to facilitate the approval of innovative and inclusive research projects.
2. **Streamlined Processes Save Resources**
   - Operationally efficient designs should be recognised and supported by ethics committees to optimise resource utilisation.
3. **Inclusive Research Requires Institutional Support**
   - Addressing health disparities necessitates institutional commitment to supporting research that prioritises underrepresented populations.

Conclusion: The MARIE project's experience highlights the need for ethics committees to adopt more informed and flexible approaches to evaluating complex and novel research proposals [231]. By addressing these challenges, the research community can ensure that groundbreaking projects like MARIE contribute to improving health outcomes for all populations.

2. This legislation promotes transparency and accountability by granting the public the right to access information held by public authorities. It requires public bodies to disclose information about their activities and respond to requests for information from the public. However, it does not cover personal data, which is addressed separately under the GDPR and the DPA.
3. **Digital Economy Act**: This comprehensive legislation addresses various aspects of digital governance, including electronic communications, data sharing, direct marketing, and cybersecurity. Part 5 of the Act specifically focuses on digital government, covering issues such as data sharing for research purposes, confidentiality of personal information, and fraud prevention.

In addition to these legislative measures, there are enforcement mechanisms in place to ensure compliance with data protection and governance standards. Breaches of ethical guidelines and data protection laws can result in penalties such as fines, restrictions on research funding, and revocation of organisational memberships. The GDPR, in particular, imposes significant fines of up to 4% of global annual turnover for non-compliance with its provisions. These regulatory frameworks and enforcement mechanisms play a crucial role in upholding ethical standards and protecting individuals' rights in the context of data usage.

The GDPR's provision for individuals to request rectification of their personal data and exercise the "right to be forgotten" is aimed at empowering individuals to have control over their personal information and protect their privacy. However, as you rightly point out, this can introduce challenges such as selection bias and hinder the effectiveness of analyses and decision-making processes. The risk of selection bias arises when individuals opt in or opt out of data collection, potentially skewing the dataset and leading to invalid analyses and suboptimal decisions. Additionally, the concept of data minimisation, while important for specific projects, may conflict with the broader potential of the data revolution to uncover unexpected insights and generate value through the integration of diverse data sources.

Unintended consequences are inevitable in complex data ecosystems, similar to the adverse effects seen in industrialisation. These consequences can range from tangible harms like financial loss and discriminatory treatment to intangible harms such as exclusion from opportunities or anxiety about data misuse. Differentiating between research studies and operational decision-making is essential, as each may have distinct requirements and considerations. Navigating these challenges requires a balanced approach that respects individuals' privacy rights while also leveraging the transformative potential of data for societal benefit. It underscores the importance of ethical considerations, transparency, and accountability in data governance practices.

Creating a checklist for ethical considerations in data-related work is indeed a prudent approach to ensure that researchers and practitioners adhere to ethical principles and legal requirements.

1. Identity ethics committees that oversee the work and obtain necessary approvals. There are two types of ethics committees that oversee research conducted in the UK. This includes university-led ethics committees that mostly oversee and approve academically led research. Research that uses NHS-based patients or NHS-sponsored studies go through the Research Ethics Committees that are part of the Health Research Authority (HRA)-UK.
2. Institutional policies and procedures in relation to data ethics, including but not limited to data administration, retention, and management.
3. Ensure compliance with national regulations and laws related to privacy, consent, discrimination, and analysis explanation requirements.
4. Maintain a detailed record of how data are modified and manipulated throughout the research.
5. Understand the origin and provenance of the data to ensure reliability and accountability.
6. Treat metadata with the same rigour as the data itself to maintain accuracy and integrity.
7. Develop an explicit data management plan that includes a transparent summary of the data collection, storage, sharing, and disposal processes.
8. Implement secure data storage practices to safeguard against unauthorised access or breaches.
9. Determine the retention period for data, considering legal requirements and research needs.
10. Specify access controls to ensure that only authorised individuals or entities have access to the data.
11. Provide a clear statistical analysis plan along with any details of using automated tools, such as specific software, machine learning, or data mining tools that may have ethical implications and potential biases.
12. Establish mechanisms for data correction and deletion to address inaccuracies or privacy concerns.
13. Clearly communicate the potential benefits of the analysis and identify stakeholders who will derive these benefits.

By systematically addressing these considerations, researchers and practitioners can promote ethical conduct, maintain data integrity, and mitigate risks associated with data-related activities.

3.4 PATIENT–PUBLIC INVOLVEMENT AND ENGAGEMENT

Patient–Public Involvement (PPI) is a vital part of continuous improvement of the data science landscape. In the realm of medicine and healthcare, data-intensive research, such as health-related big data research (HBDR), entails the aggregation and linking of data from various sources, including clinical routines, research endeavours, patient-reported data, as well as non-medical social or demographic data. This amalgamation of diverse data aims to optimise biomedical research by providing insights into health trends, treatment effectiveness, and disease prevention strategies. Within this context, concepts of patient participation and involvement are frequently invoked to justify and enhance the governance of such research endeavours. By scrutinising the role of patient participation and involvement within these research paradigms, the paper seeks to illuminate both the potential benefits and drawbacks of incorporating participatory approaches in this field.

Both PPI and by patients participating in surveys, interviews, or focus groups to provide data for analysis, interpretation, and action by others. However, the authors note that in grant applications and study protocols, PPI is often equated with qualitative research or patient opinion surveys. While collecting data from patients can be crucial for obtaining diverse or representative views, it differs from PPI, and both are often necessary. For instance, discussion with patients at a workshop might resemble data collection in a focus group, as both involve listening to patients' perspectives. However, the context and outcomes from listening vary. PPI entails researchers being in a continuing and reciprocal relationship with patients, making research decisions alongside them. In contrast, qualitative research involves researchers listening to patients to enhance understanding of a topic. Focus group discussions or qualitative interviews are recorded and transcribed, with researchers analysing and interpreting the text data to generate hypotheses and produce valid new knowledge. While qualitative and survey research adhere to systematic methodological quality standards, researchers maintain power, and patients may express views that are not always reported. In research, PPI and data collection for broader patient perspectives can be separate, combined, overlap in certain study phases, or fully integrated throughout the research process. Various combinations are possible, often seen in equitable partnership research methods like action research and research terms prefixed with "co-" such as co-learning and co-production.

Action research, originating in the 1940s as a community-led initiative, preceded the concept of co-production and gained momentum. The UK's National Institute of Health Research (NIHR), a research funder, advocates for co-production as a method of meaningfully involving patients throughout the research process. Definitions of these approaches may vary subtly and internationally, and researchers often apply them flexibly in practice. In this chapter, the term "partnership approaches" is used as an umbrella term, acknowledging the evolving roles of patients beyond mere "participants" or "subjects." Partnership research methods involve patients, clinicians, academics, and other stakeholders as equal, mutually respected partners in the research team. Being a patient partner implies equal opportunity and voice, though power differentials may exist due to factors such as pay, employment contracts, and workplace environments. As terminology evolves globally, it's more practical to describe specific patient roles, tasks, and responsibilities explicitly rather than using broad labels that can be misunderstood. For example, co-production might involve regular patient consultation or active involvement in collecting and interpreting research data. Partnership research teams decide on access to participant-level data, secure data sharing methods, and collective decision-making processes. These approaches can be resource-intensive and require leadership skills to balance equity in decision-making with scientific rigour. Negotiation skills are essential to accommodate diverse perspectives and reach consensus efficiently.

A starting point for researchers is to ascertain whether patients' priorities already exist for their topic. Many national and international organisations involve patients in identifying and publishing research priorities specific to healthcare conditions. In the UK, the James Lind Alliance (JLA) focuses on identifying and prioritising research questions for funders, supported by a register. JLA establishes Priority Setting Partnerships through collaborations between patients, carers, and clinicians. While the NIHR funds JLA advisors and infrastructure, each Priority Setting Partnership is responsible for its own funding. The JLA offers a guidebook outlining step-by-step processes to identify research uncertainties and prioritise a top ten list for various conditions. Researchers are advised to assess how priorities were established and the rigour of processes, considering that priorities can evolve over time, and some groups may not have had the opportunity to participate. If patients' priorities are unknown and a Priority Setting Partnership is not available, contacting the potential funder to discuss options may be beneficial. When researchers plan custom methods to prioritise research, it is crucial to involve patients early on to identify the topic and refine the research question for relevance; for instance, collaborating with a charity or research organisation to conduct an online survey, advertising and hosting open public workshops with patients to rank research priorities, or eliciting input from participants in qualitative interviews to identify impactful scenarios for prioritisation. Once patients have prioritised the research topic and questions, the next step involves prioritising outcomes that matter, including patient-centred outcome measures, and identifying acceptable research methods.

Researchers are encouraged to identify individuals to involve and plan potential roles, responsibilities, and tasks for their study as early as possible. Research teams can reach out to patients through formal patient groups, charities, community groups, university or health and social care patient advisory panels, national directories such as "People in Research" and "invoDIRECT," patients involved in producing guidelines like The National Institute of Health and Care Excellence, or through personal recommendations or advertisements. It is generally considered inappropriate to involve patients who are currently receiving clinical care from members of the research team. In the UK, "invoDIRECT" provides an online resource of organisations, networks, and groups supporting patient and PPI in health and social care research. Lay or professional coordinators or liaison individuals can assist, and different sources of patients may be utilised for different purposes. For example, a head office of a patient charity might nominate a person to join a study steering committee, while a local patient group could help make recruitment materials appealing and easy to understand. Participants in a preparatory survey, focus group, or qualitative interview may be invited to volunteer for patient involvement in future research, thereby making qualitative research and PPI synergistic.

Public involvement is crucial in crafting effective participant information sheets. In numerous cases, studies fail to receive initial approval due to inadequacies in their participant information sheets. Additionally, public involvement is invaluable in shaping the entire consent process, as it encompasses the interaction between the researcher and the potential participant, not just the written information provided. Involving the public in designing the consent process ensures several key benefits. Firstly, it ensures that potential participants receive the information they require and desire, tailored to their interests and concerns. This personalised approach helps to ensure that both written and verbal information are clear and easily understood, enhancing the likelihood of genuinely "informed" consent and ensuring that individuals fully comprehend the implications of participating in a project. Moreover, when conducting research with individuals from diverse backgrounds, public involvement ensures that the consent process is culturally appropriate and sensitive to community concerns. For instance, it can help prevent the use of language that may stigmatise individuals with mental health issues or disabilities. By involving the public at this stage, the recruitment process becomes more transparent and comprehensible to potential participants. Public involvement in research design plays a crucial role in ensuring that practical arrangements meet the needs of participants, as highlighted by Ennis and Wykes [232] and Jenner et al. [233]. This involvement helps to facilitate the participation of patients, members of the public, including children and young people, in research, while also ensuring that they are not overly burdened by their involvement. It serves as a demonstration of researchers' respect and appreciation for participants' time and contributions [234,235]. Practically, public involvement ensures that various aspects of research design are optimised for participants' convenience and accessibility. This may include ensuring that questionnaires are of appropriate length, relevance, and accessibility, scheduling appointments at convenient times and locations, limiting the number of assessments or invasive tests participants undergo, and ensuring that participants are not financially disadvantaged by their participation, such as covering their travel expenses (unless otherwise specified beforehand).

From an ethical standpoint, it's problematic to overlook the laborious contributions made by patients in research endeavours, especially when such efforts are couched in participatory and emancipatory language. This isn't just a matter of conceptual accuracy but also has immediate practical implications and moral consequences. When recruitment for research relies on promises of participation that aren't fulfilled or are cynically exploited to capitalise on participants' goodwill and engagement, it can severely undermine public trust in scientific endeavours, as evidenced by the case study of data care. While large datasets are indeed crucial in this type of research, the use of participatory language should never devolve into a mere tactic for enrolling research participants. Doing so would diminish the profound ethical implications inherent in true participation. Considering patients' typically high willingness to contribute biomaterials and data to research, the appropriation of participatory concepts to incentivise enrolment in data-intensive medical research like HBDR warrants scrutiny. Overall, the ethical challenge lies in establishing valid consent models that prevent the unauthorised use of data or biomaterials without participants' knowledge or against their explicit wishes. In certain research contexts, robust and transparent data protection protocols and clear information disclosure may be even more vital to patients than opportunities for active involvement in data collection processes [236,237].

In the UK, primary care services see more patients than any other part of the healthcare system, underscoring the importance of including the perspectives and insights of service recipients in primary care research. To evaluate the prevalence, quality, and impact of PPI in primary care research, we analysed documents from 200 projects and surveyed 191 researchers [238,239]. The findings revealed that approximately half of the studies incorporated PPI both in the development of research ideas and throughout the study itself [240]. Common PPI activities included designing study materials, providing input on methodologies, and overseeing the research process. However, some studies deviated from their initially planned and funded PPI activities. The extent of PPI varied depending on factors such as study design, health condition, and participant demographics. While pockets of good practice were identified, including having a dedicated PPI budget and providing support to PPI contributors, deficiencies were noted in other areas. Few projects offered training to PPI contributors, utilised PPI to inform participants about study progress, or sought PPI input on publishing findings. Researchers reported beneficial impacts resulting from PPI, particularly when good practice indicators were incorporated into the approach. The primary cost to researchers was the investment of their time, with many facing challenges in providing information about PPI activities. In collaboration with PPI contributors, we have used these findings to develop a new Cost and Consequences Framework for PPI, which outlines both the financial and non-financial costs, benefits, and potential harms associated with PPI. Additionally, we have formulated 15 co-produced recommendations aimed at enhancing the practice and delivery of PPI in primary care research.

The practices of direct-to-consumer genetic testing company 23andMe serve as a compelling example of the ethical complexities inherent in such endeavours. Beyond providing personalised genetic information to its users, the company also constructs its own research database, raising a spectrum of ethical concerns. These include issues related to participants' informed and voluntary consent, as well as their understanding of how their data will be used for specific research purposes. Particularly pertinent to our discussion is the participatory rhetoric employed by 23andMe. The company entices potential participants with slogans like "Becoming part of something bigger: Our genetic research gives everyday people the opportunity to make a difference by participating in a new kind of research — online, from anywhere." By framing participation as a means for individuals to contribute to research as part of a collective, 23andMe presents a bottom-up approach to scientific inquiry. However, this participatory facade is overshadowed by the company's underlying commercial interests. Essentially, the value of individuals' voices in research is contingent upon profitability. Goldberg highlights the pervasive intertwining of discourse and commerce on the internet, suggesting that any participation or engagement is inevitably linked to buying and selling. Despite being kept informed about ongoing research projects, participants in 23andMe are better characterised as valuable but predominantly passive data sources, rather than active contributors with a meaningful voice in shaping the direction and outcomes of research [241].

The widespread adoption of terminology such as citizen science, participation, or empowerment in online communication tools within this context begs the question of why such language holds such sway. One potential explanation lies in the perceived imminent loss of control over the use of data. In this light, online platforms that ostensibly afford patients some degree of control over their data may be seen as empowering. However, it's crucial to recognise that the power granted to participants in this scenario remains limited compared to the broader ethical-political concept of participation. It's a fallacy to assume that genuine mutual consultation and deliberation will naturally emerge from the use of online tools. In reality, achieving genuine consultation and deliberation in research may necessitate more direct forms of participation, such as including patient representatives in the governing bodies of research initiatives. Currently, this indirect mode of participation is not extensively discussed in these debates. However, given that individual-level consultation about research aims may not always be effective or ethically necessary, leveraging the potential of representation in future data-intensive research in medicine and healthcare warrants consideration.

The case of PatientsLikeMe (PLM) exemplifies a form of patient engagement where individuals not only contribute their data but also have the opportunity to form their own research cohorts. One notable instance is the Lithium study, where a group of ALS patients organised via PLM decided to take Lithium in response to a study suggesting its potential benefit in ALS treatment. By forming a cohort of 348 patients, they were able to challenge the findings of the initial study. From an ethical standpoint, this example aligns closely with the concept of empowering co-investigation, maintaining the original spirit of participation by transferring power to the participants. However, a more extensive approach to establishing a balance of power between researchers and patients would involve granting equal access to funding and knowledge production sources, such as scientific journals. Yet, granting participants the role of co-decision-makers or co-researchers presents challenges from both research-ethical and methodological perspectives. One significant concern is the potential for participants to engage in self-initiated trials involving pharmaceuticals without the safeguards typically provided by traditional research ethics, such as ethical review and ensuring free and informed consent. This lack of oversight can pose serious risks to participants, especially terminally ill patients who may be more willing to accept significant risk exposure in hopes of finding a cure or treatment. Indeed, participant-led research initiatives, while promoting inclusivity and patient empowerment, also raise concerns about the scientific validity and ethical oversight of the research process. Sampling biases, stemming from self-selection or convenient sampling methods, can distort the representativeness of the data collected. Additionally, ensuring the trustworthiness of the data and the quality of data analysis becomes more challenging when participants take a leading role in research. Even proponents of participatory research models typically advocate for ongoing cooperation between researchers and participants rather than placing patients or laypeople in a leading role throughout the research process. Therefore, initiatives in HBDR that assign patients a primary role may exceed the ethically desirable level of participation and co-determination, moving towards a more asymmetrical relationship. Given these challenges, there is a pressing need to adapt ethical oversight standards to accommodate participant-led research initiatives. This involves developing guidelines and mechanisms to ensure the scientific rigour, integrity, and ethical conduct of research led by participants while still promoting collaboration and inclusivity between researchers and participants.

The MIDATA initiative in Switzerland exemplifies a novel approach to participant involvement in research through the establishment of a non-commercial data cooperative. Unlike traditional research models where participants have limited control over their data, MIDATA empowers participants by collectively owning their data and collectively determining the conditions for its use by researchers. Additionally, participants have a say in how the revenues generated from data use by third parties are reinvested into future research endeavours. This bottom-up approach to data governance allows participants to have a significant role in shaping the conditions of data use, providing them with a form of democratic control over their data. While participants in MIDATA are primarily involved in providing data rather than directly participating in the research process, their collective decision-making power ensures that their interests and preferences are respected. Overall, initiatives like MIDATA represent a promising experiment in democratic data self-governance, offering a model where participants can actively engage in shaping the direction and governance of research initiatives while still contributing valuable data to scientific endeavours.

Simply informing participants about how their data will be used does not necessarily empower them or ensure that their interests and preferences are taken into account. True participation requires creating mechanisms for meaningful engagement, such as allowing participants to have a say in research priorities, study design, and data governance. By acknowledging these deviations from the original spirit of participation and addressing the ethical challenges they pose, researchers and policymakers can work towards creating more inclusive and ethically sound approaches to data-intensive research in medicine and healthcare. This involves moving beyond tokenistic forms of participation towards genuine collaboration and co-determination with research participants.

In the realm of data-intensive research in medicine and healthcare, there's a growing emphasis on participatory approaches, with promises of increased engagement and involvement from patients and other stakeholders. However, our analysis reveals certain deviations from the original spirit of participation, presenting ethical challenges and practical issues. Transparency about data usage is often touted as a form of participation, but from a political-ethical perspective, this falls short of more substantive forms of engagement. Moreover, there's a trend towards replacing collective deliberation and consultation with individual decision-making via online tools, which doesn't fully capture the normative essence of genuine participatory efforts. On the other hand, there are instances of overly ambitious promises of participatory involvement, such as highlighting research trials led by patients as innovative science. Striking a balance between tokenistic engagement and overly ambitious promises is crucial, grounded in a nuanced understanding of the ethical, practical, and methodological considerations. Meaningful engagement with participants, ethical considerations, practical feasibility, and continuous evaluation should guide future approaches to participation in data-intensive research. Through thoughtful consideration of these aspects, researchers and policymakers can ensure that participatory initiatives uphold ethical integrity and effectively involve stakeholders in the research process.

Firstly, data-intensive research projects must critically evaluate their motivations for embracing participatory approaches. It's essential to differentiate between instrumental uses, such as increasing data volume or financial gains, and genuinely normative reasons for involving patients to align research aims with their opinions. Bringing awareness to this distinction has practical implications for the role patients play in such projects. If participatory notions primarily serve to encourage data donation and legitimise research, participants may remain passive subjects, leading to significant mistrust if goals aren't met. Additionally, it's crucial to reflect on the ethical necessity of patients becoming involved as co-researchers. Given the challenges of data privacy and potential misuse, involving patients in the governance of research initiatives, such as advisory boards or workshops, could be highly beneficial. Secondly, as data-intensive research relies on data provided by patients, often with the intention to improve their own health, transparency is key regarding whether participation is for personal medical benefit or broader public engagement. While the boundaries between clinical care and research blur in initiatives like HBDR, it's vital to avoid therapeutic and participatory misconceptions. The latter arises when research initiatives use public engagement rhetoric without empowering patients as genuine research partners. While it may benefit individual patients to receive health status information, framing it as patient involvement in research can be misleading.

A third requirement is that research initiatives should resist depoliticising participation by denying patients real influence on research or exploiting their engagement to outsource research work and save time and money. As Prainsack [242] argue, the language used to describe such practices should acknowledge the power structures they are embedded in, referring to responsibilities devolved to patients and invited participation as "patient work." However, while Prainsack et al. criticises the invocation of participation when other collective actors should be involved, in the context of data-intensive medical research, this is only part of the issue. Patient-reported data, if patients receive sufficient information, may not inherently pose ethical problems. However, issues may arise if patients are led to believe they can control their medical destinies, while researchers or commercial agencies are actually in charge. This use of participatory rhetoric may even lower research-ethical standards, as it falsely suggests individuals hold decision-making powers. A fourth consideration is the availability of resources necessary for genuine participation. If patients are expected to participate in governing data-intensive research, projects should have sufficient financial and structural resources for effective communication and expression of opinions. Resource provision should be balanced to avoid conflicts of interest and compromises to patients' credibility. Since researchers are usually compensated for their work, acknowledgement and reimbursement of patients' contributions as citizen researchers should also be considered. Ultimately, equal access to funding and knowledge production sources would be essential for true power balance and equal status.

3.5 DATA SCIENCE AND SOCIAL POLICY

As the accessibility of data science has grown, so has its application in addressing social issues within the domain of social services. Social services encompass various programmes aimed at providing support to children, families, and individuals in need, including housing, meals, refugee resettlement, migrant services, and child protective services. These programmes, operated by government agencies, NGOs, or grassroots associations, often operate with limited resources and face diverse operational challenges. DS offers a valuable tool to understand processes, identify bottlenecks, and optimise resource utilisation within these programmes. Traditionally, decision-making in social services has been driven by policy familiarity, funding requirements, and practitioner expertise. DS methods, on the other hand, leverage data to uncover patterns and insights for knowledge discovery, complementing the knowledge-driven approach of social services. The integration of DS expands the ability to make sense of data and enhances traditional analytical methods, potentially leading to operational and programming improvements. However, caution is necessary when applying DS in the social sector to avoid oversimplification of inherent complexities. Existing DS methods may overlook nuances and unique characteristics of individual circumstances, particularly when aggregating data on a community-wide level. While DS can provide valuable insights, its deployment does not guarantee immediate improvements in service quality or quantity. Careful consideration of the validity and utility of DS insights is essential prior to deployment, given that the outcomes are only as reliable as the data used. Collaboration between data scientists and social services stakeholders is crucial in ensuring responsible and equitable DS applications. This collaboration facilitates critical discussions about potential unintended consequences and ensures that DS solutions are appropriate for real-world contexts. Given that social services cater to marginalised populations and precarious communities, it is imperative for professionals in both fields to consider the ethical dimensions of DS use and its implications, striving for solutions that are effective and ethically sound.

Data science within the public sector is burgeoning, with numerous studies extolling its importance and potential value through empirical experimentation. However, many of these studies fail to engage decision-makers and policymakers, raising doubts about the usefulness of the generated information for public decision-making processes. A handful of studies have examined the DS process from a socio-technical perspective, considering both technical aspects and the roles of actors involved. These investigations underscore the significance of how data scientists interact with data to produce knowledge. Nevertheless, existing empirical studies often overlook policymaking processes, which are characterised by greater complexity in both technical aspects and actor dynamics. Janssen and Helbig's position paper emphasises this socio-technical complexity and underscores the impact of DS advancements, highlighting the necessity for policymakers to acquire new roles and capabilities. They stress that policymakers must understand the possibilities and limitations of computational instruments and methods, assess the validity of policy models, navigate big and open data, integrate instruments and methods into public discourse, and comprehend the diverse wishes, needs, and behaviours of stakeholders.

The growing significance of "big data" is increasingly evident in today's data-driven landscape. In this era of data revolution, the ability of firms to capture and analyse data determines their profitability. Moreover, it influences the success of economies and societies in areas such as education, workforce training, healthcare, and citizen well-being. Institutions like schools and hospitals now routinely collect data to better serve their stakeholders, including students and patients. Extracting insights from this wealth of data is crucial for practitioners, administrators, and policymakers to understand societal challenges and assess the impact of existing practices and policies. Federal initiatives such as the Murray–Ryan Evidence-Based Policymaking Commission Act of 2016 and the subsequent Foundations for Evidence-Based Policymaking Act of 2018 indicate a growing centrality of administrative data in US social science and policymaking. However, the use of administrative data in the social sciences remains uneven. While fields like public health and demography frequently leverage administrative data, they are less commonly used in areas such as mental health and social behaviour. Moreover, even in domains where administrative data are prevalent, capacity constraints often limit their utility. Decision-makers may lack access to critical data, leading to incomplete information and hindering informed decision-making. In the field of education, accessing comprehensive data has historically been challenging for schools aiming to prepare students for success in college and careers. Linkages between K-12 educational systems and higher education outcomes have only recently become widespread, and connections between K-12 data systems and the labour market are still relatively uncommon. These data linkages are crucial for assessing the effectiveness of various school-based programmes such as vocational training, dropout recovery interventions, college readiness initiatives, and policies related to advanced placement courses. However, many schools lack the capacity and expertise needed to establish this infrastructure and analyse the resulting data. An article by Sean Reardon in this double issue highlights the potential value of examining nationwide data on student achievement. Reardon leverages an unprecedented administrative data file to provide insights useful for both policy decision-making and scientific understanding of child development and the impact of education. This data file, along with others like it, can address numerous important issues that were previously inaccessible for rigorous empirical scrutiny. For instance, Megan Austin, Joseph Waddington, and Mark Berends demonstrate how administrative data can shed light on the policy question of the impact of school vouchers on student achievement. Administrative data research aims to apply the data-driven approach, commonly used in fields like micro-targeting and precision medicine, to address significant societal issues. By leveraging data analytics, this research provides schools, clinics, and other public-serving institutions with valuable insights to enhance their effectiveness. However, the inability of public-sector institutions to develop the necessary infrastructure for understanding programme effectiveness may lead to inefficiencies, especially when compared to private sector entities with fewer constraints on data usage. Recent research has underscored the value of administrative data in understanding the long-term outcomes associated with various interventions. While much policy is informed by research examining relatively short-term outcomes, administrative data offer a longer-term perspective on the effects of past policies, providing a more accurate assessment of their costs and benefits. Beyond tracking individuals exposed to interventions over time, administrative data enable researchers to explore multigenerational cycles of advantage and disadvantage. This allows for the examination of descendants' outcomes across different backgrounds and the intergenerational effects of antipoverty policies and interventions. Administrative data also offer opportunities to link researcher-collected data, such as observations of student behaviour, with future administrative records, shedding light on the long-term implications of researchers' findings. This extends our understanding of longer-term policy effects and the broader intergenerational transmission of advantage and disadvantage. While standard intervention research typically concludes data collection at the end of the study, administrative records provide an efficient means to assess intervention benefits decades later, as participants' data continue to be captured post-study. The ability of administrative data to effectively transform any study into a de facto longitudinal study is particularly exciting. Recent research has demonstrated this by uncovering various long-term impacts, such as the adult income effects of kindergarten teacher quality and peer influence, the increase in adult civic participation resulting from elementary school interventions, and the positive effects of cash transfers to poor families on children's educational outcomes, mortality rates, and income. Administrative data research builds upon a longstanding tradition of survey-based research that has investigated the intergenerational transmission of advantage and disadvantage. Survey-based studies have explored processes of parent–child transmission and, in some cases, even extended to examining the roles of grandparents. However, administrative data enable researchers to extend the temporal scope of these investigations further back in time. For instance, utilising Swedish registry data, Martin Hällsten has explored the effects of not only grandparents but also great-grandparents. Similarly, research by Hyunjoon Park has leveraged Korean historical registry information to analyse the outcomes of ethnically Korean slaves, revealing significant effects on their descendants many generations after the abolition of slavery. While multigenerational data are less common in the US, exceptions such as the Utah Population Database exist. These data offer exciting new prospects for advancing our understanding of the multigenerational transmission of advantage and disadvantage, as well as the enduring costs of stigmatised identities, poverty, and disadvantage. As data infrastructure continues to develop, we anticipate seeing more studies examining how social policies targeting one generation influence the outcomes of their children and grandchildren.

Inequality in opportunities and outcomes across different groups and individuals poses one of the most complex challenges in contemporary society. These disparities often arise within spheres that are challenging to investigate using conventional survey methods or controlled experiments. For instance, in the hiring process, while correspondence studies can shed light on who receives responses from potential employers, they fall short in revealing how applicant pools are formed, which interviewees ultimately receive job offers, or whether pay disparities exist among those who are hired. Similar challenges are encountered in research on inequality within other institutional domains such as healthcare, housing, and higher education. In institutional settings, inequality is often shaped by intricate processes that determine inclusion and exclusion, as well as the hierarchical ranking of individuals within organisations. Administrative data pertaining to hiring pipelines, performance evaluations, promotion decisions, and termination practices offer valuable insights into the decision-making processes of gatekeepers within organisations. These data illuminate key aspects of entry and exit from organisations, as well as the internal dynamics governing inequality within organisational structures. A notable advantage of workplace administrative records is their ability to facilitate comparisons among individuals holding the same occupation within the same establishment. Research based on such comparisons suggests that much of the observed wage disparity across gender and race stems from sorting processes, whereby individuals performing similar work for the same employer receive largely comparable pay. Building upon this understanding, a longstanding tradition of case studies has utilised administrative data from company human resource departments to investigate inequality within these sorting processes. Researchers like Trond Petersen and Ishak Saporta have argued that, within the current institutional landscape, firms have the greatest opportunity to engage in discriminatory practices at the point of hire, leading to significant differences between men and women in hiring outcomes. Similarly, Roberto Fernandez and his collaborators have leveraged human resource data to provide crucial insights into race and gender disparities in the hiring process. Their work highlights factors such as the importance of referrals and the adjustments made by job seekers in response to perceived constraints in the job market. Recent research in this area has uncovered surprising findings, such as the egalitarian influence of executive search firms. For example, Fernandez-Mateo and Fernandez revealed the unexpected impact of such firms on reducing gender-based barriers in the biopharma industry. In the current discourse, Fernandez and Brian Rubineau utilise their extensive hiring data to offer novel analyses of network recruitment efforts and their effects on gender disparities within the biopharma sector.

3.6 IMPLICATIONS OF DATA SCIENCE-DRIVEN DECISION-MAKING

In the realm of development, decisions hold immense significance, shaping the trajectory of projects and influencing their outcomes. Despite the increasing abundance of data, many initiatives still rely on subjective factors like personal anecdotes or intuition, rather than harnessing the potential of data-driven insights. Furthermore, the traditional focus of monitoring and evaluation (M&E) processes on donor reporting and indicator tracking often overlooks their broader potential as tools for learning and informed decision-making. In this chapter, I aim to delve into the pivotal role of data in development projects, highlighting the challenges that impede its comprehensive utilisation. Additionally, I will propose solutions for development endeavours to adopt a data-driven approach to decision-making, facilitating greater impact and enhancing the communication of their achievements.

Improving the ethical implications linked to data-related decision-making necessitates a comprehensive approach engaging stakeholders across various sectors. Firstly, there's a need for heightened education and awareness campaigns to enhance data literacy and ethical consciousness among researchers, policymakers, data scientists, and the public. Transparency and accountability must also be prioritised, with organisations urged to openly disclose data collection, processing, and decision-making procedures while being held responsible for any ethical lapses. Additionally, the development and adherence to tailored ethical guidelines and frameworks are crucial, covering aspects such as privacy, consent, bias, fairness, and accountability. Establishing independent ethics committees or review boards can provide oversight and guidance to ensure ethical standards are upheld. Emphasising diversity and inclusion in data-related processes is vital to mitigate biases and ensure equitable outcomes. Ethical considerations should be integrated into the design and engineering of data systems and technologies, aiming to address biases and unintended consequences proactively. Lastly, continuous evaluation and improvement are imperative, involving regular assessments, audits, and stakeholder consultations to identify and rectify ethical shortcomings.

Consider two hypothetical projects, Project X and Project Y, to illustrate the transformative impact of data. Project X, lacking effective data utilisation, faced numerous hurdles. Decisions were based on anecdotal evidence and assumptions, leading to inefficient resource allocation and missed opportunities. Without data-driven insights, the project struggled to address emerging issues promptly, resulting in slow progress and limited learning. In contrast, Project Y embraced the power of data. They implemented robust M&E systems, collecting and analysing data throughout the project lifecycle. Utilising real-time data, they made informed decisions, adjusted strategies swiftly, and capitalised on opportunities as they arose. This data-driven approach enhanced efficiency, identified areas for improvement, and ultimately yielded superior outcomes. The examples of Project X and Project Y underscore the critical role of data in development decision-making. Data is not merely a tool; it serves as a guiding compass, directing projects towards success, efficiency, and impact. In today's data-rich environment, neglecting its potential is akin to navigating a storm without a map, resulting in wasted resources, missed opportunities, and rigidity. Conversely, projects like Project Y, embracing data-driven decision-making, unlock boundless opportunities. It enables precise navigation of development challenges, prudent resource allocation, and strategic enhancement. In the development sector, it is imperative to fully harness the potential of data. Beyond mere reports and figures, data fuels learning, innovation, and tangible impact. By leveraging data-driven insights, development projects can optimise resource allocation, adapt swiftly to changes, seize opportunities, and achieve unparalleled success.

The quality and availability of data pose significant challenges to data-driven decision-making in various projects. Issues such as inadequate data collection methods and incomplete datasets can undermine the reliability and accuracy of insights derived from data analysis, resulting in flawed conclusions and ineffective decision-making. To tackle this challenge, projects need to prioritise data quality across the entire data lifecycle and implement strategies to enhance data availability. One crucial step is to establish rigorous data collection protocols. This involves setting standardised procedures and guidelines for data collection to minimise errors and inconsistencies. Clear objectives for data collection, identification of relevant variables, and selection of appropriate methods and tools are essential components of this process, reducing the risk of collecting inaccurate or irrelevant information. Another important strategy is to establish realistic timelines for data collection. Clear deadlines and milestones ensure that the necessary data is collected on time, defining the scope of data required, establishing protocols for collection and storage, and allocating sufficient resources and personnel for the process. Timelines should also accommodate potential delays or challenges, allowing for adjustments and contingencies to be made as needed.

Ensuring the accuracy and completeness of data is crucial for maintaining data quality. Inaccurate or incomplete data can significantly impact the validity of analysis and compromise decision-making processes. To address this challenge, projects need to implement measures to validate and verify the accuracy of collected data. One approach is to cross-reference data from multiple sources to identify discrepancies and ensure consistency. Additionally, conducting data audits and employing data validation techniques, such as outlier detection or data profiling, can help identify errors and anomalies. Investing in robust data validation and cleansing processes is also essential. Data validation involves checking data for errors and inconsistencies, while data cleansing focuses on correcting or removing these issues. Automated data validation and cleansing tools can streamline these processes, reduce manual effort, and enhance the overall quality of the data.

Data visualisation serves as a crucial tool for converting raw data into actionable insights. Many projects struggle with the challenge of making data understandable and accessible to decision-makers. In response, investing in strategies to facilitate comprehension and utilisation becomes imperative, with data visualisation emerging as a key approach. By presenting complex datasets visually through charts, graphs, and interactive dashboards, data visualisation simplifies information, making it easier for decision-makers to grasp patterns, trends, and relationships within the data. These visual representations uncover insights that might otherwise remain hidden in dense tables of data. Employing user-friendly data visualisation tools with customisable interfaces empowers decision-makers to explore and interact with data in real time, facilitating more informed and timely decision-making processes. More generally, such and other techniques of exploratory statistics, as pioneered by Tukey [243], can be very useful in inducing preliminary insights and testable hypotheses from data.

Empowering project stakeholders to interpret and utilise data effectively requires a focus on promoting data literacy within the team. Data literacy encompasses the skills needed to understand, analyse, and draw meaningful insights from data, including data interpretation, statistical analysis, data visualisation, and critical thinking. Investing in data literacy programmes can enhance team members' capabilities to leverage data in decision-making processes. These initiatives may involve providing training sessions, workshops, or access to online resources tailored to different team members' needs and skill levels. Creating collaborative learning environments where individuals can share knowledge and experiences fosters a culture of data literacy within the organisation, encouraging the exchange of ideas and best practices. Additionally, projects can appoint data champions within the team who possess advanced data skills and act as advocates for data-driven decision-making. These champions guide and support team members, facilitate data analysis workshops, and promote the use of data-driven approaches throughout the project. Their role is vital in nurturing a data-driven culture and empowering stakeholders to recognise data as a valuable asset.

In conclusion, it is imperative for development projects to fully embrace the power of data in decision-making. This entails going beyond traditional donor reporting and indicator tracking and acknowledging data as a catalyst for learning, innovation, and impact. By harnessing data-driven insights, projects can efficiently allocate resources, adapt strategies, and ultimately achieve greater success. It is essential for projects to invest in robust data infrastructure, cultivate a data-driven culture, and prioritise evidence-based decision-making. Let us embark on this transformative journey together, where data serves as the cornerstone of informed and impactful decision-making.

4 Medical Statistics

KEY POINTS

- Medical statistics is a vital part of research and providing insights for optimal decision-making in any industry

4.1 INTRODUCTION TO MEDICAL STATISTICS

4.1.1 History

The history of statistics spans centuries, with roots dating back to ancient civilisations such as Babylon, Egypt, and China, where rudimentary methods of data collection and analysis were employed for tasks such as taxation, census-taking, and astronomy. However, the formal development of statistical methods as a field of study began much later. In ancient Egypt, rudimentary methods of data collection were primarily used for administrative purposes, particularly for taxation, census-taking, and resource management. These methods were essential for governing the vast and populous civilisation along the Nile River. One of the earliest known methods of data collection in ancient Egypt was the use of census records. Census-taking allowed the government to keep track of population numbers, property ownership, and labour force demographics. Records of individuals and families were often kept on papyrus scrolls, with information such as names, ages, occupations, and property holdings recorded. Another common method of data collection in ancient Egypt was the use of inventories and records of goods and resources. These inventories were crucial for managing state-owned lands, granaries, warehouses, and other resources. They provided detailed accounts of agricultural produce, livestock, commodities, and other assets owned by the state or temples. Surveying techniques were also employed for various purposes, including land measurement, irrigation planning, and construction projects. Surveyors used basic tools such as ropes, rods, and plumb bobs to measure distances, delineate boundaries, and map out terrain features. Hieroglyphic inscriptions on monuments, temples, and tombs often contain numerical and statistical information, such as dates, measurements, and counts of people, animals, or objects. These inscriptions provide valuable insights into ancient Egyptian society, economy, and culture. Overall, while the methods of data collection in ancient Egypt were rudimentary compared to modern techniques, they played a crucial role in the organisation, administration, and governance of one of the world's earliest civilisations.

In ancient China, various rudimentary methods of data collection were utilised for administrative, economic, and scientific purposes. These methods were essential for governance, taxation, resource management, and the advancement of knowledge in areas such as astronomy and medicine. Similar to ancient Egypt, census-taking

DOI: 10.1201/9781003494737-4

was a common practice in ancient China. Dynastic rulers conducted periodic censuses to assess the population size, demographics, and distribution across regions. Census records provided valuable information for taxation, conscription, and general administration. Land surveys were conducted to measure and demarcate landholdings, assess agricultural productivity, and determine tax obligations. Surveyors used basic tools such as ropes, compasses, and measuring rods to delineate boundaries, calculate land area, and map out terrain features. Government officials maintained detailed administrative records to manage state affairs, including records of land ownership, taxation, court proceedings, and official decrees. These records were often inscribed on bamboo strips, wooden tablets, or silk scrolls. Ancient Chinese astronomers meticulously observed celestial phenomena, such as the movements of the sun, moon, stars, and planets. They recorded their observations in astronomical texts, which served as valuable data for calendar-making, astrology, and navigation. Traditional Chinese medicine practitioners recorded patient information, symptoms, diagnoses, and treatment outcomes in medical texts and manuscripts. These records contributed to the accumulation of medical knowledge and the development of herbal remedies, acupuncture techniques, and diagnostic methods. Merchants, traders, and government officials conducted economic surveys to assess market trends, commodity prices, trade routes, and commercial activities. These surveys provided insights into the dynamics of ancient Chinese economies and facilitated trade and commerce. Overall, the rudimentary methods of data collection in ancient China were diverse and multifaceted, reflecting the sophisticated administrative, economic, and scientific practices of the time. While these methods may seem primitive by modern standards, they were instrumental in shaping the governance, culture, and intellectual heritage of ancient Chinese civilisation.

In ancient Babylon, rudimentary methods of data collection were integral to administrative, economic, and legal functions, essential for governance, taxation, resource management, and trade. One primary method involved the use of cuneiform tablets, which featured characters inscribed on clay using a wedge-shaped stylus. These tablets served as the medium for recording various information, including economic transactions, legal contracts, administrative decrees, and astronomical observations. Archaeological findings of thousands of cuneiform tablets provide valuable insights into Babylonian society. Administrative records were meticulously maintained by government officials, encompassing details such as land ownership, taxation, census data, and court proceedings. These records, typically etched onto cuneiform tablets, constituted the official archives of the Babylonian state. Economic activities were documented through records kept by merchants, traders, and government authorities, covering commercial transactions, commodity prices, trade routes, and inventory management. These records facilitated trade regulation, tax assessment, and the management of the empire's commercial networks. Babylonian astronomers, renowned for their precision, meticulously recorded celestial observations on cuneiform tablets. These observations, ranging from the movements of celestial bodies to the development of calendars, provided a foundation for studying astronomy and predicting astronomical events. Legal documentation was another vital aspect, with scribes recording contracts, property deeds, marriage agreements, and other legal instruments on cuneiform tablets. These documents served as evidence of ownership, rights, and obligations, stored in temple or palace archives. Additionally, mathematical tablets showcased the Babylonians' mathematical prowess, featuring advanced techniques for calculating areas, volumes, interest rates, and other mathematical problems. These tablets were utilised in various practical applications, including land surveying, construction projects, and financial transactions. In summary, the rudimentary methods of data collection in ancient Babylon were diverse and sophisticated, reflecting the advanced civilisation and administrative infrastructure of the time. The use of cuneiform writing enabled the Babylonians to record and preserve vast amounts of information, laying the groundwork for written records and bureaucratic systems in subsequent civilisations.

The 17th and 18th centuries saw significant contributions to the field. In the 17th century, John Graunt conducted pioneering work in demography and developed methods for analysing mortality data. His most significant contribution was the publication of *Natural and Political Observations Made upon the Bills of Mortality*, which was one of the earliest studies of vital statistics and population demographics. Among his key findings, Graunt noted that mortality rates varied by age, sex, occupation, and geographical location. He also observed seasonal variations in mortality and identified specific diseases that were more prevalent in urban areas. Moreover, Graunt made important contributions to the understanding of life expectancy and population growth. One of Graunt's most influential achievements was the development of life tables, which provided estimates of life expectancy based on age-specific mortality rates. These life tables became foundational tools in demography and actuarial science, enabling researchers to quantify and analyse mortality patterns in populations. Graunt's work laid the groundwork for modern demography and epidemiology, establishing the importance of statistical analysis in understanding population dynamics and public health. His methods and insights continue to influence research in population studies, epidemiology, and public policy to this day. Later in the century, John Arbuthnot applied statistical methods to study the sex ratio at birth. The 18th century witnessed the development of probability theory by mathematicians such as Jacob Bernoulli and Pierre-Simon Laplace, laying the groundwork for statistical inference. John Arbuthnot, a Scottish mathematician and physician, used applied statistical methods to study the sex ratio at birth in the early 18th century. In his groundbreaking work titled "An argument for Divine Providence, taken from the constant Regularity observed in the Births of both Sexes," Arbuthnot examined baptism records in London to investigate patterns in the ratio of male to female births. Arbuthnot's analysis began with the observation that the sex ratio at birth appeared to be remarkably consistent over time, despite fluctuations in total birth numbers. He collected and analysed baptism records spanning multiple years to quantify this phenomenon. Using statistical techniques available at the time, Arbuthnot calculated the ratio of male to female births in different years and compared these ratios to expected values based on chance alone. He found that, on average, the number of male and female births was approximately equal, suggesting a natural balance in the sex ratio. Arbuthnot then employed inferential statistics to assess the significance of his findings. He performed hypothesis tests to determine whether the observed sex ratios deviated significantly from what would be expected by random chance. His analysis provided evidence against the hypothesis that observed deviations were due to random fluctuations alone, suggesting instead that there might be underlying biological or environmental factors at play. Overall, Arbuthnot's pioneering study of the sex ratio at birth demonstrated the application of statistical methods to investigate patterns in population data. His work laid the foundation for future research in demography, epidemiology, and genetics, and his methods paved the way for the development of modern statistical techniques for analysing demographic trends.

The 19th century marked a period of rapid advancement in statistics. Sir Francis Galton introduced correlation and regression analysis and made significant contributions to the study of heredity and eugenics. Sir Francis Galton, a British polymath, made significant contributions to the fields of statistics, psychology, genetics, and eugenics in the 19th and early 20th centuries. He introduced correlation and regression analysis as statistical techniques to quantify and analyse relationships between variables. Galton's interest in correlation and regression arose from his study of heredity and the inheritance of traits. He recognised the need for methods to measure and analyse the degree of association between different characteristics within families and across generations. Galton developed the concept of correlation to quantify the degree of linear relationship between two variables. He introduced the correlation coefficient as a measure of this relationship, which ranges from −1 to 1. A correlation coefficient of 1 indicates a perfect positive relationship, −1 indicates a perfect negative relationship, and 0 indicates no relationship. Galton's work laid the foundation for modern correlation analysis, which is widely used in fields such as psychology, sociology, economics, and biology. Building upon his work on correlation, Galton developed regression analysis as a method to predict the value of one variable based on the value of another. He introduced the concept of regression toward the mean, which describes the tendency for extreme values of one variable to be followed by less extreme values of the same variable in subsequent measurements. Galton's regression techniques provided a framework for understanding and predicting patterns of inheritance and helped establish the field of quantitative genetics. Galton's research on heredity and genetics led him to propose the concept of eugenics, which advocated for the improvement of human hereditary traits through selective breeding. While his work laid the groundwork for the field of genetics, his ideas on eugenics have been widely criticised and are now viewed as controversial and unethical. However, Galton's contributions to the study of heredity and the development of statistical techniques remain significant and have had a lasting impact on science and society.

Adolphe Quetelet pioneered the application of statistics to social phenomena, leading to the emergence of social statistics. Adolphe Quetelet, a Belgian astronomer, mathematician, and statistician, is widely recognised as a pioneer in applying statistics to social phenomena, laying the foundation for the emergence of social statistics. His contributions transformed the approach to collecting, analysing, and interpreting data in the study of human societies. Firstly, Quetelet developed and refined statistical methods tailored for analysing social data. He recognised the necessity of quantitative techniques to examine complex social phenomena like crime rates, population demographics, and social inequalities. His statistical techniques, including averages, standard deviations, and correlations, enabled systematic analysis of social trends and patterns. Secondly, he introduced the concept of "social physics" to describe his approach to understanding society. Quetelet viewed society as a complex system governed by laws and regularities, akin to the laws of physics that govern the natural world. He believed that applying statistical methods to social data could reveal underlying patterns and regularities in human behaviour. Furthermore, Quetelet conducted extensive empirical research on various social phenomena, ranging from crime and mortality rates to marriage and demographic trends. He meticulously collected and analysed large datasets from sources like government records and census data, providing valuable insights into the social determinants of behaviour and outcomes. One of Quetelet's most influential concepts was the idea of the "average man." He proposed that individual variations in human characteristics could be understood in relation to the statistical average of the population. This notion laid the groundwork for establishing normative standards and social norms in modern society. Quetelet's work had a profound impact on the development of social sciences such as sociology, criminology, demography, and economics. His emphasis on empirical research, quantitative analysis, and the application of statistical methods to social data paved the way for modern social science disciplines. Quetelet's legacy continues to shape research in the social sciences and remains relevant to contemporary debates on social issues and public policy.

Karl Pearson, often referred to as the father of modern statistics, developed many statistical techniques, including the chi-squared test and Pearson correlation coefficient. Karl Pearson, a prominent British mathematician and biostatistician, significantly advanced modern statistics by introducing several pivotal statistical techniques, including the chi-squared test and the Pearson correlation coefficient. His contributions reshaped the field, establishing foundational methods that continue to underpin contemporary statistical analysis. Pearson's development of the chi-squared test in 1900 marked a watershed moment in statistical hypothesis testing. This method, designed to assess the independence of categorical variables, has become a cornerstone of statistical analysis across diverse disciplines, ranging from biology to social sciences and economics. The chi-squared test's utility extends to applications such as contingency tables, goodness-of-fit tests, and the examination of categorical data patterns. In addition to the chi-squared test, Pearson introduced the Pearson correlation coefficient, also known as Pearson's r, in 1895. This coefficient quantifies the strength and direction of linear relationships between continuous variables, offering a fundamental tool for assessing associations in data. Widely adopted in fields like psychology, sociology, economics, and biology, the Pearson correlation coefficient enables researchers to evaluate relationships between variables with precision and clarity. Pearson's contributions extended beyond specific statistical tests to encompass broader theoretical advancements in probability theory. He made significant strides in understanding probability distributions, notably the normal distribution, and contributed to the development of the central limit theorem (CLM). These theoretical insights laid essential groundwork for inferential statistics and parameter estimation methods. Among Pearson's methodological innovations was the method of moments, a systematic approach to estimating parameters of probability distributions based on distribution moments. This method revolutionised parameter estimation techniques, offering a rigorous framework for analysing data, testing hypotheses, and fitting statistical model. Despite his significant contributions to statistics, Pearson's involvement in areas like biostatistics and eugenics has sparked controversy. While his statistical work in biostatistics advanced methods for analysing biological data, his support for eugenics—particularly the notion of selective breeding to improve human hereditary traits—has been widely criticised and remains a contentious aspect of his legacy. Karl Pearson's impact on modern statistics is profound and enduring. Through his development of key statistical techniques, theoretical insights, and methodological innovations, Pearson fundamentally shaped the discipline of statistics, providing researchers with powerful tools for analysing data, testing hypotheses, and advancing scientific knowledge.

In the early 20th century, the foundations of mathematical statistics were laid by statisticians such as Ronald Fisher, Jerzy Neyman, and Egon Pearson (son of Karl Pearson). Ronald Fisher, a British statistician, is celebrated for his work on statistical inference, experimental design, and the foundations of modern statistics. Fisher developed many fundamental concepts, including the notion of maximum likelihood estimation, analysis of variance (ANOVA), and the Fisherian significance testing framework. His work established the theoretical basis for statistical hypothesis testing and laid the groundwork for modern experimental design principles. Jerzy Neyman, a Polish mathematician, collaborated closely with Egon Pearson to develop the theory of statistical hypothesis testing and the Neyman–Pearson framework. Neyman's contributions to statistical theory were vast, including his development of optimal decision rules, confidence intervals (CIs), and the concept of Type I and Type II errors. His work provided a rigorous mathematical foundation for hypothesis testing and decision-making in statistics. Egon Pearson, the son of Karl Pearson, partnered with Neyman to advance statistical theory through their joint development of the Neyman–Pearson approach to hypothesis testing. Together, they introduced concepts such as the likelihood ratio test and the principle of optimality, which revolutionised statistical inference. Pearson also made significant contributions to the theory of estimation, including the method of moments and maximum likelihood estimation. Neyman and Pearson formalised hypothesis testing and introduced concepts such as Type I and Type II errors and power. The mid-20th century witnessed the emergence of computational statistics with the advent of computers. This led to the development of new statistical techniques and the widespread application of existing methods to fields such as economics, biology, medicine, and engineering. In recent decades, the field of statistics has continued to evolve rapidly with the advent of big data, machine learning (ML), and data science. These developments have led to new methods for analysing and interpreting large and complex datasets and have expanded the role of statistics in decision-making and scientific research.

4.1.2 Why Do Clinicians Need Medical Statistics?

Identifying the study question or hypothesis is a crucial initial step in both clinical practice and clinical research, as it sets the direction for further investigation and analysis. Physicians often encounter situations where their observations prompt questions about potential associations between exposures and specific diseases, or about patterns in healthcare delivery and outcomes. For instance, in clinical practice, a physician may notice that several patients taking a particular antihypertensive therapy develop pulmonary symptoms shortly after starting the medication. This observation could lead to a question about whether there is an association between the antihypertensive therapy and the onset of pulmonary symptoms. Similarly, a cardiologist reviewing medical literature may come across studies reporting higher initial costs for patients with cardiovascular diseases cared for by specialists compared to those cared for by non-specialists. This observation might prompt a question about whether there is a difference in overall costs between specialist and non-specialist care when considering both initial and follow-up costs. Formulating clear and testable hypotheses based on these observations is essential for conducting meaningful research. These hypotheses can then guide the selection of appropriate study designs and analytical methods. Understanding the study goals from the outset is also critical, as it helps focus the research efforts and ensures that the study addresses relevant questions and objectives.

To identify study goals effectively, several questions can be considered:

1. What specific research question or hypothesis arises from the observed phenomenon or an evidence synthesis?
2. What are the objectives of the study in relation to the identified question or hypothesis?
3. Are there specific outcomes or endpoints that the study aims to investigate?
4. What are the potential implications of the study findings for clinical practice, healthcare policy, or future research?
5. How will the study contribute to existing knowledge or fill gaps in understanding in the field?

4.2 EPIDEMIOLOGY MODEL DEVELOPMENT

Epidemiology is the study of how diseases spread and affect populations. It involves examining patterns, causes, and effects of health and disease conditions within populations. Epidemiologists gather and analyse data to understand the distribution and determinants of diseases, as well as to develop strategies for prevention and control. This field plays a crucial role in public health by identifying risk factors and assessing interventions. Similar to clinical findings and pathology, the epidemiology of a disease constitutes a fundamental aspect of its basic delineation. This field possesses its unique techniques for data gathering and interpretation, along with specialised jargon for technical terminology. Many introductory epidemiology courses often commence with an emphasis on person, place, and time—the fundamental components of descriptive epidemiology. However, in our experience, these introductory courses were often the last time significant training attention was devoted to descriptive epidemiology. This may have led to the misconception that descriptive epidemiology is immune to bias and holds less significance compared to causal epidemiology. Moreover, descriptive epidemiology may not receive much recognition in academia and could encounter challenges in securing funding. We believe this undermines the field and hampers progress towards the objectives of enhancing population health and promoting health equity. The outbreak of severe acute respiratory syndrome coronavirus 2 (SARS-CoV-2) and the subsequent coronavirus disease 2019 (COVID-19) pandemic have underscored the critical role of descriptive epidemiology in addressing serious public health crises. In this commentary, we advocate for a renewed emphasis on the importance of descriptive epidemiology in the epidemiology curriculum, using SARS-CoV-2 as a compelling example. We argue that the same framework for assessing error employed in aetiological research can be applied to descriptive research, enabling a focus on both systematic and random errors. Through the lens of the current pandemic, we highlight the distinctions between causal and descriptive epidemiology and identify areas where descriptive epidemiology can make a significant impact.

The objective of this concise chapter is to furnish an introductory guide to the epidemiological approach, encompassing its terminology and methodologies. We presume that readers already acknowledge the value of addressing epidemiological inquiries. This introduction will highlight several distinguishing features of the epidemiological approach. A fundamental aspect of epidemiology involves the assessment of disease outcomes relative to a population at risk. The population at risk encompasses individuals, whether healthy or afflicted, who would be classified as cases if they contracted the disease under investigation. For instance, if a general practitioner were monitoring the frequency of patients seeking consultation for hearing loss, the population at risk would consist of individuals on their patient roster (and possibly those of their colleagues) who might seek assistance for hearing issues if they experienced them. Patients who, despite remaining on the roster, had relocated to another area and therefore would not consult the same doctor would not be considered part of the population at risk.

Key terms used in epidemiology is as follows:

1. **Incidence** refers to the number of new cases of a disease or disorder occurring within a population over a specified period.
2. **Prevalence**, on the other hand, represents the number of existing cases of a disease within a population at a particular point in time.
3. The **cost of illness** typically includes expenditures on medical care, though ideally, it should encompass additional factors such as work-related expenses, educational costs, support services required by the medical condition, and the monetary value individuals would assign to avoiding health risks.
4. The **burden of disease** extends beyond the immediate costs of treatment and measures the overall impact of a disease on society. It can be quantified in terms of years of life lost to ill health or the disparity between total life expectancy and disability-adjusted life expectancy (DALY). DALY, or Disability-Adjusted Life Year, serves as a composite measure of population health. Each DALY represents one lost year of healthy life and is employed to gauge the disparity between the current health status of a population and an ideal scenario where everyone enjoys full health until old age.

The significance of considering the population at risk is underscored by two examples. In a study examining accidents involving hospital patients, it was observed that the majority occurred among the elderly, leading the authors to conclude that "patients aged 60 and over are more susceptible to accidents." Conversely, another study, centred on hang gliding accidents, proposed a ban on flying between 11 am and 3 pm, as 73% of accidents occurred during this period. Both of these studies drew conclusions based on the same logical fallacy—the floating numerator: the number of cases was not related to the appropriate "at risk" population. Had this been taken into account, the conclusions might have differed. Variances in the numbers of accidents among patients and hang gliders likely reflect, at least in part, differences in the populations at risk. Epidemiological inferences (regarding risk) cannot be derived solely from clinical data (pertaining to the number of individuals with the condition). Implicit in any epidemiological inquiry is the concept of a target population from which conclusions are to be drawn. On occasions, measurements can be conducted on the entire target population. For instance, in a study assessing the efficacy of dust control measures in British coal mines, data on all incident cases of coal workers' pneumoconiosis nationwide were available for analysis.

The pivotal role of statistical modelling in epidemiology and public health is beyond dispute. The methodologies and tools of biostatistics are extensively utilised to comprehend disease progression, unearth its causality, and assess the efficacy of novel prevention and control strategies. Through meticulous data analysis, epidemiology steers decision-making processes, informs health and healthcare policies, and aids in the planning and provision of healthcare services for both individual and population health management. The increasing accessibility of vast healthcare databases facilitates the generation of fresh evidence concerning the effectiveness of healthcare interventions, medications, and medical devices, as well as insights into population health and health disparities. Clinical decisions founded on evidence regarding the efficacy and safety of medical interventions can significantly contribute to extending individuals' lifespans, enhancing their quality of life, and fostering appropriateness. The current Special Issue is centred on statistical methods applied in epidemiology and public health. It is advisable to broaden the evidence-based approach to encompass a value-based perspective, incorporating considerations of quality and costs from both the demand and supply sides of healthcare services. Consequently, considerable attention has also been directed towards the evaluation and cost-effectiveness of medical procedures and services. This Special Issue comprises twelve articles contributed by research teams from various corners of the globe, including Belgium, Spain, China, Canada, Austria, Romania, and Italy. These studies delve into epidemiology, public health, and health promotion, proposing suitable statistical methodologies tailored.

Of the four articles within the realm of public health, two studies concentrate on disease prevention and health promotion strategies. To elaborate, Matranga et al. [244] aim to evaluate whether the adoption of healthy behaviours correlates significantly with psychological well-being among a cohort of students in the healthcare sector. Their study indicates that students inclined towards well-being perceive healthcare professionals as role models for both their patients and the general populace. Moreover, the positive association between a virtuous lifestyle and psychological well-being implies the cultivation, enhancement, and development of individual skills to counteract unhealthy behaviours. Fujihara et al.'s [245] study delves into health promotion targeting a different demographic. Employing a prospective cohort design involving older individuals in Japan, it investigates the potential correlation between community-level social capital and the incidence of Instrumental Activities of Daily Living (IADL) disability. Findings from this investigation suggest that community-based interventions aimed at fostering community-level social capital could aid in preventing IADL disability or reducing its occurrence. Within the domain of occupational epidemiology, the Special Issue encompasses two studies examining job exposures, with one utilising extensive databases. Specifically, Maniscalco et al. [246] explore the extent to which changes in employment contribute to cardiovascular, musculoskeletal, and neuropsychological health. Using a sample of 10,530 Belgian workers over a seven-year follow-up period, the authors identify an elevated risk of cardiovascular disease and psychosocial burden associated with job changes. Verso et al. [247] address the issue of professional exposures among students. They investigate the prevalence of latent tuberculosis infection (LTBI) among undergraduate and postgraduate healthcare students at the University of Palermo, Italy, and explore the occupational risk of infection among students. The study reveals a minimal number of LTBI cases, affirming the low incidence of LTBI among Italian students. Healthcare students engaged in internships are exposed to the occupational hazard of contracting tuberculosis, necessitating effective preventive measures in university hospitals. Regarding articles within this Special Issue focused on statistical methodology, particular attention is drawn to the study by Trivelli et al. [248] elucidating the spatiotemporal distribution of cardiovascular mortality, and the study by Maniscalco et al. [249] proposing a data-driven approach to investigate the interrelationships among health indicators. These contributions are significant within the context of environmental epidemiology and health promotion. Trivelli et al.'s study seeks to establish the spatiotemporal correlation between environmental exposure to particulate matter (PM2.5 $\mu g/m^3$) and the risk of cardiovascular mortality from 2010 to 2015 in an Italian region with high levels of air pollution and human activities, employing a Bayesian smoothed approach. Their model, explained meticulously by the authors, generates a smoothed map of relative risks (RRs) and accommodates extra-Poisson variability induced by the spatiotemporal data structure. The model incorporates two Gaussian random effects: one spatially unstructured (exchangeable or white noise in the lattice) and one spatially structured (conditional autoregressive based on a Gaussian–Markov random field in the lattice). Through the smoothed RR maps, the authors demonstrate that the distribution of estimated cardiovascular disease mortality risk remained consistent across the years between 2010 and 2015, identifying evidence of three high-risk clusters for cardiovascular diseases in the Lomellina area throughout the study period.

4.3 EPIDEMIOLOGY MODEL VALIDATION AND THEIR CONSTRAINTS IN MEDICINE

4.3.1 Descriptive Epidemiology

Descriptive epidemiology lacks a standardised definition. The Centres for Disease Control and Prevention's *Field Epidemiology Manual* defines it as the task that addresses questions about the occurrence of disease, injury, or environmental hazards: What? How much? When? Where? Among whom? The Dictionary of Epidemiology describes descriptive studies as focusing more on describing associations rather than analysing and explaining causal effects, involving general descriptions of the relationship between disease and basic characteristics like age, gender, ethnicity, occupation, social class, and geographic location.

We argue that descriptive epidemiology aims to characterise the distributions of health, disease, and harmful or beneficial exposures within a well-defined population as they currently exist, including any significant differences in distribution and whether these distributions are changing over time. It also seeks to contextualise this data within historical and sociological contexts, enabling an understanding of how these contexts contribute to patterns of disease and mortality. This differs from estimating the causal effects of these contexts because it does not involve estimating disease incidence absent the historical context.

When teaching causal inference, educators often utilise a framework to guide the approach. While outlining a comprehensive framework for descriptive inference exceeds the scope of this commentary, briefly, the initial step involves posing a clear question. In descriptive epidemiology, the target quantity of interest pertains to a characteristic of the true underlying disease distribution within a well-defined target population. Similar to, and perhaps more crucially than, causal inquiries, formulating effective descriptive questions necessitates grounding them in theory regarding the disease-generating process and delineating a precise target population. Effectively addressing descriptive questions necessitates appropriate sampling, valid measurement of the outcome and any covariates, and suitable data analysis. Unlike causal inference, which centres on a contrast (absolute or relative) of disease distributions among exposure groups, assuming that covariates related to sampling are not effect measure modifiers on the relevant scale allows the sampling mechanism to be disregarded. While there may be reasons not to prioritise representative sampling for causal inquiries, such as enhancing precision, representative sampling (or stratified sampling with a clear sampling frame) is crucial in descriptive epidemiology. To evaluate the validity of a sampling strategy, the target population must be clearly defined. As descriptive epidemiology extrapolates inferences from the sampled population to the target population (rather than across exposure groups), a lack of a sampling frame or failure to define the target population renders inference nearly impossible. Although sampling need not be representative (for instance, some groups might be oversampled, with subsequent reweighting of data to adjust for oversampling), enhancing comprehension of survey sampling methods could enhance descriptive epidemiologic studies. Arguably, coursework on survey sampling methods should constitute a core component of graduate epidemiology curricula. Early research on COVID-19 illustrates how a poorly devised sampling strategy can yield flawed inference in descriptive epidemiology. Initial serological surveys recruited volunteers interested in determining their SARS-CoV-2 antibody status. These surveys likely disproportionately sampled individuals who had exhibited COVID-19-like symptoms during the Spring of 2020, resulting in prevalence estimates considerably higher than those obtained from a random population sample. Measurement error, attributable to imperfect COVID-19 antibody tests and the prevalence of false positives outweighing true positives due to low COVID-19 prevalence, likely biased the results.

However, unlike causal analyses, confounding bias is not applicable in this context (indeed, confounding bias is not defined for this question).

Descriptive questions in epidemiology inquire about the distribution of a particular outcome within a single target population under the exposure conditions that population actually experienced (i.e., only factual exposures, not counterfactual exposures). However, posing a descriptive question does not preclude consideration of the exposure conditions and historical context that contributed to the disease distribution, which can inform study design. In the context of COVID-19, descriptive questions should be informed by various theories, including those related to infectious disease transmission dynamics (especially respiratory infections), social theories on the fundamental causes of disease distribution, life-course theory, and ecosocial theory, among others. For instance, we might inquire about the proportion of the population infected with COVID-19, examining sociodemographic factors, space, and time. To address this question, it is imperative to define the target population of interest, which could be a country, a state, a community, or a specific location where transmission is anticipated due to close contact, such as schools, restaurants, or churches. Subsequently, appropriate sampling techniques must be employed to ensure that risk estimates are representative of the population. Valid measurement techniques, such as COVID-19 tests with high sensitivity and specificity, are necessary to generate accurate estimates of population prevalence or incidence of the disease. Furthermore, it's essential to decide beforehand which characteristics to examine in the data presentation. This ensures the use of valid data collection measures and, in some cases, may require modifications to sampling techniques for populations with small numbers (e.g., oversampling methods). For example, recognising systemic racism as a fundamental determinant of health may lead to prioritising questions regarding the distribution of COVID-19 by race. Similarly, understanding the unequal valuation of different "essential" professions in society may lead to prioritising the examination of COVID-19 distribution by occupation. This is pertinent considering that workers in many essential occupations were required to work in close contact with others, increasing their risk of infection, yet often received unequal protection. For instance, while shortages of personal protective equipment for medical professionals garnered widespread attention, there was not a comparable national effort to provide high-quality masks to janitorial staff in healthcare settings or workers in grocery stores.

4.3.2 Biases in Descriptive Epidemiology

In the context of descriptive epidemiology, similar to causal epidemiology, addressing random error is imperative, ideally summarised through CIs around key parameters, whether they pertain to rates, proportions, or descriptive associational measures. Moreover, like causal epidemiology, descriptive epidemiology must confront bias and systematic error. However, some biases influencing descriptive epidemiology differ from those in causal investigations. One prominent example is confounding. Unlike in causal epidemiology where analytical adjustment is crucial for controlling confounding, in descriptive epidemiology, there are instances where analytical adjustment may be beneficial, but others where it is not. In our experience, students often fail to align their study design with their question and may either over-adjust or cite "unmeasured confounding" as a limitation in their descriptive studies.

Selection bias also warrants consideration and mitigation in descriptive epidemiology. Certain selection mechanisms may not introduce bias in estimating causal parameters (e.g., selecting all cases and a sample of the study base in case-control studies), but they may impede estimation of descriptive parameters like risks or rates. Measurement error constitutes another source of bias in descriptive epidemiology. Employing well-validated tools and measurement techniques with high sensitivity and specificity to measure crucial study variables, particularly the outcome and any stratifying variables, is critical for producing valid results conducive to robust inferences and effective public health action. Although less attention has been directed towards this area, techniques like quantitative bias analysis can be applied to descriptive epidemiology to address poor measurement. Additionally, nonrandomly missing data on the outcome or key covariates used to stratify risk can also impact descriptive epidemiology.

Descriptive epidemiology stands as a cornerstone of public health, playing a pivotal role in ensuring that health and wellness are accessible to all individuals. History and epidemiologic theory, albeit often afforded limited attention in epidemiology curricula, underscore the significance of understanding the current distributions of health and illness as the outcome of decades or even centuries of injustices and inequities. Frameworks such as critical race public health praxis illuminate how existing health disparities are deeply rooted in historical and systemic injustices. The ongoing SARS-CoV-2 pandemic further exacerbates existing inequities, amplifying disparities observed in the past, both in the US and globally. Poorly conducted descriptive epidemiology, stemming from uncritical or unexamined decisions regarding data collection, population classification, or the variables included in analyses, has the potential to perpetuate narratives and power dynamics that underpin these inequities. Conversely, well-executed, theoretically grounded descriptive epidemiology empowers us with tools and evidence to actively dismantle these structures. This necessitates intentional formulation of research questions and study designs, enabling us to challenge and transform prevailing narratives and power structures, thereby fostering a more equitable and just society.

When embarking on a descriptive study, the primary question to address is, "What is the objective of this description, and does it necessitate adjustment or stratification on additional variables?" Descriptive analyses frequently involve stratifying results by relevant population characteristics to evaluate heterogeneity across and within groups, aiding in resource allocation or identifying high-risk populations. Stratification serves as a vital tool in descriptive epidemiology, enabling the identification of disparities between groups or regions. However, our choices regarding which variables to consider as strata should be guided by theory and contextual factors. Similar to the examination of effect heterogeneity, indiscriminate stratification by all available covariates risks yielding spurious association. There are compelling reasons why descriptive statistics are sometimes more informative after adjustment for certain variables, such as age, known to influence the outcome and exhibiting differential distributions across populations. Such adjustment can facilitate hypotheses regarding variations within or across populations, enabling the identification of disparities in disease distribution that might otherwise be obscured. For instance, in investigating differences in COVID mortality between doctors and nurses, adjusting for age differences allows for a focus on occupational hazards rather than age-related risks. However, in certain scenarios, age adjustment may hinder appropriate resource allocation. This is because adjusting for a significant difference, such as age, between two populations, one of which is generally older than the other, may obscure the higher disease burden in the older population, erroneously suggesting similar disease rates and resource requirements for both groups.

As an illustration, early assessments of COVID mortality by race and ethnicity erroneously adjusted for geography, thereby masking disparities attributable to systemic racism. In some instances, adjusting for location obscures the impact of policies (e.g., redlining) that influenced residential patterns and other health determinants (e.g., access to healthy foods and exposure to air pollution). Consequently, inappropriate adjustment hinders the recognition of the extent of disparities. It's worth noting that in a causal context, location could function as a confounder or mediator, depending on the circumstances. However, in descriptive epidemiology, this distinction may be less pertinent to the decision of whether to adjust; rather, the question of interest should guide this determination. In essence, comprehending how adjustment alters results and, crucially, the underlying question, is vital in guiding the decision to adjust in descriptive epidemiology. Adjustment should not be undertaken without a clear rationale for its necessity and a comprehensive understanding of its implications for result interpretation. It's imperative to move away from equating "adjustment" solely with "confounder control," which implies a causal inquiry. A thorough grasp of the utility of adjustment necessitates a nuanced approach that considers the specific objectives of the descriptive question at hand.

Observing disparities in disease distribution across populations often sparks causal hypotheses, blurring the distinction between descriptive and causal epidemiology. While there exists a continuum between the two, the prioritisation of causal epidemiology over descriptive epidemiology in training programmes is a common occurrence. Even reputable sources like the Centres for Disease Control and Prevention tend to swiftly transition from describing descriptive epidemiology as conveying the extent and pattern of a public health issue to implying it merely serves as a stepping stone towards causal inference. However, descriptive epidemiology holds intrinsic value beyond hypothesis generation. The confusion between causal and descriptive epidemiology may stem from a lack of clear differentiation between types of questions and the separation of analytical methods from specific research inquiries. The literature delineating various analytical goals and their corresponding strategies is scant but growing. Many textbooks discuss adjustment solely in the context of confounder control, overlooking other potential goals of statistical adjustment. A structured approach that begins with identifying the type of question, followed by formulating a good question within that type, and finally selecting appropriate methods is essential for producing actionable public health insights. A lack of a clear analytical plan for descriptive epidemiology can lead to flawed execution and interpretation, falling somewhere between descriptive and causal approaches. Such studies often masquerade as "risk-factor" analyses, contributing to further confusion.

For instance, media coverage of a preprint examining "risk factors" for COVID-19-related death erroneously interpreted an association between smoking and COVID-19 mortality as "protective," despite adjustment for causal intermediates and potential colliders. This highlights the importance of clarity in epidemiologic research goals, cautious interpretation of descriptive studies, clear communication of results, and the recognition of the value of descriptive epidemiology in providing meaningful insights.

PURPOSES OF DESCRIPTIVE EPIDEMIOLOGY

1. Provides a systematic approach for breaking down a health problem into its constituent elements.
2. Ensures comprehensive understanding of the fundamental dimensions of a health problem.
3. Identifies populations that are at heightened risk for the health issue under investigation.
4. Offers timely information to decision-makers, the media, the public, and other stakeholders regarding ongoing investigations.
5. Supports decision-making processes for initiating or adjusting control and prevention measure.
6. Tracks the progress of control and prevention initiatives.
7. Facilitates the generation of testable hypotheses concerning the aetiology, mode of exposure, effectiveness of control measures, and other aspects of the health problem.
8. Validates the eventual identification of causes or risk factors.

Organising descriptive data into tables, graphs, diagrams, maps, or charts offers a swift, objective, and cohesive understanding of the data. Whether these visual aids assist investigators in comprehending the data or facilitate the explanation of findings in reports or presentations to audiences, their arrangement should swiftly highlight the main patterns and any deviations from those patterns. Tables, graphs, maps, and charts share four common elements: a title, data, footnotes, and explanatory text. Throughout this chapter, additional guidelines for creating these data displays will be provided whenever a specific type of data display is introduced.

Rates adjust raw counts to account for differences in population sizes or study periods. For instance, dividing incidence by an appropriate estimate of the population results in various forms of incidence rates. Similarly, prevalent case counts divided by the population from which they originated yield a proportion known as prevalence. Ideally, the disease or health event being counted should stem from the specific population used as the denominator. However, there are situations where the population is unknown, difficult to ascertain, or unsuitable. For example, maternal mortality ratios and infant mortality rates use births in a given calendar year as the denominator for deaths in the same year, even though the deaths may be linked to births from the previous year. When evaluating the adverse effects of a vaccine or pharmaceutical, total doses distributed can serve as the denominator. Another instance is injuries from snowmobile use, which have been calculated both as ratios per registered vehicle and per crash incident. Returning to counts, expected case counts for a population can be computed by multiplying an expected rate (e.g., historical counts, enhanced surveillance, or outputs from prevention and control programs) or a target rate by the total population. This expected or target case count is then adjusted for the population and can be compared with the actual observed case counts.

Diseases or unhealthy conditions can also be assessed on a continuous scale rather than through direct counting, such as body mass index (BMI), blood lead level, blood haemoglobin, blood sugar, or blood pressure. Empirical cut-off points, like BMI $\geq$26 for overweight, can be used for classification, allowing for counts and subsequent rate calculation. However, individuals' measurements may fluctuate above or below these cut-off values. To calculate incidence, caution is necessary to prevent counting the same person multiple times with fluctuations above or below the cut-off point. This fluctuation amplifies statistical error for the prevalence estimate. A more precise approach involves computing the average and dispersion of individual measurements. These averages and dispersions can then be compared among groups, against expected values, or against target values. They can be displayed in a table or visualised using a box-and-whisker plot, which indicates the median, mean, interquartile range, and outliers.

4.3.3 Time

Time plays a crucial role in interpreting epidemiological data, as the initial exposure to a causative agent must precede the onset of disease. Typically, disease or health condition onset time is the preferred statistic for studying time patterns, although onset data may not always be available. Surveillance systems may only have report dates or other onset surrogates, and for slowly developing health conditions, a discernible onset may not exist. Conversely, injuries and acute poisonings have instantaneous and obvious onsets. The precision of exposure times also varies. Acute infections, poisonings, and injuries often have precise exposure times to different suspected agents. In contrast, chronic diseases may involve exposures spanning decades before the onset of overt disease. Other relevant events, such as underlying environmental conditions, changes in health policy, and implementation of control and prevention measures, supplement the chronological framework of a health problem. Linking disease with these events in time facilitates the calculation of key characteristics of the disease or health event. Knowing both the time of onset and the time of presumed exposure allows for the estimation of the incubation or latency period. When the causative agent is unknown, the time interval between presumed exposures and symptom onset aids in hypothesising the aetiology. For instance, the consistent time interval between rotavirus vaccination and intussusception onset helped form the hypothesis that the vaccine precipitated the disease. Similarly, knowing the incubation period enables the estimation of a time window of exposure and identification of exposures to potential causative agents during that window.

KEY POINTS

- When creating graphs using computer graphics programs like Microsoft Excel, it's important to select the appropriate graph type. For numerically scaled line graphs, use the "scatter" option instead of the "line" option.
- Adhere to mathematical principles when plotting data and scaling axes. On an arithmetic scale, equal numerical units should be represented with equal distances on an axis. Similarly, when using transformed data (e.g., logarithmic, normalised, or ranked), equal units of the transformed data should be represented with equal distances on the axis.
- Dependent variables should be represented on the vertical scale, while independent variables should be on the horizontal scale.
- Consider alternatives to joining data points with a line, such as using data markers only, a trend line of best fit, or a moving average line. Aspect ratios of approximately 2:1 work well, as extreme aspect ratios can distort data.
- Scale the graph to fill the data space and improve resolution. If excluding the zero level improves resolution, it's acceptable, but note this for the reader. However, if the zero level is integral to the data, it should be included.
- Use graphic designs that reveal the data from a broad overview to fine detail. When comparing two lines, plot their difference directly. Use visually prominent symbols to plot and emphasise the data, ensuring that overlapping plotting symbols are distinguishable.
- When plotting two or more data sets in the same space, design point markers and lines for visual discrimination and differentiate them with labels, legends, or keys. Consider using separate panels for different strata on the same graph to avoid clutter and maintain undistorted comparisons.
- When comparing two graphs of the same dependent variable, use scaling that improves comparison and resolution. Clearly indicate scale divisions and scaling units, and minimise frames, gridlines, and tick marks to avoid interfering with the data. Keep keys, legends, markers, and other annotations outside the data space.
- Proofread your graphs to ensure accuracy and clarity.
- Contact diagrams and epidemic curves are valuable tools in epidemiology for visualising and understanding the spread of diseases and health events over time. Contact diagrams could depict person-to-person transmission. Different markers are used to indicate various groups exposed or at risk, providing insight into the dynamics of disease spread within a population.
- Epidemic curves, on the other hand, are histograms that display the frequency distributions of incident cases of disease or health events

across time intervals. These curves often reveal patterns that can help identify likely modes of transmission. By plotting cases over time, epidemiologists can diagnose certain kinds of epidemic situations, such as outbreaks or clusters.

A propagated pattern typically occurs with communicable diseases that spread directly between individuals or through an intermediate vehicle. Person-to-person transmission can result in either a propagated epidemic, as seen in diseases like shigellosis, influenza, or COVID-19, or an extended point-source outbreak. When the source case is unknown, the first detected cases emerged on the 13th day of the month, followed by subsequent cases appearing at approximately three-day intervals. In such scenarios, the reproductive number (*R* value) will typically exceed one, and the shape of the epidemic curve is influenced by factors such as the disease's incubation period and environmental conditions favouring transmission. Although they often exhibit an abrupt onset, new cases emerge over a longer duration than the possible incubation period. On the other hand, propagated outbreaks are spread from person to person, potentially lasting longer than common source epidemics and resulting in multiple waves of infection if secondary and tertiary cases occur. While the classic propagated epidemic curve features a series of progressively taller peaks, each separated by an incubation period, real-life epidemic curves may vary in appearance.

Controlling an epidemic requires a multifaceted approach, tailored to the specific causative organism, source, exposure, and route of transmission. Primary prevention focuses on preventing new cases and involves interrupting transmission, protecting susceptible individuals, contact tracing, and controlling vectors or animal reservoirs. Swift implementation of these measures during a propagated epidemic can lower the reproductive rate (*R*) below 1, leading to a reduction in new cases and eventually stopping the outbreak. Various measures contribute to primary prevention, such as ensuring clean water supplies and proper sanitation to prevent cholera spread, controlling mosquito populations to reduce malaria transmission, immunising children against measles, and promoting safe sexual practices to reduce HIV transmission. Vaccines play a crucial role in protecting susceptible individuals, but their efficacy relies on high population immunisation coverage and may diminish if the virus mutates to become resistant. Secondary and tertiary prevention aim to halt transmission from established cases and carriers and treat infected individuals and animal reservoirs to prevent further spread. Control strategies may involve isolating affected areas, quarantining cases, implementing social distancing measures, and addressing the source and mode of transmission through various interventions like water source cleaning and vector control.

Characteristics of propagated epidemic curves include the following:

1. **Multiple Generation Periods**: Propagated epidemic curves encompass multiple generation periods for the causative agent, reflecting person-to-person transmission over time.

2. **Gradually Increasing Upslope**: They typically start with a single or limited number of cases and exhibit a gradually increasing upslope as the outbreak progresses, indicating ongoing transmission.
3. **Periodicity**: During the initial stages of the outbreak, a periodicity equivalent to the generation period for the agent might be evident, reflecting the interval between successive waves of transmission.
4. **Rapid Downslope**: After reaching a peak, the curve experiences a rapid downslope due to the exhaustion of susceptible hosts, leading to a decline in new cases as transmission diminishes.

4.4 EPIDEMIOLOGY MODELS FOR DATA AUGMENTATION

Stochastic epidemic models (SEMs) serve as foundational tools for analysing the transmission of infectious diseases. These models depict the progression of an epidemic by tracking the disease trajectories of individuals as they move through various stages of infection. The incorporation of stochasticity into epidemic modelling becomes crucial when disease prevalence is low or when dealing with smaller population sizes. In such scenarios, the random fluctuations in the epidemic's course significantly impact the likelihood and severity of outbreaks, as well as the insights drawn regarding its dynamics [250,251]. Furthermore, certain inquiries, such as determining the distribution of outbreak sizes or assessing the likelihood of disease eradication, cannot be adequately addressed using deterministic approaches [252]. Fitting a SEM proves challenging due to the limited availability of epidemiological data, which are often collected at discrete intervals, typically focusing on specific aspects of the disease, such as infections, and frequently capturing only a fraction of total cases. Comprehensive individual-level data, detailing the precise timings of transitions between disease states, are frequently unavailable [253]. Attempting to fit SEMs in the absence of such complete individual-level data presents a complex latent variable problem, as analytically integrating over the missing data is usually infeasible [254]. Consequently, the likelihood function based on observed data for a SEM becomes computationally intractable.

The discrete-time likelihoods described in Rampey et al. [255] and Yang et al. [256] rely solely on observed data, encompassing symptom onset dates, laboratory test results, and household structure (indicating which individuals reside in which households). These likelihoods entail summing probability components over the latent period, a characteristic often encountered in likelihoods based solely on observed data. Such intricate structures may pose challenges for standard analyses or hinder extension by alternative methods [257]. Moreover, in scenarios where data are sparse due to rare incidences and/or a multicovariate structure, iterative estimation procedures, such as the Newton–Raphson algorithm, relying solely on observed data, may exhibit sensitivity to initial estimates when locating maximum likelihood estimates. This sensitivity is also acknowledged by Yang et al. [256]. To address computational challenges associated with classical likelihood methods, data augmentation (DA) has emerged as a popular technique, as likelihood functions conditional on unobserved variables tend to be simpler [258,259]. In the context of a transmission model for infectious diseases, a fundamental aspect involves the transmission probability given contact between an infective person and a susceptible person, where contact may be defined in various ways, such as residing in the same household for one day. However, the outcome of each contact, whether infection or escape, is generally unobservable since individuals may have multiple contacts before infection occurs. In this chapter, we enhance the discrete-time likelihood proposed by Yang et al. by augmenting observed symptom onset data with the unobserved transmission outcome for each contact [256]. This augmented likelihood simplifies the form compared to one based solely on observed data and can be maximised using the EM algorithm.

Various approaches have been employed to fit SEMs with intractable likelihoods, typically categorised into four groups: martingale methods, approximation methods, simulation-based methods, and DA methods [253]. Martingale methods utilise estimating equations grounded in martingales to estimate the parameters of interest based on counting processes within the SEM, such as infections and recoveries. However, implementing these methods for SEMs with complex dynamics and partially observed count data proves challenging. Approximation methods involve replacing the SEM with a simpler model, often a Markov jump process, to render the likelihood more manageable. For example, Roberts and Stramer [260] and Cauchemez and Ferguson [261] employ diffusion processes as approximations, while Jandarov et al. [262] utilise a Gaussian process approximation of a related gravity model. Discretising time and constructing transition models for population flow between compartments at successive times represent typical simplifications, which, although computationally efficient, may not always be appropriate due to underlying assumptions. Simulation-based methods utilise the SEM to generate epidemic paths for inference, encompassing approximate Bayesian computation methods, pseudo-marginal methods, and sequential Monte Carlo methods. While these methods have been effective for fitting complex models, they are computationally demanding and prone to known pitfalls. Traditional agent-based DA methods, pioneered by O'Neill and Roberts [263] and Gibson and Renshaw [264], aim to obtain a tractable complete data likelihood by targeting the joint posterior distribution of missing data and model parameters. The "agent-based" nature of augmentation refers to introducing subject-level disease histories, rather than population-level epidemic paths, as latent variables in the model. This approach offers the advantage of incorporating household structure and subject-level covariates into the model. Recent developments in DA methods for SEMs, such as those by Pooley et al. [265], and Shestopaloff and Neal [266], have presented promising techniques applicable to epidemic count data. However, these methods may sacrifice the flexibility of agent-based DA, and in some cases, have not yet been applied to SEMs. In the study by Fintzi et al., a framework utilising agent-based DA Markov chain Monte Carlo (MCMC) has been proposed for fitting SEMs to time-series count data [267]. Fintzi et al. [267] demonstrated a manageable complete data likelihood by augmenting the data with subject-level disease histories. Their approach involves MCMC targeting the joint posterior distribution of the latent epidemic process and model parameters through alternating updates of subject-level paths and model parameters. Fintzi and colleagues suggested generating each new subject path, conditioned on the data, using a time-inhomogeneous continuous-time Markov chain with rates determined by the disease histories of other individuals [267]. These data-driven path proposals yield highly efficient perturbations to the latent epidemic path, enabling the analysis of epidemic count data even in the absence of subject-level information. In contrast, traditional agent-based DA MCMC algorithms rely on data-agnostic trans-dimensional proposals and encounter convergence issues as the amount of missing information increases. The necessity of subject-level data has thus far limited the applicability of classical DA methods in numerous scenarios. Consequently, the introduced MCMC algorithm facilitates exact Bayesian inference for SEMs fitted to datasets previously challenging to analyse with existing agent-based DA methods. Moreover, the algorithm's versatility extends beyond specific SEM dynamics or measurement processes, requiring only minimal modifications to apply to a wide range of SEMs. Fintzi et al. [267] introduced a Bayesian DA algorithm within the framework of fitting a stochastic Susceptible-Infected-Recovered (SIR) model to binomially distributed prevalence counts. Additionally, we utilise our algorithm to fit Susceptible-Exposed-Infected-Recovered (SEIR) and Susceptible-Infected-Recovered-Susceptible (SIRS) models. The SIR model delineates the progression of an epidemic by tracking the disease trajectories of individuals as they traverse three states: susceptible (S), infected/infectious (I), and recovered (R). In a basic SIR framework, each individual transitions to the infectious state immediately upon infection and gains lifelong immunity upon recovery. To simplify, we assume a closed population with homogeneous mixing and no external force of infection. Consequently, the epidemic terminates once the pool of infectious individuals is exhausted.

4.5 SYNTHETIC DATA DEVELOPMENT AND MODELLING

Data-driven approaches based on artificial intelligence (AI), ML, and statistics offer potent means to swiftly address these issues. Each day, millions of individuals generate medical data records, furnishing a wealth of data for the development of healthcare solutions and the advancement of new research. For instance, electronic medical records (EMRs) hold the potential to augment patient care, curtail expenses, expedite the identification of eligible patients, and refine research efficiency. Moreover, healthcare data can streamline clinical research procedures and enhance data precision. Within healthcare, data is also harnessed for disease progression modelling, risk assessment, and myriad other applications. The application of supervised and unsupervised ML on public health data has proven instrumental in outbreak detection, predicting hospital readmissions, discerning feature associations with outcomes, and more. Nevertheless, despite the abundant availability of healthcare data, endeavours in this field are often hampered by restricted access to healthcare records. Such records are safeguarded by privacy regulations such as the Health Insurance Portability and Accountability Act in the US and the General Data Protection Regulations in the European Union. Although these laws permit access to de-identified information, the process of de-identification can impede research, incurring substantial costs and potentially leading to severe penalties in the event of data breaches. Furthermore, traditional de-identification methods, such as age binning, may entail the loss of information, thereby compromising the utility of data for certain tasks.

Synthetic data pertains to any data not acquired through direct measurement and may be relevant to a particular scenario. In the realm of statistics, particularly population statistics, synthetic data were previously predominantly perceived as larger datasets resulting from the amalgamation of two or more smaller datasets. However, contemporary synthetic data can also be generated in instances where real data is unavailable or for specific scenarios absent in the original data. Synthetic data has found extensive utility in computational sciences and ML, serving as a method for privacy safeguarding.

Numerous research articles based on EMRs lack accompanying data, impeding future research and validation efforts. The release of synthetic healthcare data presents a viable solution to furnish timely access to EMR data while safeguarding patient privacy. Health disparities have long been a pervasive issue. The National Institute of Health (NIH) has established policies aimed at fostering more inclusive randomised clinical trials to ensure that trial outcomes encompass diverse subgroups. To foster the development of equitable analysis and unbiased predictive models, it is imperative that synthetic versions of healthcare data accurately represent diverse minority subgroups. Drawing inspiration from fairness research in ML, this challenge is referred to as the "synthetic data fairness problem." Persistent health disparities among different demographics pose ongoing challenges. Inadequate representation of subgroups in synthetic data could lead to inaccurate analyses, resulting in conclusions and predictive models that fail to generalise to real-world data. In EMRs, health outcomes are often influenced by covariates such as age, gender, race, obesity, and comorbidities. In the context of ML fairness, these covariates are commonly termed "protected attributes." To achieve "fairness," a synthetic data model must ensure that the synthetic data accurately mirror the real data across various subgroups defined by these covariates or protected attributes. For instance, in the American Time Usage Study (ATUS), an individual's average sleep duration is influenced by their age. Consequently, the synthetic data must accurately reflect the distribution of subjects across different age groups and faithfully represent sleep patterns within each subgroup.

Synthetic healthcare data proves valuable when it achieves three key objectives: (1) safeguarding patient privacy, (2) demonstrating high utility by producing high-quality ML models, and (3) closely resembling the real data from which it originates. While this approach has shown effectiveness at a general level, exploration into covariates has been limited. In our recent research, we delved into covariate analysis for evaluating synthetic data using time-series metrics to underscore the significance of covariate-level resemblance. This prompts the question: Does a given synthetic generation method exhibit fairness towards subgroups within real data, or does it exhibit discrimination against certain protected classes to strike a balance between these aspects of synthetic data generation? We contend that while utility, resemblance, and privacy are pivotal in synthetic data generation, they must be accompanied by (4) fairness measures tailored to each aspect. Resemblance in synthetic data generation gauges the degree of similarity between the real data (used to train the synthetic data generator) and the synthetic data produced by the model. One might argue for making synthetic data closely resemble the available real data; however, this could lead to overfitting and breach the imperative of preserving privacy by replicating examples too faithfully. Instead, the focus should be on aligning the distribution of synthetic data with that of the underlying real data, rather than replicating exact training samples. Thus, there exists a trade-off between resemblance (of synthetic data to real training data) and privacy, akin to the trade-off between fit and robustness. Yet, evading overfitting merely constitutes a prerequisite for achieving privacy-preserving data; additional measures are necessary to obfuscate data and safeguard privacy, which can, in turn, impact utility.

A synthetic data generation method must capture the inherent trends and patterns in real data while simultaneously safeguarding the privacy of subjects across all subgroups. To achieve this resemblance, it's imperative to ensure that synthetically generated data don't deviate significantly from real data to the extent that it discriminates against certain protected subgroups. This necessitates the application of innovative fairness metrics that gauge equity in synthetic data resemblance. We propose assessing this fairness in resemblance through representational rates and time-series resemblance analysis at the covariate level. It's crucial to delineate the disparity between the definitions of "resemblance" and "representation" in the context of this work. "Resemblance," as previously mentioned, pertains to how closely synthetic data align with real data, whereas "representation" is employed in the fairness context, indicating how adequately or inadequately a given subgroup is represented based on fairness metrics. Fairness should permeate every facet of synthetic health data and be assessed for each generation method. We advocate for incorporating fairness evaluation at every step of synthetic health data generation. Hence, in this chapter, we introduce metrics for "fairness in resemblance" of synthetic data with real data. Additionally, we touch upon "fairness in utility" and "fairness in privacy," although comprehensive examination of these aspects is deferred as potential future work.

Fairness analysis of synthetically generated healthcare data is indispensable for maintaining the utility of synthetic data utilised in lieu of real medical data. Conducting fairness metrics at the covariate level offers a thorough comprehension of this generated synthetic data, facilitating a clearer explanation of its utility and resemblance. This chapter sheds light on the bias present in published synthetic datasets towards certain protected attributes through three case studies of healthcare datasets. Undoubtedly, the issue of fairness is multifaceted, with numerous existing definitions of fairness underscored by the constraint that not all can be simultaneously satisfied. Consequently, we present two methods for measuring synthetic healthcare fairness, recognising the limitation that these are not exhaustive metrics addressing all definitions of fairness nor do they comprehensively encapsulate the myriad measures of similarity between real and synthetic data. We propose this chapter as a stepping stone for future research in this domain, potentially devising more robust metrics for evaluating fairness in synthetic healthcare data and integrating them as a routine component of synthetic data assessment.

There could be metrics for evaluating fairness in synthetic healthcare data, providing insights at the covariate level. Subsequently, showing the disparities. There is evidence to suggest that synthetic data may underscore the imperative for examining covariate-level fairness in synthetically generated healthcare data. Synthetic data generation involves crafting realistic-looking data through specific methodologies.

In the healthcare domain, the generation of synthetic data necessitates maintaining the privacy of patients in the original data while achieving a high level of utility and resemblance. Generative adversarial networks (GANs) such as medGAN and HealthGAN offer promising solutions that obviate the need for real health data once fully trained. HealthGAN, in particular, purports to balance utility, resemblance, and fairness, as demonstrated in recent research catering to categorical, binary, and temporal data. Thus, we concentrate on analysing several available synthetic datasets generated by HealthGAN for this study. ML models trained on biased data have exhibited discriminatory behaviour based on factors such as gender and race. Recently, synthetic data generation methods have begun to incorporate fairness as a crucial aspect of equitable data generation. Differentially private GANs aim to uphold privacy and mitigate fairness concerns but have shown to compromise synthetic image quality and utility. Other approaches have assessed synthetic data fairness by training models on the data and calculating fairness metrics like demographic parity and equality of odds, revealing disparities and diminished fairness outcomes. Group fairness metrics such as parity gap and recall gap have also been scrutinised on downstream models generated from synthetic data. The authors of Fairness GAN utilised error rate, demographic parity, and equality of opportunity as fairness metrics, while Equalised Odds has been employed for learning fairness in differentially private settings. However, research on the fairness of subgroups of covariates remains limited, suggesting a potential area for further exploration in synthetic health data generation.

To assess inequities in healthcare data, researchers have devised metrics to compare the observed enrolment rates of protected subgroups against a reference group, such as enrolment fractions, or to gauge the proportion of the target population eligible for trials, exemplified by the GIST metric. Our recent work has contributed theorems for establishing scalable randomised controlled trial (RCT) versions of ML metrics, which quantify the equities of protected subgroups concerning any community or population-level targets. The term "fairness" in the context of synthetic health data generation encompasses various definitions found in the ML literature, each accompanied by corresponding metrics. However, according to the impossibility theorem of fairness, not all metrics can be satisfied simultaneously, as each entails specific trade-offs. In the realm of synthetic health data generation, "fairness" is defined as the generation method's ability to accurately capture the distribution of real data subgroups across all protected attributes. In essence, a fair synthetic health data generation method would yield similar subgroup statistics and trends, resulting in real and synthetic data distributions that closely match across all protected subgroups. Even if quality metrics applied to the entire synthetic dataset are satisfactory, a dataset could still be deemed unfair if it inadequately represents the distribution of small protected subgroups, despite accurately representing the distribution of a majority subgroup. Therefore, an "equity metric" should quantify any undesirable bias in synthetic data compared to real data. In this context, we define the equity metric in terms of "disparate impact," which measures the bias in two different groups receiving significantly different outcomes, as it has been the focus of numerous recent publications. For RCTs, we have previously devised a set of metrics to gauge RCT representativeness using representational rates based on ML fairness metrics. In ML, disparate impact is employed to measure the fairness of a trained classification function. It evaluates each data point's influence on the outcome and helps ascertain whether certain groups are disproportionately affected by the model's predictions. This approach was discussed by Qi and colleagues [268] and Bellamy et al. [269]:

$$X \in R^d.$$

With,

$$Y \in \{0,1\}c.$$

That could have a prediction label as below to develop a prediction label:

$$Y' \in \{0,1\}.$$

The assumption is as follows:

$$Y=1$$

The desired positive outcome in this context remains consistent with previous works. Protected attributes encompass any subset of the *d* attributes capable of distinguishing the population into distinct groups, where parity in outcomes is sought. A protected subgroup is delineated by one or more protected attributes through a binary membership function:

$$g(x).$$

If

$$g(x) = 1,$$

where the x is within the protected subgroup,

$$g(x)=0.$$

This means *x* could be redefined. In ML fairness, disparate impact evaluates the positive prediction rate of both the protected and unprotected groups, necessitating their similarity under the "80 percent rule" as outlined by the US Equal Employment Opportunity Commission (EEOC). According to this rule, the positive outcome prediction for a specific subgroup should be at least 80% of that for the other subgroups to attain fairness.

$$\frac{P(y' = 1 | g(x) = 1)}{P(y' = 1 | g(x) = 0)} > 0.8$$

These probabilities are estimated through frequencies evaluated on training data and the predictions made by the ML classifier on the same training data. Our proposed approach is built upon the log disparity metric, which quantifies the representativeness of RCTs, as developed by Qi et al. [268] It operates on the assumption of a theoretical sample of subjects R, drawn equitably from a target population, and an observed sample of subjects S, recruited in the RCT. The observed sample may or may not exhibit equity. By employing a general mapping from ML fairness to RCTs, the ML disparate impact metric is transformed into its RCT counterpart, log disparity, to gauge the representativeness of the subgroup:

$$g(x) = 1.$$

In the context of the actual clinical trial sample S compared to the target population sample R, the log disparity metric for RCTs is calculated as follows:

$$\text{Log}\left[\frac{\text{odds }\left(g(x)=1\right)\middle| x \in S}{\text{odds }\left(g(x)=1\right)\middle| x \in R}\right].$$

4.6 INTRODUCTION TO CLINICAL TRIAL STATISTICS

Statistical concerns encompass every stage of a trial, ranging from its inception through design and protocol development, ongoing monitoring and conduct, data management, analysis, and the final reporting of results. These concepts can often pose challenges for those without a statistical background. Nonetheless, it's crucial for clinicians participating in clinical trials to grasp key statistical principles to ensure the trial's integrity is maintained.

Research indicates a notable rise in the complexity of statistical techniques within medical literature [270]. Moreover, studies highlight the insufficiency of current medical training in biostatistics [271,272]. In a survey by West and Ficalora, over two-thirds of clinicians disagreed or strongly disagreed with the assertion that the current level of biostatistical training in medicine suffices. Clinicians often appear willing to draw conclusions that lack support from the data [273]. Wulff et al. [274] reported that the statistical knowledge of most physicians is so limited that they struggle to draw accurate conclusions from analyses presented in medical journals. Furthermore, evidence suggests that researchers frequently misuse statistical methods due to a poor grasp of statistical concepts [275], with Glantz [276] suggesting that around half of the articles in medical journals employing statistical methods do so incorrectly.

4.7 GAUSSIAN METHODOLOGY AND APPLICATION IN CLINICAL EPIDEMIOLOGY

The Gaussian methodology, rooted in the principles of normal distribution, occupies a pivotal role in the field of clinical epidemiology. Named after Carl Friedrich Gauss, the normal distribution underpins many statistical methods, providing a foundation for understanding variability and assessing the significance of findings. This critical overview explores the theoretical underpinnings, practical applications, and limitations of Gaussian methodology in clinical epidemiology.

4.7.1 Theoretical Foundations of Gaussian Methodology

The Gaussian or normal distribution is characterised by its bell-shaped curve, symmetrical around the mean. Defined by two parameters—mean (μ) and standard deviation (σ)—it describes a probability distribution where approximately 68% of values lie within one standard deviation, 95% within two, and 99.7% within three. The ubiquity of the normal distribution in biological phenomena, such as blood pressure, body temperature, and lipid levels, arises from the CLT. The CLT posits that, given a sufficiently large sample size, the distribution of the sample mean approximates normality regardless of the underlying population distribution.

In clinical epidemiology, Gaussian methodology serves as the cornerstone for numerous statistical analyses, including hypothesis testing, regression modelling, and CI estimation. Its utility is augmented by its compatibility with parametric methods, which assume normality to derive robust inferential conclusions.

4.7.2 Applications in Clinical Epidemiology

1. **Hypothesis Testing and Inferential Statistics**

   Gaussian methods form the backbone of hypothesis testing, allowing researchers to determine whether observed data provide sufficient evidence to reject a null hypothesis in favour of an alternative hypothesis. The application of Gaussian principles in this domain is extensive, particularly through *t*-tests, *z*-tests, and ANOVA [275,277].

   - ***t*-Tests**: *t*-Tests assess whether the means of two groups differ significantly, assuming the data are approximately normally distributed. For instance, in clinical trials comparing the efficacy of two treatments, a *t*-test evaluates whether the difference in mean outcomes between the groups exceeds what might be expected by chance alone.
   - ***z*-Tests**: *z*-Tests are employed when sample sizes are large, and the population variance is known. They test whether a sample mean differs significantly from a population mean, which is crucial in quality control and benchmarking studies.
   - **ANOVA**: ANOVA extends *t*-tests to compare means across three or more groups. It partitions overall variability into between-group and within-group components, allowing researchers to ascertain whether group membership explains a significant portion of the variability. For example, ANOVA is frequently used in epidemiological studies to compare biomarker levels across different population subgroups.
   - ***p*-Values and Significance**: A critical element of hypothesis testing is the *p*-value, which quantifies the probability of observing data as extreme as those collected if the null hypothesis is true. Gaussian assumptions underpin the derivation of *p*-values, ensuring their validity when data follow normal distributions.

   The Gaussian approach also facilitates the calculation of test statistics (e.g., *t*-statistics, *F*-statistics), which follow known probability distributions under the null hypothesis. This predictability enables precise quantification of evidence against the null hypothesis. Inferential statistics based on Gaussian methods extend to estimating population parameters from sample data. CIs, discussed further below, provide a probabilistic range for these estimates, enhancing the interpretability of results.

2. **Regression Modelling**

Regression modelling is a cornerstone of statistical analysis in clinical epidemiology, enabling researchers to investigate relationships between variables, test hypotheses, and draw inferential conclusions. By leveraging mathematical models, regression analysis provides insights into the magnitude, direction, and significance of associations, while accounting for confounding factors. This section examines the role of regression modelling in hypothesis testing and inferential statistics, with a focus on its methodological foundations and applications [122,278,279].

Fundamentals of Regression Modelling

Regression analysis involves estimating the relationship between a dependent variable (outcome) and one or more independent variables (predictors). In clinical epidemiology, regression models are frequently used to quantify the impact of exposures, treatments, or risk factors on health outcomes. Common regression techniques include the following:

1. **Linear Regression**: Assumes a linear relationship between the dependent and independent variables, often used for continuous outcomes such as blood pressure or cholesterol levels.
2. **Logistic Regression**: Models the probability of a binary outcome (e.g., disease presence or absence) as a function of predictors.
3. **Cox Proportional Hazards Regression**: Evaluates the association between predictors and the hazard of an event occurring over time, commonly employed in survival analysis.

Hypothesis Testing in Regression Modelling

Regression models facilitate hypothesis testing by providing a framework to evaluate the significance of associations between predictors and outcomes. This involves specifying a null hypothesis (typically that a regression coefficient equals zero) and testing whether observed data provide sufficient evidence to reject it. Key components include the following:

1. **Regression Coefficients**: Each predictor in the model is assigned a regression coefficient, representing the estimated change in the outcome variable per unit change in the predictor. For example, in a study examining smoking and lung function, the coefficient for smoking might represent the reduction in forced expiratory volume per pack-year smoked.
2. **Test Statistics and *p*-Values**:
   - Test statistics, such as the *t*-statistic in linear regression or the Wald statistic in logistic regression, are calculated for each coefficient to assess its significance.
   - *p*-Values indicate the probability of observing the data (or something more extreme) if the null hypothesis is true. A small *p*-value suggests that the predictor is significantly associated with the outcome.

3. **Overall Model Significance**: In addition to individual predictors, the overall fit of the regression model can be tested. The examples are as follows:
   - In linear regression, the *F*-test evaluates whether the model explains a significant portion of the variability in the outcome.
   - In logistic regression, the likelihood ratio test compares the fit of nested models, assessing whether adding predictors improves explanatory power.

Inferential Statistics in Regression Modelling

Regression modelling extends beyond hypothesis testing to provide inferential insights about population-level associations. Inferential statistics derived from regression models include the following:

1. **Confidence Intervals**:
   - CIs for regression coefficients indicate the range of values within which the true effect size is likely to lie, with a specified level of confidence (e.g., 95%).
   - Narrow CIs reflect precise estimates, whereas wide CIs suggest greater uncertainty. In clinical research, CIs help contextualise statistical significance in terms of clinical relevance.
2. **Adjusted Effects**:
   - Regression models account for confounding by including multiple predictors simultaneously, enabling the estimation of adjusted effects.
   - For instance, in an analysis of obesity and diabetes, including covariates such as age, sex, and socioeconomic status ensures that observed associations are not confounded by these factors.
3. **Prediction and Extrapolation**:
   - Regression models are used to predict outcomes based on specific predictor values. For example, clinicians may estimate a patient's cardiovascular risk using a multivariable regression equation.
   - These predictions are particularly valuable in personalised medicine and resource allocation.
4. **Interaction Effects**:
   - Interaction terms in regression models evaluate whether the effect of one predictor depends on the level of another. For example, an interaction between treatment and age might reveal differential treatment efficacy across age groups.

Applications in Clinical Epidemiology

Regression modelling is indispensable in clinical epidemiology for addressing complex research questions. Examples include the following:

1. **Risk Factor Analysis**:
   - Investigating the relationship between modifiable risk factors (e.g., diet, exercise) and health outcomes using linear or logistic regression.
   - Studies on the role of hypertension in stroke risk frequently employ regression to quantify the strength of association.

2. **Health Disparities Research**:
   - Identifying and quantifying disparities in health outcomes across demographic groups.
   - Multivariable regression models are used to adjust for socioeconomic factors and disentangle the contributions of race, income, and access to healthcare.
3. **Treatment Efficacy Studies**:
   - Assessing the impact of interventions in RCTs.
   - Regression models evaluate whether treatment effects persist after adjusting for baseline characteristics and potential confounders.

Limitations and Considerations

While regression modelling is a powerful tool, it is not without limitations. Key considerations include the following:

1. **Assumption Violations**:
   - Linear regression assumes normality of residuals, homoscedasticity, and independence, which may not always hold in clinical data.
   - Logistic regression assumes independence of observations and correct model specification.
2. **Multicollinearity**:
   - High correlations among predictors can destabilise coefficient estimates, reducing interpretability and precision.
3. **Overfitting**:
   - Including too many predictors relative to the sample size can lead to overfitting, where the model captures noise rather than true associations.
4. **Causal Inference**:
   - Regression models describe associations but do not establish causality without rigorous design considerations, such as randomisation or instrumental variables.

Future Directions and Innovations

Advances in computational power and statistical techniques are enhancing the capabilities of regression modelling. Bayesian regression, ML-based regression, and regularisation methods (e.g., Lasso, Ridge) offer flexible and robust alternatives for analysing complex datasets. These innovations are particularly relevant in precision medicine, where high-dimensional data necessitate sophisticated modelling approaches.

Regression modelling is integral to hypothesis testing and inferential statistics in clinical epidemiology. By providing a rigorous framework for evaluating associations, adjusting for confounding, and making predictions, regression models contribute to the generation of actionable insights in public health and clinical practice. Nevertheless, careful attention to assumptions, limitations, and ethical considerations is essential to ensure the validity and relevance of findings.

3. **CIs Estimation**

CI estimation is a fundamental aspect of statistical inference, offering a robust method for quantifying the precision and uncertainty of parameter estimates in clinical epidemiology. Unlike point estimates, which provide a single value for a parameter, CIs delineate a range within which the true population parameter is likely to lie, given a specified confidence level (e.g., 95%). This section explores the principles, applications, and limitations of CIs estimation in hypothesis testing and inferential statistics [280–282].

Principles of CIs Estimation

CIs are derived from sample data under the assumption that the sampling distribution of the estimate follows a known statistical distribution, such as the Gaussian or *t*-distribution. The key components of a CIs include the following:

1. **Point Estimate**: The best single-value estimate of the parameter, such as the sample mean or proportion.
2. **Margin of Error**: Reflects the variability of the estimate, calculated as the product of the standard error and a critical value from the appropriate distribution.
3. **Confidence Level**: Indicates the probability that the interval will contain the true population parameter if the study were repeated multiple times (e.g., 95% confidence level implies 95 out of 100 intervals would capture the true parameter).

Mathematically, a CIs for a population mean that is is expressed as

$$\text{CI} = \bar{x} \pm z\,\text{SE},$$

where $\bar{x}$ is the sample mean, z is the critical value, and SE is the standard error of the mean.

CIs in Hypothesis Testing

CIs play a complementary role to hypothesis testing by providing a range of plausible values for a parameter rather than a binary decision. Key applications include the following:

1. **Assessing Statistical Significance**:
   - A CIs that excludes the null hypothesis value (e.g., zero for differences or one for ratios) implies statistical significance at the corresponding confidence level.
   - For instance, in a clinical trial comparing two treatments, if the 95% CI for the difference in mean outcomes does not include zero, the null hypothesis of no difference can be rejected.
2. **Interpreting Effect Size**:
   - While *p*-values indicate whether an effect exists, CIs provide additional information about its magnitude and clinical relevance.
   - Narrow CIs suggest precise estimates, whereas wide intervals indicate greater uncertainty, necessitating caution in interpretation.
3. **Equivalence and Non-Inferiority Testing**:
   - In equivalence and non-inferiority studies, CIs are used to determine whether a treatment's effect lies within a pre-specified margin of clinical acceptability.

- For example, a new drug may be considered non-inferior if the CI for the difference in efficacy falls entirely within a defined equivalence margin.

CIs in Inferential Statistics

CIs estimation underpins inferential statistics by facilitating population-level generalisations based on sample data. Specific applications include the following:

1. **Comparing Group Means**:
   - CIs are commonly employed to compare means across groups. For example, in a study evaluating blood pressure between treatment and control groups, the CI for the mean difference quantifies the likely range of the true difference.
   - If the interval is narrow and excludes zero, the results support a meaningful difference between groups.
2. **Proportions and Risk Ratios**:
   - In epidemiological studies, CIs for proportions, odds ratios, and risk ratios provide insight into associations between exposures and outcomes.
   - For example, the 95% CI for an odds ratio of 2.5 might be (1.8, 3.4), indicating a statistically significant and clinically relevant increase in odds.
3. **Meta-Analysis**:
   - CIs are integral to pooling results in meta-analyses. They provide a measure of the precision of the combined effect estimate, aiding in the interpretation of heterogeneity across studies.
4. **Public Health Decision-Making**:
   - In health policy, CIs guide resource allocation by quantifying uncertainty in cost-effectiveness analyses, prevalence estimates, and burden of disease metrics.

Advantages of CIs Estimation

CIs offer several advantages over point estimates and hypothesis testing alone:

1. **Contextualisation of Results**:
   - CIs provide a richer understanding of data by incorporating both magnitude and uncertainty, enabling more informed decision-making.
   - For instance, a significant p-value may correspond to a clinically trivial effect, whereas a CIs conveys whether the effect size warrants clinical action.
2. **Avoidance of Dichotomous Thinking**:
   - By presenting a range of plausible values, CIs discourage overreliance on arbitrary thresholds (e.g., $p < 0.05$) and promote nuanced interpretations.
3. **Reproducibility and Transparency**:
   - CIs facilitate replication and comparison across studies by standardising the presentation of uncertainty.

Limitations and Challenges

Despite their utility, CIs are not without limitations:

1. **Dependency on Assumptions**:
   - CIs rely on the validity of underlying assumptions, such as normality and independence of observations. Violations may lead to inaccurate intervals.
   - For non-Gaussian data, transformations or bootstrapping methods may be required to construct reliable intervals.
2. **Misinterpretation**:
   - CIs are often misconstrued as providing a probability that the parameter lies within the interval, which is incorrect. Instead, they reflect the long-run proportion of intervals that capture the true parameter.
3. **Sensitivity to Sample Size**:
   - Small sample sizes yield wide CIs, reflecting greater uncertainty. Conversely, large samples may produce narrow intervals that overemphasise trivial effects.

Emerging Approaches and Innovations

Advancements in statistical methodologies are enhancing the accuracy and interpretability of CIs:

1. **Bootstrap CIs**:
   - Non-parametric bootstrapping techniques generate CIs without relying on distributional assumptions, making them particularly useful for skewed or complex data.
2. **Bayesian Credible Intervals**:
   - Bayesian approaches offer an alternative to frequentist CIs by incorporating prior information into interval estimation. Credible intervals provide a direct probabilistic interpretation of parameter uncertainty.
3. **Simulation-Based Methods**:
   - Monte Carlo simulations are increasingly used to construct CIs in scenarios with complex data structures or computationally intensive models.

CIs estimation is a cornerstone of hypothesis testing and inferential statistics, enabling researchers to quantify uncertainty, assess significance, and draw meaningful conclusions in clinical epidemiology. By providing a range of plausible parameter values, CIs complement traditional *p*-values and enhance the interpretability of statistical findings. However, careful attention to assumptions, sample size, and reporting practices is essential to ensure their validity and utility. As methodological innovations continue to evolve, CIs will remain indispensable in advancing evidence-based decision-making in healthcare.

4. **Risk Prediction and Diagnostic Modelling**

Risk prediction and diagnostic modelling are fundamental components of clinical epidemiology, providing tools to estimate the likelihood of health outcomes and assess the diagnostic utility of clinical markers.

These models integrate statistical principles with clinical knowledge to support hypothesis testing, inferential statistics, and decision-making. This section explores the methodologies, applications, and challenges associated with risk prediction and diagnostic modelling in clinical research [283–285].

Principles of Risk Prediction and Diagnostic Modelling

Risk prediction involves estimating the probability of an individual developing a particular outcome, often based on multiple risk factors. Diagnostic modelling, by contrast, assesses the ability of tests or biomarkers to distinguish between individuals with and without a specific condition. Both approaches rely on regression-based methodologies, including the following:

1. **Logistic Regression**:
   - Commonly used for binary outcomes, logistic regression estimates the odds of an event occurring as a function of predictor variables. The coefficients represent the log odds ratios associated with each predictor.
   - For example, logistic regression may evaluate the impact of smoking, hypertension, and age on the likelihood of myocardial infarction.
2. **Cox Proportional Hazards Regression**:
   - Frequently applied in survival analysis, this model assesses the time to an event, such as disease recurrence or mortality, while accounting for censored data.
   - Predictors are expressed as hazard ratios, which quantify the RR of the event for different levels of the predictor.
3. **ML Algorithms**:
   - Emerging methods, such as random forests and neural networks, offer flexible approaches for risk prediction and diagnostic modelling, particularly in high-dimensional data settings.

Hypothesis Testing in Risk Prediction and Diagnostic Modelling

1. **Evaluating Predictor Significance**:
   - Risk prediction models allow hypothesis testing of individual predictors to determine their contribution to outcome variation. For example, in a model assessing diabetes risk, a hypothesis might evaluate whether BMI significantly predicts the probability of diabetes onset.
   - Statistical tests, such as Wald tests or likelihood ratio tests, assess the null hypothesis that a predictor's coefficient equals zero (no effect).
2. **Assessing Model Performance**:
   - Hypothesis testing is employed to evaluate the overall performance of risk prediction models. Metrics such as the likelihood ratio test compare nested models, assessing whether additional predictors significantly improve model fit.
   - For example, adding genetic markers to a clinical risk score can be tested to determine whether they enhance predictive accuracy.

3. **Calibration and Goodness-of-Fit**:
   - Calibration assesses how well predicted probabilities align with observed outcomes. Hypothesis tests, such as the Hosmer–Lemeshow test, evaluate whether deviations between observed and predicted probabilities are statistically significant.
4. **Hypothesis Testing in Diagnostic Accuracy**:
   - Diagnostic models evaluate the performance of biomarkers or tests using measures such as sensitivity, specificity, and the area under the receiver operating characteristic (ROC) curve.
   - Hypotheses about diagnostic accuracy can be tested by comparing AUC values or sensitivity/specificity between competing diagnostic tools.

Inferential Statistics in Risk Prediction and Diagnostic Modelling

Inferential statistics play a critical role in interpreting the results of predictive and diagnostic models, enabling generalisation from sample data to the broader population. Applications include the following:

1. **CIs for Risk Estimates**:
   - CIs quantify the uncertainty of risk predictions, providing a range within which the true risk is likely to lie.
   - For example, a model estimating a ten-year cardiovascular risk of 15% might report a 95% CI of 12%–18%, highlighting the precision of the prediction.
2. **Adjusted Risk Estimates**:
   - Multivariable modelling adjusts for confounders, allowing the estimation of independent effects of predictors on the outcome. Adjusted estimates are critical for drawing valid inferences in observational studies.
   - For instance, adjusting for age, sex, and socioeconomic status ensures that the reported effect of a dietary intervention on diabetes risk is not confounded by these variables.
3. **Prognostic Index Development**:
   - Inferential statistics support the development of prognostic indices, which combine multiple predictors into a single score. CIs for the index coefficients ensure their stability and reliability.
4. **Risk Stratification and Decision Thresholds**:
   - Risk models stratify individuals into categories (e.g., low, moderate, and high risk) to guide clinical decisions. Inferential statistics assess the validity of stratification thresholds, ensuring that they optimise sensitivity and specificity.

Applications in Clinical Epidemiology

Risk prediction and diagnostic modelling are extensively applied in clinical research and practice:

1. **Public Health Risk Assessment**:
   - Predictive models estimate population-level risks for conditions such as diabetes, cancer, or cardiovascular disease, informing screening and prevention strategies.

2. **Personalised Medicine**:
   - Individualised risk predictions enable tailored interventions, such as selecting high-risk patients for preventive therapies or enhanced monitoring.
3. **Diagnostic Tool Evaluation**:
   - Models evaluate the utility of new diagnostic tests or biomarkers. For example, ROC analysis might compare the performance of a novel blood test against a standard imaging modality.
4. **Clinical Trial Enrolment**:
   - Predictive models identify patients likely to benefit from experimental treatments, improving the efficiency and ethical conduct of trials.

Limitations and Challenges

Risk prediction and diagnostic modelling face several methodological and practical challenges:

1. **Overfitting**:
   - Complex models with many predictors risk overfitting, capturing noise rather than true associations. Cross-validation and penalisation techniques (e.g., Lasso, Ridge regression) mitigate this issue.
2. **Sample Size and Generalisability**:
   - Small sample sizes reduce model reliability, while models developed in specific populations may lack generalisability to other settings or demographics.
3. **Model Interpretation**:
   - Complex models, particularly those from ML, often lack transparency, complicating the interpretation and application of findings in clinical practice.
4. **Bias and Confounding**:
   - Residual confounding and selection bias can distort model estimates, necessitating rigorous study design and sensitivity analyses.

Future Directions

Advances in computational methods and data availability are driving innovations in risk prediction and diagnostic modelling:

1. **Integration of Omics Data**:
   - Incorporating genomic, proteomic, and metabolomic data enhances model precision and enables the discovery of novel predictors.
2. **Dynamic Modelling**:
   - Time-varying models incorporate longitudinal data to predict risks that evolve over time, such as the progression of chronic diseases.
3. **Explainable AI**:
   - Efforts to improve the interpretability of ML models aim to bridge the gap between predictive power and clinical usability.

Risk prediction and diagnostic modelling are indispensable tools in hypothesis testing and inferential statistics, enabling the quantification and interpretation of health risks and diagnostic utility. These models inform public health strategies, clinical decision-making, and research innovation. However, their reliability depends on rigorous methodology, transparent reporting, and careful consideration of limitations. Continued advancements in statistical techniques and computational tools will further enhance their utility in improving patient outcomes and advancing population health.

4.7.3 Limitations and Challenges

Despite its widespread utility, the Gaussian methodology is not without limitations. Several challenges arise when applying Gaussian-based approaches in clinical epidemiology, particularly in scenarios where underlying assumptions are violated.

1. **Non-Normality of Data**
   Many biological and clinical datasets deviate from normality, exhibiting skewness or kurtosis. Non-Gaussian distributions are particularly common in outcomes such as hospital stays, where data are right-skewed, or in rare diseases, where small sample sizes preclude normal approximations. The reliance on Gaussian assumptions in such contexts can lead to biased estimates and inaccurate conclusions.
2. **Outlier Sensitivity**
   Gaussian methods are highly sensitive to outliers, which disproportionately influence means and standard deviations. Outliers can distort hypothesis tests, regression models, and CIs, undermining the robustness of findings. Robust statistical techniques, such as median-based methods or transformations (e.g., log transformations), are often necessary to address this issue.
3. **Over-Reliance on Parametric Methods**
   The assumption of normality underpins many parametric methods, but over-reliance on these approaches may limit their applicability in non-Gaussian scenarios. Non-parametric methods, such as the Mann–Whitney U test or Kaplan–Meier survival analysis, provide alternatives that are less dependent on distributional assumptions, albeit often at the cost of statistical power.
4. **Complexity in Multivariable Settings**
   In multivariable models, the Gaussian assumption applies not only to individual variables but also to residuals and joint distributions. Ensuring these conditions is challenging in complex datasets with multiple predictors and interactions. Violations can lead to model misspecification, compromising the interpretability and generalisability of results.

4.7.4 Emerging Approaches and Alternatives

To address the limitations of Gaussian methodology, several emerging approaches and alternatives have gained prominence:

1. **Data Transformation and Normalisation**
   Transformations, such as log, square root, or Box-Cox transformations, are commonly applied to achieve approximate normality in skewed data.

These techniques enable the continued use of Gaussian-based methods while mitigating the effects of non-normality.

2. **Robust Statistical Methods**

   Robust methods, including quantile regression and bootstrap resampling, provide alternatives that are less sensitive to deviations from normality. These approaches enhance the reliability of analyses in datasets with outliers or non-Gaussian distributions.

3. **Bayesian Methods**

   Bayesian statistics offers a flexible framework that does not rely on strict distributional assumptions. By incorporating prior knowledge and uncertainty into the analysis, Bayesian methods are particularly useful in small-sample studies and scenarios with complex data structures.

4. **Non-Parametric Techniques**

   Non-parametric methods, which do not assume specific distributions, are increasingly employed in clinical epidemiology. Techniques such as kernel density estimation and permutation tests provide robust alternatives for analysing non-Gaussian data.

4.7.5 Ethical and Practical Considerations

The application of Gaussian methodology in clinical epidemiology must be guided by ethical and practical considerations. Ensuring the validity of assumptions is critical to avoid misleading conclusions that may adversely affect patient care. Transparent reporting of methods, including sensitivity analyses, enhances the reproducibility and credibility of findings.

Moreover, epidemiologists must balance statistical rigour with clinical relevance, prioritising approaches that yield actionable insights. Collaborative efforts between statisticians and clinicians can facilitate the selection of appropriate methodologies tailored to specific research questions.

Gaussian methodology remains a cornerstone of clinical epidemiology, offering powerful tools for understanding variability, testing hypotheses, and predicting outcomes. However, its applicability is contingent on the validity of underlying assumptions, and its limitations necessitate careful consideration. By embracing emerging alternatives and adhering to ethical principles, epidemiologists can leverage Gaussian methodology to generate robust and meaningful insights, advancing the science of population health.

4.8 BAYESIAN METHODOLOGY AND APPLICATION IN CLINICAL EPIDEMIOLOGY

Bayesian methodology offers a flexible and robust framework for statistical analysis, providing a principled way to incorporate prior knowledge with observed data. Rooted in Bayes' theorem, this approach has gained increasing traction in clinical epidemiology for addressing complex questions, handling uncertainty, and integrating evidence from diverse sources. This overview critically examines Bayesian methodology's theoretical foundations, applications, advantages, and challenges, with an emphasis on its role in advancing epidemiological research.

4.8.1 Theoretical Foundations of Bayesian Methodology

Bayes' theorem is the cornerstone of Bayesian methodology, expressed mathematically as:

$P(\theta \mid D) = [P(D \mid \theta) \times P(\theta)]/P(D)$

where,

- $P(\theta \mid D)$ is the posterior probability, representing the updated belief about a parameter (θ) after observing data (D)
- $P(D \mid \theta)$ is the likelihood, reflecting the probability of the observed data given the parameter value
- $P(\theta)$ is the prior probability, encapsulating existing knowledge or beliefs about the parameter before observing the data; and
- P(D) is the marginal likelihood or evidence, which normalises the posterior distribution.

Bayesian analysis updates prior beliefs with data-driven evidence to produce a posterior distribution, providing a full probabilistic description of uncertainty. Unlike frequentist methods, Bayesian approaches interpret probabilities as degrees of belief rather than long-run frequencies, making them particularly suitable for clinical decision-making and personalised medicine.

4.8.1.1 Applications in Clinical Epidemiology

Bayesian methodology has diverse applications in clinical epidemiology, spanning study design, data analysis, and evidence synthesis. Key applications include the following:

1. **Evidence Synthesis and Meta-Analysis**

   Bayesian methods excel in combining evidence from multiple studies, accommodating heterogeneity and uncertainty more naturally than frequentist approaches. Hierarchical Bayesian models allow for partial pooling of information, enabling the integration of disparate sources while accounting for study-level variability.

   For example, in a meta-analysis of vaccine efficacy, Bayesian models can incorporate varying baseline risks across populations, producing posterior distributions that reflect a weighted synthesis of evidence. The use of credible intervals (CIs) instead of confidence intervals enhances interpretability, providing probabilistic statements about parameter estimates [286].

2. **Risk Prediction and Stratification**

   Bayesian models support the development of personalised risk prediction tools, integrating prior knowledge with patient-specific data. This approach is particularly valuable for rare diseases or conditions with limited data, where traditional methods often struggle to produce reliable estimates.

   For instance, in cardiovascular risk prediction, Bayesian models incorporate prior distributions derived from epidemiological studies, refining predictions as more data becomes available. These models account for uncertainty in parameter estimates, improving the reliability of risk stratification in clinical settings [287].
3. **Missing Data and Causal Inference**

   Bayesian methods offer robust solutions for handling missing data and conducting causal inference. Multiple imputation using Bayesian models generates plausible values for missing observations, accounting for uncertainty in the imputation process. This approach avoids biases associated with complete-case analyses, enhancing the validity of conclusions.

   In causal inference, Bayesian models integrate prior knowledge about causal structures with observational data, enabling estimation of treatment effects even in the presence of confounding. Directed acyclic graphs often guide model specification, ensuring alignment with epidemiological theory [288].
4. **Adaptive Trial Designs**

   Bayesian methodology underpins adaptive clinical trials, where interim analyses guide modifications to the trial design. Bayesian adaptive trials allow for real-time updating of probability distributions, enabling dynamic changes in sample size, randomisation ratios, or stopping rules based on accruing data.

   For example, oncology trials frequently use Bayesian approaches to identify optimal dosing regimens or terminate trials early for efficacy or futility. This flexibility enhances trial efficiency, ethical considerations, and resource allocation [289].
5. **Longitudinal and Hierarchical Modelling**

   Bayesian methods are particularly well suited for analysing longitudinal and hierarchical data. In longitudinal studies, Bayesian models account for individual-level variability over time, enabling precise estimation of trends and treatment effects.

   Hierarchical Bayesian models facilitate multilevel analyses, incorporating nested structures such as patients within clinics or regions. These models provide robust estimates by borrowing strength across levels, addressing issues of small sample sizes at lower levels of the hierarchy [290].

4.8.1.2 Advantages of Bayesian Methodology

Bayesian approaches offer several advantages over frequentist methods:

1. **Flexibility**: Bayesian models handle complex data structures, missing data, and non-standard distributions with ease.

2. **Integration of Prior Knowledge**: Priors allow for the incorporation of previous evidence, enhancing the efficiency and interpretability of analyses, particularly in resource-limited settings.
3. **Probabilistic Interpretation**: Posterior distributions provide direct probabilistic statements about parameters, aiding decision-making under uncertainty.
4. **Adaptability**: Real-time updating of beliefs enables dynamic analyses, as in adaptive trials or sequential monitoring.
5. **Transparency**: Bayesian models explicitly account for uncertainty, offering a comprehensive framework for evaluating robustness and sensitivity.

4.8.1.3 Challenges and Limitations

Despite its strengths, Bayesian methodology presents several challenges:

1. **Subjectivity of Priors**: The choice of priors can influence results, leading to debates about their objectivity. While non-informative priors mitigate this concern, they may dilute the benefits of Bayesian analysis.
2. **Computational Intensity**: Bayesian methods often require advanced computational techniques, such as MCMC, which can be resource-intensive and time-consuming.
3. **Interpretational Complexity**: Bayesian analyses produce richer outputs than frequentist methods, but their interpretation requires statistical expertise, potentially limiting accessibility for non-specialists.
4. **Regulatory Acceptance**: Regulatory agencies may favour frequentist approaches, necessitating additional justification for Bayesian analyses in clinical trials [291].

4.8.1.4 Future Directions and Innovations

Advancements in computational power and methodological development are expanding the scope of Bayesian applications. Emerging trends include the following:

1. **Bayesian ML**: Integrating Bayesian inference with ML algorithms enhances model interpretability and uncertainty quantification in high-dimensional data.
2. **Bayesian Networks**: These probabilistic graphical models are increasingly used for causal inference, risk prediction, and decision support in complex systems.
3. **Big Data and Real-World Evidence**: Bayesian methods are well suited for analysing real-world data, accommodating heterogeneity and missingness inherent in large datasets.

Bayesian methodology represents a transformative paradigm in clinical epidemiology, offering unparalleled flexibility, precision, and adaptability for addressing diverse research questions. By integrating prior knowledge with observed data, Bayesian approaches enhance the robustness and interpretability of findings, supporting evidence-based decision-making. However, widespread adoption requires addressing challenges related to computation, interpretation, and regulatory acceptance. As methodological innovations continue to evolve, Bayesian methodology is poised to play an increasingly pivotal role in advancing population health.

4.9 CASE STUDY: MEDICAL DEVICE INTERVENTIONS FOR NON-CANCER CHRONIC LOWER BACK PAIN – EVIDENCE FROM A SYSTEMATIC REVIEW AND META-ANALYSIS

The study explores the efficacy of medical devices in managing non-cancer chronic pain, focusing primarily on lower back pain. The systematic review and meta-analysis include 13 studies with 875 participants, encompassing a range of study designs such as RCTs, feasibility trials, and crossover studies. The meta-analysis specifically includes six studies with 173 participants, investigating the effects of various medical devices, including transcutaneous electrical nerve stimulation, pulsed electromagnetic therapy (PEMT), and transcranial direct current stimulation (tDCS). While the findings provide evidence of pain reduction, methodological limitations and heterogeneities challenge the generalisability of results [292].

KEY FINDINGS

1. **Efficacy of Medical Devices**:
   - Pain reduction was evident in some studies, with TICT and PEMT showing significant results in chronic low back pain patients (pooled mean difference of −4.2 and −0.87, respectively).
   - Disability levels showed significant improvement, with an average reduction of 7.44 points on the Oswestry Disability Index (ODI) for device-treated groups.
   - Sleep quality improvements with tDCS were not statistically significant, potentially due to unmeasured confounders such as pre-existing sleep disorders or other comorbidities.
2. **Subgroup Analyses**:
   - Subgroups based on geographical location, gender, age, and pain type revealed disparities. Studies conducted in Korea showed a statistically significant pooled efficacy for pain reduction, whereas other regions lacked adequate representation.
   - Gender subgroup analysis highlighted underrepresentation of women in clinical trials, despite their higher prevalence of chronic pain and differences in pain perception and analgesic response.
   - Devices were primarily evaluated for chronic low back pain, neglecting other chronic pain conditions like pelvic or neuropathic pain.
3. **Statistical Heterogeneity**:
   - High heterogeneity ($I_2 = 87\%$) was identified across studies, particularly in pain reduction outcomes, influenced by variations in assessment tools, study design, and sample sizes.

- Sensitivity analysis demonstrated that removing specific studies significantly altered pooled results, suggesting that inconsistencies in methodologies impact robustness.

CRITICAL METHODOLOGICAL CONSIDERATIONS

1. **Study Design Limitations**:
   - A significant proportion of studies relied on small sample sizes, reducing statistical power and generalisability.
   - Limited longitudinal data restrict the understanding of long-term efficacy and sustainability of device-based interventions.
   - Lack of standardisation in outcome measures, with various self-reported tools (e.g., visual analogue scales [VAS], ODI, BPI), introduces biases related to recall, mood, and external influences.
2. **Sample Characteristics**:
   - Important demographic and clinical variables, such as BMI, comorbidities, and medication use, were often unreported, impeding subgroup analysis and contextual understanding of findings.
   - Many studies excluded relevant populations or failed to stratify results adequately by age, gender, or socioeconomic status, further limiting applicability.
3. **Data Heterogeneity and Bias**:
   - High variability in assessment tools and study protocols led to inconsistencies in reported outcomes. For instance, VAS and face pain rating scales yielded divergent results due to differing assessment modalities.
   - Publication bias was detected, with smaller studies disproportionately contributing to pooled results and favouring positive findings.
4. **Generalisation Challenges**:
   - Geographical representation was skewed, with a majority of studies conducted in Korea and limited representation from diverse populations or low-resource settings.
   - The limited focus on lower back pain excludes other chronic pain conditions, highlighting the need for broader exploration of medical device efficacy.
5. **Regulatory and Reporting Gaps**:
   - The lack of uniform reporting guidelines across studies and insufficient disclosure of conflicts of interest or funding sources compromise the transparency and reliability of findings.
   - The methodological rigour of included studies varied, with many failing to include multidisciplinary teams or comprehensive patient assessments.

RECOMMENDATIONS FOR FUTURE RESEARCH

1. **Standardisation and Comprehensive Reporting**:
   - Employ core outcome sets and standardised tools for chronic pain assessment to reduce heterogeneity and improve comparability across studies.
   - Ensure comprehensive reporting of demographic, clinical, and procedural details to enable more granular subgroup analyses.

2. **Inclusion of Underrepresented Populations**:
   - Address gender disparities and include diverse populations to enhance the external validity of findings.
   - Expand research focus beyond lower back pain to encompass other chronic pain conditions.
3. **Improved Study Designs**:
   - Conduct larger, multicentre RCTs with robust sample sizes to strengthen the evidence base.
   - Incorporate longitudinal data collection to assess long-term outcomes and the sustainability of interventions.
4. **Addressing Bias and Heterogeneity**:
   - Use advanced statistical techniques, such as Bayesian models, to handle heterogeneity and integrate prior evidence effectively.
   - Evaluate publication bias rigorously and encourage transparent dissemination of negative or null results.

While the findings suggest that medical devices offer potential for managing chronic pain, the limitations in study design, sample diversity, and standardisation undermine the reliability of the conclusions. Future research must address these methodological shortcomings to generate robust, generalisable evidence that informs clinical practice and policymaking.

5 Application Development Using Data Science

5.1 DIGITAL MEDICINE TOOL DEVELOPMENT

The evolution of digital medicine tools represents a pivotal advancement in healthcare, addressing critical gaps in access, personalisation, and efficiency of medical care. These tools harness innovations in data science, artificial intelligence (AI), and user-centred design to enhance the diagnosis, treatment, and monitoring of diverse medical conditions. Their development aligns with the growing global emphasis on precision medicine and the democratisation of healthcare.

5.1.1 Addressing Unmet Needs in Healthcare

The healthcare landscape faces numerous challenges, including limited accessibility, inefficiencies in service delivery, and disparities in health outcomes across populations. Traditional models of care often fail to fully address the needs of vulnerable groups, such as those in rural areas, low-resource settings, or underserved communities, exacerbating inequities in health access and outcomes. Digital medicine tools offer transformative potential to overcome these barriers by leveraging technology to reimagine how care is delivered and experienced.

5.1.1.1 Expanding Access to Care

Digital medicine tools, such as telemedicine platforms, mobile health applications, and wearable devices, enable healthcare services to transcend geographical constraints. Individuals in remote or underserved regions can access medical expertise and evidence-based interventions without the need to travel long distances or face extended wait times. This expanded access is particularly valuable in addressing conditions that require continuous monitoring or timely intervention, such as diabetes management, mental health support, or infectious disease outbreaks.

5.1.1.2 Bridging Resource Gaps

Healthcare systems in low-resource settings often face shortages of medical personnel, diagnostic infrastructure, and therapeutic options. Digital medicine tools can mitigate these challenges by augmenting existing resources. For instance, AI-driven decision-support systems assist clinicians in making accurate diagnoses, even in resource-constrained environments. Similarly, mobile diagnostic tools and remote monitoring systems enable frontline health workers to deliver care with greater precision and efficiency.

DOI: 10.1201/9781003494737-5

5.1.1.3 Empowering Patients and Communities

Traditional healthcare models frequently place patients in passive roles, relying heavily on healthcare providers to manage their conditions. Digital tools empower individuals to take an active role in their health through self-monitoring and personalised insights. Tools like symptom trackers and health education platforms enable users to better understand their conditions, adhere to treatment plans, and make informed decisions about their care. Furthermore, digital tools can foster community engagement and collective health improvements by facilitating peer support networks and disseminating culturally relevant health information.

5.1.1.4 Enhancing Health System Efficiency

Digital medicine tools streamline healthcare processes, reducing administrative burdens and optimising resource allocation. For example, electronic health records (EHRs) and automated appointment scheduling systems improve workflow efficiency for healthcare providers. Additionally, digital triage systems can prioritise patients based on the severity of their condition, ensuring timely intervention and reducing the strain on emergency services.

5.1.1.5 Addressing Health Disparities

Health inequities persist due to systemic factors, including socioeconomic status, geographic location, and cultural barriers. Digital medicine tools can address these disparities by tailoring interventions to the specific needs of diverse populations. For example, multilingual health apps and culturally sensitive telemedicine services ensure inclusivity and relevance, making care accessible and effective for marginalised groups. By incorporating localised data and feedback, these tools can further adapt to the unique healthcare challenges faced by specific communities.

5.1.1.6 Resilience in Crisis Situations

Digital medicine tools have demonstrated their utility during public health emergencies, such as the COVID-19 pandemic, where they enabled the rapid dissemination of information, remote diagnosis, and the continuation of essential health services. Their scalability and adaptability make them indispensable in responding to future crises, including natural disasters, epidemics, or humanitarian emergencies, ensuring continuity of care when traditional healthcare systems are disrupted.

By addressing these unmet needs, digital medicine tools pave the way for a more equitable, efficient, and responsive healthcare ecosystem that places the individual at the centre of care.

5.1.2 Personalisation through Data-Driven Insights

The integration of machine learning (ML) algorithms and large-scale health data enables the personalisation of medical interventions. Digital tools can analyse individual-level data, including genetic, physiological, and behavioural parameters, to tailor recommendations and improve clinical outcomes. Such approaches not only enhance efficacy but also foster patient engagement by delivering bespoke health solutions.

The integration of ML algorithms and large-scale health data has revolutionised the ability to deliver personalised medical interventions, enabling a shift from traditional "one-size-fits-all" approaches to bespoke healthcare solutions. By analysing individual-level data, including genetic, physiological, behavioural, and environmental parameters, digital tools can provide precise, context-specific recommendations that improve clinical outcomes and optimise patient satisfaction. This personalisation leverages the growing availability of diverse data sources and the computational power of advanced analytics to address the complexity of individual health needs.

5.1.2.1 Genomic and Biomarker Insights

Advances in genomics and high-throughput sequencing technologies have made it possible to integrate genetic data into digital health platforms. ML algorithms can identify genetic variations associated with specific diseases or responses to treatment, enabling interventions that are tailored to an individual's unique genetic profile. For example, pharmacogenomics—a field that examines how genetic differences influence drug metabolism—has enabled the development of digital tools that guide personalised drug prescriptions, reducing the risk of adverse drug reactions and enhancing therapeutic efficacy [293].

Incorporating biomarkers, such as blood glucose levels or inflammatory markers, into digital platforms further enables real-time tracking of health status. Predictive models can use these biomarkers to assess disease progression and recommend early interventions, as demonstrated in conditions like diabetes, cardiovascular diseases (CVD), and certain cancers [140].

5.1.2.2 Behavioural and Psychosocial Data

Behavioural data, such as physical activity patterns, dietary habits, and sleep quality, provide critical insights into an individual's lifestyle and its impact on health outcomes. Digital tools equipped with wearable sensors and mobile applications collect continuous behavioural data, which can be analysed to generate personalised recommendations for preventive and therapeutic measures. For instance, ML algorithms can identify deviations from healthy behaviours and deliver tailored interventions to encourage adherence to lifestyle modifications or treatment plans.

Psychosocial factors, including mental health status and social determinants of health, are also increasingly integrated into personalisation frameworks. By capturing data on stress levels, emotional well-being, and social support networks, digital tools can provide holistic care that addresses both physical and mental health needs.

5.1.2.3 Dynamic and Adaptive Learning

The capacity of ML models to learn dynamically from new data further enhances their personalisation capabilities. These models can adapt over time to reflect changes in an individual's health status or treatment response, ensuring that recommendations remain relevant and effective. For example, adaptive algorithms used in digital therapeutics for managing chronic diseases can adjust treatment plans based on real-time data from wearable devices or patient-reported outcomes, thereby improving adherence and efficacy.

5.1.2.4 Patient Engagement and Empowerment

Personalisation also fosters patient engagement by delivering health solutions that are perceived as relevant and actionable. Tailored feedback, coupled with clear, individualised goals, enhances motivation and adherence to treatment regimens. Personalised digital platforms often include interactive features, such as virtual coaching or peer support networks, which further empower patients to actively participate in their healthcare journey.

5.1.2.5 Challenges and Future Directions

Despite the promise of personalisation through data-driven insights, challenges remain, including ensuring the quality and completeness of health data, addressing algorithmic biases, and maintaining data privacy and security. Future efforts must prioritise the integration of diverse data sources, including underrepresented populations, to improve generalisability and equity in personalised care. Collaboration between researchers, clinicians, and technology developers will be essential to overcoming these barriers and advancing the application of personalisation in digital medicine.

5.1.3 Enhancing Early Detection and Prevention

The advent of digital medicine tools has significantly expanded the possibilities for early disease detection and prevention. These technologies leverage continuous monitoring, real-time feedback, and advanced analytics to identify early signs of disease and support timely interventions. By providing actionable insights into an individual's health trajectory, these tools enable proactive management of risk factors, ultimately reducing the burden of chronic and preventable diseases.

5.1.3.1 Continuous Monitoring and Early Detection

Wearable devices, such as smartwatches and fitness trackers, are at the forefront of early detection efforts. These devices are equipped with sensors capable of monitoring a wide range of biomarkers, including heart rate, blood pressure, glucose levels, and sleep patterns. Continuous data collection allows for the identification of subtle physiological changes that may signal the onset of disease. For instance, abnormal variations in heart rate variability or blood pressure could indicate early signs of cardiovascular conditions, prompting further diagnostic evaluation [294].

Similarly, digital tools designed for diabetes management use continuous glucose monitoring systems to detect patterns in blood sugar levels. This real-time data empowers individuals and healthcare providers to implement preventive measures, such as dietary adjustments or medication titration, to mitigate disease progression [295].

5.1.3.2 Predictive Analytics and Risk Stratification

The integration of ML algorithms into digital medicine tools enhances their ability to predict disease risk. By analysing large datasets from diverse populations, predictive models can identify individuals at high risk for developing conditions such as diabetes, hypertension, or depression. For example, algorithms analysing lifestyle data, genetic predisposition, and environmental factors can calculate a personalised risk score, guiding targeted prevention strategies [140].

Risk stratification capabilities also enable healthcare systems to prioritise resources and interventions for high-risk populations. This is particularly relevant in public health initiatives aimed at addressing non-communicable diseases, which account for a significant portion of global morbidity and mortality.

5.1.3.3 Proactive Interventions and Behavioural Modification

Digital medicine tools facilitate early and effective interventions by promoting behavioural modifications that reduce disease risk. Mobile health applications often include personalised coaching features, providing users with tailored recommendations for improving physical activity, diet, and stress management. Evidence suggests that such interventions are effective in preventing lifestyle-related conditions, such as obesity and metabolic syndrome [296].

Additionally, digital tools can deliver automated reminders and motivational messages to encourage adherence to preventive measures, such as vaccination schedules or screening programmes. These features have been particularly successful in improving participation rates in cancer screening and immunisation efforts.

5.1.3.4 Mental Health and Psychological Well-Being

Early detection and prevention of mental health disorders represent a critical area of application for digital medicine tools. Mobile applications and wearable devices can monitor psychological markers, such as sleep disturbances, activity levels, and mood fluctuations, which are often early indicators of mental health conditions. These tools provide real-time feedback and recommendations, enabling individuals to seek timely professional support [297].

Moreover, digital platforms offering cognitive behavioural therapy and mindfulness training have been shown to reduce the risk of developing anxiety and depression in high-risk populations. Such tools are particularly valuable in addressing barriers to mental healthcare, such as stigma and limited access to providers.

5.1.3.5 Challenges and Future Directions

While digital medicine tools hold immense promise for early detection and prevention, several challenges must be addressed. Ensuring the accuracy and reliability of wearable sensors, minimising false-positive rates, and maintaining data privacy are critical to building trust and promoting widespread adoption. Furthermore, the integration of these tools into clinical workflows and healthcare systems remains a work in progress.

Future research should focus on validating the effectiveness of digital medicine tools through randomised controlled trials (RCTs) and real-world implementation studies. Collaboration between technology developers, healthcare providers, and regulatory bodies will be essential to maximise their impact on public health.

5.1.4 Supporting Evidence-Based Practice

The development of digital medicine tools must be firmly rooted in rigorous scientific methodologies to ensure their safety, efficacy, and acceptability. RCTs, observational studies, and usability testing are essential to establish their validity. Furthermore, co-design approaches, involving end-users and healthcare professionals, are critical to ensuring the tools are fit for purpose and culturally sensitive.

5.1.5 Ethical and Regulatory Considerations

As digital medicine tools increasingly integrate into healthcare systems, adherence to ethical principles and regulatory frameworks is paramount. Ensuring data privacy, equity of access, and transparency in algorithmic decision-making are vital to fostering trust and minimising harm. Collaborations with regulatory bodies can expedite the pathway to clinical adoption while maintaining rigorous standards of patient safety.

Digital medicine tools are transformative innovations that bridge gaps in healthcare delivery, empower patients, and support clinicians in delivering high-quality, personalised care. Their development requires a multidisciplinary approach, integrating expertise in healthcare, engineering, and social sciences. By prioritising evidence-based design and addressing ethical considerations, these tools can catalyse a paradigm shift towards more equitable and effective healthcare systems.

5.2 MOBILE APPLICATIONS AS CLINICIAN DECISION AIDS

The integration of mobile applications into clinical practice has emerged as a transformative advancement in modern healthcare. These digital tools act as decision aids for clinicians by providing access to evidence-based guidelines, diagnostic algorithms, and real-time patient data. Their adoption addresses several challenges in contemporary medicine, including information overload, variability in clinical decision-making, and the demand for personalised patient care. This chapter explores the scientific underpinnings, applications, benefits, and challenges associated with mobile applications as clinician decision aids.

5.2.1 Role of Mobile Applications in Clinical Decision Support

Mobile applications are designed to assist clinicians by synthesising complex medical information into actionable insights. These tools leverage algorithms, ML, and cloud-based databases to deliver real-time recommendations that are tailored to individual patient profiles. Examples include apps for differential diagnosis, risk stratification, drug prescribing, and procedure selection.

- **Access to Evidence-Based Guidelines**
  Mobile applications provide instant access to up-to-date clinical guidelines and best practices. Tools such as UpToDate, BMJ Best Practice, and Medscape integrate peer-reviewed evidence to support informed decision-making at the point of care. This capability is particularly valuable in rapidly evolving fields such as oncology or infectious diseases, where guidelines are frequently updated.
- **Diagnostic Support**
  Applications like Isabel and VisualDx employ diagnostic algorithms to assist in the formulation of differential diagnoses. These tools rely on

patient-specific data—such as symptoms, demographics, and test results—to generate a ranked list of possible conditions, enhancing diagnostic accuracy and reducing cognitive biases.

- **Medication Management**
  Mobile apps such as Epocrates and Medscape provide drug databases, dosage calculators, and interaction checkers, helping clinicians avoid prescribing errors and optimise pharmacotherapy. These features are critical for ensuring patient safety, particularly in polypharmacy scenarios.
- **Risk Stratification and Predictive Analytics**
  Applications like MDCalc and QxMD incorporate validated scoring systems, such as the CHADS2 score for atrial fibrillation or the CURB-65 score for pneumonia, to assess patient risk and guide treatment decisions. Some apps utilise predictive models to forecast disease progression or treatment response, enabling proactive care.

5.2.2 Benefits of Mobile Decision Aids

- **Enhanced Efficiency**
  Mobile applications streamline clinical workflows by reducing the time required to retrieve information and perform calculations. For instance, automated scoring systems eliminate the need for manual computation, freeing up clinicians to focus on patient care.
- **Standardisation of Care**
  By providing evidence-based recommendations, mobile apps help minimise variability in clinical practice. Standardisation reduces the risk of medical errors and improves patient outcomes, particularly in high-stakes scenarios like emergency medicine or critical care.
- **Personalisation of Patient Care**
  Mobile applications facilitate personalised medicine by integrating patient-specific data into decision-making processes. This approach aligns with the principles of precision medicine, ensuring that interventions are tailored to individual needs and characteristics [140].
- **Continuing Medical Education**
  Many decision-support apps incorporate educational content, such as summaries of recent research, case studies, and interactive quizzes. These features promote lifelong learning and keep clinicians abreast of advances in their field.

5.2.3 Challenges and Limitations

- **Data Privacy and Security**
  Mobile applications often process sensitive patient information, raising concerns about data privacy and compliance with regulations such as General Data Protection Regulation (GDPR) or HIPAA. Robust encryption and secure storage protocols are essential to mitigate these risks [298].

- **Algorithm Bias**
  The quality of recommendations generated by mobile apps depends on the datasets used to train their algorithms. If these datasets lack diversity, the resulting tools may perpetuate healthcare disparities by delivering less accurate recommendations for underrepresented populations [116].
- **Integration with Clinical Workflows**
  The usability of mobile applications is contingent on their seamless integration into existing EHRs and clinical workflows. Poor interoperability can lead to clinician frustration and reduced adoption rates [299].
- **Reliability and Validation**
  Not all mobile applications undergo rigorous validation before being marketed. The lack of regulatory oversight for certain tools may result in the dissemination of inaccurate or outdated information, potentially compromising patient safety [300].

5.2.4 Future Directions

The role of mobile applications as clinician decision aids is likely to expand with advancements in AI, ML, and wearable technology. Future developments may include the following:

- **Integration with Wearable Devices**
  Real-time data from wearable sensors could enhance the predictive capabilities of mobile apps, enabling dynamic monitoring and early intervention for conditions such as heart failure or diabetes.
- **Natural Language Processing (NLP)**
  NLP algorithms may allow clinicians to interact with apps using conversational queries, improving usability and reducing cognitive load.
- **Global Health Applications**
  Mobile apps tailored to low-resource settings could address critical healthcare disparities by providing decision support in areas with limited access to specialist care.

5.3 REAL-WORLD DATA TOOL FOR REAL-TIME DATA GATHERING

Real-world data (RWD) tools represent a critical advancement in contemporary healthcare, enabling the continuous collection, analysis, and utilisation of data from diverse sources outside the controlled settings of RCTs. These tools provide actionable insights into patient behaviours, treatment patterns, and health outcomes in real-world contexts, thereby addressing gaps in traditional research methodologies. By leveraging advancements in digital technologies, such as mobile applications, wearable devices, and EHRs, RWD tools facilitate real-time data gathering and decision-making, significantly enhancing clinical practice and research.

5.3.1 The Nature and Importance of RWD

RWD encompasses information collected from routine healthcare delivery and everyday patient interactions. Sources include EHRs, claims and billing data, disease registries, and patient-reported outcomes [301]. Unlike RCTs, which are often limited by strict inclusion criteria and controlled environments, RWD provides a comprehensive view of healthcare utilisation and outcomes in diverse, heterogeneous populations.

Real-time data gathering using RWD tools has become increasingly important for capturing dynamic and evolving health phenomena. This capability is particularly relevant for chronic disease management, pharmacovigilance, and public health surveillance, where timely interventions can significantly alter health trajectories.

5.3.1.1 Key Applications of RWD Tools

1. **Chronic Disease Monitoring**
   RWD tools enable continuous monitoring of chronic conditions, such as diabetes, hypertension, and asthma. Mobile health applications and wearable devices collect physiological data, such as blood glucose levels or blood pressure, in real time. These data are transmitted to healthcare providers, allowing for immediate adjustments to treatment plans and enhanced patient engagement.
2. **Pharmacovigilance and Drug Safety**
   Real-time data gathering through RWD tools facilitates post-market surveillance of pharmaceutical products. Adverse drug reactions and safety signals can be detected earlier, ensuring timely regulatory action and patient safety. For instance, mobile applications designed for patient-reported outcomes enable the prompt reporting of side effects, complementing traditional pharmacovigilance systems.
3. **Public Health and Epidemiology**
   RWD tools have been instrumental in tracking disease outbreaks and informing public health interventions. During the COVID-19 pandemic, mobile apps and wearable devices were used to monitor symptoms, mobility patterns, and vaccination status, providing critical insights into disease spread and the effectiveness of containment measures.
4. **Precision Medicine and Personalised Care**
   By integrating genomic, behavioural, and environmental data, RWD tools enable personalised care pathways. Predictive analytics derived from real-time data allow clinicians to anticipate disease progression and tailor interventions to individual patients, aligning with the goals of precision medicine [140].
5. **Clinical Research and Trial Augmentation**
   RWD tools support decentralised and hybrid clinical trials by collecting patient data outside traditional research settings. This approach reduces the logistical burden on participants and increases the generalisability of trial findings. Furthermore, real-time data integration enhances interim analyses and adaptive trial designs.

5.3.2 Technological Advancements in RWD Tools

The effectiveness of RWD tools is underpinned by technological innovations, including the following:

1. **Wearable Devices**
   Devices such as smartwatches and biosensors continuously collect physiological data, including heart rate, activity levels, and sleep patterns. Advances in sensor technology and wireless communication have improved the accuracy and reliability of these devices, making them indispensable for real-time health monitoring.
2. **Mobile Health Applications**
   Mobile apps provide a user-friendly interface for data entry and visualisation. Features such as symptom trackers, medication reminders, and teleconsultation capabilities enhance user engagement and facilitate the seamless transfer of RWD to healthcare providers.
3. **Cloud Computing and Data Analytics**
   The scalability and processing power of cloud-based platforms enable the storage and analysis of large, complex datasets. ML algorithms applied to RWD facilitate predictive modelling and pattern recognition, supporting evidence-based decision-making.

5.3.3 Benefits of Real-Time Data Gathering with RWD Tools

1. **Timely Interventions**
   Real-time data gathering enables healthcare providers to identify and address health issues as they arise, reducing the likelihood of complications and hospitalisations.
2. **Enhanced Patient Engagement**
   By providing immediate feedback and actionable insights, RWD tools empower patients to take an active role in managing their health.
3. **Improved Research Efficiency**
   The integration of RWD tools into clinical research reduces costs and accelerates timelines by minimising the need for in-person visits and manual data collection.
4. **Broader Inclusivity**
   Unlike traditional trials, which often exclude vulnerable populations, RWD tools capture data from diverse demographic groups, enhancing the representativeness of findings.

5.3.4 Challenges and Limitations

Despite their potential, RWD tools face several challenges:

1. **Data Quality and Integration**
   Variability in data quality and the lack of standardisation across sources can hinder the reliability of insights derived from RWD tools.

2. **Privacy and Security Concerns**
   The use of RWD tools necessitates robust measures to protect patient confidentiality and comply with data protection regulations, such as the GDPR.
3. **Algorithm Bias**
   ML models used in RWD tools are susceptible to biases in training data, which can lead to disparities in healthcare delivery.
4. **Adoption and Usability**
   Successful implementation requires addressing barriers to adoption, including technological literacy, provider acceptance, and infrastructure limitations.

The future of RWD tools lies in their seamless integration into healthcare ecosystems and their ability to harness emerging technologies. Advancements in AI, NLP, and blockchain will further enhance the accuracy, security, and usability of these tools. Collaborative efforts among stakeholders—including researchers, policymakers, and technology developers—will be essential to fully realise the potential of RWD tools in transforming healthcare.

5.4 PRECISION MEDICINE TOOL FOR PREDICTING OUTCOMES

Precision medicine, an innovative approach to healthcare, emphasises tailoring medical interventions to the unique characteristics of each patient. Advances in genomic technologies, AI, and data science have enabled the development of precision medicine tools capable of predicting clinical outcomes with remarkable accuracy. These tools integrate diverse data sources, including genetic, environmental, and lifestyle factors, to generate individualised risk assessments, treatment plans, and prognostic insights. Their application has the potential to revolutionise disease prevention, diagnosis, and management by facilitating proactive and personalised healthcare.

Precision medicine rests on the principle that genetic, phenotypic, and environmental variations significantly influence an individual's health outcomes and response to treatment. Traditional "one-size-fits-all" approaches often fail to account for this heterogeneity, leading to suboptimal care and adverse outcomes. Predictive tools in precision medicine utilise algorithms and ML models to analyse vast datasets, identifying patterns and correlations that inform clinical decisions [302].

5.4.1 Components of Precision Medicine Tools for Predicting Outcomes

1. **Genomic and Molecular Profiling**
   Genomic data plays a pivotal role in precision medicine tools. Next-generation sequencing technologies enable the identification of genetic mutations, epigenetic modifications, and molecular markers associated with specific diseases or treatment responses. For example, in oncology, genomic profiling can predict tumour behaviour, therapeutic efficacy, and survival outcomes [303].

2. **Integration of Multi-Omics Data**
   Beyond genomics, precision medicine tools incorporate data from other "omics" domains, such as transcriptomics, proteomics, and metabolomics. The integration of multi-omics datasets enhances the predictive accuracy of these tools by capturing the complex interactions between biological systems. This approach is particularly valuable in complex diseases such as cancer, cardiovascular conditions, and neurodegenerative disorders [304].
3. **ML and Predictive Analytics**
   MLML algorithms underpin the predictive capabilities of precision medicine tools. Supervised learning models analyse historical data to predict outcomes such as disease progression or treatment response, while unsupervised learning identifies previously unrecognised subgroups within populations. These tools can dynamically update their predictions as new data becomes available, ensuring ongoing relevance [140].
4. **RWD Integration**
   The inclusion of RWD, such as EHRs, wearable device outputs, and patient-reported outcomes, enhances the clinical applicability of precision medicine tools. By reflecting the diversity of real-world patient populations, these data sources improve the generalisability and reliability of predictions [301].

5.4.1.1 Applications of Predictive Tools in Precision Medicine

1. **Cancer Treatment and Prognosis**
   Precision medicine tools are widely used in oncology to predict patient outcomes and guide therapeutic decisions. For instance, molecular profiling of breast cancer tumours using tools like Oncotype DX® enables the prediction of recurrence risk and the likelihood of benefit from adjuvant chemotherapy [305]. Similar tools, such as FoundationOne® CDx, provide comprehensive genomic profiling to inform targeted therapy selection.
2. **CVD Risk Prediction**
   Predictive tools in cardiology assess an individual's risk of developing CVD based on genetic and clinical data. Polygenic risk scores, derived from genome-wide association studies, quantify the cumulative effect of genetic variants on CVD risk, enabling earlier interventions and personalised management [306].
3. **Pharmacogenomics and Drug Response Prediction**
   Pharmacogenomic tools predict an individual's response to specific medications based on genetic variants affecting drug metabolism. For example, variations in the CYP2C19 gene influence the efficacy of clopidogrel, a commonly prescribed antiplatelet drug. Incorporating pharmacogenomic data into clinical practice can minimise adverse drug reactions and optimise therapeutic outcomes [307].
4. **Neurological and Psychiatric Disorders Therapy**
   In neurology and psychiatry, precision medicine tools aid in predicting disease progression and treatment outcomes. For instance, amyloid and tau biomarkers, combined with genetic data, are used to forecast the likelihood of cognitive decline in Alzheimer's disease patients [308].

5.4.1.2 Benefits of Predictive Tools in Precision Medicine

1. **Improved Diagnostic Accuracy**
   Predictive tools enhance the precision of diagnoses by identifying disease subtypes and underlying pathophysiological mechanisms, enabling targeted interventions.
2. **Personalised Risk Stratification**
   By quantifying individual risk levels, these tools support tailored preventive strategies, reducing the incidence and severity of diseases.
3. **Optimised Treatment Selection**
   Predictive models guide the selection of therapies with the highest likelihood of success for each patient, minimising trial-and-error approaches and associated costs.
4. **Enhanced Patient Outcomes**
   The application of precision medicine tools leads to improved clinical outcomes, including increased survival rates, reduced complications, and enhanced quality of life.

5.4.1.3 Challenges and Limitations

1. **Data Quality and Standardisation**
   The accuracy of predictions depends on the quality and consistency of input data. Variability in data collection methods and incomplete datasets can compromise tool performance.
2. **Ethical and Privacy Concerns**
   The use of genetic and health data raises significant ethical considerations, including the risk of data misuse and discrimination. Robust data governance frameworks are essential to mitigate these risks.
3. **Algorithm Bias**
   Predictive models may reflect biases in the datasets used for their development, leading to disparities in healthcare delivery. Ensuring diversity in training datasets is critical for equitable application.
4. **Integration into Clinical Practice**
   Effective implementation of precision medicine tools requires seamless integration with existing healthcare systems and clinician workflows, which can be technologically and logistically challenging.

Advancements in AI, multi-omics integration, and RWD analytics will continue to refine the predictive accuracy of precision medicine tools. Collaborative efforts among researchers, clinicians, and policymakers are essential to ensure their ethical development, equitable application, and widespread adoption. Future innovations may include the use of digital twins—virtual representations of patients that simulate disease progression and treatment responses—paving the way for fully personalised healthcare.

5.5 SOFTWARE DEVELOPMENT USING DATA SCIENCE PRINCIPLES

The integration of data science principles into software development has transformed the way applications are designed, built, and optimised. Data-driven methodologies enable the development of intelligent, adaptive, and scalable software systems that cater to the dynamic demands of users and industries. By leveraging techniques such as ML, statistical analysis, and big data processing, developers can build software solutions that are not only efficient but also capable of deriving actionable insights from data.

5.5.1 Key Principles of Data Science in Software Development

1. **Data-Driven Design**

   Data-driven design focuses on using empirical evidence to guide software development decisions. User data, application performance metrics, and market trends are analysed to inform feature development, user interface design, and system architecture. This approach ensures that software solutions are closely aligned with user needs and expectations [309].
2. **Iterative Development and Continuous Learning**

   Data science principles align well with agile software development methodologies. Iterative development cycles, combined with continuous feedback loops, enable developers to refine software incrementally based on RWD. Techniques such as A/B testing and multivariate testing are commonly employed to evaluate the impact of new features or changes [310].
3. **Predictive and Prescriptive Analytics**

   Incorporating predictive analytics into software systems allows for forecasting future trends and behaviours, enabling proactive decision-making. Prescriptive analytics extends this capability by recommending specific actions based on predictive insights, enhancing the software's decision-support capabilities.
4. **Scalability and Big Data Processing**

   Modern software systems must process vast amounts of data efficiently. Data science principles guide the design of scalable architectures that can handle large datasets, often leveraging distributed computing frameworks like Apache Hadoop or Apache Spark. Such systems ensure reliability and performance under high workloads [311].
5. **Integration of ML Models**

   The integration of ML models into software applications enables automation, personalisation, and enhanced functionality. For example, recommendation systems, NLP tools, and predictive maintenance modules are increasingly embedded into software products, providing advanced capabilities [113].

5.5.1.1 Applications of Data Science in Software Development

1. **User-Centred Software Design**

   Data science tools, such as user behaviour analytics and sentiment analysis, enable developers to design software solutions tailored to user needs. By analysing interaction patterns and feedback, developers can optimise user interfaces and experiences, ensuring usability and satisfaction.

2. **Automation of Software Testing**
   Data science principles are employed to automate software testing processes, improving the detection of bugs and performance issues. ML algorithms can identify patterns in testing data, enabling predictive error detection and prioritisation of test cases.
3. **Real-Time Analytics in Software Systems**
   Software applications, particularly those in e-commerce, healthcare, and finance, integrate real-time analytics to provide instantaneous insights and decision support. Data streams are processed and analysed in real time using tools such as Apache Kafka, ensuring responsiveness and adaptability [153].
4. **Fraud Detection and Security**
   Data science techniques, including anomaly detection and clustering, are used to develop software systems capable of identifying fraudulent activities and security breaches. These systems continuously monitor user behaviour and system logs, flagging deviations that indicate potential threats [312].
5. **Optimisation and Resource Management**
   Software solutions in logistics, supply chain management, and cloud computing use data science for optimisation. Techniques like linear programming, genetic algorithms, and simulation modelling enhance resource allocation, scheduling, and operational efficiency [313].

5.5.1.2 Benefits of Incorporating Data Science Principles

1. **Improved Decision-Making**
   Data science principles enable software systems to support evidence-based decision-making by analysing historical and real-time data.
2. **Enhanced Adaptability**
   By learning from user interactions and external data sources, software systems can adapt dynamically to changing requirements and conditions.
3. **Increased Efficiency and Accuracy**
   Automation of processes and predictive modelling reduce manual effort and improve the accuracy of software functionalities.
4. **Scalable and Future-Proof Systems**
   Data science-driven architectures are designed to scale seamlessly, accommodating future growth and technological advancements.

5.5.1.3 Challenges in Data Science-Driven Software Development

1. **Data Quality and Availability**
   The effectiveness of data science applications in software development depends on the quality and completeness of the underlying data. Poor-quality data can lead to inaccurate models and unreliable software functionalities [314].
2. **Complexity in Model Integration**
   Incorporating sophisticated ML models into software systems requires expertise in both data science and software engineering. Ensuring seamless integration without compromising performance is a significant challenge [315].

3. **Ethical and Privacy Concerns**
   The use of user data raises concerns about privacy and ethical considerations. Compliance with regulations, such as the GDPR, is essential to maintain user trust and legal conformity [316].
4. **Resource Constraints**
   Developing and deploying data-intensive applications demand substantial computational and financial resources. Optimising resource usage is crucial for cost-effective software development.

5.5.1.4 Future Directions

The integration of data science principles into software development is expected to evolve with advancements in AI, quantum computing, and edge computing. Future developments may include the following:

1. **Enhanced Automation with AI**
   AI-driven tools will further automate software development tasks, including coding, testing, and debugging, improving productivity and reducing errors.
2. **Explainable AI (XAI)**
   As ML models become integral to software systems, the focus will shift towards XAI to enhance transparency and trust in decision-making processes.
3. **Collaborative Software Development Platforms**
   Data science-driven platforms will facilitate collaboration among developers, data scientists, and domain experts, streamlining workflows and fostering innovation.

5.6 SIMULATION TOOLS FOR MEDICAL EDUCATION

Simulation tools have become indispensable in medical education, offering safe, controlled, and replicable environments for learners to develop clinical skills, improve decision-making, and enhance teamwork. These tools range from high-fidelity mannequins to virtual reality (VR) platforms and AI-driven systems, catering to a diverse spectrum of educational needs. This chapter critically examines the types, benefits, and challenges of simulation tools in medical education, drawing on current research and evidence to provide a comprehensive understanding of their role in modern healthcare training.

Simulation-based education (SBE) is built on the principle of experiential learning, enabling students to practise and refine skills in realistic yet safe environments. Unlike traditional teaching methods, SBE allows learners to confront high-pressure situations, such as resuscitation or trauma care, without the risk of patient harm. By replicating real-world conditions, SBE supports the development of cognitive, psychomotor, and affective domains, fostering competence and confidence in healthcare professionals.

5.6.1 Types of Simulation Tools in Medical Education

1. **High-Fidelity Mannequin Simulators**

   High-fidelity mannequins are advanced tools capable of replicating complex physiological responses, such as cardiac rhythms, respiratory patterns, and pupil reactions. These simulators are widely used for scenarios requiring advanced clinical decision-making, such as cardiac arrest management or anaesthesia training [317].

   Critical Discussion: While high-fidelity mannequins provide unmatched realism, they are resource-intensive, requiring substantial financial investment and ongoing maintenance. Additionally, their effectiveness depends on the quality of the scenario design and the competency of the facilitators. Poorly executed simulations may lead to disengagement and suboptimal learning outcomes [318]. Moreover, access to these simulators is often limited in low-resource settings, perpetuating disparities in medical education.
2. **VR and Augmented Reality (AR) Simulations**

   VR and AR technologies provide immersive, interactive environments for medical training. VR offers fully virtual settings for practising procedures like laparoscopic surgery, while AR overlays digital information onto the physical environment, enhancing real-world training experiences [319].

   Critical Discussion: VR and AR simulations excel at exposing learners to rare or high-risk situations, such as mass casualty incidents or complex surgeries. However, the lack of tactile feedback in VR and the high cost of AR devices remain significant limitations. Additionally, technical challenges, such as latency or compatibility issues, may detract from the learning experience [320]. Standardisation of VR/AR content is needed to ensure uniformity in training outcomes across institutions.
3. **Task Trainers**

   Task trainers are designed for practising specific procedural skills, such as intravenous cannulation, suturing, or catheterisation. These tools are widely used in early medical training due to their cost-effectiveness and focused scope.

   Critical Discussion: Although task trainers are effective for skill acquisition, their lack of contextual realism limits their ability to develop clinical reasoning. Combining task trainers with scenario-based simulations can address this gap by providing context and reinforcing decision-making skills.
4. **Computer-Based Simulations and Virtual Patients**

   Computer-based simulations use algorithms to replicate patient conditions, allowing learners to practise diagnostics and treatment planning. Virtual patient systems, in particular, simulate interactions with patients, enhancing communication and decision-making skills [321].

   Critical Discussion: These tools are accessible and scalable, making them suitable for large-scale training. However, they often lack the interpersonal and tactile dimensions of clinical practice. Additionally, the quality of computer-based simulations is highly variable, with some tools failing to align with evidence-based guidelines.

5. **AI-Driven Simulations**

   AI-powered simulation tools use ML to adapt scenarios based on learner performance, providing personalised feedback and dynamic difficulty adjustment. These systems are particularly useful for assessing higher-order competencies, such as critical thinking and adaptability [140].

   Critical Discussion: While AI-driven tools hold promise for creating highly personalised learning experiences, their development and deployment are constrained by ethical concerns, data privacy regulations, and the risk of algorithmic bias. Further research is required to validate their effectiveness across diverse learner populations.

5.6.2 Benefits of Simulation Tools in Medical Education

1. **Enhancing Patient Safety**

   By allowing learners to practise without risking patient harm, simulation fosters a safer healthcare environment. This is particularly critical for high-stakes scenarios, such as surgical emergencies or trauma care [322].

2. **Fostering Interprofessional Collaboration**

   Simulation scenarios often involve multidisciplinary teams, promoting interprofessional education. This improves communication, clarifies roles, and enhances teamwork, which are essential for high-quality care delivery [323].

3. **Boosting Competence and Confidence**

   Simulation provides learners with repeated opportunities to refine their skills, which enhances competence and builds confidence. Studies have consistently shown that SBE is superior to traditional methods in improving clinical performance [324].

5.6.3 Challenges and Limitations of Simulation Tools

1. **Resource Constraints**

   High-fidelity simulators, VR platforms, and AI-driven tools require substantial financial and infrastructural investment. Institutions in low-resource settings may struggle to adopt these technologies, creating disparities in access to quality education [318].

2. **Standardisation Issues**

   A lack of uniform standards for simulation scenarios and assessment metrics limits the comparability and reproducibility of training outcomes across institutions [325].

3. **Transferability to Clinical Practice**

   Despite their realism, simulations cannot fully replicate the complexities of real-world clinical environments. Continuous exposure to clinical settings is necessary to reinforce simulation-based learning.

5.6.4 Future Directions

1. **Hybrid Simulations**
   Combining physical and digital elements to create more realistic and engaging training environments.
2. **Data-Driven Optimisation**
   Leveraging big data and AI to design adaptive, evidence-based scenarios tailored to individual learners.
3. **Global Collaboration**
   Establishing international guidelines for SBE to ensure equitable access and consistent quality across institutions.

5.7 ROBOTIC SURGERY USING DATA APPLICATIONS

Robotic surgery, a rapidly advancing domain in modern medicine, leverages sophisticated technologies to enhance the precision, safety, and efficacy of surgical interventions. Data applications play an integral role in robotic surgery, enabling advancements in intraoperative decision-making, surgical planning, and postoperative analysis. This chapter critically examines the integration of data-driven technologies in robotic surgery, highlighting their capabilities, limitations, and transformative potential in reshaping the field of surgery. The discussion draws upon peer-reviewed evidence to provide an in-depth analysis suitable for a comprehensive academic resource.

Robotic surgery involves the use of robotic systems to perform complex surgical procedures with enhanced precision and control. These systems, such as the da Vinci Surgical System, combine high-definition 3D visualisation, robotic arms, and advanced instrumentation. The integration of data applications into robotic systems enhances their functionality by incorporating real-time analytics, ML, and predictive modelling. This combination facilitates better surgical planning, minimises intraoperative errors, and optimises patient outcomes [326].

5.7.1 Data-Driven Preoperative Planning

Preoperative planning is a critical component of robotic surgery, and data applications significantly enhance this process by enabling detailed visualisation and simulation.

1. **Imaging and Anatomical Modelling**
   Data from advanced imaging modalities such as computed tomography, magnetic resonance imaging, and 3D ultrasound are integrated into robotic systems to create detailed anatomical models. These models assist surgeons in visualising patient-specific anatomy, identifying critical structures, and planning precise surgical approaches [327].

   Critical Discussion: While imaging-based planning improves surgical accuracy, the effectiveness of these models depends on the quality of imaging data and the algorithms used for reconstruction. Variability in imaging quality across institutions can impact the consistency of preoperative plans.

Additionally, the computational demands of generating high-resolution models may limit their use in resource-constrained settings.

2. **ML in Risk Stratification**

   ML algorithms analyse patient data to predict surgical risks and complications. By incorporating data on patient demographics, comorbidities, and previous surgical outcomes, these models enable surgeons to anticipate potential challenges and optimise perioperative management [328].

   Critical Discussion: Although ML-based risk stratification has shown promise, its accuracy is contingent on the quality and diversity of training datasets. Biases in datasets can result in inaccurate predictions for underrepresented populations, raising concerns about the equity of these tools.

5.7.2 Intraoperative Data Applications

1. **Real-Time Imaging and Navigation**

   Robotic systems incorporate intraoperative imaging, such as fluoroscopy or AR, to provide real-time visualisation of surgical fields. Data overlays assist in identifying anatomical landmarks and tracking surgical instruments with submillimetre accuracy.

   Critical Discussion: Real-time navigation reduces the likelihood of intraoperative errors and enhances the precision of procedures, particularly in minimally invasive and delicate surgeries. However, challenges such as imaging artefacts and delayed processing times can compromise the reliability of these systems.

2. **Haptic Feedback and Sensor Integration**

   The integration of sensors into robotic systems provides tactile feedback to surgeons, compensating for the loss of physical sensation in robotic-assisted procedures. Data collected from force sensors and accelerometers enhances the surgeon's ability to gauge tissue resistance and manipulate instruments safely [329].

   Critical Discussion: While haptic feedback improves the safety and ergonomics of robotic surgery, its fidelity is often limited by the resolution of sensors and the responsiveness of feedback systems. Research is ongoing to develop high-fidelity haptic technologies that closely replicate human tactile perception.

3. **AI-Assisted Decision Support**

   AI algorithms analyse intraoperative data to provide real-time recommendations. For example, computer vision algorithms detect anatomical structures or pathologies, guiding surgeons during complex procedures [330].

   Critical Discussion: AI-assisted decision support enhances the accuracy of surgical interventions but raises concerns about surgeon reliance on automated systems. Maintaining a balance between human expertise and AI guidance is critical to preserving surgical judgement.

5.7.3 Postoperative Analysis and Outcome Prediction

1. **Postoperative Data Analytics**

   Data collected during robotic surgeries, including instrument trajectories and tissue interactions, are analysed postoperatively to evaluate surgical performance and identify areas for improvement. These analytics contribute to continuous learning and skill refinement [331].

   Critical Discussion: While postoperative analytics provide valuable insights, their implementation requires robust data storage and processing infrastructure. Data privacy concerns also arise, necessitating stringent measures to protect patient and procedural information.

2. **Predictive Modelling for Recovery and Complications**

   Predictive models use intraoperative and patient-specific data to forecast postoperative recovery trajectories and complication risks. These predictions enable personalised post-surgical care plans, improving patient outcomes [332].

   Critical Discussion: Although predictive modelling shows promise, its application in clinical practice is limited by uncertainties in model reliability and the need for extensive validation studies. Additionally, clinicians must interpret model outputs cautiously to avoid overreliance on predictions.

5.7.4 Benefits of Data Applications in Robotic Surgery

1. **Enhanced Precision and Safety**

   Data applications improve surgical precision by integrating detailed anatomical visualisations, real-time feedback, and decision-support systems. These enhancements reduce intraoperative errors and improve patient safety [333].

2. **Improved Training and Skill Assessment**

   Data collected during robotic procedures provides objective metrics for assessing surgical performance, enabling targeted training interventions and continuous professional development [334].

3. **Personalised Surgical Care**

   The integration of patient-specific data enables personalised surgical approaches, improving outcomes and minimising complications [328].

5.7.5 Challenges and Future Directions

1. **Technical and Operational Barriers**

   The integration of data applications into robotic systems requires significant computational resources and technical expertise. Ensuring interoperability between different software and hardware systems is also a challenge [335].

2. **Ethical and Privacy Considerations**

   The use of patient data raises ethical concerns, including the need for informed consent and compliance with data protection regulations such as GDPR. Balancing data utility with privacy safeguards is critical.

3. **Advancements in AI and ML**

   Future developments in AI and ML are expected to enhance the predictive and decision-making capabilities of robotic systems. Collaborative efforts between clinicians, engineers, and data scientists are essential to drive innovation and ensure clinical relevance.

5.8 COGNITIVE PERFORMANCE APPLICATION

The advent of cognitive performance applications represents a significant advancement in understanding, enhancing, and managing human cognitive functions. These applications are designed to assess, monitor, and improve cognitive abilities such as memory, attention, problem-solving, and decision-making through digital platforms. Integrating advances in neuroscience, data analytics, and AI, these tools hold promise for both clinical and non-clinical applications, including healthcare, education, and workplace productivity. This chapter provides a critical examination of cognitive performance applications, discussing their foundations, applications, limitations, and future potential.

5.8.1 THE FOUNDATIONS OF COGNITIVE PERFORMANCE APPLICATIONS

1. **Theoretical Basis**

   Cognitive performance applications are grounded in cognitive psychology and neuroscience, which describe how cognitive processes operate and interact. These applications often target domains such as executive function, working memory, and attention, guided by theories like Baddeley's working memory model or Kahneman's dual-process theory of thinking [336,337]. By operationalising these theories, cognitive performance applications translate abstract constructs into measurable and trainable parameters.

   Critical Discussion: Despite their theoretical grounding, many applications simplify cognitive constructs to ensure usability and scalability. This reductionism may limit the ecological validity of the tools, as they often fail to capture the complexity of cognitive processes in real-world contexts.
2. **Technological Advancements**

   Advances in AI, ML, and big data analytics have enabled the development of sophisticated algorithms that adapt to user performance, provide personalised feedback, and predict cognitive outcomes. For example, neurofeedback systems utilise electroencephalography (EEG) data to offer real-time insights into brain activity, supporting cognitive training and rehabilitation [338].

   Critical Discussion: While technological advancements enhance the functionality of cognitive performance applications, they also introduce challenges, including algorithmic biases, data privacy concerns, and the need for extensive validation.

5.8.2 Applications of Cognitive Performance Tools

1. **Clinical Applications**

    Cognitive performance applications are increasingly used in diagnosing and managing neurocognitive disorders, including Alzheimer's disease, attention-deficit/hyperactivity disorder, and traumatic brain injury. For example, tools like Cogstate and Cambridge Cognition's CANTAB provide objective measures of cognitive impairment, aiding early diagnosis and treatment planning [339].

    Critical Discussion: While these tools offer significant potential, their reliability and validity in diverse populations remain areas of concern. Many applications are developed using data from homogeneous populations, limiting their generalisability and potentially introducing health inequities.
2. **Educational Enhancement**

    Cognitive performance applications are used to support learning and academic achievement. Tools like Lumosity and Elevate employ gamified exercises to improve memory, attention, and problem-solving skills in students.

    Critical Discussion: Although widely adopted, the efficacy of these applications in enhancing long-term cognitive skills remains debated. Studies suggest that cognitive training effects are often limited to tasks within the application, with minimal transfer to broader cognitive domains [340].
3. **Workplace Productivity**

    In professional settings, cognitive performance tools aim to optimise productivity, decision-making, and stress management. Applications such as Peak and BrainHQ are marketed to professionals seeking to maintain cognitive sharpness and improve focus.

    Critical Discussion: While promising, the evidence supporting workplace applications is largely anecdotal or industry-sponsored, raising questions about their empirical validity. Independent, peer-reviewed studies are necessary to establish their effectiveness in real-world workplace settings.
4. **Sports and Peak Performance**

    Cognitive performance tools are increasingly integrated into sports psychology to enhance athletes' focus, reaction time, and decision-making under pressure. Applications often incorporate biofeedback and visual-spatial training to optimise performance.

    Critical Discussion: Although these tools show potential, their impact on actual performance metrics, such as game statistics or injury prevention, requires further empirical investigation.

5.8.3 Benefits of Cognitive Performance Applications

1. **Personalisation and Accessibility**

    Cognitive performance tools offer personalised training regimens based on individual needs, making them accessible to a wide audience. Mobile applications and cloud-based platforms ensure that users can engage with these tools anytime and anywhere [341].

2. **Objective and Quantifiable Metrics**
   By leveraging digital data, these tools provide objective measures of cognitive function, enabling precise tracking of improvements and declines over time.
3. **Support for Cognitive Decline Prevention**
   Cognitive performance applications can support ageing populations in maintaining mental acuity, delaying the onset of cognitive decline, and improving quality of life.

5.8.4 Limitations and Challenges

1. **Lack of Generalisability**
   The efficacy of cognitive performance applications often fails to extend beyond the specific tasks trained within the application. This lack of "far transfer" limits their utility in real-world scenarios [340].
2. **Validation and Regulatory Oversight**
   Many cognitive performance tools are released without rigorous validation or adherence to regulatory standards, raising concerns about their reliability and safety [339].
3. **Ethical and Privacy Concerns**
   The collection and storage of user data pose significant ethical challenges. Ensuring compliance with data protection regulations such as the GDPR is critical to maintaining user trust.
4. **Digital Divide**
   The reliance on digital platforms may exclude populations with limited access to technology or low digital literacy, exacerbating health inequities.

5.8.5 Future Directions

1. **Integration with Wearable Technology**
   The integration of cognitive performance tools with wearable devices, such as smartwatches and EEG headsets, will enable continuous monitoring of cognitive states and real-time feedback.
2. **AI and Adaptive Learning**
   Advances in AI will enable the development of more sophisticated adaptive learning algorithms, ensuring that cognitive training regimens remain challenging and personalised.
3. **Evidence-Based Development**
   Future cognitive performance applications must prioritise evidence-based design, with robust validation studies to ensure reliability, efficacy, and safety across diverse populations.
4. **Global Accessibility**
   Efforts to reduce the digital divide through affordable, multilingual, and culturally sensitive applications will ensure equitable access to cognitive performance tools worldwide.

6 Governance and Regulatory Approvals

6.1 BACKGROUNDS

Data science is a rapidly evolving field of study. Use of data science solutions primarily driven by real-world problems and often driven by the said industry requirements. The notion of industry-driven data science solutions requires simple solutions to interventions such as software or other applicators such as mobile apps. The scope and purpose of these applications largely decide the governance requirements and its alignment to regulations.

For example, within the healthcare industry, patient data is highly sensitive and its use to inform better development of interventions and tool to improve health outcomes, the regulatory and governance requirements could be complex and specific. This is vital to understand when using data gathered under research constraints versus routinely gathered clinical data that may be used to inform knowledge and practice gaps across multiple populations in multiple countries. Health outcomes have begun to improve within low- and middle-income countries, although novel challenges continue to be a problem with growing public expectations and the implementation of new health goals due to increases in the global populous, clinical or otherwise. The current trajectory of healthcare demand is also raising concerns over the implementation of new medicinal products, medical devices, and other clinical interventions within urban and rural settings, rising costs, and quality assurance provided for research conducted to test new interventions. Thus, governance and regulatory applicability incur at a number of time points.

6.2 QUALITY ASSURANCE, QUALITY CONTROL, AND QUALITY MANAGEMENT

Quality assurance in data science is about ensuring that the data being used for analysis is of high quality and suitable for the intended purpose. Quality assurance in data science involves ensuring that the data used for analysis is accurate, reliable, and appropriate for the intended purpose, as follows:

1. **Accurate**: Accurate data is fundamental in various fields, ensuring the integrity of analyses, models, and decision-making processes. It refers to information devoid of errors, inconsistencies, or biases, offering a true representation of the phenomenon it depicts. Accuracy encompasses correctness, precision, consistency, completeness, and relevance. Firstly, accurate data must be factually correct, devoid of any inaccuracies or mistakes. It reflects the actual values, measurements, or observations without distortion. Precision ensures

DOI: 10.1201/9781003494737-6

exactness, providing clear and unambiguous descriptions or measurements. Consistency across different sources, time periods, or observations is crucial to maintain reliability and trustworthiness. Accurate data is complete, lacking any missing values or gaps that could compromise its usefulness. Completeness ensures that all necessary information for analysis or decision-making is available. Finally, accurate data is relevant, aligning with the objectives of the analysis and providing meaningful insights.

2. **Reliable**: Reliable data can be depended upon to make decisions or draw conclusions. It means the data is consistent and trustworthy, and it won't produce widely varying results under similar conditions. Reliable data is information that can be trusted and depended upon to be consistent and accurate over time and across different contexts. It is data that consistently produces the same or similar results under similar conditions, and it reflects the true state of the phenomenon it represents, including a variety of characteristics. Reliable data remains consistent across various sources, time periods, or observations. It produces the same or similar results when analysed repeatedly, providing confidence in its reliability. Reliable data is precise and provides exact measurements or descriptions without ambiguity. Precision ensures that the data can be relied upon for making informed decisions or drawing conclusions. Reliable data can be reproduced or replicated by others using the same methods or procedures. It allows for independent verification and validation of results, enhancing trust and confidence in the data. Reliable data is valid and relevant to the problem or question being addressed. It aligns with the objectives of the analysis and provides meaningful insights that can inform decision-making processes.
3. **Acceptable for Intended Purpose**: Data should be relevant to the problem or question being addressed. It should also meet any specific requirements or criteria set for the analysis. The data selected is directly related to the problem or question being addressed. It provides information that is pertinent and meaningful in the context of the analysis. The data is suitable for the intended use or analysis methodology. It meets any specific requirements, criteria, or constraints set for the analysis, such as data format, quality, or scope. For example, if the objective is to analyse customer preferences for a new product, appropriate data would include information such as past purchase history, demographic characteristics, and survey responses related to product preferences. Using data that is irrelevant or unrelated to customer preferences would not be appropriate for the intended purpose.

This process includes various steps to verify the quality of data, such as data cleaning, data validation, and data profiling.

1. **Data Cleaning**: This is the process of identifying and correcting errors, inconsistencies, or missing values in the dataset. Cleaning the data ensures that it is accurate and reliable for analysis. It is a crucial step in the data preparation phase of the data science workflow. Initially, data cleaning entails identifying errors or anomalies within the dataset. This may include various

issues such as missing values, incorrect data types, outliers, duplicates, or inconsistencies in formatting. Detecting these discrepancies is crucial for laying the groundwork for effective data cleaning. One of the primary tasks in data cleaning is handling missing values, which are common occurrences in datasets. Missing values can arise due to a multitude of factors, such as data entry errors or equipment malfunctions. Strategies for managing missing values typically involve either imputation, where missing values are replaced with estimated values based on other data, or deletion, which involves removing rows or columns containing missing values. In addition to missing values, data cleaning also focuses on rectifying inconsistencies present within the dataset. These inconsistencies may stem from different data sources or entry methods, resulting in variations in formatting or coding. Standardising data formats, correcting typos, and reconciling discrepancies are integral aspects of this process. Another crucial facet of data cleaning involves identifying and removing duplicate records or entries within the dataset. Duplicate entries can skew analysis results and inflate statistical measures, making their identification and elimination imperative for ensuring the integrity of the dataset. Data cleaning addresses outliers—data points that substantially deviate from the rest of the dataset. Outliers have the potential to distort analysis results and may require correction, removal, or separate treatment based on the context of the analysis. Data cleaning encompasses validating the accuracy and integrity of the data through various checks and validations. This may involve cross-referencing data with external sources, conducting logical checks, or performing consistency checks to verify the reliability of the dataset.

2. **Data Validation**: Data validation involves checking the integrity and quality of the data. This includes verifying data formats, ensuring that data falls within expected ranges, and checking for relationships between different data fields. Data validation focuses on confirming that the data is correctly formatted or structured. This entails ensuring that data fields adhere to expected formats, such as dates, numbers, or text, and comply with any formatting requirements set for them. Data validation entails validating that data values fall within anticipated ranges or limits. For example, numeric data must fit within predetermined minimum and maximum values, while date data should fall within a specified timeframe. Data validation maintains the integrity of the data by identifying inconsistencies or irregularities. It involves examining for logical errors or discrepancies between interconnected data fields to ensure data coherence and precision.
3. **Data Profiling**: Data profiling involves analysing the structure and content of the data to understand its characteristics. This helps in identifying any anomalies or patterns in the data that may need further investigation.

6.3 DATA GOVERNANCE

Data governance entails the comprehensive management of data availability, usability, integrity, and security within an organisation. It involves establishing processes, policies, standards, and guidelines to ensure the effective management of data assets throughout their lifecycle. Key elements of data governance encompass data quality management, ensuring accuracy, consistency, and reliability of data, alongside data security measures to safeguard against unauthorised access and cyber threats. It also encompasses data privacy considerations, ensuring compliance with regulations and organisational policies regarding personal or sensitive information. Data stewardship involves assigning responsibilities for managing and maintaining data assets to specific individuals or teams. Additionally, data architecture is pivotal in designing the structure and organisation of data to align with business requirements and objectives. Data lifecycle management ensures systematic handling of data from creation to archival or disposal. Compliance with regulatory requirements is also crucial, ensuring that data management practices adhere to relevant laws, regulations, and industry standards. Effective data governance enables organisations to maximise the value of their data assets, minimise risks, and ensure responsible and ethical use of data, thereby facilitating informed decision-making processes by providing accurate and timely information to stakeholders.

Data governance constitutes a foundational aspect of any organisation engaged in handling big data, fostering uniform business processes and accountabilities across the board. It delineates the categories of data requiring meticulous control through the organisation's data governance framework. This framework establishes explicit regulations regarding the roles of personnel with data access or responsibility, necessitating consensus across various departments within the organisation. For instance, safeguarding the privacy of patient information and medical records holds particular significance in the healthcare sector. Entities like hospitals or individual medical practices must diligently secure patient data as it traverses through their operations. A well-crafted, top-tier data governance initiative typically encompasses a dedicated governance team, a steering committee serving as the governing authority, and a cohort of data stewards. Data stewards fulfil a supervisory function within the organisation's data governance framework. Their primary responsibility is to uphold the quality and suitability of the organisation's data assets. Recognised as specialists, they contribute to the development and execution of data assets while proposing enhancements to the data governance process. Collaboratively, these individuals establish the standards and policies governing data, with the data stewards primarily overseeing the implementation and enforcement procedures. Senior executives and representatives from the organisation's management, in conjunction with IT and data management teams, also play integral roles in data governance efforts.

In the US, part of the challenge lies in striking a delicate balance where data used for research purposes can be handled safely and securely, ensuring that evidence can be generated without compromising legitimate interests. The advancements in health information storage and technology, as discussed elsewhere in this compilation, have rendered the pursuit of this equilibrium more promising. Now, it is feasible to manage research within secure data enclave environments, which enhances the viability of achieving this balance. The critical question arises regarding the duration of the social and legal adjustment required to fully leverage this technology, a query that has surfaced repeatedly in health policy discussions as new technologies reshape the healthcare landscape. Notably, technology has reshaped societal expectations concerning the professional standard of care, consequently instigating significant legal transformations [342]. Presently, this scenario remains consistent, particularly with the enactment of the American Recovery and Reinvestment Act (ARRA) of 2009, inclusive of the HITECH Act, and the focus of healthcare reform on enhancing efficiency, performance, and comparative effectiveness research. The Patient Protection and Affordable Care Act (PPACA) underscores the significance of health information in generating essential knowledge for enhancing quality, reducing costs, and fostering population health. This legislative emphasis indicates a burgeoning interest in health information, suggesting a swift evolution in this domain.

The 2007 Request for Information (RFI) signified the Agency for Healthcare Research and Quality's (AHRQ) endeavour, under its extensive agency mandate, to facilitate technological advancements aimed at enhancing healthcare quality. The RFI aimed to gather insights on the establishment of a National Health Data Stewardship Entity (NHDSE) to support a performance measurement and reporting initiative, as recommended by the Institute of Medicine in a previous report. Seeking stakeholder input, the RFI solicited public comments on the structure, functions, and roles of a data stewardship entity, with terms like "stewardship" and "stewardship entity" left undefined. AHRQ specifically requested feedback on the characteristics and functions of an NHDSE, highlighting areas of agency interest such as public–private governance, mission, and the adoption of uniform operating rules and standards for sharing and aggregating quality and efficiency data. The envisioned entity was not to be an extension of AHRQ itself but rather an independent body with certain powers, including data collection and holding, and advising agencies on research priorities and evaluation methodologies. The proposed entity was envisioned to transcend mere technical functions, venturing into policy development and advisement. To this end, AHRQ outlined a set of proposed principles, including objectivity, independence in governance, knowledge-based conduct, responsiveness, trustworthiness, adaptability, transparency, timeliness, collaborative style, and sustainability. AHRQ sought feedback on the necessity and value of such an entity, its roles and responsibilities, challenges and risks in its creation and sustenance, stakeholder governance models, conflict avoidance methods, priority areas of activity, and the suitability of existing organisations for fulfilling such a role.

A data steward assumes responsibility for managing available data. However, this responsibility is shrouded in uncertainty. Concerns arise, particularly for those well-versed in privacy and confidentiality issues, regarding the potential for data stewardship to expose healthcare-generated data for broader system-wide use. These concerns extend beyond patient rights, delving into the business aspects of healthcare. Like any business, healthcare relies on safeguarding information that may carry business, legal, or social ramifications. The government holds the authority to establish a data steward, as evidenced by the creation of a Federal Coordinating Council for Comparative Effectiveness Research under health reform. Government entities routinely collect and utilise healthcare data to inform their practices, leveraging powers related to taxation, expenditure, and commerce regulation. Extensive healthcare data is reported to federal agencies via programmes like Medicare and Medicaid, and disciplinary actions against physicians by hospitals are similarly documented and analysed. Additionally, public health agencies at various levels of government collect, store, and utilise personal information as part of their public health effort. Despite the government's capacity to gather healthcare data, several factors prompt a cautious approach towards utilising this information to make more informed decisions regarding resource allocation or population health advancement. These factors include ongoing concerns about privacy and security safeguards, as well as the substantial interests of healthcare industry stakeholders who may resist disclosure despite significant federal investment in healthcare. Government officials increasingly recognise the need for greater knowledge, yet the healthcare industry has managed to introduce legal protections to shield their actions from public scrutiny. Examples include the Patient Safety Quality Improvement Act, which establishes a federal privilege against disclosing "patient safety work product," and special exemptions from public reporting for Medicare Part D prescription drug plans.

Many experts highlight the imperfections of existing privacy and security standards. Amendments to the HIPAA Privacy Rule, as outlined in the ARRA, aim to bolster these standards. These amendments expand the scope of entities subject to the Privacy Rule, enhance security measures, impose penalties for breach notification failures, and augment patients' rights to withhold consent for certain data uses. The Common Rule, which governs research, provides additional safeguards against unauthorised data usage. A study by the Institute of Medicine [343] proposed simplifying data usage in research, including reforms allowing health information custodians to disclose personally identifiable health information without consent to "prescribed persons or entities" that implement privacy and confidentiality safeguards. Similar practices in the UK, supported by robust data stewardship and technological advancements, underpin such progressive standards. Various federal and state laws address access to and use of specific data types, such as genetic information or information related to mental illness or addiction disorders. These laws often require specific informed consent for data usage, posing additional challenges. The evolution of these laws is likely to hinge on the safety and security track record established by data stewards, as well as the perceived value of enhanced data access in contrast to the associated risks of aggregating patient and provider data for health system evidence.

6.4 DATA CODES OF PRACTICE AND FRAMEWORKS

When utilising personal data, adherence to the principles outlined in the European Union (EU) General Data Protection Regulation (GDPR) and the Data Protection Act 2018 (DPA 2018) is mandatory. The DPA 2018 not only incorporates elements of the GDPR but also transposes the Law Enforcement Directive into UK law. Furthermore, it establishes distinct processing regimes for activities that lie beyond the scope of EU legislation. The definition of personal data is provided in Section 3(2) of the DPA 2018, with a more comprehensive explanation available in Article 4 of the GDPR.

The pertinent chapters of Part 5 of the Digital Economy Bill, concerning public service delivery, debt, and fraud, define personal information as data that pertains to and identifies a specific individual or body corporate. According to this definition, information "identifies" a particular person if the person's identity is either explicitly stated in the information, deducible from the information itself, or deducible from the information in combination with other available data. Contrastingly, the Data Protection Act 1998 (DPA 1998) defines personal data as information relating to a living individual who can be identified from that data or from data likely to come into the possession of the data controller. This definition under the DPA encompasses not only factual data but also opinions about an individual and indications of intentions concerning that individual. It's important to note that the definition of personal information excludes data about the internal administrative arrangements of the specified body permitted to disclose or receive data under these permissive powers.

The definitions of "personal information" outlined in the Bill are aimed at ensuring careful handling of information shared through its provisions. While the definition of "personal information" under the Bill may differ from the definition of "personal data" in the DPA, all information shared and utilised under the public service delivery, debt, and fraud provisions must adhere to the framework of rules established in the DPA, particularly the Data Protection Principles. Additionally, specific safeguards have been introduced in the Bill to guarantee appropriate handling of personal information. The provisions related to public service delivery, debt, and fraud are subject to the DPA, including criminal offences concerning the unlawful obtaining or disclosure of personal data outlined in Section 55. Moreover, the Bill introduces new criminal offences to prevent the unlawful disclosure of personal information. Individuals convicted under these offences could face a maximum penalty of up to two years in prison, an unlimited fine, or both. These maximum penalties align with those existing offences governing data use by HMRC and DWP, emphasising the Government's commitment to safeguarding citizens' data. Traditionally, data sharing has involved bulk transfers within and between public authorities. However, advancements in technology have significantly influenced data-sharing practices. Application Programming Interfaces (APIs) serve as standards enabling software components to interact and exchange data. APIs facilitate interaction between applications and datasets across organisational and geographical boundaries, allowing public authorities to identify or verify eligibility for services and other objectives through less intrusive methods, such as binary checks against specific datasets. Although this method is generally safer and less intrusive, as large data transfers are avoided and underlying data sharing is eliminated when eligibility is checked, information is still being shared. Thus, those involved in data sharing in these manners require legal powers to do so.

6.5 DEVELOPING DATA GOVERNANCE AND REGULATORY FRAMEWORKS

In an era marked by exponential growth in data generation, the development of robust data governance and regulatory frameworks has become imperative. Data governance refers to the policies, procedures, and standards that ensure the proper management, integrity, and security of data assets. Regulatory frameworks complement governance by establishing legal and ethical guidelines to protect data and promote its responsible use. Together, these frameworks underpin the effective utilisation of data, particularly in fields such as healthcare, finance, and artificial intelligence (AI). This chapter explores the principles, methodologies, and challenges in developing data governance and regulatory frameworks, with a focus on their scientific foundations and applications.

6.5.1 Foundations of Data Governance

6.5.1.1 Definition and Scope

Data governance encompasses a comprehensive system of policies, processes, and tools designed to manage data availability, usability, integrity, and security. It addresses the entire data lifecycle, from collection and storage to analysis and dissemination [344,345]. Key elements include the following:

1. **Data Stewardship**:
    - Designating roles and responsibilities for data management.
    - Ensuring accountability for data quality and compliance.
2. **Data Quality Management**:
    - Establishing standards for accuracy, consistency, and completeness.
    - Implementing regular audits and validation processes.
3. **Data Security and Privacy**:
    - Safeguarding data against unauthorised access and breaches.
    - Complying with privacy regulations, such as the GDPR.
4. **Data Sharing and Interoperability**:
    - Facilitating secure and efficient data exchange across systems and organisations.
    - Adopting standardised formats and protocols.

6.5.1.2 Scientific Foundations

The development of data governance frameworks is informed by multiple disciplines, including the following:

- **Computer Science**: Techniques in cryptography, database management, and system architecture form the technical basis for governance.
- **Ethics**: Principles of autonomy, beneficence, and justice guide the responsible use of data.
- **Law**: Legal frameworks provide enforceable standards and recourse for data misuse.
- **Management Science**: Strategies for organisational change and stakeholder engagement support effective implementation.

6.5.2 Regulatory Frameworks: Principles and Approaches

6.5.2.1 Principles of Regulation

Effective regulatory frameworks are grounded in principles that balance innovation with protection. These are as follows:

1. **Transparency**:
   - Requiring organisations to disclose data practices, including collection, usage, and sharing.
   - Enhancing public trust and accountability.
2. **Fairness and Equity**:
   - Preventing discrimination and ensuring equitable access to data-driven benefits.
   - Addressing biases in algorithmic decision-making.
3. **Proportionality**:
   - Tailoring regulations to the level of risk associated with data use.
   - Avoiding unnecessary burdens on innovation.
4. **Harmonisation**:
   - Aligning national and international regulations to facilitate cross-border data flows.
   - Promoting consistency across sectors.

6.5.2.2 Approaches to Regulation

1. **Prescriptive Regulation**:
   - Specifies detailed requirements for compliance.
   - **Example**: GDPR mandates specific measures for data protection, including breach notification and consent [346].
2. **Principles-Based Regulation**:
   - Focuses on high-level principles rather than prescriptive rules.
   - **Example**: The UK Data Ethics Framework provides guidelines for ethical data use without dictating specific practices [347].
3. **Co-Regulation**:
   - Combines government oversight with industry self-regulation.
   - **Example**: The International Organization for Standardization (ISO) standards for information security.
4. **Responsive Regulation**:
   - Adapts to emerging technologies and societal needs.
   - **Example**: Regulatory sandboxes for testing innovations in a controlled environment.

6.5.3 Challenges in Developing Frameworks

6.5.3.1 Data Complexity and Volume

The unprecedented growth in data generation presents significant challenges for governance and regulation. Modern organisations must navigate the intricacies of managing vast quantities of data that vary in structure, source, and velocity [348,349]. The primary challenges include the following:

1. **Integrating Structured and Unstructured Data from Diverse Sources**:
   - **Heterogeneity of Data**: Structured data, such as relational databases, coexist with unstructured formats like images, videos, and text.

Harmonising these disparate formats requires sophisticated data integration tools and techniques.

- **Data Silos**: Organisations often store data in isolated systems, creating barriers to interoperability and holistic analysis. Breaking down silos involves implementing enterprise-wide data governance policies and adopting interoperable standards.
- **Semantic Interoperability**: Ensuring that data from diverse sources convey consistent meanings necessitates the use of ontologies and metadata standards. For example, the healthcare sector employs Health Level Seven (HL7) and Fast Healthcare Interoperability Resources (FHIR) standards to achieve semantic alignment across electronic health records (EHRs).

Critical Reflection: While technological advances, such as cloud-based data warehouses and AI-powered data integration platforms, facilitate progress, their deployment requires substantial investments. Smaller organisations or those in low-resource settings may face difficulties adopting these technologies, exacerbating the digital divide.

2. **Managing Real-Time Data Streams in Internet of Things (IoT) Applications**:
   - **Velocity of Data**: The proliferation of IoT devices generates continuous, high-velocity data streams, necessitating real-time processing and analytics. Examples include sensor data from smart homes, autonomous vehicles, and industrial monitoring systems.
   - **Data Overload**: Real-time data processing poses challenges in prioritising critical information while filtering irrelevant or redundant data. This is particularly crucial in safety-critical domains, such as aviation or healthcare monitoring.
   - **Infrastructure Requirements**: Managing real-time streams requires robust infrastructure, including edge computing and distributed systems, to process data closer to the source and reduce latency.

   Critical Reflection: While IoT applications promise transformative benefits, such as predictive maintenance and personalised healthcare, they also introduce vulnerabilities. Real-time data streams are prone to cyberattacks, necessitating stringent security measures. Moreover, regulatory frameworks must address the ownership and privacy concerns associated with continuously collected personal data.

6.5.4 Balancing Innovation and Protection

The pursuit of innovation often intersects with the imperative to protect individual rights, particularly in domains such as AI and healthcare. While technological advancements promise transformative benefits, they also pose significant ethical, legal, and societal challenges. This critical appraisal evaluates the complexities of balancing innovation and protection in these fields, focusing on algorithmic opacity in AI and data privacy concerns in healthcare. Frameworks must encourage technological advancements while safeguarding rights. Striking this balance is particularly challenging in the following:

6.5.4.1 AI: Algorithmic Opacity and Accountability

6.5.4.1.1 Promise of Innovation

AI systems, particularly machine learning (ML) models, have revolutionised sectors by enabling predictive analytics, automation, and personalised experiences. Their capabilities include diagnosing diseases, optimising supply chains, and even judicial decision-making. However, these systems often operate as black boxes, with decision-making processes that are opaque even to their developers.

6.5.4.1.2 Challenges of Algorithmic Opacity

1. **Lack of Transparency**:
   - Many AI systems, especially deep learning models, lack interpretability. Stakeholders cannot easily trace how input data translates into outputs, complicating accountability for erroneous or biased decisions.
   - For example, in predictive policing algorithms, opacity has led to discriminatory outcomes without clear mechanisms to identify or rectify biases.
2. **Bias and Discrimination**:
   - Training data often reflect historical inequities, embedding biases within AI systems. Without transparency, identifying and addressing these biases becomes challenging.
   - Disparities in facial recognition algorithms, which perform poorly on darker skin tones, illustrate the societal risks of unaccountable AI systems.
3. **Regulatory Gaps**:
   - Existing regulatory frameworks often lag behind technological advancements. The lack of enforceable standards for explainability and fairness exacerbates risks.
   - For instance, the EU's AI Act aims to classify and regulate AI systems by risk levels, but its implementation faces delays and industry resistance.

6.5.4.1.3 Strategies to Balance Innovation and Protection

1. **Mandating Explainability**:
   - Regulatory frameworks must require AI systems to include explainability as a core feature, ensuring decisions can be traced and understood.
   - Techniques such as Local Interpretable Model-agnostic Explanations (LIME) and SHapley Additive exPlanations (SHAP) offer potential solutions.
2. **Ethical AI by Design**:
   - Embedding ethical principles into the AI development lifecycle ensures fairness, accountability, and transparency.

- Initiatives like the IEEE Global Initiative on Ethics of Autonomous and Intelligent Systems provide actionable guidelines for developers.

3. **Independent Auditing and Oversight**:
    - Independent audits of AI systems can identify biases and assess compliance with ethical standards.
    - Mechanisms for redress, such as appeals against automated decisions, empower affected individuals.

Critical Reflection: Balancing innovation and protection in AI requires proactive regulatory measures that do not stifle technological growth. Achieving this balance necessitates global collaboration to establish harmonised standards while fostering accountability and transparency.

6.5.4.2 Healthcare: Accelerating Innovation and Protecting Privacy

6.5.4.2.1 Promise of Innovation

Healthcare innovation thrives on data sharing, enabling breakthroughs in precision medicine, early diagnosis, and population health management. Collaborative data ecosystems, such as those underpinning genomic research and pandemic response efforts, exemplify the transformative potential of shared health data.

6.5.4.2.2 Challenges of Data Sharing and Privacy

1. **Data Sensitivity**:
    - Health data are among the most sensitive types of personal information, encompassing medical histories, genetic data, and behavioural patterns. Breaches of such data carry profound consequences, including identity theft and discrimination.
    - For example, the 2017 NHS data breach exposed vulnerabilities in systems handling sensitive patient information.
2. **Consent and Autonomy**:
    - Obtaining informed consent for data use is complex in large-scale research initiatives, where future uses of data may not be foreseeable.
    - This complexity is evident in biobanking projects, where participants often consent to broad, unspecified future research.
3. **Inequities in Access**:
    - Data sharing often benefits well-resourced institutions while excluding marginalised communities, exacerbating health disparities.
    - For instance, low-income countries face barriers to accessing shared genomic data due to technological and financial constraints.

6.5.4.2.3 Strategies to Balance Innovation and Protection

1. **Privacy-Preserving Technologies**:
    - Techniques such as federated learning and differential privacy enable data sharing while minimising exposure of sensitive information.
    - Federated learning allows AI models to be trained across distributed data sources without centralising data, preserving patient privacy.

2. **Robust Governance Frameworks**:
   - Governance structures that ensure ethical oversight and accountability are critical. These include data access committees and public involvement in decision-making.
   - The UK's National Data Guardian provides a model for balancing data sharing with patient trust and transparency.
3. **Global Data Equity**:
   - Collaborative frameworks must address disparities in access and representation. For example, initiatives like the Global Alliance for Genomics and Health (GA4GH) promote equitable sharing of genomic data across borders.
   - Capacity-building efforts, such as training programmes and infrastructure development, empower underrepresented regions to participate in and benefit from shared data ecosystems.

Critical Reflection: In healthcare, innovation and privacy are not mutually exclusive but interdependent. Effective governance frameworks and privacy-preserving technologies can enable transformative progress while safeguarding individual rights.

Balancing innovation and protection in AI and healthcare requires nuanced, multifaceted approaches that address unique challenges in each field. In AI, tackling algorithmic opacity demands a combination of explainable technologies, ethical frameworks, and robust oversight. In healthcare, the emphasis must be on governance structures, privacy-preserving technologies, and equitable access. Achieving this balance will require interdisciplinary collaboration, proactive regulation, and a commitment to ethical principles, ensuring that technological advancements serve society equitably and responsibly.

6.5.5 Global Disparities and Harmonisation

The development of regulatory frameworks for data governance faces significant challenges due to global disparities in technological capacity and governance maturity. These disparities not only impede equitable progress but also create vulnerabilities that undermine international collaboration and data protection. This critical appraisal explores the complexities of addressing global disparities and the importance of harmonising regulations to enable international collaboration and prevent regulatory arbitrage. Regulatory frameworks must address disparities in technological capacity and data governance maturity. Harmonising regulations across jurisdictions is vital for the following:

6.5.5.1 Global Disparities in Technological Capacity and Data Governance Maturity

6.5.5.1.1 Technological Capacity

Technological capacity varies widely across nations, particularly between high-income and low-income countries. Disparities in access to infrastructure, expertise, and resources significantly affect the ability of nations to implement robust data governance frameworks.

1. **Infrastructure Gaps**:
    - Low-resource countries often lack the digital infrastructure needed to collect, store, and analyse data securely. This impedes their ability to participate in international data-sharing initiatives, such as genomic research or climate modelling.
    - For example, in sub-Saharan Africa, limited internet connectivity and outdated hardware hinder the adoption of advanced data technologies.
2. **Expertise and Workforce Development**:
    - A shortage of skilled professionals in data science, cybersecurity, and regulatory compliance limits the capacity to manage complex data governance systems.
    - Countries with robust educational systems and investment in STEM fields, such as the US and Germany, contrast starkly with regions where technical training is scarce.
3. **Policy and Legal Frameworks**:
    - Nations at different stages of economic and technological development often exhibit disparities in the maturity of their data governance policies. For instance, while the EU has implemented the comprehensive GDPR, many developing countries are still drafting foundational legislation.

Critical Reflection: Efforts to close technological capacity gaps require international collaboration and targeted investments. High-income countries and global organisations must prioritise capacity-building initiatives in low-resource regions, ensuring equitable access to technological advancements.

6.5.5.1.2 Data Governance Maturity

Governance maturity varies due to historical, cultural, and political factors. Countries with advanced governance systems often implement stringent data protection measures, while others struggle to enforce even basic privacy standards.

1. **Cultural and Ethical Differences**:
    - Perceptions of privacy and data ownership vary globally, complicating the development of standardised governance frameworks. For example, collectivist societies may prioritise communal benefits over individual privacy, influencing governance models.
    - Ethical concerns about data sovereignty and exploitation further complicate cross-border data sharing, particularly in low-income countries that may lack robust protections against misuse.
2. **Political Will and Resources**:
    - In nations where political stability is fragile, data governance is often deprioritised. Limited resources and competing priorities, such as healthcare and education, further impede progress.
    - Countries with authoritarian regimes may exploit data governance frameworks to suppress dissent, contrasting with democratic nations that prioritise transparency and accountability.

Critical Reflection: Addressing governance maturity disparities requires adaptive frameworks that respect cultural differences while promoting universal principles of fairness, transparency, and accountability.

6.5.5.2 Harmonising Regulations across Jurisdictions

The harmonisation of data governance regulations is essential for enabling international collaboration and preventing regulatory arbitrage. However, achieving this harmonisation presents substantial challenges due to varying legal systems, economic interests, and cultural values.

6.5.5.2.1 Enabling International Collaboration and Data Sharing

1. **Standardisation**:
   - Developing global standards for data protection, interoperability, and ethical use is vital for fostering trust and collaboration. Initiatives such as the ISO provide a foundation for aligning governance practices.
   - For example, the HL7 and FHIR standards enable seamless data exchange in healthcare systems across borders.
2. **Trust-Building Mechanisms**:
   - Trust frameworks, such as the EU-US Privacy Shield (now invalidated but replaced with newer agreements), are critical for ensuring data-sharing agreements comply with varying regulatory requirements.
   - Transparent reporting and accountability measures enhance confidence among stakeholders, promoting sustainable international collaborations.
3. **Equitable Access and Representation**:
   - Harmonisation efforts must include underrepresented nations and communities, ensuring equitable participation in global data ecosystems.
   - The Global Alliance for Genomics and Health (GA4GH) exemplifies efforts to include diverse stakeholders in shaping data governance policies.

Critical Reflection: While harmonisation fosters collaboration, it risks favouring well-resourced nations if not carefully managed. Ensuring equitable representation and addressing power imbalances are crucial for inclusive progress.

6.5.5.2.2 Preventing Regulatory Arbitrage

Regulatory arbitrage occurs when organisations exploit inconsistencies in governance frameworks across jurisdictions to evade stringent regulations. This undermines global efforts to protect data and exacerbates inequalities.

1. **Exploitation of Weak Frameworks**:
   - Organisations often relocate operations or store data in countries with less stringent data protection laws to reduce compliance costs.
   - For instance, data centres are frequently established in jurisdictions with lenient regulations, raising concerns about privacy and accountability.

2. **Impact on Competition**:
   - Regulatory inconsistencies create an uneven playing field, disadvantaging organisations operating in regions with robust governance frameworks.
   - Small and medium-sized enterprises (SMEs) may struggle to compete with larger corporations that leverage regulatory arbitrage to lower operational costs.
3. **Mitigation Strategies**:
   - Bilateral and multilateral agreements can reduce disparities by aligning regulatory standards. The GDPR's extraterritorial provisions, which apply to organisations outside the EU that process EU citizens' data, serve as a model for combating arbitrage.
   - International cooperation, such as through the United Nations or the World Trade Organization (WTO), can promote uniform enforcement of data governance standards.

Critical Reflection: Preventing regulatory arbitrage requires a collective commitment to enforcing harmonised standards. However, the imposition of extraterritorial regulations must be balanced against concerns of sovereignty and fairness, particularly for low-resource nations.

Balancing global disparities in technological capacity and data governance maturity with the need for harmonisation is a complex but essential task. While international collaboration and standardisation offer pathways to equitable progress, efforts must account for cultural differences, ethical considerations, and economic inequities. Preventing regulatory arbitrage requires robust, enforceable standards that ensure accountability without stifling innovation. By fostering inclusive dialogue and prioritising capacity-building, global stakeholders can create governance frameworks that promote both protection and progress in the data-driven era.

6.5.6 Ethical and Social Considerations

The development and implementation of data governance frameworks must address profound ethical and social concerns. As data becomes increasingly central to decision-making across sectors, issues such as bias and discrimination and public scepticism about data collection and surveillance present significant challenges. This critical appraisal evaluates these concerns and explores strategies to mitigate their impact. Frameworks must address societal concerns, including the following:

6.5.6.1 Bias and Discrimination in Data-Driven Decision-Making

6.5.6.1.1 The Problem of Bias

Bias in data-driven decision-making arises when the datasets or algorithms used reflect and perpetuate existing inequalities. This issue is particularly prevalent in ML systems, which learn patterns from historical data that may encode societal prejudices.

1. **Sources of Bias**:
   - **Data Bias**: Historical data often reflect systemic inequalities, leading to biased outcomes when used in predictive models. For example, in hiring algorithms, historical bias against women in certain roles can perpetuate gender discrimination.
   - **Algorithmic Bias**: Design choices, such as feature selection or weighting, can introduce or amplify bias. Black-box algorithms, whose inner workings are opaque, exacerbate this issue by making it difficult to identify and rectify discriminatory patterns.
   - **Feedback Loops**: Systems that reinforce biased decisions through repeated use can create self-fulfilling cycles of inequality. For example, predictive policing systems disproportionately target minority communities based on historical crime data.
2. **Impact of Bias**:
   - Discriminatory outcomes in critical areas such as healthcare, finance, and criminal justice erode public trust and exacerbate social inequalities.
   - For instance, facial recognition technologies have been shown to misidentify individuals from minority groups at disproportionately high rates, leading to unjust consequences in law enforcement.

6.5.6.1.2 Strategies to Address Bias

1. **Bias Audits and Impact Assessments**:
   - Regular audits of datasets and algorithms can identify sources of bias. Bias impact assessments, akin to environmental impact assessments, can evaluate the societal implications of data-driven systems before deployment
   - **Example**: The AI Now Institute advocates for mandatory algorithmic impact assessments in high-stakes applications.
2. **Fairness Metrics**:
   - Incorporating fairness metrics into algorithm design can mitigate bias. These metrics, such as equal opportunity or demographic parity, ensure equitable treatment across demographic groups.
3. **Inclusive Design and Representation**:
   - Engaging diverse stakeholders during system design helps identify and address potential biases. For example, including underrepresented groups in the development of healthcare algorithms can ensure more equitable outcomes.

Critical Reflection: While technical interventions are necessary, addressing bias requires broader societal change. Efforts to reduce bias must be complemented by policies that tackle systemic inequalities, ensuring that data-driven decision-making promotes social justice.

6.5.6.2 Public Scepticism about Data Collection and Surveillance

6.5.6.2.1 The Problem of Scepticism

Public scepticism about data collection and surveillance stems from concerns over privacy violations, misuse of data, and lack of transparency. High-profile data breaches and revelations about mass surveillance have heightened these concerns.

1. **Erosion of Privacy**:
    - The widespread collection of personal data, often without explicit consent, raises significant privacy concerns. For example, data collected from social media platforms for behavioural targeting has been criticised for its intrusive nature.
    - Advances in technology, such as biometric data collection and location tracking, amplify these concerns by enabling unprecedented levels of surveillance.
2. **Lack of Transparency**:
    - Many organisations fail to provide clear information about how data is collected, stored, and used. Complex terms of service agreements often obscure data practices, undermining informed consent.
3. **Distrust in Institutions**:
    - Public distrust is exacerbated by perceived misuse of data by governments and corporations. For instance, the Cambridge Analytica scandal, which involved the misuse of Facebook data for political campaigns, significantly eroded trust in data governance.

6.5.6.2.2 Strategies to Address Public Scepticism

1. **Transparent Data Practices**:
    - Organisations must adopt transparent data practices, including clear communication about data collection, usage, and sharing.
    - Initiatives such as privacy dashboards, which allow individuals to view and control their data, empower users and build trust.
2. **Strengthening Consent Mechanisms**:
    - Consent processes must be simplified and made more meaningful. Dynamic consent models, which allow individuals to update their preferences over time, offer a promising approach.
    - **Example**: In healthcare research, dynamic consent platforms enable patients to decide how their data is used at different stages of a study.
3. **Accountability and Oversight**:
    - Independent oversight bodies can hold organisations accountable for ethical data practices. Public reporting requirements, such as those mandated by the GDPR, enhance accountability.
    - Mechanisms for redress, such as the right to erasure or compensation for misuse, further strengthen public confidence.

4. **Public Education and Engagement**:
   - Efforts to improve data literacy can empower individuals to make informed decisions about data sharing. Public engagement initiatives, such as citizen assemblies on data governance, can foster trust and inclusivity.

Critical Reflection: Addressing public scepticism requires a shift from a compliance-driven approach to a trust-centric model of data governance. Transparency, accountability, and engagement must be prioritised to rebuild public confidence in data practices [187].

Ethical and social considerations, such as bias and discrimination and public scepticism, are critical challenges in developing effective data governance frameworks. Mitigating bias in data-driven decision-making requires technical interventions, inclusive design, and systemic change to address underlying inequalities. Similarly, addressing public scepticism demands transparency, robust consent mechanisms, and active public engagement. By prioritising these considerations, governance frameworks can foster trust, equity, and accountability in the data-driven age [350].

6.5.6.2.3 Future Directions and Innovations

1. **Adaptive Governance**

   Frameworks must evolve to accommodate emerging technologies and societal needs [351]. Adaptive governance involves the following:
   - Continuous monitoring and evaluation of regulatory impact.
   - Stakeholder engagement to anticipate and address challenges.
2. **Decentralised Models**

   Decentralised data governance, enabled by technologies like blockchain, offers the following benefits:
   - Enhanced transparency and trust.
   - Greater user control over personal data.
3. **Ethical AI and Data Sovereignty**

   Developing frameworks that prioritise ethical considerations and data sovereignty will ensure the following:
   - Fair and accountable use of data.
   - Empowerment of individuals and communities to manage their data.

The development of data governance and regulatory frameworks is a multidisciplinary endeavour requiring collaboration across technical, legal, and ethical domains. By addressing challenges such as data complexity, global disparities, and ethical concerns, these frameworks can foster innovation while safeguarding rights. Future advancements in adaptive governance, decentralised models, and ethical AI will play a pivotal role in shaping a data-driven society that prioritises equity, accountability, and trust.

6.6 AUDITS AND REGULATORY INSPECTION PREPARATION

Audits and regulatory inspections serve as critical mechanisms for ensuring compliance, building stakeholder trust, and improving organisational processes. These evaluations assess adherence to legal and regulatory frameworks, industry standards, and internal policies, playing a central role in organisational governance and risk management. This discussion explores their importance with scientific rigour, focusing on compliance, stakeholder trust, and process improvement, and provides a critical reflection on their effectiveness.

6.6.1 Ensuring Compliance

6.6.1.1 Purpose and Scope

Audits and inspections are fundamental tools for verifying that organisations meet the requirements set forth by laws, regulations, and industry standards. Compliance ensures that operations align with legal obligations, mitigates risks associated with non-conformance, and fosters organisational integrity.

1. **Legal and Regulatory Compliance**:
    - Regulatory frameworks, such as the GDPR, mandate periodic audits to assess compliance with data privacy and protection requirements. These audits verify that organisations manage personal data responsibly, ensuring lawful processing, secure storage, and timely breach notifications.
    - For instance, GDPR audits evaluate adherence to principles of data minimisation and accountability, requiring evidence of documentation, consent management, and data subject rights fulfilment.
2. **Industry Standards**:
    - Industry-specific standards, such as ISO/IEC 27001 for information security management, necessitate regular audits to confirm the implementation of robust controls. Compliance with these standards demonstrates an organisation's commitment to safeguarding sensitive information.
3. **Internal Policies**:
    - Internal audits assess conformity with organisational policies, ensuring consistency in practices across departments. For example, internal evaluations of cybersecurity protocols may uncover lapses in employee adherence to password policies or incident reporting procedures.

Impact of Compliance Audits: Compliance audits reduce the risk of legal penalties, reputational damage, and operational disruptions. Moreover, they create a culture of accountability, emphasising the importance of ethical and lawful conduct across all levels of the organisation.

6.6.2 Building Stakeholder Trust

6.6.2.1 Transparency as a Pillar of Trust

Transparent audit practices enhance the credibility of organisations by demonstrating their commitment to ethical and responsible governance. Stakeholders, including customers, employees, investors, and regulatory bodies, value organisations that prioritise accountability.

1. **Customer Confidence**:
   - Customers are increasingly aware of their data privacy rights and expect organisations to handle their information responsibly. Regular audits provide assurance that businesses comply with privacy laws and protect customer data.
   - For instance, e-commerce platforms that pass PCI DSS (Payment Card Industry Data Security Standard) audits reassure customers about the security of their payment information.
2. **Employee Assurance**:
   - Transparent audits foster a culture of trust within organisations. Employees are more likely to engage with and adhere to policies when they perceive that the organisation values ethical practices and complies with regulations.
   - Clear communication of audit findings and follow-up actions can further reinforce this trust.
3. **Investor and Regulatory Confidence**:
   - Investors view audit results as indicators of financial stability and governance quality. Organisations with strong audit records are more likely to attract investments.
   - Regulatory bodies, too, are more inclined to engage collaboratively with organisations that demonstrate consistent compliance and transparency in their audit practices.

Reputation Management: Organisations that consistently meet audit standards gain a competitive edge by establishing themselves as reliable and trustworthy. Conversely, failing audits or withholding audit results can damage reputations and erode stakeholder confidence.

6.6.3 Improving Processes and Reducing Risks

6.6.3.1 Identification of Weaknesses

Audits are instrumental in identifying gaps in governance frameworks, operational processes, and risk management strategies. By uncovering vulnerabilities, audits provide a roadmap for corrective actions and continuous improvement.

1. **Governance Weaknesses**:
   - Audits evaluate the effectiveness of governance structures, such as the role of data protection officers (DPOs) under GDPR or the adequacy of information security committees in organisations certified under ISO/IEC 27001.
   - For example, audits might reveal inadequate reporting lines or insufficient training for governance teams, highlighting areas for organisational restructuring.
2. **Operational Risks**:
   - Inspections of operational processes often identify inefficiencies or non-compliance. For instance, audits in manufacturing sectors may reveal deviations from safety protocols, while audits in financial institutions may identify gaps in anti-money laundering (AML) controls.
3. **Data Management Practices**:
   - Inadequate data management practices, such as unencrypted data storage or poor access control, are frequently highlighted in audits. Addressing these issues mitigates the risk of data breaches and enhances overall security.

6.6.3.2 Implementation of Corrective Actions

The insights from audits guide the development and implementation of corrective measures. For example, organisations may introduce automated monitoring tools, enhance staff training programmes, or revise internal policies to address identified gaps.

6.6.3.3 Proactive Risk Reduction

By identifying risks before they manifest as crises, audits contribute to organisational resilience. Proactive risk management reduces the likelihood of financial losses, regulatory penalties, and reputational harm.

6.6.4 Critical Reflection

6.6.4.1 Effectiveness Depends on Organisational Commitment

While audits and inspections are essential, their effectiveness hinges on the organisation's commitment to addressing findings and integrating recommendations into long-term strategies. Merely conducting audits without meaningful follow-up undermines their value and perpetuates risks.

6.6.4.2 Challenges in Implementation

1. **Resource Constraints**:
   - Smaller organisations may struggle to allocate resources for regular audits, particularly when compliance requirements are complex or costly.
2. **Audit Fatigue**:
   - Frequent audits across various domains can lead to disengagement and reduced quality of preparation, diluting the effectiveness of the process.

6.6.4.3 Opportunities for Continuous Improvement

1. **Technology Integration**:
   - Leveraging advanced technologies, such as AI for anomaly detection or blockchain for audit trails, can enhance the efficiency and reliability of audits.
2. **Stakeholder Involvement**:
   - Engaging stakeholders in the audit process, such as through feedback mechanisms, can provide valuable insights and foster a collaborative approach to governance.

Audits and regulatory inspections are indispensable for ensuring compliance, building stakeholder trust, and improving organisational processes. They verify adherence to legal and ethical standards, enhance transparency, and provide actionable insights for risk mitigation. However, their success relies on the organisation's dedication to addressing findings, allocating resources effectively, and embedding audit practices within a broader culture of accountability. By recognising these dynamics, organisations can leverage audits not only as compliance tools but also as catalysts for continuous improvement and strategic growth.

6.6.5 Challenges in Audit and Inspection Preparation: A Critical Discussion

Preparing for audits and regulatory inspections is a complex process that requires meticulous planning, cross-departmental coordination, and a deep understanding of evolving regulatory frameworks. Several challenges impede organisations' ability to meet these requirements, including navigating dynamic regulatory landscapes, addressing resource constraints, managing data complexity, and mitigating audit fatigue. This discussion critically examines these challenges and explores strategies to overcome them, using scientific reasoning and examples.

6.6.5.1 Dynamic Regulatory Landscape

6.6.5.1.1 Complexity of Regulations

Organisations operating in multiple jurisdictions must comply with a diverse array of regulatory requirements, often characterised by overlaps, contradictions, and ambiguities. Regulatory frameworks such as the GDPR in the EU and the California Consumer Privacy Act (CCPA) in the US exemplify this complexity. While both laws address data privacy, their scopes, terminologies, and enforcement mechanisms differ significantly.

1. **Overlapping Requirements**:
   - For instance, GDPR mandates a lawful basis for data processing and robust consent mechanisms, while CCPA emphasises consumer rights to data access, deletion, and opting out of sales. Organisations operating in both jurisdictions must harmonise their practices to comply with both regulations simultaneously.

- This requires maintaining multiple data governance policies, increasing administrative burden and risk of non-compliance.

2. **Conflicting Standards**:
   - Some regulatory frameworks may conflict, creating uncertainty in compliance strategies. For example, cross-border data transfers between regions with differing privacy laws, such as the EU and the US, face legal and operational challenges.
   - The invalidation of the EU-US Privacy Shield in 2020 highlighted these conflicts, forcing organisations to adopt alternative mechanisms like Standard Contractual Clauses.

6.6.5.1.2 Navigational Strategies

1. **Global Compliance Frameworks**:
   - Organisations can establish unified compliance frameworks based on widely accepted principles, such as those outlined by ISO/IEC standards, to address regulatory variations.
2. **Regulatory Intelligence Systems**:
   - Leveraging regulatory intelligence tools that monitor changes in laws across jurisdictions can help organisations stay informed and responsive.
3. **Engaging Legal Experts**:
   - Consulting regional legal experts ensures nuanced understanding and adherence to local requirements.

Critical Reflection: While regulatory diversity reflects regional priorities and values, greater international harmonisation of laws could reduce complexity and foster global compliance. Collaborative initiatives, such as the OECD Guidelines on the Protection of Privacy and Transborder Flows of Personal Data, exemplify steps in this direction.

6.6.5.2 Resource Constraints

6.6.5.2.1 Challenges for SMEs

SMEs face significant resource limitations in audit preparation, including constrained budgets, inadequate staffing, and limited access to compliance expertise.

1. **Budgetary Constraints**:
   - Robust audit preparation often requires investment in advanced tools, training programmes, and external consultants. For SMEs with tight budgets, these expenses can be prohibitive.
   - For instance, deploying automated compliance monitoring systems may be feasible for large organisations but challenging for SMEs.
2. **Staffing Limitations**:
   - SMEs may lack dedicated compliance teams, relying instead on generalist staff who juggle multiple responsibilities. This reduces the focus and expertise available for thorough audit preparation.

- Staff turnover further exacerbates this issue, leading to knowledge gaps and inconsistent practices.

6.6.5.2.2 *Mitigation Strategies*

1. **Scalable Solutions**:
   - Adopting cost-effective, scalable tools, such as cloud-based compliance platforms, enables SMEs to streamline audit preparation within their budgetary constraints.
2. **Collaborative Models**:
   - SMEs can participate in industry consortia or cooperative compliance initiatives to share resources and best practices.
3. **Training and Upskilling**:
   - Offering targeted training programmes equips staff with the necessary skills to manage audits effectively, reducing reliance on external consultants.

Critical Reflection: Addressing resource constraints in SMEs requires systemic support, including government grants, subsidies, and accessible training programmes. Public–private partnerships could also facilitate shared access to compliance resources.

6.6.5.3 Data Complexity

6.6.5.3.1 *The Challenges of Modern Data Ecosystems*

The exponential growth of data in volume, variety, and velocity complicates audit preparation, particularly in organisations handling large-scale or diverse datasets.

1. **Volume**:
   - Organisations generate and store massive amounts of data across distributed systems, increasing the difficulty of identifying relevant records for audits.
   - For example, multinational corporations may need to audit data spread across numerous cloud servers, on-premise databases, and third-party systems.
2. **Variety**:
   - Data exists in structured (e.g., databases), semi-structured (e.g., JSON files), and unstructured (e.g., emails, videos) formats, necessitating specialised tools for integration and analysis.
   - Healthcare organisations, for instance, must reconcile data from EHRs, imaging systems, and wearable devices to ensure compliance with health data regulations.
3. **Velocity**:
   - Real-time data streams, such as those generated by IoT devices, require continuous monitoring and auditing. Ensuring the integrity of these dynamic datasets is a significant challenge.

6.6.5.3.2 Solutions for Managing Data Complexity

1. **Data Mapping and Classification**:
   - Implementing data mapping tools to identify and classify data assets aids in locating relevant information quickly during audits.
2. **Centralised Data Management**:
   - Establishing centralised data repositories simplifies access and governance. Data warehouses or data lakes can consolidate diverse datasets for easier management.
3. **Advanced Analytics**:
   - Leveraging AI and ML for anomaly detection and predictive analytics enhances the ability to identify potential non-compliance in large datasets.

Critical Reflection: Data complexity necessitates investment in cutting-edge technologies and cross-functional collaboration. Organisations must prioritise data governance as a strategic initiative, integrating it into their broader compliance frameworks.

6.6.5.4 Audit Fatigue

6.6.5.4.1 Impact of Frequent Audits

Organisations subject to repeated audits across various domains may experience audit fatigue, reducing engagement and preparation quality.

1. **Diminished Staff Morale**:
   - Employees tasked with repeated audit preparation may feel overwhelmed, leading to disengagement and errors.
   - For instance, compliance teams in financial institutions may be audited for AML, cybersecurity, and financial reporting within a single year.
2. **Reduced Preparation Quality**:
   - Frequent audits can result in a focus on meeting minimum requirements rather than addressing systemic issues. This short-term approach undermines the effectiveness of audits in driving improvement.

6.6.5.4.2 Strategies to Mitigate Audit Fatigue

1. **Audit Coordination**:
   - Coordinating audits to avoid redundancy and streamline processes reduces duplication of effort. For example, integrated audits can combine assessments for overlapping requirements.
2. **Rotational Scheduling**:
   - Implementing rotational audit schedules distributes the workload more evenly, allowing staff time to focus on remediation and improvement.
3. **Automated Tools**:
   - Automation of repetitive audit tasks, such as data collection and reporting, reduces the burden on staff and improves consistency.

Critical Reflection: While audit fatigue is a legitimate concern, it can be mitigated through strategic planning and resource allocation. Organisations must view audits as opportunities for learning and improvement rather than burdensome obligations.

The challenges of audit and inspection preparation—navigating a dynamic regulatory landscape, addressing resource constraints, managing data complexity, and combating audit fatigue—underscore the need for proactive and systematic approaches. Organisations must invest in scalable technologies, foster collaboration, and cultivate a culture of compliance to address these challenges effectively. By integrating audits into a broader framework of continuous improvement, organisations can enhance resilience, accountability, and operational excellence.

6.6.6 Strategies for Effective Audit and Inspection Preparation

Audits and regulatory inspections are critical for ensuring compliance, identifying operational weaknesses, and fostering accountability. Effective preparation requires a systematic approach, combining comprehensive compliance frameworks, technological tools, organisational readiness, external expertise, and continuous improvement. This discussion explores strategies for optimising audit and inspection readiness using scientific reasoning and practical examples.

6.6.6.1 Developing a Comprehensive Compliance Framework

A robust compliance framework serves as the foundation for audit preparation, ensuring consistency and alignment with regulatory requirements and industry best practices.

6.6.6.1.1 Centralised Policies and Procedures

Establishing clear, standardised policies is essential for maintaining organisational coherence and ensuring that all activities comply with legal and regulatory standards.

1. **Policy Development**:
    - Policies should cover all aspects of operations, including data handling, storage, sharing, and security protocols.
    - **Example**: A comprehensive data protection policy aligned with GDPR mandates ensures consistent handling of personal data, such as obtaining consent, maintaining access logs, and securing storage systems.
2. **Standardisation**:
    - Standardised procedures reduce ambiguity, enabling employees to adhere to consistent practices across departments and geographies.
    - **Example**: A standard operating procedure for managing third-party vendor compliance ensures uniformity in evaluating contracts and data-sharing agreements.

6.6.6.1.2 Risk Assessments

Regular risk assessments help organisations identify potential vulnerabilities and prioritise corrective actions before audits.

1. **Cybersecurity Risk Analysis**:
   - Assessing cybersecurity risks ensures that critical vulnerabilities, such as outdated firewalls or weak password protocols, are addressed proactively.
   - **Example**: Regular penetration testing identifies system weaknesses, reducing the likelihood of data breaches during inspections.
2. **Operational Risk Evaluation**:
   - Evaluating operational risks, such as gaps in employee training or supply chain weaknesses, prepares organisations to address audit findings effectively.

Critical Reflection: Developing a compliance framework requires continuous updates to reflect evolving regulatory requirements and technological advancements. Leadership commitment is vital for embedding these practices within organisational culture.

6.6.6.2 Leveraging Technology for Compliance

Technological tools streamline audit preparation by automating processes, improving accuracy, and enhancing efficiency.

6.6.6.2.1 Automated Monitoring and Reporting

Automation reduces manual effort and ensures real-time tracking of compliance metrics.

1. **Compliance Dashboards**:
   - Tools such as data governance platforms monitor access logs, detect anomalies, and provide audit trails, ensuring transparency and accountability.
   - **Example**: Automated dashboards can alert organisations to unauthorised access attempts, enabling immediate corrective actions.
2. **Real-Time Reporting**:
   - Automated reporting tools generate compliance reports on demand, simplifying preparation for audits.
   - **Example**: A cloud-based system can produce GDPR compliance reports detailing data processing activities and breach response timelines.

6.6.6.2.2 Document Management Systems

Centralising documentation simplifies audit preparation and ensures version control.

1. **Central Repositories**:
   - Cloud-based systems store policies, audit findings, and related documentation in a single repository, facilitating easy retrieval and updates.
   - **Example**: Version-controlled systems prevent discrepancies in compliance documents across departments.
2. **Integration with Regulatory Portals**:
   - Integration with regulatory portals streamlines submission processes, reducing the administrative burden of audits.

Critical Reflection: While technology enhances efficiency, it requires upfront investment and training. Organisations must ensure that tools are scalable and adaptable to future needs.

6.6.6.3 Building Organisational Readiness

Organisational readiness is critical for smooth and effective audit preparation. It involves fostering a culture of compliance and ensuring collaboration across departments.

6.6.6.3.1 Internal Audits

Conducting regular internal audits simulates external inspections and identifies gaps proactively.

1. **Preparation Simulations**:
   - Mock audits assess the readiness of processes, documentation, and staff for regulatory inspections.
   - **Example**: Organisations following ISO 27001 conduct internal audits to prepare for external certification, ensuring adherence to information security standards.
2. **Remediation Plans**:
   - Findings from internal audits inform corrective action plans, strengthening compliance frameworks.

6.6.6.3.2 Training and Awareness

Ongoing education ensures that employees understand their roles and responsibilities in audit processes.

1. **Workshops and Seminars**:
   - Workshops on specific regulations, such as GDPR or PCI DSS, improve employee knowledge and engagement.
   - **Example**: DPOs can deliver training on consent management and breach notification protocols.
2. **Role-Specific Training**:
   - Tailored training ensures that employees in critical roles, such as IT or legal, are equipped to handle specific compliance challenges.

6.6.6.3.3 Cross-Functional Collaboration

Collaboration across departments ensures a holistic approach to compliance.

1. **Interdepartmental Committees**:
   - Committees comprising IT, HR, and legal teams ensure that compliance efforts are cohesive and comprehensive.
   - **Example**: Joint efforts between IT and HR can address gaps in employee data protection and cybersecurity protocols.

Critical Reflection: Building readiness requires leadership support and employee buy-in. Organisations must create incentives for compliance, such as recognition programmes for departments with exemplary audit performance.

6.6.6.4 Engaging External Expertise

External experts provide specialised knowledge and objective insights to enhance audit preparation.

6.6.6.4.1 Third-Party Consultants

Consultants with expertise in regulatory compliance can review policies, conduct mock audits, and provide recommendations.

1. **Specialised Reviews**:
    - External GDPR consultants can evaluate data protection practices, ensuring compliance with regulatory requirements.
    - **Example**: Consultants might recommend encrypting sensitive data or updating vendor contracts to align with GDPR.
2. **Industry-Specific Expertise**:
    - Consultants with domain expertise can address unique compliance challenges, such as FDA regulations in healthcare or AML requirements in finance.

6.6.6.4.2 Benchmarking and Peer Learning

Learning from industry peers and best practices improves audit readiness.

1. **Industry Forums**:
    - Participating in forums or associations facilitates knowledge sharing and benchmarking.
    - **Example**: Membership in industry-specific associations, such as ISACA, provides access to resources and networking opportunities.
2. **Case Studies**:
    - Reviewing case studies of successful audits offers practical insights into best practices.

Critical Reflection: While external expertise enhances readiness, organisations must ensure that consultants align with their strategic goals and compliance culture.

6.6.6.5 Post-Audit Follow-Up

6.6.6.5.1 Action Plans

Developing action plans based on audit findings demonstrates accountability and continuous improvement.

1. **Corrective Actions**:
    - Addressing gaps in access controls, security protocols, or documentation improves future compliance.
    - **Example**: Implementing multifactor authentication addresses weaknesses identified in cybersecurity audits.

2. **Timelines and Accountability**:
   - Setting clear timelines and assigning responsibilities ensure timely completion of action plans.

6.6.6.5.2 Feedback Mechanisms

Gathering feedback from auditors and staff refines audit preparation processes.

1. **Debriefs**:
   - Post-audit debriefs highlight lessons learned and inform improvements.
   - **Example**: Staff feedback might reveal gaps in training that require additional resources.
2. **Continuous Improvement**:
   - Regularly updating policies and procedures ensures sustained compliance and readiness for future audits.

Critical Reflection: Post-audit follow-up is an opportunity to reinforce a culture of accountability. Organisations must view audits as tools for growth rather than punitive measures.

Effective audit and inspection preparation requires a comprehensive approach that integrates compliance frameworks, technology, organisational readiness, external expertise, and continuous improvement. By adopting these strategies, organisations can enhance their audit readiness, ensure regulatory compliance, and maintain operational integrity. Leadership commitment and a culture of compliance are essential to embedding these practices into everyday operations, ultimately aligning audits with broader organisational growth and ethical responsibility.

6.7 CASE STUDY

Case Study: GCP Violations in the Trial

1. **Inadequate Informed Consent Process**
   - **Violation**: Participants were not fully informed about the potential risks of the investigational drug, including its effects on bone mineral density and fertility. The consent forms used technical jargon that many participants could not understand.
   - **Impact**: Several participants withdrew from the trial upon experiencing severe side effects, citing that they were unaware of these risks. This undermined the ethical foundation of the study and eroded trust in the trial.
2. **Poor Participant Monitoring**
   - **Violation**: Regular health checks mandated by the protocol were inconsistently conducted. Several participants reported worsening symptoms, including severe pelvic pain, which were not adequately addressed.
   - **Impact**: One participant developed a serious adverse event (osteoporosis), which went undetected until the trial's conclusion. This event could have been mitigated with proper monitoring, raising concerns about participant safety.

3. **Incomplete Documentation**
    - **Violation**: Site investigators failed to maintain accurate and complete records of participant data, including medication adherence and adverse events.
    - **Impact**: Missing and inconsistent data compromised the reliability of the trial's findings, raising questions about the drug's efficacy and safety profile.
4. **Protocol Deviations**
    - **Violation**: Investigators at one site altered the dosing schedule to accommodate participant preferences, contrary to the protocol. Another site enrolled participants who did not meet the inclusion criteria, such as individuals with a history of severe osteoporosis.
    - **Impact**: These deviations introduced variability in the trial data, undermining its scientific validity and the generalisability of its findings.
5. **Lack of Training and Oversight**
    - **Violation**: Site personnel lacked adequate training in GCP and the specific requirements of the trial protocol. Additionally, the sponsor failed to provide regular oversight or respond to site-specific issues.
    - **Impact**: Mismanagement at several sites contributed to widespread non-compliance with trial procedures, further jeopardising data integrity and participant safety.

CONSEQUENCES OF GCP NON-COMPLIANCE

1. **Regulatory Repercussions**
    - Regulatory authorities, including the FDA and EMA, suspended the trial following an inspection that uncovered widespread GCP violations. The sponsor faced fines and a halt to further drug development activities.
2. **Ethical and Legal Implications**
    - Participants filed lawsuits against the sponsor, alleging negligence and harm. Ethical breaches, such as inadequate informed consent, damaged the sponsor's reputation and undermined public trust in clinical research.
3. **Data Integrity Issues**
    - The trial's data were deemed unreliable, delaying the drug's potential approval and requiring the sponsor to redesign the trial with additional safeguards. This setback increased development costs and delayed access to a potentially beneficial therapy for patients with endometriosis.

LESSONS LEARNED

1. **Strengthen Informed Consent Procedures**
    - Simplify consent forms using plain language and ensure participants fully understand the risks and benefits of participation. Regularly update consent materials based on emerging trial data.
2. **Enhance Participant Monitoring**
    - Implement robust monitoring systems, such as EHRs and wearable devices, to ensure timely detection of adverse events. Conduct regular training for site staff on monitoring protocols.

3. **Maintain Accurate Documentation**
   - Use centralised electronic data capture systems to ensure consistent and complete documentation. Regular audits can identify and address documentation gaps promptly.
4. **Enforce Protocol Adherence**
   - Establish clear mechanisms for reporting and addressing protocol deviations. Conduct regular site visits to ensure compliance and provide guidance on protocol complexities.
5. **Prioritise GCP Training and Oversight**
   - Provide comprehensive GCP training to all site personnel before the trial begins. Sponsors should maintain regular communication with sites and conduct periodic inspections to ensure adherence to protocols and regulations.

CONCLUSION

This case study illustrates the consequences of poor adherence to Good Clinical Practice in a drug trial for endometriosis. The trial's GCP violations jeopardised participant safety, compromised data integrity, and delayed the development of a potentially transformative therapy. By learning from these failures, sponsors and investigators can implement stronger safeguards to ensure ethical and scientifically sound clinical trials, ultimately advancing the field of endometriosis treatment and improving patient outcomes.

7 Decision Support

It is a cliché that we all make decisions all the time, but it is not an untrue cliché. When it comes to one's health, it is quite easy to see that. Your patient had some breakfast today? That was the outcome of a decision (or probably of several decisions). Did they walk to work or to pick up their children from school, or did they take the car? Another few decisions there. And did they make it to tennis practice in the evening, or did they decide to do it ... well... sometime later this week? Are they complying to their medication regime and are they taking the medication properly? You get the point. And of course, health practitioners, of all people, know that much of their treatment of patients is the product of decision-making. Sure, there are tests to order and run and protocols and pathways to consult and follow, but sometimes you must judge, choose, or estimate; in short, you must decide. Hopefully, your decision-making is based on good evidence and sound reasoning, but there might always be the patient with a combination of symptoms you just have not seen or heard about before, or who might create a feeling of uncertainty to you about their situation. Let alone that, as we will discuss in this chapter, protocols and pathways are often just rules and algorithms for making decisions.

These points are of course not new. The field of health, or medical, decision-making has been around for some time [352]. This makes good sense because individual health outcomes, as well as healthcare system outcomes, have been linked to the decision-making of all stakeholders [353]. This chapter aims to dissect how academic decision theory, here broadly construed to also include other fields such as data science and machine learning, has been shaping practice, assess what this theory has contributed, and make informed suggestions about how it might further support medical decision-making. As is often the case in academia, decision theory has many faces. We start with classical decision theory.

7.1 CLASSICAL DECISION THEORY

One can always trace a scientific endeavour to the ancients, but for classical decision theory, one can start later. In the 16th and 17th centuries, prominent polymaths in Italy and France, such as Gerolamo Cardano and Blaise Pascal, saw that the emerging tools of probability could be applied to playing games of chance and skill, with coin, dice, and cards [352]. This modern theory of probability starts from obvious empirical facts such that, in the long run, a coin will land half of the time heads and half of the time tails (assuming that it is what is called a "fair" or "unbiased" coin). Well, according to the same logic, a dice will show an even number half of the time, and it will show a two or a four each one-sixth of the time. Logic and arithmetic then allow us to calculate more complicated probabilities by decomposing them into elementary events, as the ones described below. It was all about counting back then; sophisticated counting, but counting nevertheless. In the 18th century, the revered

DOI: 10.1201/9781003494737-7

Bayes thought more abstractedly about how one might revise a probability in the light of new information, with an approach that was more than vindicated and is in the core of data science today. A hundred years later, another Brit, mathematician Boole, clearly laid out the kind of logic that is necessary for probability calculations.

Are you superstitious? Here's a strange coincidence for you: The contributions of Blaise Pascal, Thomas Bayes, and George Boole all occurred on similar dates: 1654, 1754, and 1854 [354]. Next, fast forward to the 20th century. In 1954 (no kidding), American statistician Jimmie Savage brought Bayesian probability theory together with the concerns of economics and operations research about maximising the value that comes from making decisions, or as it is also often called, utility. He provided mathematical axioms that are seemingly compelling such as that if you prefer option A to B and B to C then you must also prefer A to C, and that are jointly logically equivalent to the doctrine that "rational" decision-making means to maximise one's subjective expected utility. At the time this book is written, it has been 70 years from Savage's (1954) classic contribution [355]. There are, of course, amendments, refinements, and objections to it, but it remains the Bible of classical decision theory. Ron Howard has aptly called it the old-time religion [356].

The present chapter respects the pioneering contributions of the classical decision doctrine, and retains some of its concepts, but goes beyond it and synthesises it with alternative decision theories—staying on the religious motif, one of this book's authors has called those heretics and heathens!—that focus on employing simple rules of thumb, or heuristics, for making decisions [357]. As you can see by peeping into the section titles, the likes of machine learning feature in the mix too. But we are getting ahead of ourselves. We first need to clarify the basics of classical decision theory and prepare the ground for the theories of heuristics and the subsequent synthesis. To do so, let us first describe the basics of classical decision theory with a medical example.

7.1.1 The Basics

Cindy is an amateur basketball enthusiast. During a pick-up game with friends, she jumps to make a basket with a fancy lay-up, only to subsequently land on top of the foot of another player. The details of the incident are somewhat fuzzy in Cindy's memory, but she thinks that she might have turned her ankle upon landing, and since then she has been feeling some pain in the malleolar zone of the foot, and her ankle looks like it is starting to swell. Cindy applied a pack of ice on the affected area and she is sitting courtside now, contemplating her options. Should she slowly bike home and see how it goes? Or should she have her friends take her to the emergency department of the nearby hospital?

Classical decision theory has, since the 1960s and the work of Howard and others, developed a practical arm, called decision analysis. Decision analysis relies on determining the ingredients of any given decision problem, which are (1) the set of possible options, (2) the possible consequences of each option, expressed numerically as utilities, and (3) the numerical probability of each consequence. Based on these ingredients, the worth of each option to Cindy, which classical decision theory calls subjective expected utility, can be computed. Then Cindy is gently nudged to choose the option with the higher worth, or if she is not ready to commit to this option yet, to go back to the drawing board. Below, we show how this work might unfold in action.

Cindy has identified two options: home or emergency. There might of course be more options, but let us ignore this complication for now. Her next step is to determine the possible consequences of each option. Let us say that she conceives two possibilities for the home option: (1) the symptoms recede and within hours she is essentially back to normality, or (2) there is more and more swelling and pain. Again, there might be more consequences, but Cindy's more pressing concern is to assign values to these consequences. For the sake of the argument, let us assume that, on a scale from 0 to 10 with 10 being best, return to normality scores a utility of 9 (some little damage that was not attended to by a healthcare practitioner must have occurred, but that is fine for Cindy) and more swelling and pain scores 3 (it could be worse, but this is not good either, Cindy thinks). The final step for the home option is to estimate the probabilities of these two consequences. This does look like a leap of faith but based on previous personal injuries and the experiences of others, Cindy might manage to attach a probability of, say, 20%, or 0.2, to the return to normality, and thus also a probability of 80%, or 0.8, to more swelling and pain. Savage's calculus suggests that the worth of the home option to Cindy, in other words, her subjective expected utility, equals $0.2 \times 9 + 0.8 \times 3 = 4.2$ [355].

Similar work must be carried out for the emergency option, but you see how it would go, so no reason to repeat it. Now, what do you think of this analysis? Would Cindy be able to do it? Should she trust the results? If it were you, would you be able to do such a decision analysis, and would you trust it? These are trick questions in a way, as they have no right answers. But one can provide arguments both ways, and researchers have been doing so, as we discuss below.

7.1.2 A Critique

In terms of pros, decision analysis is attractive in that it introduces a reasonable structure for making decisions that includes expressive concepts such as options, consequences, probabilities, and utilities, and shows a way of computing the worth of options. This structure can help decision-makers organise their thoughts, figure out what information they would need and want to have, and arrive at a candidate option that they may choose (the option with the higher worth). Another advantage of decision analysis is that it is not dogmatic, but merely suggestive. It does provide a first candidate, but this is just meant to be food for thought; if this candidate option does not fully satisfy the decision-maker, they are welcome to ponder why is that, and possibly redo the analysis by, say, updating some of the information of even changing the set of options. The success of decision analysis processes would of course depend on the ability and openness of the decision-maker and the decision analyst to communicate with each other, reach a shared understanding of the problem, and eventually arrive at a satisfying decision. In sum, decision analysis has a scientific theoretical basis, but it should also be practiced as an art.

In terms of cons, decision analysis has been criticised for being too complex and, at the same time, too unrealistic. As Cindy's case highlights, a lot is demanded of decision-makers. They must identify effective decision options and provide accurate estimates of the options' parameters. Can decision-makers realistically put in the amount and quality of work required? How can one be sure that they have done so, at least to a sufficient extent? Considering just the probabilities required might suffice to show just how tall the order is. How can Cindy know the probability of more swelling and pain? Does it even make sense to talk of such a probability? According to an increasing number of theorists and practitioners, most decisions must be made under radical uncertainty, which is uncertainty that cannot meaningfully be reduced to probability. Mervyn King, former governor of the Bank of England, and John Kay, inaugural dean of Oxford Business School, urge us to resist the "lure of probabilities" and make decisions based on coherent and insightful narratives. King and Kay [358] discuss the case of President Obama who refused to base his decision of whether to bomb a location where Osama bin Laden might have been hiding, on probabilities, and commented that "probabilities disguised uncertainty as opposed to actually providing you with more useful information" (p. 160). Sometimes sensitivity analyses, which consider several settings of probabilities and utilities and compare the resulting decisions, can be useful, but clearly not always.

What can one do? Should we give up on classical decision theory and decision analysis? This chapter argues for enhancement, rather than elimination. Elements of decision analysis that may be retained are the existence of some structure and the lack of dogmatism, and elements that may be replaced are unrealistic information demands and a blind obedience to an idealised calculus of optimisation. In this section, we have merely touched upon the ideal of optimisation. Developing an objection to this ideal means discussing theories of pragmatic heuristics, as we do in the next section.

7.2 ALTERNATIVE THEORIES: DECISION HEURISTICS

A heuristic is a simple rule for getting things done. In applied mathematical disciplines, such as operations research, a heuristic is a technique for solving a problem with the computational resources that are realistically available. This solution might not always be what is theoretically expected to be the best one, but it is a practical possibility that addresses the problem at hand. A well-known example is the travelling salesperson problem, wherein an agent must visit all cities in a given set, and do so by minimising the total distance travelled. For instance, if there are three cities, A, B, and C, so that the distance between A and B equals 50 km, between A and C 100 km, and between B and C 75 km, one might ask what the minimum total distance travelled is, starting from A, so that all three cities are visited. The best solution is to first travel from A to B and then from B to C, which yields a total distance of (50 + 75) km = 125 km, because travelling first to C and then to B amounts to (100 + 75) km = 175 km. Now, this travelling salesperson problem is an easy one as the best solution can be found by these few, simple computations.

But imagine a problem with tens, hundreds, thousands, or millions of cities as it may be the case in the real world; the number of possible routes to evaluate grows very fast and not only human minds, but not even artificial ones (computers) can determine the best solution by such evaluation [359]. An appropriate response in such cases is to devise a reasonable rule for solving the problem that can be realistically applied to any number of cities. For instance, the travelling salesperson can resolve to always visit next the city closest to the one they are currently in. In the previous example, this will again lead to the best solution of 125 km but that would not necessarily be the case in all problems, as for example when there is a fourth city *D*, with a distance of 25 km to *B* and 85 km to *C* (and unconnected to *A*). In such a case, it would be better to travel from *A* to *C* to *B* to *D* (200 km) as opposed to travel from *A* to *B* to *C* to *D* (210 km). The heuristic of always travelling to the next solution provides a solution that is easy to find even for huge problems, but that is not guaranteed to be the best solution. Nevertheless, it is not clear at all what else one can do.

The above discussion casts heuristics in the usual light—at least in standard behavioural decision research—which is that they are useful, but they are second-best [360]. In this narrative, we need heuristics because we cannot attain the actual best. This interpretation of heuristics is sometimes the right one. But not always. In fact, research in the last few decades is showing that the second-best view of heuristics tends to hold mostly in textbook-style, idealised problems such as the travelling salesperson problem as it was framed above. In this frame, there was certainty that the task of the salesperson will always be exactly as the problem says. But can that really be true? Let us probe a bit deeper.

7.2.1 The Need for Heuristics

In practice, will distances always be what we think they are? No. Some routes might become unavailable due to natural or human-caused disasters, weather, strikes, and other disruptions. And some vehicles, such as lorries, are not permitted or able to travel on specific routes. All in all, it looks like there would be plenty of sources of uncertainty related to distance. Furthermore, consider the motivation for minimising the total travel distance in the first place. Does everyone care about driving less? True, it might well be that one is after total travel time and uses distance as a proxy to time. This is reasonable, but it may introduce additional uncertainty, due to the sensitivity of travel time on conditions not directly related to distance such as traffic and road conditions.

Let us now move away from the travelling salesperson problem per se and attempt to abstract lessons for modelling and solving decision problems more generally. Upon reflection, one sees that several, even many, if not most, decision problems feature uncertainty. In healthcare, this is quite clear. Consider Cindy's ankle decision problem again. As we argued, there is uncertainty around probabilities of key events such as whether there will be more swelling and pain. King and Kay, following a long tradition of thinkers [358], of which an early one is Frank Knight, co-founder of the famous Chicago School of Economics, insist on the prevalence of such uncertainty in real-world decisions. Uncertainty about probabilities is often called radical uncertainty [361].

A thesis that is being formed for decades is that radical uncertainty is more successfully handled by pragmatic heuristics, rather than classical decision theory [362,363]. This thesis was put convincingly on the table in the 1970s by psychologists and management theorists such as Robyn Dawes, Hillel Einhorn, Robin Hogarth, and Spyros Makridakis [364]. In a series of appreciated but also somewhat ignored articles, these researchers showed that simple models can predict an unknown future better than more complex and more mathematically sophisticated models. These simple models map directly to intuitive heuristics that laypeople as well as professionals often employ, spontaneously or as a result of deliberation or training. Two of these heuristics are simplifications of linear models, such as ordinary regression.

For example, say that you want to predict the recovery time from an ankle sprain, based on three variables, ability to bear weight, swelling, and age. Of course, for such a scheme to make sense, the variables—predicting (independent) and predicted (dependent)—must be put on the same scale, say from 0 to 10. Instead of using a weighted linear combination of variables, one might simply (*i*) tally the variables without weighting them; or alternatively, (*ii*) only use the single most informative of the variables, say ability to bear weight. Summing things and singling one thing out of many are two simple approaches that people intuitively gravitate to.

Mathematically, say that recovery time is symbolised by y and ability to bear weight, swelling, and age by, respectively, x_1, x_2, and x_3. A full linear model, such as regression, would then be represented by

$$y = w_0 + w_1x_1 + w_2x_2 + w_3x_3,$$

whereas the two heuristics (*i*) and (*ii*) can be written as

$$y = x_1 + x_2 + x_3; \; y = x_1.$$

Not only do the heuristics look simpler and are, at least to some people, easier to understand and learn than the linear model, but they are also simpler to implement. The linear model requires the estimation of four parameters (the four weights $w_0, w_1, w_2,$ and w_3), say by minimising the sum of squared errors, whereas the heuristics are parameter-free. This extra machinery in the linear model can be taken as a sign of mathematical sophistication but, interestingly, it does not buy much in practice. The work of Dawes, Einhorn, and Hogarth showed that linear regression does not always predict more accurately than tallying, and in fact, there is a range of conditions satisfied in practice where tallying predicts more accurately. Perhaps not that surprisingly to you after having read the previous parts of this chapter, one such condition is low predictability of the dependent variable, which could be due to the lack of ample, high-quality independent variables. And Makridakis and Hogarth found that regression may also be outperformed by a single variable, again under low predictability.

In such situations, optimisation cannot beat intuition. Nevertheless, this fact is itself counterintuitive (pun intended), and has not yet penetrated theory, at least not to the extent that it should. As Hogarth remarked, sometimes "simple is hard to accept" [365]. This is often the case in practice too. While practitioners would themselves come up with a simple model, they might hesitate to trust the advice of a decision analyst or consultant who would recommend such a model [366].

A boost to the heuristics thesis and the acceptance of the usefulness of simple models was initiated in the 1990s by an interdisciplinary network of decision researchers led by Gerd Gigerenzer and Peter Todd and continues to develop. This research program has also made contact with healthcare decision support. Let us first outline this view of heuristics.

7.2.2 Fast-and-Frugal Heuristics

Unlike classical decision theory that takes a top-down approach, the heuristics view of human decision-making goes from the bottom up. The top-down view builds mathematical axioms about how an idealised person should use theoretically available information about values and probabilities to maximise their expected utility, and hopes that this approach will generalise well in the real world where not all required information is indeed available. In contrast, the bottom-up approach studies how an actual person makes do with the practical limits in information to make a decision that, according to reasonable criteria, is better than the alternatives, and uses such findings to build a theory of effective heuristics. In other words, the decision theorist insists on optimising in a small version of the world, whereas the heuristic practitioner realises that they can only satisfice in the real world.

It is important to notice that it is an empirical question which of the two approaches would perform better in real decision problems; that is, the second-best view of heuristics necessarily applies only to small worlds. For those of you eager to know what the results of such empirical research are, the short answer is that, as it is often the case in science, it depends. There are conditions under which classical decision theory and related statistical machine learning models outperform heuristics. Roughly, these conditions refer to decision problems where ample and high-quality information is available as when the situation is relatively stable and meaningful statistics can be collected [367]. Examples might include predicting election results in secure and thriving democracies, or medical outcomes in the absence of health crises such as pandemics. On the other hand, there are also conditions that favour simple heuristics over more complex and mathematically sophisticated algorithms. Again roughly, such conditions refer to decisions where the available information is limited in volume and quality, possible because the situation keeps changing. Political complications might make the prediction of elections harder for information-greedy models but possible by simple rules such as tallying as was the case in the 2016 US Presidential Election. And not only pandemics such as COVID-19 could not be predicted by sophisticated models, but influenza incidence has also been more accurately nowcasted by a single variable. We will provide more detail on these two cases [363] and other findings at the end of this subsection. But, before that, let us develop further the heuristics view.

The heuristics view is founded on knowledge of how real agents make real decisions. A part of this knowledge comes from fields such as behavioural ecology, which studies non-human animals [368]. Such animals might behave similarly to humans but reside in relatively much simpler contexts that might allow one to more clearly observe their decision processes. For instance, consider the Norway rat. Its decision-making mainly refers to avoiding predators, finding mates, and staying nourished. Consider this rat's rule for what to eat. It relies on the recognition heuristic, which states that the rat should only eat food it, or its co-specifics, have tried before (and did not get sick from). The recognition heuristic is an example of a fast-and-frugal heuristic, which means that it uses only a few pieces of information (frugal; here only one piece of information, recognition) and processes these pieces in simple ways, hence also being fast. Fast-and-frugal heuristics typically violate the basic tenets of classical decision theory about deciding based on expected utility. The recognition heuristic, for example, does not consider all options and does not calculate any measure of worth, such as expected utility, for any option. Other examples of animals that appear to be using fast-and-frugal heuristics abound, as reviewed by biologist John Hutchinson and Gerd Gigerenzer, and include the honeybee and the ant *Leptothorax albipennis*, who both use slightly more involved heuristics than the Norway rat [368]. The bee chooses one among many flowers to pollinate based on different attributes of the inflorescences (the complete head of the flower) that each correlates with nectar volume and sugar weight, such as whether an inflorescence has been visited before or not and morphological characteristics such as size. The ant uses one variable only to estimate the size of a cavity that is a potential nest, but this variable is intelligently constructed by the ant itself: the ant circles the cavity twice while laying a pheromone trail each time, and then records the overlap between the trails as a proxy for size.

A lesson from the fast-and-frugal decision-making of non-human animals is the use of a few variables/attributes that are relatively easily accessible to each animal species and are then combined simply. Introspection, observation, and more controlled studies in the lab and in the wild (outside the lab, in the field) suggest that a first instinct, or sometimes a more measured response, of people is to employ a similar approach. People routinely use the recognition heuristic to make decisions about their dinner (which restaurant and which food), and they do the same in all sorts of other contexts, such as deciding how to invest their money. We use information that is relatively easy for us to access perceptually such as face recognition and process such information with our basic cognitive capacities such as comparing or summing numbers or singling one number out of many [362].

Traditionally, such heuristic processes were celebrated in the psychological sciences, but in the last five decades, they have been sometimes criticised as naïve and error-prone. The work of famous psychologists, including Amos Tversky and Daniel Kahneman, is often seen as a point of initiation of such claims, but, as often in academia, the emergence of a shared belief is a complicated process. Those interested in such debates can look up literature on the so-called heuristics-and-biases research program [360]. The position of this program to the old-time religion of classical decision theory is, according to Howard, that of heretics. At any rate, a commonly held belief is that using heuristics such as the tallying and singling out of variables is inaccurate. The fast-and-frugal-heuristics research program, however, has produced empirical evidence that goes against this narrative, as the two following examples demonstrate (as promised, from politics and health). This heuristic program plays the role of heathens.

Predicting Elections: To predict whether Hillary Clinton or Donald Trump would win the 2016 US Presidential Election, statistician Nate Silver leveraged "big data" from polls and past elections. He predicted a 71.4% chance of Clinton winning the 2016 election, as did polls and prediction markets about who had the clearly better chance of winning. Historian Allan Lichtman, on the other hand, predicted that Trump would win. He relied on his own historical analysis of US Presidential Elections from 1860 to 1980 and, blending theories of politics, economics, sociology, and psychology, derived a tallying heuristic that uses the following 13 binary variables—which Lichtman aptly called keys (to the White House)—each phrased so that it is either true or false [369].

Key 1: Incumbent-party mandate. Incumbent party holds more seats in the House of Representatives after this midterm election than in the previous one.
Key 2: Nomination contest. No serious contest for the incumbent party nomination.
Key 3: Incumbency. Incumbent-party candidate is the sitting president.
Key 4: Third party. No significant third party or independent campaign.
Key 5: Short-term economy. Economy not in recession during the campaign.
Key 6: Long-term economy. Real annual per capita economic growth during the term equals or exceeds mean growth during two previous terms.
Key 7: Policy change. Incumbent administration effects major changes in national policy.
Key 8: Social unrest. No sustained social unrest during the term.
Key 9: Scandal. Incumbent administration untainted by major scandal.
Key 10: Foreign or military failure. Incumbent administration suffers no major failure in foreign or military affairs.
Key 11: Foreign or military success. Incumbent administration achieves a major success in foreign or military affairs.
Key 12: Incumbent charisma. Incumbent-party candidate is charismatic or national hero.
Key 13: Challenger charisma. The challenging-party candidate is not charismatic or national hero.

Lichtman's tallying heuristic is that *if six or more keys are false, the challenger will win.* As an example of how the heuristic operates, consider the 2012 election where Mitt Romney challenged Barack Obama. Lichtman counted all keys as true except 1, 6, and 12, and correctly predicted that Obama will win. Some keys, such as whether the candidate is the sitting president, require no judgement, while others, such as charisma, do. In late September of 2016, Lichtman considered the keys to be settled and he counted them. Six keys 1, 3, 4, 7, 11, and 12 were false, and the correct prediction that Trump will win was made. Now, you might be wondering what happened after 2016. In 2020, Lichtman's tallying heuristic was correct again, although arguably this was less of a feat as this election result was less surprising than the 2016 result. In 2024, in the heavily contested election between Donald Trump and Kamala Harris, Lichtman, in an entertaining video made by *The New York Times* (https://www.youtube.com/watch?v=xE22XjWEyQE&t=39s), again went out on a limb and predicted that Harris will win; alas, he was, for the first time, wrong [370].

Predicting Influenza: Let o_t be the observed incidence of influenza for period (here, week) t and p_t be the prediction for t. The recency heuristic predicts $p_t = o_{t-1}$.

This is, sometimes derogatorily, called naïve forecasting since it implements the straightforward idea that this week's influenza incidence will equal the most recently observed incidence. But, as they say, sometimes naïveté is the mark of genius, and this seems to be the case in a study where the recency heuristic was pitted against the mighty Google Flu Trends, an early poster child of big data analytics where billions of query terms were used to build a linear model with tens of attributes (no more detail is known because this model is proprietary).

A general model tested was $p_t = o_{t-1} + a(o_{t-1} - o_{t-2})$, where a is a parameter controlling the extent to which the latest trend $(o_{t-1} - o_{t-2})$ is damped. Setting $a = 0$ means ignoring the trend and using the recency heuristic. The parameter a was estimated as 0.44 by minimising the mean absolute error, $\text{MAE} = \frac{1}{n}\sum_{t=1}^{n}|p_t - o_t|$ of forecasting the data from the US Centers for Disease Control and Prevention from March 17, 2004 to March 17, 2007.

An alternative approach to fixing the value of a is to consider the trend-recency heuristic that says $p_t - o_{t-1} = o_{t-1} - o_{t-2}$, and hence $p_t = o_{t-1} + (o_{t-1} - o_{t-2})$. This heuristic corresponds to $a = 1$ in the general model, which means no trend damping.

Table 7.1 provides the mean absolute error on a test set from March 18, 2007 to August 9, 2015, for the trend-damping model, the trend-recency and recency heuristics, as well as linear regression on the most recent observation, Google Flu Trends, and the benchmark model of always predicting zero.

From Table 7.1 we see that incorporating or damping trends only slightly improves forecasting accuracy beyond the recency heuristic. Beyond this study, using a recency-based model, with or without trends, might be a robust choice. For instance, in Austria, using a simple trend model led to more accurate COVID-19 forecasts than those produced by a team of experts advising the government who relied on a combination of more sophisticated models such as extended or agent-based susceptible, infected, recovered/removed models, and state-space epidemiological models. It is also interesting to note that, along with the excitement at the possibility of combining simplicity, transparency, and accuracy, there has been some resistance to such findings, as can be seen in a debate and rebuttal on this research, as published in the leading forecasting venue, *International Journal of Forecasting* (https://www.sciencedirect.com/journal/international-journal-of forecasting/vol/38/issue/2).

TABLE 7.1
Performance of Models for Predicting Influenza

Model	MAE
Trend-damping model	0.17
Trend-recency heuristic	0.19
Recency heuristic	0.20
Linear regression	0.20
Google Flu Trends	0.38
Benchmark: Predict zero	1.80

In sum, much as classical decision theory, fast-and-frugal heuristics can and have been applied across a host of decision tasks, such as choices under risk and uncertainty, multi-attribute choices, estimations, classifications, and predictions. Some of these tasks are also domains in which very powerful algorithms from statistics and machine learning have been applied. Such research allows one to compare the three approaches, conceptually and empirically, and consider possible divisions of labour and even a synthesis. The next two sections are dedicated to exactly those two issues.

7.3 MACHINE LEARNING FOR DECISION-MAKING

Machine learning is a branch of artificial intelligence that aims at building machines that can improve their future performance by utilising feedback based on their past performance. It has a relatively long history, with the first successful illustration of its power coming in the 1950s with the work of computer scientist Arthur Samuel. Samuels, at the time working at IBM, built an algorithm that could learn to play checkers by itself up to a better-than-average level; in Samuels [33], he also coined the term machine learning. Checkers is a board game, and it can be seen as an instance of sequential decision-making, wherein prior decisions may affect decisions in the future. The field, as all dynamic and powerful ones, has many facets including signal processing and pattern recognition in which it has recently, with the advent of deep neural networks, reached impressive performance [363]. Around a decade back, some feats of human cognition, such as face recognition or playing very complicated games like Go, were unmatched by computers, but this is no longer the case.

In some sense, many or even most cognitive tasks involve some kind of decision-making, and in this sense machine learning is indeed a decision-making field. But the connection of machine learning is stronger for some decision tasks than others. In terms of the tasks we have been considering in this chapter, one might say that machine learning has had a very strong bearing on tasks of classification and prediction. Models such as decision trees, random forests, support vector machines, linear regressions, neural and Bayesian networks are some of the names you might have heard of and are discussed in other chapters in this book. The 2016 election and influenza incidence are examples of prediction tasks. Obviously predicting better can enable better decision-making as well. But it can be misleading to draw a direct and strong link between the two; for example, sometimes prediction is quite different from decision, let alone that predicting might be almost impossible but that does not mean that one should give up on deciding too. For instance, the emergence and development of COVID-19 could not be predicted well, but crucial decisions still needed to be made about what protective equipment to use, whether to put lockdowns in place, and so on [370].

In this subsection, we focus on classification tasks. This task category is a very central one in decision-making, and in fact, with some ingenuity, other decision tasks can often be reformulated as a classification task. This is indeed the case with Cindy's choice that we opened the chapter with. We initially framed the decision as a choice between staying home and keeping an eye on her ankle injury or going to the emergency to be assessed by a healthcare practitioner, and possibly have some tests done and treatments be recommended. But one could just as well reframe the choice as a classification of Cindy's case into one of two categories (classes): low risk of complications, which would map to the choice of staying home, and high risk of complications, which would map to the choice of going to the emergency ward. Now, because indeed classification tasks play such a central role in healthcare, practitioners have had an interest in inferring, designing, and using understandable and actionable heuristics for making classifications, in domains such as diabetes, cardiovascular disease, mental health, and obstetrics, to name a few. Let us stick with orthopaedics and Cindy's case here. Assume first that Cindy did decide to go to the emergency as the pain in the malleolar region could not be ignored anymore. Now it is time for the health practitioner to make some decisions. A key decision is whether an ankle radiograph should be performed. A known guide for doing so is to apply one of the Ottawa ankle rules. As we shall see immediately below, there are multiple ways of presenting the radiograph rule. Let us start from a presentation of this rule as a combination of two fast-and-frugal heuristics, a single-variable heuristic and a tallying heuristic.

The first variable involved in the Ottawa ankle radiograph rule is the variable x_0 coding the symptom of pain in the malleolar region, where $x_0 = 1$ if there is pain and $x_0 = 0$ if not. There are also three more binary variables, each referring to an another possible symptom: Bone tenderness at the posterior edge of the distal 6 cm or the tip of the lateral malleolus (x_1), bone tenderness at the posterior edge of the distal 6 cm or the tip of the medial malleolus (x_2), and inability to bear weight for at least four steps both immediately after injury and at the time of evaluation (x_3), where again each attribute x_i receives a score of 1 if it refers to a symptom that is present and a score of 0 if the symptom is absent. The Ottawa rule says that an ankle radiograph should be given if there is malleolar pain and at least one of the other three symptoms is present. Thus, formally, the rule can be represented as follows:

Perform an ankle radiograph only if $x_0 = 1$ and $x_1 + x_2 + x_3 \geq 1$.

In practice, the rule is often represented as a table with text that communicates the same meaning as presented above (https://www.roshreview.com/blog/rapid-review-ottawa-ankle-rules/).

In the approach of fast-and-frugal heuristics, wherein understandability and transparency by all stakeholders are especially valued, the Ottawa ankle radiograph rule would be represented graphically. Figure 7.1 provides a so-called fast-and-frugal decision tree. Except that it is a picture, this representation also has the advantage of combining the two heuristics (single-cue and tallying) into one. The outcome of course of all three representations would be the same as long as the heuristics are executed correctly. Perhaps the tree representation has an added advantage in that it clearly displays the process leading to the outcome. Displaying the process can also make the rule faster to execute because if the malleolar-pain variable is queried first, it is possible that a classification be made immediately (no pain means no radiograph), and no further work is needed. Note also that the other three variables can be ordered within the tree in any sequence that would be more agreeable to the healthcare practitioner, or potentially more efficient for the whole system.

Fast-and-frugal trees for several other medical conditions have been developed, including for the detection of ischaemic heart disease, diabetes risk assessment,

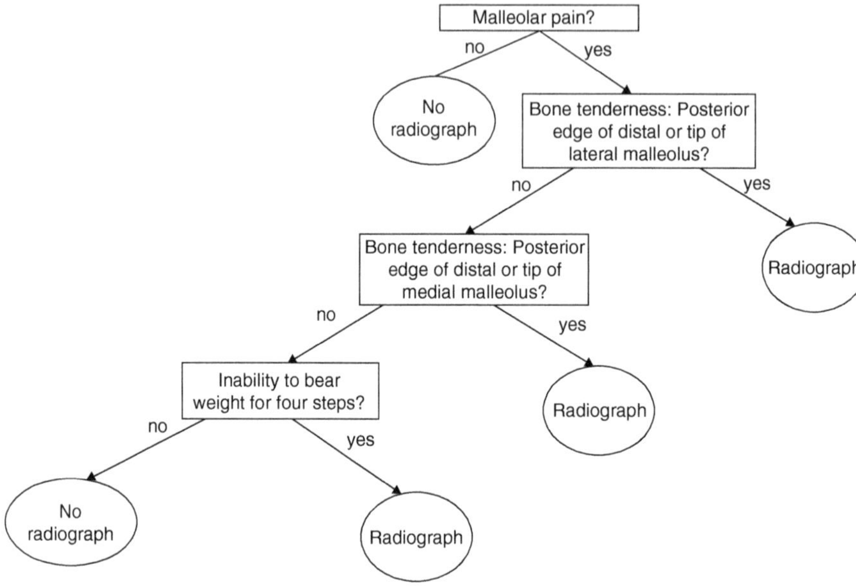

FIGURE 7.1 The Ottawa ankle radiograph rule as a fast-and-frugal decision tree.

depression diagnosis [363], and foetal monitoring [371]. This of course begs the question: How do these simple decision trees compare, in terms of accuracy, to more complex trees or forests, and other machine learning classification algorithms? Table 7.2 summarises the results of studies that utilised several datasets to compare simple heuristics with more complex models (in each study, the name of the first author is given; performance is in all cases measured in percentage points of predictive accuracy; CART stands for Leo Breiman's classification-and-regression trees; the label "regression" stands for different versions of this statistical model in different studies; linear, logistic, and regularised, from top to bottom).

TABLE 7.2
Some Results of Comparisons between Simple and More Complex Decision Models

Study	Number of Datasets	Simple Heuristics (%)	Machine Learning Models (%)
Czerlinski [375]	20	Fast-and-frugal tree: 76 Tallying: 69	Regression: 76
Martignon and Hoffrage [376]	30	Fast-and-frugal tree: 75	CART: 76
Şimşek [377]	51	Fast-and-frugal tree: 78	Regression: 79
Katsikopoulos [363]	64	Fast-and-frugal tree: 79 Tallying: 79	CART: 79 Random Forest: 82

These results show that, on the average, the performance difference between simple heuristics and machine learning models is not that large. Of course, the picture varies with each dataset; in all four studies, there are datasets in which one or the other class of algorithms is more accurate. This means that it would be very useful to have a theory that a priori delineates the types of datasets in which heuristics or more complex models are expected to be more accurate. This theory exists under the name of ecological rationality. We already mentioned elements of ecological rationality in the guise of conditions that match models with datasets, such as different ways for capturing the degree of uncertainty or unpredictability in a dataset. A somewhat simplified, but potentially very useful and insightful, summary of ecological rationality is that simple heuristics are a more suitable choice when the task at hand is relatively easy or relatively difficult. The intuition here is that easy tasks can be attacked by many models and hence why should we not choose a simpler one? and that difficult tasks require solutions that are not information-greedy. Conversely, for decision tasks that are of an intermediate difficulty, more complex models might be a better choice because there is enough information available that it pays off to try and build such a more complex model.

7.4 SYNTHESIS: DERIVING AND EVALUATING CLINICAL PATHWAYS

So, beyond deciding, classifying, and predicting, how does the theory of fast-and-frugal heuristics play into medical practice? Practitioner and researcher Benjamin Djulbegovic has shown resourcefulness in bringing the two worlds together. For example, Djulbegovic and his colleagues have strongly argued that fast-and-frugal trees can serve as a systematic approach to translating medical evidence to clinical practice guidelines [372]. This work also includes advances in fast-and-frugal-tree methodology, such as presenting conceptual ideas and statistical techniques on how to incorporate thresholds in these trees [373].

Now, a common critique of attempts to import decision algorithms into clinical practice pertains to the purported overemphasis of rigid rules to the expense of more unstructured medical intuition. This can be a very valid concern, especially when the algorithms are non-transparent "black-boxes," as is often the case with so-called big data analytics [226]. Fast-and-frugal trees, as we saw in this chapter, do not suffer from lack of transparency, but do they translate to accurate clinical guidance? This is of course ultimately an empirical question to be investigated on a case-by-case basis. Djulbegovic et al. [374] provided an answer in the case of anti-coagulant treatment of COVID-19 hospitalised patients. They found that fast-and-frugal-tree-based clinical practice guidelines shortened hospital stay and helped avoid admission to intensive care units.

References

1. Stigler SM. *The History of Statistics: The Measurement of Uncertainty before 1900*: Harvard University Press; 1986.
2. Hassani H, Unger S, Beneki C. Big data and actuarial science. *Big Data and Cognitive Computing*. 2020;4(4):40.
3. Alfaro ME, Zoller S, Lutzoni F. Bayes or bootstrap? A simulation study comparing the performance of Bayesian Markov chain Monte Carlo sampling and bootstrapping in assessing phylogenetic confidence. *Molecular Biology and Evolution*. 2003;20(2):255–66.
4. Kitchin R. Big data, new epistemologies and paradigm shifts. *Big Data & Society*. 2014;1(1):2053951714528481.
5. Sarker IH. Data science and analytics: An overview from data-driven smart computing, decision-making and applications perspective. *SN Computer Science*. 2021;2(5):377.
6. Fathian K, Jin J, Wee S-G, Lee D-H, Kim Y-G, Gans NR. Camera relative pose estimation for visual servoing using quaternions. *Robotics and Autonomous Systems*. 2018;107:45–62. https://doi.org/10.1016/j.robot.2018.05.014.
7. Seo E-H, Park C-S, Kim D, Song J-B,. Quaternion-based orientation estimation with static error reduction. In *Proceedings of the 2011 IEEE International Conference on Mechatronics and Automation (ICMA)*: Beijing, China; 2011. pp. 1624–1629. https://doi.org/10.1109/ICMA.2011.5985957
8. Wang C, Huang K, Shi W. An accurate and efficient quaternion-based visualization approach to 2D/3D vector data for the mobile augmented reality map. *ISPRS International Journal of Geo-Information*. 2022;11(7):383. https://doi.org/10.3390/ijgi11070383
9. Liu J, Zhang X, Liu H, Yuan Y, Zhu Z, Yu Q. New method for camera pose estimation based on line correspondence. *Science China Technological Sciences*. 2013;56(11):2787–97.
10. Cao L. Data science: A comprehensive overview. *ACM Computing Surveys (CSUR)*. 2017;50(3):1–42.
11. Saltz JS, Krasteva I. Current approaches for executing big data science projects—a systematic literature review. *PeerJ Computer Science*. 2022;8:e862.
12. Myatt GJ. *Making Sense of Data: A Practical Guide to Exploratory Data Analysis and Data Mining*: John Wiley & Sons; 2007.
13. Naidu G, Zuva T, Sibanda EM, editors. A review of evaluation metrics in machine learning algorithms. *Computer Science On-Line Conference*; 2023: Springer.
14. Agrawal K, Nargund N, editors. Deep learning in industry 4.0: Transforming manufacturing through data-driven innovation. *International Conference on Distributed Computing and Intelligent Technology*; 2024: Springer.
15. Mgendi G. Unlocking the potential of precision agriculture for sustainable farming. *Discover Agriculture*. 2024;2(1):87.
16. Liu DYT, Bartimote-Aufflick K, Pardo A, Bridgeman AJ. Data-driven personalization of student learning support in higher education. In Peña-Ayala, A. Editor *Learning Analytics: Fundaments, Applications, and Trends: A View of the Current State of the Art to Enhance e-Learning*: Springer; 2017. pp. 143–69.
17. Ogundeko-Olugbami O, Ogundeko O, Lawan M, Foster E. Harnessing data for impact: Transforming public health interventions through evidence-based decision-making. *World Journal of Advanced Research and Reviews*. 2025;25(1):2085–103.

18. Ali SK, Khan H, Shah J, Nadeem Ahmed K. An electronic health record system implementation in a resource limited country—lessons learned. *Digital Health.* 2023;9:20552076231203660.
19. Fraser HS, Mugisha M, Remera E, Ngenzi JL, Richards J, Santas X, et al. User perceptions and use of an enhanced electronic health record in Rwanda with and without clinical alerts: Cross-sectional survey. *JMIR Medical Informatics.* 2022;10(5):e32305.
20. Nzarama GM, Mukabalisa A, Sibomana L, Perjons E, Johannesson P. Interoperability of electronic health record systems in Rwandan healthcare system. *Journal of Health Informatics in Developing Countries.* 2024;18(1):1.
21. Uwera T, Venkateswaran M, Bhutada K, Papadopoulou E, Rukundo E, Tumusiime DK, et al. Electronic immunization registry in Rwanda: Qualitative study of health worker experiences. *JMIR Human Factors.* 2024;11(1):e53071.
22. Fraser HS, Mugisha M, Bacher I, Ngenzi JL, Seebregts C, Umubyeyi A, et al. Factors influencing data quality in electronic health record systems in 50 health facilities in Rwanda and the role of clinical alerts: Cross-sectional observational study. *JMIR Public Health and Surveillance.* 2024;10(1):e49127.
23. Anton N, Doroftei B, Curteanu S, Catalin L, Ilie O-D, Târcoveanu F, et al. Comprehensive review on the use of artificial intelligence in ophthalmology and future research directions. *Diagnostics.* 2022;13(1):100.
24. Brown N, Ertl P, Lewis R, Luksch T, Reker D, Schneider N. Artificial intelligence in chemistry and drug design. *Journal of Computer-Aided Molecular Design.* 2020;34(7):709–15.
25. Badillo S, Banfai B, Birzele F, Davydov II, Hutchinson L, Kam-Thong T, et al. An introduction to machine learning. *Clinical Pharmacology & Therapeutics.* 2020;107(4):871–85.
26. Majumdar DD. Trends in pattern recognition and machine learning. *Defence Science Journal.* 1985;35(July (3)):327–51.
27. Kubat M. *An Introduction to Machine Learning*: Springer; 2017.
28. Aggarwal M, Murty M. Deep learning. *Machine Learning in Social Networks: Embedding Nodes, Edges, Communities,* and Graphs: Springer; 2020. pp. 35–66.
29. Schmidhuber J. Deep learning in neural networks: An overview. *Neural Networks.* 2015;61:85–117.
30. Hu YH, Hwang J-N. Editors. Introduction to neural networks for signal processing. *Handbook of Neural Network Signal Processing*: CRC Press; 2018. pp. 1–30.
31. Angermueller C, Pärnamaa T, Parts L, Stegle O. Deep learning for computational biology. *Molecular Systems Biology.* 2016;12(7):878.
32. McCulloch WS, Pitts W. A logical calculus of the ideas immanent in nervous activity. *The Bulletin of Mathematical Biophysics.* 1943;5(4):115–33.
33. Samuel AL. Some studies in machine learning using the game of checkers. *IBM Journal of Research and Development.* 1959;3(3):210–29.
34. Rosenblatt F. The perceptron, a perceiving and recognizing automaton:(Project Para): Cornell Aeronautical Laboratory; 1957.
35. Kelley HJ. Gradient theory of optimal flight paths. *ARS Journal.* 1960;30(10):947–54.
36. Dreyfus S. The numerical solution of variational problems. *Journal of Mathematical Analysis and Applications.* 1962;5(1):30–45.
37. Fukushima K. Neocognitron: A self-organizing neural network model for a mechanism of pattern recognition unaffected by shift in position. *Biological Cybernetics.* 1980;36(4):193–202.
38. Fukushima K. Neocognitron: A hierarchical neural network capable of visual pattern recognition. *Neural Networks.* 1988;1(2):119–30.
39. Rumelhart DE, Hinton GE, Williams RJ. Learning representations by back-propagating errors. *Nature.* 1986;323(6088):533–6.

40. Cortes C, Vapnik V. Support-vector networks. *Machine Learning.* 1995;20(3):273–97.
41. Hochreiter S, Schmidhuber J. Long short-term memory. *Neural Computation.* 1997;9(8):1735–80.
42. Ilievski A, Zdraveski V, Gusev M, editors. How CUDA powers the machine learning revolution. *2018 26th Telecommunications Forum (TELFOR)*; 2018: IEEE, Serbia, Belgrade.
43. Deng J, Dong W, Socher R, Li L-J, Li K, Fei-Fei L, editors. Imagenet: A large-scale hierarchical image database. *2009 IEEE Conference on Computer Vision and Pattern Recognition*; 2009: IEEE, Miami, FL.
44. Krizhevsky A, Sutskever I, Hinton GE. ImageNet classification with deep convolutional neural networks. Advances in neural information processing systems. 2012;25.
45. Le QV, editor. Building high-level features using large scale unsupervised learning. *2013 IEEE International Conference on Acoustics, Speech and Signal Processing*; 2013: IEEE, Vancouver, BC.
46. Jorda M, Valero-Lara P, Pena AJ. Performance evaluation of cuDNN convolution algorithms on NVIDIA Volta GPUs. *IEEE Access.* 2019;7:70461–73.
47. Taigman Y, Yang M, Ranzato MA, Wolf L, editors. Deepface: Closing the gap to human-level performance in face verification. *Proceedings of the IEEE Conference on Computer Vision and Pattern Recognition*; 2014.
48. Goodfellow I, Pouget-Abadie J, Mirza M, Xu B, Warde-Farley D, Ozair S, et al. Generative adversarial networks. *Communications of the ACM.* 2020;63(11):139–44.
49. Gandomi A, Haider M. Beyond the hype: Big data concepts, methods, and analytics. *International Journal of Information Management.* 2015;35(2):137–44.
50. Brazma A, Kapushesky M, Parkinson H, Sarkans U, Shojatalab M. [20] Data storage and analysis in ArrayExpress. *Methods in enzymology.* 2006;411:370–86.
51. Lo Y-C, Ren G, Honda H, Davis KL. Artificial intelligence-based drug design and discovery. In Amalia Stefaniu, Azhar Rasul and Ghulam Hussain, editors *Cheminformatics and Its Applications*; 2019.
52. Edgar R, Domrachev M, Lash AE. Gene Expression Omnibus: NCBI gene expression and hybridization array data repository. *Nucleic Acids Research.* 2002;30(1):207–10.
53. Wang Z, Jensen MA, Zenklusen JC. A practical guide to the cancer genome atlas (TCGA). In Mathé, E., Davis, S. Editors *Statistical Genomics: Methods and Protocols*: Springer; 2016. pp. 111–41.
54. LeCun Y, Touresky D, Hinton G, Sejnowski T, editors. A theoretical framework for back-propagation. *Proceedings of the 1988 Connectionist Models Summer School*; 1988. Pittsburgh, PA.
55. Gaman M, Ionescu RT. Combining deep learning and string kernels for the localization of Swiss German tweets. arXiv preprint arXiv:201003614. 2020.
56. Sumathi S, Suganya K, Swathi K, Sudha B, Poornima A, Varghese CA, et al. A review on deep learning-driven drug discovery: Strategies, tools and applications. *Current Pharmaceutical Design.* 2023;29(13):1013–25.
57. Kuhn R, Padua D. *Parallel Processing, 1980 to 2020*; 2022. Springer Nature.
58. Kljucaric L, George AD. Deep learning inferencing with high-performance hardware accelerators. *ACM Transactions on Intelligent Systems and Technology.* 2023;14(4):1–25.
59. Ambler AP, Barrow HG, Brown CM, Burstall RM, Popplestone RJ. A versatile system for computer-controlled assembly. *Artificial Intelligence.* 1975;6(2):129–56.
60. Muggleton S. Alan Turing and the development of Artificial Intelligence. *AI Communications.* 2014;27(1):3–10.
61. Barrow HG, Tenenbaum JM. Interpreting line drawings as three-dimensional surfaces. *Artificial Intelligence.* 1981;17(1–3):75–116.
62. Buchanan B, Feigenbaum E, Sridharan N. Heuristic theory formation: Data interpretation and rule formation. *Machine Intelligence.* 1972;7:267–90.

63. Church A. An unsolvable problem of elementary number theory. *American Journal of Mathematics*. 1936;58(2):345–63.
64. Popplestone R, Dale E, Michie D. POP-1: An on-line language. *Machine Intelligence*. 1968;2.
65. Davies DW. The bombe a remarkable logic machine. *Cryptologia*. 1999;23(2):108–38.
66. Fleck J. Development and establishment in artificial. *Scientific Establishments and Hierarchies*. 2012;6:169.
67. Feigenbaum EA. Themes and case studies of knowledge engineering. *Expert Systems in the Micro-Electronic Age*. 1979;1:3–25.
68. Fikes RE, Nilsson NJ. STRIPS: A new approach to the application of theorem proving to problem solving. *Artificial Intelligence*. 1971;2(3–4):189–208.
69. Schank R, DeJong G. Purposive understanding. *Machine Intelligence*. 1979;9:459–65.
70. Scott JJ. A chess-playing program. *Machine Intelligence*. 1969;4:255–65.
71. Shannon CE. A mathematical theory of communication. *The Bell System Technical Journal*. 1948;27(3):379–423.
72. Shapiro EY. *Algorithmic Program Debugging*: Yale University; 1982.
73. Shortliffe EH, Buchanan BG. A model of inexact reasoning in medicine. *Mathematical Biosciences*. 1975;23(3–4):351–79.
74. Turing AM. Computing machinery and intelligence. In Robert Epstein, Gary Roberts, Grace Beber, editors *Parsing the Turing Test: Philosophical and Methodological Issues in the Quest for the Thinking Computer*: Springer; 2007. pp. 23–65.
75. Turing AM. On computable numbers, with an application to the Entscheidungsproblem. *Journal of Mathematics*. 1936;58(345–363):5.
76. Valiant L. A theory of the learnable. *Communications of the ACM*. 1984; 27(11):1134–42.
77. Warren DH, Pereira LM, Pereira F. Prolog-the language and its implementation compared with Lisp. *ACM SIGPLAN Notices*. 1977;12(8):109–15.
78. Gonçalves B. Can machines think? The controversy that led to the Turing test, 1946–1950. 2021.
79. Copeland BJ. Early AI in Britain: Turing et al. *IEEE Annals of the History of Computing*. 2023;45(3):19–31.
80. Todd D. Mobile robots. *Fundamentals of Robot Technology: An Introduction to Industrial Robots, Teleoperators and Robot Vehicles*: Springer; 1986. pp. 171–204.
81. Todd PM, Gigerenzer G. *Ecological rationality: Intelligence in the World*: OUP USA; 2012.
82. Nilsson NJ. John Mccarthy. National Academy of Sciences. 2012:1–27.
83. Moor J. The Dartmouth College artificial intelligence conference: The next fifty years. *AI Magazine*. 2006;27(4):87-.
84. Wang S, Summers RM. Machine learning and radiology. *Medical Image Analysis*. 2012;16(5):933–51.
85. Kassahun Y, Yu B, Tibebu AT, Stoyanov D, Giannarou S, Metzen JH, et al. Surgical robotics beyond enhanced dexterity instrumentation: A survey of machine learning techniques and their role in intelligent and autonomous surgical actions. *International Journal of Computer Assisted Radiology and Surgery*. 2016;11(4):553–68.
86. Sheikhtaheri A, Sadoughi F, Hashemi Dehaghi Z. Developing and using expert systems and neural networks in medicine: A review on benefits and challenges. *Journal of Medical Systems*. 2014;38(9):110.
87. van IJzendoorn DG, Szuhai K, Briaire-de Bruijn IH, Kostine M, Kuijjer ML, Bovée JV. Machine learning analysis of gene expression data reveals novel diagnostic and prognostic biomarkers and identifies therapeutic targets for soft tissue sarcomas. *PLoS Computational Biology*. 2019 Feb 20;15(2):e1006826

88. Li J, Yuan X, March ME, Yao X, Sun Y, Chang X, Hakonarson H, Xia Q, Meng X, Li J. Identification of target genes at Juvenile idiopathic arthritis GWAS loci in human neutrophils. *Frontiers in Genetics*. 2019 Mar 27;10:181.
89. Han Y, Yang J, Qian X, Cheng WC, Liu SH, Hua X, Zhou L, Yang Y, Wu Q, Liu P, Lu Y. DriverML: A machine learning algorithm for identifying driver genes in cancer sequencing studies. *Nucleic Acids Research*. 2019 May 7;47(8):e45.
90. Xu Z, Yang L, Zhang X, Zhang Q, Yang Z, Liu Y, Wei S, Liu W. Discovery of potential flavonoid inhibitors against COVID-19 3CL proteinase based on virtual screening strategy. *Frontiers in Molecular Biosciences*. 2020 Sep 29;7:556481.
91. Delanerolle G, Yang X, Shetty S, Raymont V, Shetty A, Phiri P, et al. Artificial intelligence: A rapid case for advancement in the personalization of gynaecology/obstetric and mental health care. *Women's Health*. 2021;17:17455065211018111.
92. Gradus JL, Rosellini AJ, Horváth-Puhó E, Street AE, Galatzer-Levy I, Jiang T, Lash TL, Sørensen HT. Prediction of sex-specific suicide risk using machine learning and single-payer health care registry data from Denmark. *JAMA Psychiatry*. 2020 Jan;77(1):25–34.
93. Walsh CG, Ribeiro JD, Franklin JC. Predicting risk of suicide attempts over time through machine learning. *Clinical Psychological Science*. 2017 May;5(3):457–69.
94. Galatzer-Levy IR, Karstoft KI, Statnikov A, Shalev AY. Quantitative forecasting of PTSD from early trauma responses: A machine learning application. *Journal of Psychiatric Research*. 2014 Dec 1;59:68–76.
95. Månsson KN, Frick A, Boraxbekk CJ, Marquand AF, Williams SC, Carlbring P, Andersson G, Furmark T. Predicting long-term outcome of Internet-delivered cognitive behavior therapy for social anxiety disorder using fMRI and support vector machine learning. *Translational Psychiatry*. 2015 Mar;5(3):e530.
96. Kessler RC, Warner CH, Ivany C, Petukhova MV, Rose S, Bromet EJ, Brown III M, Cai T, Colpe LJ, Cox KL, Fullerton CS. Predicting suicides after psychiatric hospitalization in US Army soldiers: The Army Study to Assess Risk and Resilience in Servicemembers (Army STARRS). *JAMA Psychiatry*. 2015 Jan;72(1):49–57.
97. Chen Y, Stewart JW, Ge J, Cheng B, Chekroud A, Hellerstein DJ. Personalized symptom clusters that predict depression treatment outcomes: A replication of machine learning methods. *Journal of Affective Disorders Reports*. 2023 Jan 1;11:100470.
98. Lichtenberg JM, Şimşek Ö. Regularization in directable environments with application to Tetris. In *International Conference on Machine Learning;* 2019 May 24 (pp. 3953–62). PMLR.
99. Rosellini AJ, Liu S, Anderson GN, Sbi S, Tung ES, Knyazhanskaya E. Developing algorithms to predict adult onset internalizing disorders: An ensemble learning approach. *Journal of Psychiatric Research*. 2020 Feb 1;121:189–96.
100. Goodfellow I, Bengio Y, Courville A, Bengio Y. *Deep Learning*: MIT Press Cambridge; 2016.
101. LeCun Y, Bengio Y, Hinton G. Deep learning. *Nature*. 2015;521(7553):436–44.
102. Silver D, Huang A, Maddison CJ, Guez A, Sifre L, Van Den Driessche G, et al. Mastering the game of Go with deep neural networks and tree search. *Nature*. 2016;529(7587):484–9.
103. Zhu XJ. Semi-supervised learning literature survey. 2005.
104. Cho K, Van Merriënboer B, Bahdanau D, Bengio Y. On the properties of neural machine translation: Encoder-decoder approaches. arXiv preprint arXiv:14091259. 2014.
105. Devlin J, Chang M-W, Lee K, Toutanova K, editors. Bert: Pre-training of deep bidirectional transformers for language understanding. *Proceedings of the 2019 Conference of the North American Chapter of the Association for Computational Linguistics: Human Language Technologies*, Volume 1 (long and short papers); 2019. Minneapolis, MN.

106. Goodfellow IJ, Pouget-Abadie J, Mirza M, Xu B, Warde-Farley D, Ozair S, et al. Generative adversarial nets. Advances in neural information processing systems. 2014;27.
107. Hinton GE, Salakhutdinov RR. Reducing the dimensionality of data with neural networks. *Science*. 2006;313(5786):504–7.
108. Hochreiter S, Bengio Y, Frasconi P, Schmidhuber J. Gradient flow in recurrent nets: The difficulty of learning long-term dependencies. *A Field Guide to Dynamical Recurrent Neural Networks*. IEEE Press; 2001.
109. Kingma DP, Welling M. Auto-encoding variational bayes. arXiv preprint arXiv:13126114. 2013.
110. Vaswani A, Shazeer N, Parmar N, Uszkoreit J, Jones L, Gomez AN, et al. Attention is all you need. Advances in neural information processing systems. 2017;30.
111. Denney KB. *Assessing Clinical Software User Needs for Improved Clinical Decision Support* Tools: Walden University; 2015.
112. Berg M. Implementing information systems in health care organizations: Myths and challenges. *International Journal of Medical Informatics*. 2001;64(2–3):143–56.
113. Domingos P. A few useful things to know about machine learning. *Communications of the ACM*. 2012;55(10):78–87.
114. Schwartz A, Elstein AS. Clinical reasoning in medicine. *Clinical Reasoning in the Health Professions*. 2008;3:223–34.
115. Kuhn M, Johnson K. *Applied Predictive Modeling*: Springer; 2013.
116. Obermeyer Z, Powers B, Vogeli C, Mullainathan S. Dissecting racial bias in an algorithm used to manage the health of populations. *Science*. 2019;366(6464):447–53.
117. Middleton B, Sittig DF, Wright A. Clinical decision support: A 25 year retrospective and a 25 year vision. *Yearbook of Medical Informatics*. 2016;25(S 01):S103–S16.
118. Russell SJ, Norvig P. *Artificial Intelligence: A Modern Approach*;[the intelligent agent book]: Prentice Hall; 1995.
119. Yeung AWK, Torkamani A, Butte AJ, Glicksberg BS, Schuller B, Rodriguez B, et al. The promise of digital healthcare technologies. *Frontiers in Public Health*. 2023;11:1196596.
120. Berner ES. *Clinical Decision Support Systems*: Springer; 2007.
121. Breiman L. Random forests. *Machine Learning*. 2001;45(1):5–32.
122. Hosmer Jr DW, Lemeshow S, Sturdivant RX. *Applied Logistic Regression*: John Wiley & Sons; 2013.
123. Jain AK, Murty MN, Flynn PJ. Data clustering: A review. *ACM Computing Surveys (CSUR)*. 1999;31(3):264–323.
124. Sengupta A, Roy S, Ranjan G. LJST: A semi-supervised joint sentiment-topic model for short texts. *SN Computer Science*. 2021;2(4):256.
125. Topol E. *Deep Medicine: How Artificial Intelligence Can Make Healthcare Human Again*: Hachette UK; 2019.
126. Eccles R. Understanding the symptoms of the common cold and influenza. *The Lancet infectious diseases*. 2005;5(11), 718–725.
127. Bastian H, Glasziou P, Chalmers I. Seventy-five trials and eleven systematic reviews a day: How will we ever keep up? *PLoS Medicine*. 2010;7(9):e1000326.
128. CASP U. Critical Appraisal Skills Programme (CASP) checklist: 10 questions to help you make sense of a qualitative research. Oxford: CASP UK; 2018.
129. Grol R, Wensing M, Eccles M, Davis D. *Improving Patient Care: The Implementation of Change in Health Care*: John Wiley & Sons; 2013.
130. Greenhalgh TM, Dijkstra P. *How to Read a Paper: The Basics of Evidence-based Healthcare*: John Wiley & Sons; 2024.
131. Sackett D, Haynes B, Marshall T, Morgan W. Evidence-based medicine. *The Lancet*. 1995;346(8983):1171–2.

132. Sackett DL, editor. Evidence-based medicine. *Seminars in Perinatology*; 1997: Elsevier.
133. Sackett DL, Rosenberg WM, Gray JM, Haynes RB, Richardson WS. Evidence based medicine: What it is and what it isn't. *British Medical Journal Publishing Group*. 1996;312(7023):71–2.
134. Guyatt GH, Oxman AD, Vist GE, Kunz R, Falck-Ytter Y, Alonso-Coello P, et al. GRADE: An emerging consensus on rating quality of evidence and strength of recommendations. *BMJ*. 2008;336(7650):924–6.
135. Greenhalgh T, Howick J, Maskrey N. Evidence based medicine: A movement in crisis? *BMJ*. 2014;348:1–7.
136. Moher D, Liberati A, Tetzlaff J, Altman DG. Preferred reporting items for systematic reviews and meta-analyses: The PRISMA statement. *BMJ*. 2009;339.
137. Balshem H, Helfand M, Schünemann HJ, Oxman AD, Kunz R, Brozek J, et al. GRADE guidelines: 3. Rating the quality of evidence. *Journal of Clinical Epidemiology*. 2011;64(4):401–6.
138. Haynes RB, Sackett DL, Richardson WS, Rosenberg W, Langley GR. Evidence-based medicine: How to practice & teach EBM. *Canadian Medical Association Journal*. 1997;157(6):788.
139. Friedman J. The elements of statistical learning: Data mining, inference, and prediction. (No Title). 2009.
140. Topol EJ. High-performance medicine: The convergence of human and artificial intelligence. *Nature Medicine*. 2019;25(1):44–56.
141. Pencina MJ, Goldstein BA, D'Agostino RB. Prediction models—development, evaluation, and clinical application. *New England Journal of Medicine*. 2020;382(17):1583–6.
142. Friedman LM, Furberg CD, DeMets DL, Reboussin DM, Granger CB. *Fundamentals of Clinical Trials*: Springer; 2015.
143. Grimes DA, Schulz KF. An overview of clinical research: The lay of the land. *The Lancet*. 2002;359(9300):57–61.
144. Schulz KF, Grimes DA. Generation of allocation sequences in randomised trials: Chance, not choice. *The Lancet*. 2002;359(9305):515–9.
145. Wang SV, Schneeweiss S, Berger ML, Brown J, de Vries F, Douglas I, et al. Reporting to improve reproducibility and facilitate validity assessment for healthcare database studies V1. 0. *Value in Health*. 2017;20(8):1009–22.
146. Pocock SJ. *Clinical Trials: A Practical Approach*: John Wiley & Sons; 2013.
147. Berry SM, Carlin BP, Lee JJ, Muller P. *Bayesian Adaptive Methods for Clinical Trials*: CRC Press; 2010.
148. Woodcock J, LaVange LM. Master protocols to study multiple therapies, multiple diseases, or both. *New England Journal of Medicine*. 2017;377(1):62–70.
149. Park JJH, Siden E, Zoratti MJ, Dron L, Harari O, Singer J, et al. Systematic review of basket trials, umbrella trials, and platform trials: A landscape analysis of master protocols. *Trials*. 2019;20(1):572.
150. Esteva A, Kuprel B, Novoa RA, Ko J, Swetter SM, Blau HM, et al. Dermatologist-level classification of skin cancer with deep neural networks. *Nature*. 2017;542(7639):115–8.
151. Rajpurkar P, Irvin J, Zhu K, Yang B, Mehta H, Duan T, et al. Chexnet: Radiologist-level pneumonia detection on chest x-rays with deep learning. arXiv preprint arXiv:171105225. 2017.
152. Wang C, Xu P, Zhang L, Huang J, Zhu K, Luo C. Current strategies and applications for precision drug design. *Frontiers in Pharmacology*. 2018;9:787.
153. Chen M, Mao S, Liu Y. Big data: A survey. *Mobile Networks and Applications*. 2014;19(2):171–209.
154. Davenport TH, Harris JG. *Analytics and Big Data: The Davenport Collection (6 Items)*: Harvard Business Review Press; 2014.

155. Raghupathi W, Raghupathi V. Big data analytics in healthcare: A survey. *Journal of King Saud University-Computer and Information Sciences*. 2014;30(4):391–405.
156. Redman T. *Data Driven: Creating a Data Culture*. Harvard Business Press; 2008.
157. Bycroft C, Freeman C, Petkova D, Band G, Elliott LT, Sharp K, et al. The UK Biobank resource with deep phenotyping and genomic data. *Nature*. 2018;562(7726):203–9.
158. Herrett E, Gallagher AM, Bhaskaran K, Forbes H, Mathur R, Van Staa T, et al. Data resource profile: Clinical practice research datalink (CPRD). *International Journal of Epidemiology*. 2015;44(3):827–36.
159. Medina CRR, Lyon M, Davies E, McCarthy D, Reid V, Khanna A, et al. Clinical indications associated with new opioid use for pain management in the United Kingdom: Using national primary care data. *Pain*. 2025;166(3):656–66.
160. Nab L, Schaffer AL, Hulme W, DeVito NJ, Dillingham I, Wiedemann M, et al. OpenSAFELY: A platform for analysing electronic health records designed for reproducible research. *Pharmacoepidemiology and Drug Safety*. 2024;33(6):e5815.
161. de Lusignan S, Jones N, Dorward J, Byford R, Liyanage H, Briggs J, et al. The Oxford Royal College of general practitioners clinical informatics digital hub: Protocol to develop extended COVID-19 surveillance and trial platforms. *JMIR Public Health and Surveillance*. 2020;6(3):e19773.
162. Floridi L, Taddeo M. What is data ethics? *Philosophical Transactions of the Royal Society A: Mathematical, Physical and Engineering Sciences*. 2016;374. p. 20160360.
163. Kramer AD, Guillory JE, Hancock JT. Experimental evidence of massive-scale emotional contagion through social networks. *Proceedings of the National Academy of Sciences*. 2014;111(24):8788–90.
164. United States. National Commission for the Protection of Human Subjects of Biomedical, and Behavioral Research. *The Belmont Report: Ethical Principles and Guidelines for the Protection of Human Subjects of Research*: The Commission; 1978.
165. Morse SA, Weirich E. Select agent regulations. Microbial Forensics: Elsevier; 2011. pp. 199–220.
166. Metcalf J, Crawford K. Where are human subjects in big data research? The emerging ethics divide. *Big Data & Society*. 2016;3(1):2053951716650211.
167. Appelbaum PS, Roth LH, Lidz CW, Benson P, Winslade W. False hopes and best data: Consent to research and the therapeutic misconception. *The Hastings Center Report*. 1987;17(2):20–4.
168. Metcalf J. Ethics codes: History, context, and challenges. *Council for Big Data, Ethics, and Society*. 2014:1–15.
169. Drew C. Data science ethics in government. *Philosophical Transactions of the Royal Society A: Mathematical, Physical and Engineering Sciences*. 2016;374(2083):20160119.
170. Hand DJ. *Measurement Theory and Practice*: Arnold; 2004.
171. Greenwood D, Stopczynski A, Sweatt B, Hardjono T, Pentland A. The new deal on data: A framework for institutional controls. *Privacy, Big Data, and the Public Good: Frameworks for Engagement*. 2014;1:192–210.
172. Finck M, Pallas F. They who must not be identified—distinguishing personal from non-personal data under the GDPR. *International Data Privacy Law*. 2020;10(1):11–36.
173. ICO. What is personal data?–A quick reference guide. 2012.
174. Schwab K, Marcus A, Oyola J, Hoffman W, Luzi M, editors. Personal data: The emergence of a new asset class. *An Initiative of the World Economic Forum*; 2011: World Economic Forum, Cologny, Davos, Switzerland.
175. Hand DJ. Aspects of data ethics in a changing world: Where are we now? *Big Data*. 2018;6(3):176–90.
176. Leon LFA. A blueprint for market construction? Spatial data infrastructure (s), interoperability, and the EU Digital Single Market. *Geoforum*. 2018;92:45–57.

177. Van Asbroeck B, Debussche J, César J. Building the European data economy: Data ownership. *White Paper, Bird and Bird*. 2017.
178. Markham AN, Tiidenberg K, Herman A. Ethics as methods: Doing ethics in the era of big data research—introduction. *Social Media+ Society*. 2018;4(3):2056305118784502.
179. Cuquet M, Fensel A. The societal impact of big data: A research roadmap for Europe. *Technology in Society*. 2018;54:74–86.
180. Bynum TW. Computer and information ethics. *The Stanford encyclopedia of philosophy*. 2008.
181. Floridi L. *The Ethics of Information*: Oxford University Press (UK); 2013.
182. Miller KW, Taddeo M. *The Ethics of Information Technologies*: Routledge; 2020.
183. Dahl O-J, Dijkstra EW, Hoare CAR. *Structured Programming*: Academic Press Ltd.; 1972.
184. Parker DB. Rules of ethics in information processing. *Communications of the ACM*. 1968;11(3):198–201.
185. Moor JH. What is computer ethics? *Metaphilosophy*. 1985;16(4):266–75.
186. Floridi L. Information ethics, its nature and scope. *ACM Sigcas Computers and Society*. 2005;35(2):3-.
187. Mittelstadt BD, Floridi L. The ethics of big data: Current and foreseeable issues in biomedical contexts. *The Ethics of Biomedical Big Data*. 2016:445–80.
188. Kirkpatrick R. A new type of philanthropy: Donating data. *Harvard Business Review*. 2013;21.
189. Brey PA. Anticipatory ethics for emerging technologies. *NanoEthics*. 2012;6(1):1–13.
190. Camfield L. Rigor and ethics in the world of big-team qualitative data: Experiences from research in international development. *American Behavioral Scientist*. 2019;63(5):604–21.
191. Cass S. Researcher charged with data theft. *Nature Medicine*. 1999;5(5):474.
192. Chang RM, Kauffman RJ, Kwon Y. Understanding the paradigm shift to computational social science in the presence of big data. *Decision Support Systems*. 2014;63:67–80.
193. Connelly R, Playford CJ, Gayle V, Dibben C. The role of administrative data in the big data revolution in social science research. *Social Science Research*. 2016;59:1–12.
194. Curty RG. Factors influencing research data reuse in the social sciences: An exploratory study. *International Journal of Digital Curation*. 2016;11(1):96–117.
195. Danaher J, Nyholm S, Earp BD. The quantified relationship. *The American Journal of Bioethics*. 2018;18(2):3–19.
196. Duchin M. Geometry v. gerrymandering. In Mircea Pitici, editor *The Best Writing on Mathematics*; 2019: Princeton University Press. pp. 1–11.
197. European Commission. Ethics in social science and humanities. Bruxelles/Luxembourg. 2018.
198. Feldman S, Shaw L. The epistemological and ethical challenges of archiving and sharing qualitative data. *American Behavioral Scientist*. 2019;63(6):699–721.
199. Foster I, Ghani R, Jarmin RS, Kreuter F, Lane J. *Big Data and Social Science: A Practical Guide to Methods and Tools*: Chapman and Hall/CRC; 2016.
200. Hosseini M, Wieczorek M, Gordijn B. Ethical issues in social science research employing big data. *Science and Engineering Ethics*. 2022;28(3):29.
201. Franzke AS, Bechmann A, Ess CM, Zimmer M. Internet research: Ethical guidelines 3.0. 2020.
202. Frey WR, Patton DU, Gaskell MB, McGregor KA. Artificial intelligence and inclusion: Formerly gang-involved youth as domain experts for analyzing unstructured twitter data. *Social Science Computer Review*. 2020;38(1):42–56.
203. Anderson C. The end of theory: The data deluge makes the scientific method obsolete. *Wired Magazine*. 2008;16(7):16–07.

204. Ajana B. Digital health and the biopolitics of the Quantified Self. *Digital Health*. 2017;3:2055207616689509.
205. Attewell P, Monaghan D. *Data Mining for the Social Sciences: An Introduction*: University of California Press; 2015.
206. Barocas S, Selbst AD. Big data's disparate impact. *California Law Review*. 2016;104:671.
207. Kosinski M, Stillwell D, Graepel T. Private traits and attributes are predictable from digital records of human behavior. *Proceedings of the National Academy of Sciences*. 2013;110(15):5802–5.
208. Kramer DB, Xu S, Kesselheim AS. Regulation of medical devices in the United States and European Union. *The Ethical Challenges of Emerging Medical Technologies*: Routledge; 2020. pp. 41–8.
209. Kreitmair K, Cho MK. The neuroethical future of wearable and mobile health technology. *Neuroethics: Anticipating the Future*. 2017:80–107.
210. Barrowman N. Why data is never raw. *The New Atlantis*. 2018(56):129–35.
211. Wacquant L. Symbolic power and group-making: On Pierre Bourdieu's reframing of class. *Journal of Classical Sociology*. 2013;13(2):274–91.
212. Bourdieu P, Wacquant LJ. *An Invitation to Reflexive Sociology*: University of Chicago Press; 1992.
213. Boyd KM. Why the biomedical research ethics model is inappropriate for social sciences: A response to 'Responsible to Whom? Obligations to participants and society in social science research' by Matt Sleat. *Finding Common Ground: Consensus in Research Ethics across the Social Sciences*: Emerald Publishing Limited; 2017. pp. 55–60.
214. Brandom R. Shadow profiles are the biggest flaw in Facebook's privacy defense. *The Verge*. 2018;11.
215. Kitchin R, McArdle G. What makes Big Data, Big Data? Exploring the ontological characteristics of 26 datasets. *Big Data & Society*. 2016;3(1):2053951716631130.
216. Gitelman L. *Raw Data Is an Oxymoron*: MIT Press; 2013.
217. González-Bailón S. Social science in the era of big data. *Policy & Internet*. 2013;5(2):147–60.
218. Hargittai E. Potential biases in big data: Omitted voices on social media. *Social Science Computer Review*. 2020;38(1):10–24.
219. Hesse A, Glenna L, Hinrichs C, Chiles R, Sachs C. Qualitative research ethics in the big data era. *American Behavioral Scientist*. 2019;63(5):560–83.
220. Resnik DB. *The Ethics of Science: An Introduction*: Routledge; 2005.
221. Hossain N, Scott-Villiers P. Ethical and methodological issues in large qualitative participatory studies. *American Behavioral Scientist*. 2019;63(5):584–603.
222. Hoy MB. Personal activity trackers and the quantified self. *Medical Reference Services Quarterly*. 2016;35(1):94–100.
223. Kerr NL. HARKing: Hypothesizing after the results are known. *Personality and Social Psychology Review*. 1998;2(3):196–217.
224. Hollingshead W, Quan-Haase A, Chen W. Ethics and privacy in computational social science: A call for pedagogy. *Handbook of Computational Social Science, Volume* 1: Routledge; 2021. pp. 171–85.
225. Delanerolle G, McCauley M, Hirsch M, Zeng Y, Cong X, Cavalini H, et al. The prevalence of mental ill-health in women during pregnancy and after childbirth during the Covid-19 pandemic: A systematic review and Meta-analysis. *BMC Pregnancy and Childbirth*. 2023;23(1):76.
226. Katsikopoulos K, Canellas M. Decoding human behavior with big data? Critical, constructive input from the decision sciences. *AI Magazine*. 2022;43(1):126–38.

227. Dignum V, Crawford K. Atlas of AI: Power, Politics, and the Planetary Costs of Artificial Intelligence. NATURE PORTFOLIO HEIDELBERGER PLATZ 3, BERLIN, 14197, GERMANY; 2021.
228. Hand DJ, Yu K. Idiot's Bayes—not so stupid after all? *International Statistical Review*. 2001;69(3):385–98. https://doi.org/10.1111/j.1751-5823.2001.tb00465.x
229. Katsikopoulos KV, Simsek O, Buckmann M, Gigerenzer G. *Classification in the wild: The science and art of transparent decision making*: MIT Press; 2021.
230. Delanerolle G, Cavalini H, Taylor J, Hinchliff S, Talaulikar V, Zingela Z, et al. An exploration of the mental health impact among menopausal women: The MARIE Project Protocol (International Arm). medRxiv. 2023:2023.11. 26.23299012.
231. Delanerolle G, Phiri P, Elneil S, Talaulikar V, Eleje GU, Kareem R, et al. Menopause: A global health and wellbeing issue that needs urgent attention. *The Lancet Global Health*. 2025;13(2):e196–e8.
232. Ennis L, Wykes T. Impact of patient involvement in mental health research: Longitudinal study. *The British Journal of Psychiatry*. 2013;203(5):381–6.
233. Jenner MK, Gilchrist M, Baker GC. Practical considerations in improving research through public involvement. *Research Involvement and Engagement*. 2015;1(1):3.
234. Archard D, Montgomery J, Caney S, Clancy T, Edwards J, Gallagher A, et al. Nuffield Council on Bioethics. *of Global Bioethics*. 2016:135.
235. Staley K, Elliott J. Public involvement could usefully inform ethical review, but rarely does: What are the implications? *Research Involvement and Engagement*. 2017;3(1):30.
236. Lipworth W, Mason PH, Kerridge I, Ioannidis JP. Ethics and epistemology in big data research. *Journal of Bioethical Inquiry*. 2017;14(4):489–500.
237. Liu H, Guo G. Opportunities and challenges of big data for the social sciences: The case of genomic data. *Social Science Research*. 2016;59:13–22.
238. Warsh J. PPI: Understanding the difference between patient and public involvement. *The American Journal of Bioethics*. 2014;14(6):25–6.
239. Florin D, Dixon J. Public involvement in health care. *BMJ*. 2004;328(7432):159–61.
240. Blackburn S, McLachlan S, Jowett S, Kinghorn P, Gill P, Higginbottom A, et al. The extent, quality and impact of patient and public involvement in primary care research: A mixed methods study. *Research Involvement and Engagement*. 2018;4(1):16.
241. Chen F. 23andMe and the FDA: Negotiating conceptions of benefit in the direct-to-consumer genetic testing regulatory debate 2014. Doctoral dissertation.
242. Prainsack B. *Personalized medicine: Empowered patients in the 21st century? Personalized medicine*: New York University Press; 2017.
243. Tukey JW. *Exploratory data analysis*: Springer; 1977.
244. Matranga D, Restivo V, Maniscalco L, Bono F, Pizzo G, Lanza G, et al. Lifestyle medicine and psychological well-being toward health promotion: A cross-sectional study on Palermo (Southern Italy) undergraduates. *International Journal of Environmental Research and Public Health*. 2020;17(15):5444.
245. Fujihara S, Tsuji T, Miyaguni Y, Aida J, Saito M, Koyama S, et al. Does community-level social capital predict decline in instrumental activities of daily living? A JAGES prospective cohort study. *International Journal of Environmental Research and Public Health*. 2019;16(5):828.
246. Maniscalco L, Schouteden M, Boon J, Matranga D, Godderis L. The impact of a change in employment on three work-related diseases: A retrospective longitudinal study of 10,530 belgian employees. *International Journal of Environmental Research and Public Health*. 2020;17(20):7477.
247. Verso MG, Serra N, Ciccarello A, Romanin B, Di Carlo P. Latent tuberculosis infection among healthcare students and postgraduates in a Mediterranean Italian area: What correlation with work exposure? *International Journal of Environmental Research and Public Health*. 2020;17(1):137.

248. Trivelli L, Borrelli P, Cadum E, Pisoni E, Villani S. Spatial-temporal modelling of disease risk accounting for PM2. 5 exposure in the province of Pavia: An area of the Po Valley. *International Journal of Environmental Research and Public Health.* 2021;18(2):658.
249. Maniscalco L, Miceli S, Bono F, Matranga D. Self-perceived health, objective health, and quality of life among people aged 50 and over: Interrelationship among health indicators in Italy, Spain, and Greece. *International Journal of Environmental Research and Public Health.* 2020;17(7):2414.
250. Keeling MJ, Rohani P. *Modeling Infectious Diseases in Humans and Animals*: Princeton University Press; 2008.
251. Allen LJ. An introduction to stochastic epidemic models. In Fred Brauer, Pauline Driessche, Jianhong Wu, Editors Mathematical Epidemiology: Springer; 2008. pp. 81–130.
252. Britton T. Stochastic epidemic models: A survey. *Mathematical Biosciences.* 2010;225(1):24–35.
253. O'Neill PD. Introduction and snapshot review: Relating infectious disease transmission models to data. *Statistics in Medicine.* 2010;29(20):2069–77.
254. O'Neill PD. A tutorial introduction to Bayesian inference for stochastic epidemic models using Markov chain Monte Carlo methods. *Mathematical Biosciences.* 2002;180(1–2):103–14.
255. Rampey Jr AH, Longini Jr IM, Haber M, Monto AS. A discrete-time model for the statistical analysis of infectious disease incidence data. *Biometrics.* 1992; 48(1):117–28.
256. Yang Y, Longini Jr IM, Halloran ME. A data-augmentation method for infectious disease incidence data from close contact groups. *Computational Statistics & Data Analysis.* 2007;51(12):6582–95.
257. O'neill J, Spash CL. Conceptions of value in environmental decision-making. *Environmental Values.* 2000;9(4):521–36.
258. Van Dyk DA, Meng X-L. The art of data augmentation. *Journal of Computational and Graphical Statistics.* 2001;10(1):1-50.
259. Paap R. What are the advantages of MCMC based inference in latent variable models? *Statistica Neerlandica.* 2002;56(1):2–22.
260. Roberts GO, Stramer O. On inference for partially observed nonlinear diffusion models using the Metropolis–Hastings algorithm. *Biometrika.* 2001;88(3):603–21.
261. Cauchemez S, Ferguson NM. Likelihood-based estimation of continuous-time epidemic models from time-series data: Application to measles transmission in London. *Journal of the Royal Society Interface.* 2008;5(25):885–97.
262. Martínez-Flórez G, Bolfarine H, Gómez HW. The log-power-normal distribution with application to air pollution. *Environmetrics.* 2014;25(1):44–56.
263. O'Neill PD, Roberts GO. Bayesian inference for partially observed stochastic epidemics. *Journal of the Royal Statistical Society Series A: Statistics in Society.* 1999;162(1):121–9.
264. Gibson GJ, Renshaw E. Estimating parameters in stochastic compartmental models using Markov chain methods. *Mathematical Medicine and Biology: A Journal of the IMA.* 1998;15(1):19–40.
265. Pooley C, Bishop S, Marion G. Using model-based proposals for fast parameter inference on discrete state space, continuous-time Markov processes. *Journal of The Royal Society Interface.* 2015;12(107).
366. Shestopaloff AY, Neal RM. *Sampling latent states for high-dimensional non-linear state space models with the embedded HMM method*; 2018.
267. Fintzi J, Cui X, Wakefield J, Minin VN. Efficient data augmentation for fitting stochastic epidemic models to prevalence data. *Journal of Computational and Graphical Statistics.* 2017;26(4):918–29.

268. Qi M, Cahan O, Foreman MA, Gruen DM, Das AK, Bennett KP. Quantifying representativeness in randomized clinical trials using machine learning fairness metrics. *JAMIA Open*. 2021;4(3): 1–11.
269. Bellamy RK, Dey K, Hind M, Hoffman SC, Houde S, Kannan K, et al. AI Fairness 360: An extensible toolkit for detecting and mitigating algorithmic bias. *IBM Journal of Research and Development*. 2019;63(4/5):4-1.
270. Horton NJ, Switzer SS. Statistical methods in the journal. *New England Journal of Medicine*. 2005;353(18):1977–9.
271. West CP, Ficalora RD, editors. *Clinician attitudes toward biostatistics. Mayo clinic proceedings*; 2007: Elsevier.
272. Windish DM, Huot SJ, Green ML. Medicine residents' understanding of the biostatistics and results in the medical literature. *Jama*. 2007;298(9):1010–22.
273. Berwick DM, Fineberg HV, Weinstein MC. When doctors meet numbers. The *American Journal of Medicine*. 1981;71(6):991–8.
274. Wulff HR, Andersen B, Brandenhoff P, Guttler F. What do doctors know about statistics? *Statistics in Medicine*. 1987;6(1):3–10.
275. Altman DG, Bland JM. Statistics notes: The normal distribution. *BMJ*. 1995;310(6975):298.
276. Glantz SA. Biostatistics: how to detect, correct and prevent errors in the medical literature. *Circulation*. 1980;61(1):1–7.
277. Kirkwood BR, Sterne JA. *Essential Medical Statistics*: John Wiley & Sons; 2010.
278. Kleinbaum DG, Klein M. *Survival Analysis a Self-Learning Text*: Springer; 1996.
279. Vittinghoff E, Shiboski SC, Glidden DV, McCulloch CE. *Regression Methods in Biostatistics: Linear, Logistic, Survival, and Repeated Measures Models*: Springer; 2005.
280. Altman DG, Bland JM. Uncertainty beyond sampling error. *BMJ*. 2014;349: g7065.
281. Rothman KJ, Greenland S, Lash TL. *Modern Epidemiology*: Wolters Kluwer Health/ Lippincott Williams & Wilkins Philadelphia; 2008.
282. Cumming G, Finch S. Inference by eye: Confidence intervals and how to read pictures of data. *American Psychologist*. 2005;60(2):170.
283. EW S. *Clinical Prediction Models: A Practical Approach to Development, Validation, and Updating*. New York: Springer; 2009.
284. Harrell FE, Levy DG. Regression modeling strategies. R package version. 2022:6.3-0.
285. Moons KG, Altman DG, Reitsma JB, Ioannidis JP, Macaskill P, Steyerberg EW, et al. Transparent Reporting of a multivariable prediction model for Individual Prognosis or Diagnosis (TRIPOD): Explanation and elaboration. *Annals of Internal Medicine*. 2015;162(1):W1–W73.
286. Sutton AJ, Abrams KR. Bayesian methods in meta-analysis and evidence synthesis. *Statistical Methods in Medical Research*. 2001;10(4):277–303.
287. Greenland S. Bayesian perspectives for epidemiological research: I. Foundations and basic methods. *International Journal of Epidemiology*. 2006;35(3):765–75.
288. Carpenter JR, Bartlett JW, Morris TP, Wood AM, Quartagno M, Kenward MG. *Multiple Imputation and Its Application*: John Wiley & Sons; 2023.
289. Berry DA. Bayesian clinical trials. *Nature Reviews Drug Discovery*. 2006;5(1):27–36.
290. Gelman A, Hill J. *Data Analysis Using Regression and Multilevel/Hierarchical Models*: Cambridge University Press; 2007.
291. Spiegelhalter DJ, Abrams KR, Myles JP. *Bayesian Approaches to Clinical Trials and Health-Care Evaluation*: John Wiley & Sons; 2004.
292. Shetty A, Delanerolle G, Deng C, Thillainathan A, Cavalini H, Yang X, et al. A systematic review and Bayesian meta-analysis of medical devices used in chronic pain management. *Scientific Reports*. 2024;14(1):13549.

293. Shendure J, Findlay GM, Snyder MW. Genomic medicine–progress, pitfalls, and promise. *Cell.* 2019;177(1):45–57.
294. Steinhubl SR, Muse ED, Topol EJ. Can mobile health technologies transform health care? *JAMA.* 2013;310(22):2395–6.
295. Chaudhury A, Duvoor C, Reddy Dendi VS, Kraleti S, Chada A, Ravilla R, et al. Clinical review of antidiabetic drugs: Implications for type 2 diabetes mellitus management. *Frontiers in Endocrinology.* 2017;8:6.
296. Jakicic JM, Davis KK, Rogers RJ, King WC, Marcus MD, Helsel D, et al. Effect of wearable technology combined with a lifestyle intervention on long-term weight loss: The IDEA randomized clinical trial. *JAMA.* 2016;316(11):1161–71.
297. Torous J, Nicholas J, Larsen ME, Firth J, Christensen H. Clinical review of user engagement with mental health smartphone apps: Evidence, theory and improvements. *BMJ Mental Health.* 2018;21(3):116–9.
298. Meingast M, Roosta T, Sastry S, editors. Security and privacy issues with health care information technology. *2006 International Conference of the IEEE Engineering in Medicine and Biology Society*; 2006: IEEE.
299. Bates DW, Saria S, Ohno-Machado L, Shah A, Escobar G. Big data in health care: Using analytics to identify and manage high-risk and high-cost patients. *Health Affairs.* 2014;33(7):1123–31.
300. Buijink AWG, Visser BJ, Marshall L. Medical apps for smartphones: Lack of evidence undermines quality and safety. *BMJ Evidence-Based Medicine.* 2013;18(3):90–2.
301. Ashley EA. Towards precision medicine. *Nature Reviews Genetics.* 2016;17(9):507–22.
302. Collins FS, Varmus H. A new initiative on precision medicine. *New England Journal of Medicine.* 2015;372(9):793–5.
303. Hasin Y, Seldin M, Lusis A. Multi-omics approaches to disease. *Genome Biology.* 2017;18(1):83.
304. Sherman RE, Anderson SA, Dal Pan GJ, Gray GW, Gross T, Hunter NL, et al. Real-world evidence—what is it and what can it tell us. *New England Journal of Medicine.* 2016;375(23):2293–7.
305. Paik S, Shak S, Tang G, Kim C, Baker J, Cronin M, et al. A multigene assay to predict recurrence of tamoxifen-treated, node-negative breast cancer. *New England Journal of Medicine.* 2004;351(27):2817–26.
306. Inouye M, Abraham G, Nelson CP, Wood AM, Sweeting MJ, Dudbridge F, et al. Genomic risk prediction of coronary artery disease in 480,000 adults: Implications for primary prevention. *Journal of the American College of Cardiology.* 2018;72(16):1883–93.
307. Caudle KE, Dunnenberger HM, Freimuth RR, Peterson JF, Burlison JD, Whirl-Carrillo M, et al. Standardizing terms for clinical pharmacogenetic test results: Consensus terms from the Clinical Pharmacogenetics Implementation Consortium (CPIC). *Genetics in Medicine.* 2017;19(2):215–23.
308. Jack Jr CR, Bennett DA, Blennow K, Carrillo MC, Dunn B, Haeberlein SB, et al. NIA-AA research framework: Toward a biological definition of Alzheimer's disease. *Alzheimer's & Dementia.* 2018;14(4):535–62.
309. Kohavi R, Tang D, Xu Y. *Trustworthy Online Controlled Experiments: A Practical Guide to A/B Testing*: Cambridge University Press; 2020.
310. Fitzgerald B, Stol K-J. Continuous software engineering: A roadmap and agenda. *Journal of Systems and Software.* 2017;123:176–89.
311. Zaharia M, Chowdhury M, Franklin MJ, Shenker S, Stoica I, editors. Spark: Cluster computing with working sets. *2nd USENIX Workshop on Hot Topics in Cloud Computing (HotCloud 10)*: Boston, MA; 2010.
312. Bhattacharyya S, Jha S, Tharakunnel K, Westland JC. Data mining for credit card fraud: A comparative study. *Decision Support Systems.* 2011;50(3):602–13.
313. Mitchell M. *An Introduction to Genetic Algorithms*: MIT Press; 1998.

314. Provost F, Fawcett T. *Data Science for Business: What You Need to Know About Data Mining and Data-Analytic Thinking*: O'Reilly Media, Inc.; 2013.
315. Sculley D, Holt G, Golovin D, Davydov E, Phillips T, Ebner D, et al. Hidden technical debt in machine learning systems. Advances in neural information processing systems. 2015;28.
316. Nissenbaum H. Privacy in context: Technology, policy, and the integrity of social life. *Privacy in Context*: Stanford University Press; 2009.
317. Dieckmann P, Gaba D, Rall M. Deepening the theoretical foundations of patient simulation as social practice. *Simulation in Healthcare*. 2007;2(3):183–93.
318. Cheng A, Lang TR, Starr SR, Pusic M, Cook DA. Technology-enhanced simulation and pediatric education: A meta-analysis. *Pediatrics*. 2014;133(5):e1313–e23.
319. Tang KS, Cheng DL, Mi E, Greenberg PB. Augmented reality in medical education: A systematic review. *Canadian Medical Education Journal*. 2020;11(1):e81.
320. Elendu C, Amaechi DC, Okatta AU, Amaechi EC, Elendu TC, Ezeh CP, et al. The impact of simulation-based training in medical education: A review. *Medicine*. 2024;103(27):e38813.
321. Cook DA, Triola MM. Virtual patients: A critical literature review and proposed next steps. *Medical Education*. 2009;43(4):303–11.
322. Ziv A, Ben-David S, Ziv M. Simulation based medical education: An opportunity to learn from errors. *Medical Teacher*. 2005;27(3):193–9.
323. Reeves S, Fletcher S, Barr H, Birch I, Boet S, Davies N, et al. A BEME systematic review of the effects of interprofessional education: BEME Guide No. 39. *Medical Teacher*. 2016;38(7):656–68.
324. McGaghie WC, Issenberg SB, Cohen ER, Barsuk JH, Wayne DB. Does simulation-based medical education with deliberate practice yield better results than traditional clinical education? A meta-analytic comparative review of the evidence. *Academic Medicine*. 2011;86(6):706–11.
325. Nestel D, Groom J, Eikeland-Husebø S, O'Donnell JM. Simulation for learning and teaching procedural skills: The state of the science. *Simulation in Healthcare*. 2011;6(7):S10–S3.
326. Sgarbura O, Vasilescu C. The decisive role of the patient-side surgeon in robotic surgery. *Surgical Endoscopy*. 2010;24(12):3149–55.
327. Cho H-J, Lloyd T, Zammit A, Sadasivan AP, Wagels M, Sutherland A. Radiologically derived 3D virtual models for neurosurgical planning. *Journal of Clinical Neuroscience*. 2024;123:23–9.
328. Chen Y, Huang S, Chen T, Liang D, Yang J, Zeng C, et al. Machine learning for prediction and risk stratification of lupus nephritis renal flare. *American Journal of Nephrology*. 2021;52(2):152–60.
329. Culbertson H, Schorr SB, Okamura AM. Haptics: The present and future of artificial touch sensation. *Annual Review of Control, Robotics, and Autonomous Systems*. 2018;1(1):385–409.
330. Takayanagi T, Hashimoto R, Chen C-C, Izumi K. The impact and feasibility of self-confidence shaping for AI-assisted decision-making. arXiv preprint arXiv:250214311. 2025.
331. Chang Y-J, Hung K-C, Wang L-K, Yu C-H, Chen C-K, Tay H-T, et al. A real-time artificial intelligence-assisted system to predict weaning from ventilator immediately after lung resection surgery. *International Journal of Environmental Research and Public Health*. 2021;18(5):2713.
332. Liu X, Fang M, Wang K, Zhu J, Chen Z, He L, et al. Machine learning-based model to predict severe acute kidney injury after total aortic arch replacement for acute type A aortic dissection. *Heliyon*. 2024;10(13).

333. Hashimoto DA, Rosman G, Rus D, Meireles OR. Artificial intelligence in surgery: Promises and perils. *Annals of Surgery*. 2018;268(1):70–6.
334. Hung AJ, Liu Y, Anandkumar A. Deep learning to automate technical skills assessment in robotic surgery. *JAMA Surgery*. 2021;156(11):1059–60.
335. Schiller G, Blum A, Hecht R, Oertel H, Ferber U, Meinel G. Urban infill development potential in Germany: Comparing survey and GIS data. *Buildings & Cities*. 2021;2(1): 36-54.
336. Baddeley A. Working memory: Looking back and looking forward. *Nature Reviews Neuroscience*. 2003;4(10):829–39.
337. Watson K. D. Kahneman. (2011). Thinking, fast and slow. New York, NY: Farrar, Straus and Giroux. 499 pages. *Canadian Journal of Program Evaluation*. 2011;26(2):111–3.
338. Enriquez-Geppert S, Huster RJ, Herrmann CS. EEG-neurofeedback as a tool to modulate cognition and behavior: A review tutorial. *Frontiers in Human Neuroscience*. 2017;11:51.
339. Papp KV, Walsh SJ, Snyder PJ. Immediate and delayed effects of cognitive interventions in healthy elderly: A review of current literature and future directions. *Alzheimer's & Dementia*. 2009;5(1):50–60.
340. Simons DJ, Boot WR, Charness N, Gathercole SE, Chabris CF, Hambrick DZ, et al. Do "brain-training" programs work? *Psychological Science in the Public Interest*. 2016;17(3):103–86.
341. Rabipour S, Raz A. Training the brain: Fact and fad in cognitive and behavioral remediation. *Brain and Cognition*. 2012;79(2):159–79.
342. Jacobson PD. Medical liability and the culture of technology: Project on Medical Liability in Pennsylvania; 2004.
343. Gostin LO, Levit LA, Nass SJ. *Beyond the HIPAA privacy rule: enhancing privacy, improving health through research*. 2009.
344. Khatri V, Brown CV. Designing data governance. *Communications of the ACM*. 2010;53(1):148–52.
345. Otto B. A morphology of the organisation of data governance. 2011.
346. Zarsky TZ. Incompatible: The GDPR in the age of big data. *Seton Hall Law Review*. 2016;47:995.
347. Gellert R. Data protection: A risk regulation? Between the risk management of everything and the precautionary alternative. *International Data Privacy Law*. 2015;5:3.
348. Hashem IAT, Yaqoob I, Anuar NB, Mokhtar S, Gani A, Khan SU. The rise of "big data" on cloud computing: Review and open research issues. *Information Systems*. 2015;47:98–115.
349. Riggins FJ, Wamba SF, editors. Research directions on the adoption, usage, and impact of the internet of things through the use of big data analytics. *2015 48th Hawaii International Conference on System Sciences*; 2015: IEEE, Kauai, HI.
350. Heeks R, Shekhar S. Datafication, development and marginalised urban communities: An applied data justice framework. *Information, Communication & Society*. 2019;22(7):992–1011.
351. Zwitter A, Gstrein OJ. Big data, privacy and COVID-19–learning from humanitarian expertise in data protection. *Journal of International Humanitarian Action*. 2020;5(1):4.
352. Sox HC, Higgins MC, Owens DK, Schmidler GS. *Medical Decision Making*: John Wiley & Sons; 2024.
353. Djulbegovic B, Guyatt GH. Progress in evidence-based medicine: A quarter century on. *The Lancet*. 2017;390(10092):415–23.
354. Gigerenzer G. In the year 2054: Innumeracy defeated. In Peter Sedlmeier, Tilmann Betsch, editors *Etc: Frequency Processing and Cognition*: Oxford University Press; 2002. pp. 55–66.
355. Savage LJ. *The Foundations of Statistics*: Courier Corporation; 1972.

356. Howard RA. Heathens, heretics, and cults: The religious spectrum of decision aiding. *Interfaces*. 1992;22(6):15–27.
357. Katsikopoulos KV. Analyzing decisions under uncertainty: Simple tools of the heathens. In F. Federspiel, G. Montibeller and M. Seifert, editors Behavioral Decision Analysis: Springer; 2024. pp. 65–79.
358. King M, Kay J. *Radical Uncertainty: Decision-Making for an Unknowable Future*: Hachette UK; 2020.
359. Reb J, Luan S, Gigerenzer G. *Smart Management: How Simple Heuristics Help Leaders Make Good Decisions in an Uncertain World*: MIT Press; 2024.
360. Tversky A, Kahneman D. Judgment under Uncertainty: Heuristics and Biases: Biases in judgments reveal some heuristics of thinking under uncertainty. *Science*. 1974;185(4157):1124–31.
361. Knight FH. *Risk, Uncertainty and Profit*: Рипол Классик; 1921.
362. Gigerenzer GE, Hertwig RE, Pachur TE. *Heuristics: The Foundations of Adaptive Behavior*: Oxford University Press; 2011.
363. Katsikopoulos KV, Simsek O, Buckmann M, Gigerenzer G. *Classification in the Wild: The Science and Art of Transparent Decision Making*: MIT Press; 2021.
364. Katsikopoulos KV, Durbach IN, Stewart TJ. When should we use simple decision models? A synthesis of various research strands. *Omega*. 2018;81:17–25.
365. Hogarth RM. When simple is hard to accept. 2012.
366. Goodwin P. Commentary on "Transparent modelling of influenza incidence": The need to justify complexity. *International Journal of Forecasting*. 2022;38(2):628–9.
367. Katsikopoulos KV. *What Is Cognitive Operations? Cognitive Operations: Models that Open the Black Box and Predict our Decisions*: Springer; 2023. pp. 1–10.
368. Hutchinson JM, Gigerenzer G. Simple heuristics and rules of thumb: Where psychologists and behavioural biologists might meet. *Behavioural Processes*. 2005;69(2):97–124.
369. Lichtman AJ. *Predicting the Next President: The Keys to the White House, 2024*: Bloomsbury Publishing PLC; 2024.
370. Ioannidis JP, Cripps S, Tanner MA. Forecasting for COVID-19 has failed. *International Journal of Forecasting*. 2022;38(2):423–38.
371. Pereira S, Bakker P, Zaima A, Ghi T, Kessler J, Timonen S, et al. Is the fetus fit for labor? Introducing fast-and-frugal trees (FFTrees) to simplify triage of women for STAN monitoring: An interobserver agreement comparison with traditional classification. *Acta Obstetricia et Gynecologica Scandinavica*. 2024;103(1):68–76.
372. Djulbegovic B, Hozo I, Dale W. Transforming clinical practice guidelines and clinical pathways into fast-and-frugal decision trees to improve clinical care strategies. *Journal of Evaluation in Clinical Practice*. 2018;24(5):1247–54.
373. Djulbegovic B, Hozo I. *Threshold Decision-Making in Clinical Medicine: With Practical Application to Hematology and Oncology*: Springer Nature; 2023.
374. Djulbegovic B, Hozo I, Lizarraga D, Thomas J, Barbee M, Shah N, et al. Evaluation of a fast-and-frugal clinical decision algorithm ('pathways') on clinical outcomes in hospitalised patients with COVID-19 treated with anticoagulants. *Journal of Evaluation in Clinical Practice*. 2023;29(1):3–12.
375. Czerlinski J, Gigerenzer G, Goldstein DG. How good are simple heuristics? In Gigerenzer, G., Todd, P.M., and the ABC Research Group Editors. *Simple Heuristics that make us Smart*. New York: Oxford University Press; 1999. pp. 97–118.
376. Martignon L, Hoffrage U. Fast, frugal, and fit: simple heuristics for paired comparison. *Theory and Decision*. 2002;52(1):29–71.
377. Şimşek Ö. Linear decision rule as aspiration for simple decision heuristics. In *Advances in neural information processing systems (NeurIPS 26)*; 2013. pp. 2904–2912.

Index

E

F

G

H

I

K

L

M

N

O

P

Q

R

S

T

U

V

W

For Product Safety Concerns and Information please contact our EU
representative GPSR@taylorandfrancis.com
Taylor & Francis Verlag GmbH, Kaufingerstraße 24, 80331 München, Germany

www.ingramcontent.com/pod-product-compliance
Ingram Content Group UK Ltd.
Pitfield, Milton Keynes, MK11 3LW, UK
UKHW020011200926
475702UK00014B/1816
9781032786063